People & Peaks

of Willmore Wilderness Park

1800s to mid-1900s

Co-Published by the Willmore Wilderness Foundation &
Whitefox Circle Inc. Printed May 2007.
Copyright © 2007 Willmore Wilderness Foundation and Whitefox Circle Inc.

Distributed by Willmore Wilderness Foundation
Box 93, 4210 Pine Plaza, Grande Cache, Alberta, Canada
(780) 827-2696 - www.WillmoreWilderness.com

EDITORIAL CONTENT
Researched and written by Susan Feddema-Leonard RN
Chief Editor – Estella Cheverie
Editorial Consultant - Roger Brunt

COVER/BOOK DESIGN/LAYOUT/PHOTOGRAPHY
Susan Feddema-Leonard, Whitefox Circle Inc.
Box 537 Grande Cache, Alberta ToE oYo
(780) 827-6404 - www.WhitefoxCircle.com

PRINTER
Printed and bound by Friesens Printers, Winnipeg, Canada

LIBRARY AND ARCHIVES CANADA CATALOGUING IN PUBLICATION
Feddema-Leonard, Susan, 1952

      People & Peaks of Willmore Wilderness Park,

      1800s to mid 1900s / Susan Feddema-Leonard ;

      Estella Cheverie, editor.

Includes bibliographical references and index.
ISBN 978-0-9783377-0-4

      1. Willmore Wilderness Park (Alta.)—History.

      2. Willmore Wilderness Park (Alta.)—Biography.

      I. Cheverie, Estella, 1936

      II. Willmore Wilderness Foundation

      III. Title.

      IV. Title: People & Peaks of

          Willmore Wilderness Park, 1800s to mid 1900s.

FC3665.W5F44 2007   971.23'32   C2007-902145-X

Front cover:
'Trail Men' from left to right:
 Felix Plante, courtesy of Jim Babala
 Jack Brewster, courtesy of Jasper Yellowhead Museum & Archive PA 7 - 25
 Stan Kitchen, courtesy of Gerry Kitchen
 Tom Vinson, courtesy of Tom & Yvette Vinson
 Tom McCready, courtesy of Fay McCready
 Judd Groat, courtesy of Dusty Groat.

Main Image: Winifred Lakes in Willmore Wilderness Park
Photo by Susan Feddema-Leonard taken in 2006

Spine:
'Trailman' Albert Norris, courtesy of Tom & Yvette Vinson.

Back cover:
'Trail Men' from left to right:
 Roy Hargreaves, courtesy Ishbel Cochrane
 Henry Joachim, courtesy Victoria Moberly
 Deome Findlay, courtesy Rose Findlay
 Art Allen, courtesy Linda Hokanson,
 Glen Kilgour by Susan Feddema-Leonard
 Mac Elder by Susan Feddema-Leonard.

Tree carving at Many Faces Camp 2004
located on Me and Charlie Creek
by Susan Feddema-Leonard.

Wild Tiger Lily by Susan Feddema-Leonard.
High Country Vacation Horses at Kvass Flats by Susan Feddema-Leonard.

Page i: Tom Vinson's outfit at Eagle's Nest Pass
Photo courtesy of Yvette and Tom Vinson, Circa 1940.

Pictured right: Two Whitetail Bucks 2006 by Susan Feddema-Leonard.
Pictured on page iv: Willmore Waterfall 2005 by Susan Feddema-Leonard.
Pictured on page v: Packtrain courtesy of Victoria Moberly - circa 1940.
Pictured on page vi: Sweat Lodge 2005 by Susan Feddema-Leonard.
Pictured on xvi: Mountain Aster, Wild Rose & Fireweed by S. Feddema-Leonard.
Pictured on xvii: Mountain Teepee & Tennessee Horse by S. Feddema-Leonard.
Pictured on page xviii: Mountain Flowers 2005 by Susan Feddema-Leonard.
Pictured on page xix: top to bottom. Photos portraying the "Willmore Spirit"
— Deer Family, Baby Birds, Cow Bird & Bighorn Ram
by Susan Feddema-Leonard 2006.

Dedicated to the

Metis Nation of Alberta Local Council 1994 Grande Cache

Aseniwuche Winewak Nation of Canada

understanding our past ...

determines our ability to shape our present

and influence our future

table of contents

People & Peaks
of Willmore Wilderness Park

On both pages
Mountain Flowers 2006
by Susan Feddema-Leonard.

INTRODUCTION:

Willmore Park is located directly north of Jasper National Park and its western boundary follows the Great Continental Divide. This area is an untouched alpine frontier. The park is 4,597 sqare kilometers of pristine wilderness, which has traditionally been hunted, trapped and accessed by horseback. The Willmore Wilderness Foundation recognized that there was very little information about this mountain region and is endeavouring to provide more information on Alberta's 'best kept secret.'

As the years passed and changes came to the eastern slopes of the Rockies, it became apparent that there was not a voice for the mountain people. There was also very little written material on Willmore Wilderness Park. In order to remedy this, a group of interested people decided to form the Willmore Wilderness Foundation. Their primary objective was to clear historic packtrails in the Park. Other objectives included preparing publications and providing educational programming. The most important goal was to maintain the Willmore Wilderness Act which allows hunting, trapping and horse use in the Park.

This first book on the People & Peaks of Willmore Wilderness Park reflects the events, and characters who traveled the trails, from the early 1800s to the mid-1900s. A subsequent book will reflect the outfitters in the post-war era. The men and women portrayed in this book are only a few of the indigenous people, trappers, outfitters, guides and cooks who were the pioneers in the outfitting industry of Alberta. There are many more mountain people not mentioned in the pages of this manuscript. The Willmore Wilderness Foundation is in the process of preparing successive editions that will bring to life the stories of others who have lived and worked in this magnificent Rocky Mountain Park.

We wish to thank the following organizations and individuals who have donated their time and energy to bring this old-time knowledge to publication. The first book is always the hardest to publish and the Willmore Wilderness Foundation is very grateful to those who provided support.

Pictured left:
Larry Nelles on horseback at Kvass Flats
in Willmore Wilderness Park.

Photo by Susan Feddema-Leonard
taken in July 2004.

PARTNERSHIPS:

This publication would not be possible without the support of those who believed in this project. We wish to thank those individuals and organizations who believe enough in this undertaking, to support the publication of the People & Peaks of Willmore Wilderness Park. Very little has been written on the history of Willmore Wilderness Park and we believe that this publication will help increase understanding of this area.

We anticipate publishing more books on Willmore Wilderness Park and we look for future opportunities to partner new projects. If you are interested, we would encourage you to call our toll free number at 1.866.WILMORE or 1.866.945.6673.

Gold: Talisman Energy
       High Point Consulting - Mark Engstrom
       Whitefox Circle Inc. - WhitefoxCircle.com
       High Country Vacations - HorsebackTheRockies.com & Packtrails.com
       Prime Property Management - Grande Prairie - primepm@telusplanet.net
       Sheep Creek Back Country Lodge & Cabins - SheepCreek.net

Silver: Alberta Equestrian Federation- albertaequestrian.com
       Alberta Professional Outfitters Society (APOS) - apos.ab.ca
       Alberta Conservation Association - ab-conservation.com

Bronze: DunRite Roofing, Deb & Alvin Luger ... Cold Lake, AB
       Northern Alberta Chapter: Safari Club International (NAC SCI)

Honourable Mentions

Edna Bryanton ... Breton, AB	Dan & Deenie Leonard ... Buick, B.C.
Estella & Hank Cheverie ... Grande Cache, AB	Rick & Nancy McCabe ... Grande Prairie, AB
Mac Cochrane ... Valemount, B.C.	Fay McCready ... Jasper, AB
Sheila & Joe Couture ... Jasper, AB	Catherine McPhee ... Parksville, B.C.
Nona Foster ... Stavely, AB	Phillip & Leanne Minton ... Jasper, AB
Sawridge Inn and Conference Centre Jasper	Reg Morley ... Rocky Mtn House, AB
Viv & Doug Gaudin ... Edmonton, AB	Ross & Deborah Peck ... Hudson's Hope, B.C.
Dale Harke ... Hinton, AB	Leon Ramstad ... Bashaw, AB
Ralph & Debbie Hope ... Red Deer, AB	Chuck Stojan ... Sexsmith, AB
Travis Jaburek ... Falun, AB	Bobby & Sunni Turner ... Cochrane, AB
Cindy LeClercq ... Hinton, AB	Bryan and Sherry Woronuk ... Rycroft, AB
Angela & Jim Leonard ... High River, AB	Maggie Ellen ... Hinton, AB
Bill & Rhonda Leonard ... Innisfail, AB	Jim & Bev Bruhm - Fort McMurray, AB

FOREWORD:

The first time I viewed the Willmore Wilderness Park, I was so utterly grateful to the Honourable Norman Willmore, the then Minister of Natural Resources, in whose name this wonderfully beautiful park was created by the government of Alberta. Comprising some 4,597 square kilometers of virtually untouched beauty, it is backed by majestic mountains with such historic names as Lougheed, de Veber, Hardisty and Talbot—after the first Alberta Senators. Although hunting, trapping and trail riding are allowed, the intrusion of motor-driven vehicles is forbidden, thus preserving the silence to allow those who wish to appreciate the goodness of God's own creation without disturbance.

In the year 2002, the Willmore Wilderness Preservation and Historical Foundation was formed by a group of individuals. Members have volunteered to inventory and catalogue old cabins, graves, carvings on trees, historical campsites and trails. Databases are being created—which include GPS coordinates, photographs and oral histories. This information is being catalogued and stored for further study. The work of trail clearing has been particularly difficult because of huge windfalls over many miles of mountain terrain—complicated by the historic no-burn policy of the Alberta Government in the 1900s. Just finding the traditional trails has been difficult and only managed through the special talents of our outfitters and aboriginal guides, who seemed to possess paranormal abilities in their identification of blazes and other old sign.

Efforts have been made to look at the very early history of this magnificent park, its geology, its natural history and its occupation. I have been asked to write this foreword for the People & Peaks of Willmore Wilderness Park—which promises to provide the readers with a detailed historical account of this marvelous wilderness country.

During the first year of operation, the Willmore Wilderness Foundation received Official Income Tax status from Revenue Canada—so that those who wish to contribute to the Foundation will be able to receive tax benefits with receipts. For those few people who have experienced the Willmore and its intense beauty and tranquility, the Foundation is requesting that generous contributions be made for this most worthwhile work.

Finally, there are some people who have contributed hugely to the work of the Foundation and deserve special mention. These people are Bazil Leonard and Susan Feddema-Leonard together with their working crews. They have sacrificed generously so that the work of the Foundation could proceed.

Julian Kinisky, Founding President
Willmore Wilderness
Preservation & Historical Foundation

Pictured above:
Julian Kinisky builds a log corral at Kvass Flats. He was founding President of the Willmore Wilderness Foundation from 2002 - 2004. He was a meteorologist, a TV weatherman and later an alderman for Edmonton City Council. Julian passed away in Grande Cache on September 30, 2004. He wrote the Foreword prior to his passing.

Pictured left:
Elk Sisters - July 2005.

Photos by Susan Feddema-Leonard.

AUTHOR'S NOTES:

I first moved to Grande Cache in 1977 and have since developed an intimate relationship with the eastern slopes of the Rocky Mountains. Both the people and peaks of Willmore Wilderness Park mesmerized me and influenced the very essence of my life. Shortly after settling in Grande Cache, I met and fell in love with Bazil Leonard, a Willmore Wilderness outfitter. Throughout the years, we have raised our family on horseback, teaching them the traditional lifestyle of the nomadic mountain ways. The essence of the wilderness was ingrained into our children's souls when we took the infants by horseback into the deep recesses of the Rockies. The tent camps were, and still are, our home. During the winter months, Grande Cache became a temporary residence—when we were not trapping.

Larry Nelles, a skilled horse trainer, was the one who inspired me to write about the mountain people and encouraged me to talk to Tom Vinson. Tom directed me to contact several other old-time cowboys—and the book spiraled from there. I soon became aware that it was critical to make contact with the mountain men and women before the information that they held within their souls was lost forever. The pioneer outfitters, guides, cooks, trappers and aboriginal descendants of the Rocky Mountain Cree had a valuable story to tell about survival in the Canadian Rockies. Those interviewed provided insight into how the peoples of Mt. Robson region, Jasper National Park, Willmore Wilderness Park and Kakwa Wildland Park are interconnected. There were no boundaries between these breathtaking wilderness areas in days gone by.

This first publication has been made possible by the hard work of others who have been a tremendous support to the Willmore Wilderness Foundation. Since the conception of the book, Estella Cheverie has spent countless hours editing the transcripts for clarity. Special thanks to Hank Cheverie for his patience and tolerance while Estella worked during this period. During the early stages, Jaeda Mae Feddema transcribed the manuscripts—Gina Goldie Graphics shared some preliminary design consultation, and Gordy Schreiber was a tremendous help in preparing working proofs of the book. Gwen Edge, Graphic Designer for Alberta Sustainable Resources provided the Willmore map and Judy Fushtey of Broken Arrow Solutions was the pre-press consultant. Bazil Leonard spent many hours reading the transcripts for typos and errors, while Brian and Deana Bildson did the final proofing. Roger Brunt of Salt Spring Island guided us with respect to the final editing touches.

This publication will provide a glimpse of the magic and majesty of Willmore Wilderness Park. The chapters include 'first person' notes, transcripts, journals or interviews. The people interviewed speak for themselves, in their own words, with very little change from the original audiotapes. The only changes made were to increase clarity for the reader—and such changes were signed off by all those interviewed. Please remember that history is really 'his story'. Everyone has his or her own unique perspective of reality. I am sure there are readers who will remember circumstances differently from those outlined in this manuscript; however, all are entitled to their own truths—as they see it.

Susan Feddema-Leonard RN

Pictured above:
Susan Feddema-Leonard
Photo by
Jaeda Mae Feddema
taken January 2007.

Estella Cheverie
Photo by
Susan Feddema-Leonard
taken September 2003.

Pictured on left page:
Horses at Boulder Creek
by Susan Feddema-Leonard.

AUTHOR'S BIOGRAPHY

The author was born Susan Patricia Gaudin—with an historic surname. She is proudly a member of the Gaudin family whose famous Theobold Gaudin was the 23rd Commander of the Knights Templar. Susan's father was in the Royal Canadian Air Force, so she was exposed to traveling at an early age. This undoubtedly contributed to her broad outlook of the world, its people and environment.

Susan is a Registered Nurse who has taken extensive post-nursing education in family therapy, under the "Mother of Family Therapy," Virginia Satir. The courses she undertook had a foundation that focused on the study of "family trees" and the use of them in understanding "self, family, community and beyond." Understanding genealogies in an historical context has allowed Feddema-Leonard to reconstruct the social fabric of the mountain people, their families and community spanning more than one hundred and fifty years.

The author's love of horses, since she was a child, eventually led her to horses, the trails and the mountains of Grande Cache where she finally felt in her element and at home. There, she met her soul mate, outfitter, Bazil Leonard in the early 1980s. The couple has a blended family with nine children, all of whom were raised in the Rocky Mountain Wilderness. Susan has spent the past twenty-five years traveling the mountain trails of Willmore Wilderness and Kakwa Wildland Parks, working alongside Bazil. Many of the guides and cooks that she traveled with were indigenous to the area. Susan was quick to embrace the traditional lifestyle, learning the old ways, medicines and herbs of the Rockies.

Susan is currently involved in her independent nursing practice, as well as in writing, photography, creating PowerPoint presentations, and expanding to video productions. All of this is in conjunction with running an office, raising a family and assisting in the outfitting/trapping business, which includes twenty to thirty head of horses.

Editor, Estella Cheverie
Grande Cache, Alberta

ACCOLADES

March 25, 2007

We know that Canada, especially western Canada, was pioneered by hunters, trappers and mountain people and, of course, by Canada's First Nations peoples. But seldom are we provided with a modern-day, close-up view of the day-to-day lives and activities of these people, whose courage, resourcefulness and humour (often in the face of, what would be for lesser stock, overwhelming calamity) is captured here in the pages of The People & Peaks of Willmore Wilderness Park.

In private correspondence, author Susan Feddema-Leonard wrote to me: "You birth your story—then begins the work of chiseling and shaping the initial thoughts, finally refining them into a work of art." That's exactly what Leonard has achieved, a work of art that not only brings to life in words and fine photography (much of it by Leonard herself) one of Canada's most beautiful and little-known wilderness areas, but pays tribute to the brave folk who opened up, and now fight to preserve, the Willmore Wilderness.

This fine book not only provides a much-needed historical record of this area, it pays homage to the men and women who, confronted by trackless wilderness, grizzly bears, swollen rivers and chest-deep snows, saw not adversity, but challenge and opportunity. To them all, and to Susan Feddema-Leonard for capturing these voices before they are forever silenced by time, I tip my hat.

Roger Brunt, Salt Spring Island,
award-winning journalist/columnist and director of
The North American School of Outdoor Writing
http://www.linksnorth.com/outdoorwriting/index.html

WILLMORE WILDERNESS
Preservation & Historical Foundation:

The mountain men and women of the Mt. Robson, Jasper, Willmore and Kakwa areas had, and still have, exceptional abilities and knowledge. If one were to liken their aptitude in today's education system standards, they would be recognized with a PhD in bush knowledge. These trail people exercised refined skills in survival, tracking, hunting, horsemanship, trapping and fishing. An example of this is when one aboriginal elder showed me how to make a candle out of lard and a tea towel, when the candle supply was depleted. This simple technique afforded our camp two nights of light, which was superior to the candles we had previously been using. Survival in remote places took ingenuity and common sense.

Sadly, the expertise of the mountain people was often ignored by many in the professional community who came to study this unique wilderness area. These educated men and women often patronized the locals with their scientific rhetoric, while failing to include this valuable resource in their scientific studies.

The early indigenous people used historic trails that traversed the heights of land and river valleys, and which furnished a tried-and-true travel corridor. The Rockies have a difficult landscape to negotiate. In places there is dangerous muskeg, quicksand and crevices to navigate. The old pack trails provided a superior network, which allowed the transport of goods and people. In the early 1900s, the Alberta Government actively cleared the trail system, because they saw it an important duty to keep the arteries of this region in good condition. Over the past fifty years, the trails have been neglected, which has resulted in downed timber creating impossible travel conditions for hiker, horseman and wildlife alike.

The *Willmore Wilderness Foundation* was formed as a grass roots movement to address these concerns. Its primary mandate is to clear trails—and to record and preserve the old time knowledge that the mountain people have gained. The *Willmore Wilderness Foundation* now has national and international membership, which is rapidly growing. It is a Registered Charitable Organization under the Revenue Canada Act.

As you will read in the following pages, the Willmore Wilderness Act is a legacy that our early outfitters, guides and trappers fought for. If we want the right to hunt, fish, trap and ride horses in this Park as the early trail men did, we need to be the watchdog for this unique piece of legislation. *The Willmore Wilderness Foundation* is a voice for this region, and this manuscript is but one way in which the voices of the mountain people can be heard.

CHAPTER ONE:
The Beginnings

The Rocky Mountains have a rich history of people living in her valleys. Ancient signs of human habitation in and around Willmore Wilderness Park are widespread. From 1974 to 1979, archaeological digs uncovered evidence that people had been living in the Willmore area for at least ten thousand years. Remnants of human encampments at Grande Cache Lake confirmed that human habitation did indeed exist long ago. More recent signs show that life was teeming in the area during the 1700s and 1800s. Aboriginal people, fur traders, and natural resource prospectors have long utilized the region.

The indigenous Rocky Mountain People were exceptional at moving through the mountainous terrain traveling on horseback and carrying their supplies on packhorses. These people hunted and trapped and were self-sufficient. The mountain region was an excellent place to hunt sheep, buffalo, moose, and deer. They trapped high-quality furs, which were traded for food, tools, guns and blankets.

In the early 1800s, the white man wanted to find natural corridors through the Canadian Rockies—so the search began. The Indians had been traveling through these natural passageways for generations. One of the first attempts to find a practical route to the Pacific Ocean was through what is now called Howse Pass. Although David Thompson has been credited with the first crossing of this Pass in 1807, his employer, the North West Company, had sent an advance party over the pass in 1806. This trail-blazing trip was made by Jacques (Jacco) Findlay, a man named MacMaster, and two others. They drew a sketch of their route, and upon their return to Rocky Mountain House, presented it to Thompson. This helped to guide Thompson on his first passage in 1807, during which he officially mapped the area. However, the pass was named after Joseph Howse, even though it was not until 1809 that he crossed it for his employer, the Hudson's Bay Company.[1]

---

[1] This is an interesting but ironic story. History celebrates David Thompson's crossing of Howse pass in 1807 and there will be bi-centennial celebrations of the event in 2007. However, the North West Company, in anticipation of Thompson's proposed trip, arranged with Jacco Findlay to go through in 1806 to test its feasibility – which he did, along with his family. Howse made the first crossing for the Hudson's Bay Company in 1809 – two years after Thompson and three years after Jacco Findlay – but the Pass was named after Howse

Pictured top:
"Campfire Cuisine."
Photo courtesy
of Jacquie Hanington.

Pictured left:
Smoky River Valley.
Photo by
Susan Feddema-Leonard.

Jacco's descendants would eventually play a key role in the Jasper and Grande Cache saga. Isadore Findlay, great-grandson of Jacco, and his family were some of the indigenous people forced out of the Jasper area when it became a National Park.

David Thompson reached the Brûlé Lake area on the Athabasca River on December 5, 1810 where he camped for about three weeks to hunt, and build sleds. Led by his Iroquois guide, Thomas, he crossed Athabasca Pass on January 10, 1811, mapping the route, which would become a viable way to the west coast of Canada. Passes such as Howse, Athabasca, Eagle and Yellowhead were discovered with the help of the local Native Indians, who knew the country.

The first reports of Iroquois in the Athabasca Valley were recorded in 1814, resulting in their bloodlines running deep in the veins of the area's indigenous people. The Wanyandies were some of the first Iroquois to come west. In fact, Vincent *(Basa)* Wanyandie landed a job with Henry John Moberly, a Hudson's Bay Factor at Jasper House. He was born in 1858 and was the son of Jean Baptiste Wanyandie *(1821-1874)* and the grandson of fur trader, Ignace Wanyandie, one of the first Iroquois who guided the first explorers west.

"Vincent (Basa) *Wanyandie's hunting skills were in demand, because Jasper House was the central post for provisioning the fur brigades as they came and went."*[2] According to Mac Elder, a retired Jasper Park warden and former Willmore Wilderness guide, the Athabasca Valley had been hunted out in the late 1700s. Mac stated in a November 12, 2006 interview, *"When Jasper House was a fur trading post on the Athabasca River in early to mid-1800s the people who ran the post had hunted out the main valley near Jasper. For many years the post needed to go north to hunt for meat. They went to places like Willow Creek and Rock Lake and packed meat back down to Jasper House."*[3] Basa Wanyandie was hired specifically to go into these remote areas and keep the main post supplied with meat.

Basa was a nickname that his family and friends used in place of Vincent. They had a hard time pronouncing Vincent, so *Vasa* or *Basa* was used instead. *"Vincent* (Basa) *Wanyandie was the only full-blooded Indian in the Smoky River country and was proud of this distinction. He was born near Jasper House in 1850. Though he could not speak English, he was the recognized leader of the Natives in this area. There was some mild rivalry between him and Ewan Moberly for this claim to leadership, which was on a strictly informal basis—yet it was, nevertheless, clearly*

---

2   History of Hinton by Hazel Hart - Page 16

3   The first Jasper House or Rocky Mountain House post was built in 1813 at the north end of Brûlé Lake.
The post was moved upriver to just below Jasper Lake on the west side of the Athabasca in 1824.
The game was often in short supply during the days of the fur trade and accounts indicate that
hunting trips extended to the Smoky River. The time period would have been as the early to mid-
1800s. There is no record of fur trading in the 1700s – only after Thompson returned in 1811 and 1812.

understood even by the Moberlys. All white men who were well acquainted with the Natives recognized this leadership and dealt with Vincent (Basa) on that footing."[4]

Basa married Isabelle Karakuntie who was born in 1866. One of their sons, Daniel Wanyandie was born in 1890. In the late 1800s, Basa decided to move his family and followers to the Smoky and Kakwa River valleys, where they lived undisturbed until the formation of Grande Cache in 1969. Descendants of Basa would become well-known guides in years to come. His sons, grandsons and great-grandsons would become renowned for their tracking, hunting, trapping, horsemanship, and mountain skills. Many of Basa's descendants currently reside at Wanyandie Flats and at Mile 119 on the Smoky River, while some reside at Susa Creek Co-op east of Grande Cache. He lived his life as a mountain man and is buried at McDonald Flats near Grande Cache.

Some of the indigenous families, like the present-day Wanyandies, have striking features of the Iroquois. *"Many of them stand over six feet, broad-shouldered and erect, big men with aquiline noses and strong features; while the Cree are short in stature, with round faces and snub noses. The Iroquois who came west were select men".*[5] The Rocky Mountain People, called the Aseniwuche Winewak, have long acknowledged their family ties with the Iroquois, Cree, Beaver, and Stoney.

Some of the other Iroquois families also included the Karakunties and Gauthiers. One notable man by the name of Michael Gauthier made a lobstick, for the railroad surveyors of the day. A lobstick was a tree stripped of branches, leaving only the top visible, so as to be a marker. The Indians climbed up and removed all branches below the top. The "Lobstick" on the bank of the Athabasca River below the cemetery east of Jasper was believed to have been cut by Michael Gauthier, who lived at Henry House Flats. He cut this to identify a meeting place in 1872 with Walter Moberly[6], C.P.R. surveyor and Sanford Fleming, Engineer/Chief of C.P.R. Descendants of Michael Gauthier live in Grande Cache today. Two of his progeny are Leah *(Belcourt)* McLane—and her sister, Loretta Belcourt, who has been a counselor for Native Counseling Services of Alberta since 1980.

Jasper House was named for Jasper Haws who was the manager of the North West Company post on Brule Lake from 1814 to 1917. The fur trade kept expanding and by 1821 the Hudson's Bay Company had expanded into the Smoky River valley, as there was an abundance of fur to trap on the Smoky and its tributaries.

Pictured above:
The "Moberly Lobstick." This tree is one bare of branches below the top. The Indians climbed up and removed all branches below the top. This tree was living when this picture was taken and identified by Curly Phillips and one of the Moberly men. The "Lob Tree" or "Lobstick" is on the bank of the Athabasca River, east of Jasper. It was believed to have been cut by Michael Gauthier, who lived at Henry House Flats, for the meeting in 1872 of Walter Moberly, C.P.R. surveyor and Sanford Fleming, Engineer/Chief of C.P.R. The latter was traveling from the east, and Moberly from the west.

Photo & caption courtesy Jasper Yellowhead Museum & Archives PA 18-54

4 Packsaddles to Tête Jaune Cache - James G. MacGregor - Page 149
5 Packsaddles to Tête Jaune Cache - James G. MacGregor - Page 149
6 Walter Moberly was Henry John Moberly's brother.

By 1840, Colin Fraser was in charge of Jasper House with a mandate to facilitate the fur trade. A great number of horses were kept at the post to ensure the movement of furs. Henry John Moberly succeeded Colin Fraser as the Hudson's Bay Factor in Jasper House from 1855 to 1861. Evidence that there were well-traveled trails in the foothills and eastern slopes is found in Henry John Moberly's journals. Henry John provides an account of his first trip to the Rockies in his book, *When Fur Was King.* He wrote, *"We commenced our hunting along the foothills, and as hunting in the locality had been followed for years , we had good road, or "pitching trails," as they were called for the reason that whole camps travelled them and pitched at accustomed intervals where feed for horses was plentiful. Sometimes we made only a few miles, sometimes a fairly long move, remaining two or three weeks at each camp until the vicinity was hunted out and meat was dried and cached."*

Henry John married Suzanne Karakuntie who was the daughter of Louis Karakuntie (Kwarakwante), an Iroquois and freeman.[7] The couple had two sons by the names of Ewan and John. Ewan was baptized on August 28, 1860 and John on December 30, 1861. Although Henry and Suzanne were officially married at Lac Ste. Anne in 1861, Henry John left her there and she evidently returned to Jasper to live. It was difficult for many of the fur traders when it came time to leave their posts—as life with a Native wife outside the trading post was seen as a problem. Many of the fur traders left their Indian wives behind, and Henry John was no exception. Suzanne and her boys remained on the land in Jasper. She died in 1905 and was buried on her son, Ewan's farm near the present town of Jasper.

Ewan's and John's sons and grandsons would play a big role in the guiding and outfitting of both Willmore Wilderness Park and Jasper National Park. They were considered the best guides and packers in the area. Henry John Moberly died in 1932 in Duck Lake, Saskatchewan at the age of ninety-seven.

By 1880, the Canadian Pacific Railroad was moving west towards Calgary and there was a need for experienced trail men and packers to move supplies to the survey camps.[8] The expansion of the railroad resulted in tourists wanting to travel deeper into the mountain wilderness. 'Necessity is the mother of invention'—and it wasn't long before a profession called outfitting was born in the Banff region of the Rockies. *"The first outfitter who stands out in history is Tom Wilson who, in 1881, joined the survey of what is now the Stoney Indian Reserve near Banff, Alberta. He quickly learned how to pack a horse and followed old Indian trails up the Bow Valley. Tom Wilson befriended a group of Stoney Indians. One young man by the name of Gold Seeker guided*

---

7   The Certificate of Marriage for Henry Moberly and Suzanne Karakuntie has more recently come to light. It was signed by Albert Lacombe on the 9th of October 1861.

8   CPR line went through Calgary, later Banff and Laggan, now known as Lake Louise.

Tom to a beautiful lake that became known as Lake Louise. Tom believed that he was the first white man to have ever seen the lake." [9]

In 1887, development of Lake Louise commenced and the Canadian Pacific Railroad began advertising unlimited opportunities for hunting, fishing and mountain wilderness scenery. Tom Wilson officially began a new career that fall in Banff. He guided a party on a thirty-day hunting trip, which established the new profession of guiding and outfitting. By the late 1890s, Tom was a major outfitter employing men to outfit mountaineering groups, explorers and hunting parties. Men like Billy Warren, Jimmy Simpson, Bill Peyto, Fred Stephens and Jack Otto worked for Wilson learning the trade. Fred Stevens and Jack Otto would shortly play a big role in the outfitting business in the Jasper and Willmore areas.

In 1901 and 1902, A.O. Wheeler, born in Ireland and a surveyor by trade, was placed in charge of surveying various peaks in the Rockies. Wheeler had been trained in photogrammetry, which was a method of conducting camera-assisted surveys. Photographs had to be taken from the summits of mountains in order to carry out a triangulation of images. As he climbed the mountain peaks, he developed a passion for the Canadian Rockies—and this love of the mountains was a motivating factor in his forming the Alpine Club of Canada. In order to get the Club off the ground, Wheeler depended on the generosity of Banff-based outfitters, Bill Brewster and Tom Wilson to volunteer their horses, equipment and guides for its first year of operation. Brewster and Wilson made a pledge at a founding meeting in Winnipeg,

Pictured above:
Ewan & Madeline *(nee Findlay)* Moberly.
The older boy is Lactap Moberly,
and the young boy is Joe Moberly.

Photo courtesy of the
Jasper Yellowhead
Museum & Archives
PA 20-29

Manitoba in 1906; however Brewster withdrew his offer later that year. This resulted in a long lasting friction between the two men. Despite this fact, the Alpine Club of Canada was successful because of the generosity of the outfitting community, specifically Tom Wilson.

By the turn of the century, Fred Stephens ventured out on his own to become the first man to investigate the Yellowhead country. In 1901 and 1903, he headed north from Lake Louise but was unsuccessful in his endeavours. In 1905, he traveled west from his home in Lacombe to explore the Yellowhead. Not only was he successful, but also he visited the area on a regular basis for many years. In later times, Fred Stephens outfitted from a location near Entrance, Alberta.

In 1902, Wilson had competitors by the name of Bill and Jim Brewster of *W. & J. Brewster, Guides and Packers*. As adolescents, the brothers were known to have skipped school, spending time hunting and fishing with William Twin, a Stoney Indian who had befriended them. Jim and Bill had received a good foundation from a skilled mountain man. By 1904, the Banff-based *Brewster Brothers* had outfitted a party in the country north of where the Sunwapta joins the Athabasca River. This trip put pressure on the outfitting industry to explore the undeveloped north country.

In 1905, the Brewsters' Banff operation had grown to two hundred and fifty head of horses and their business was growing by leaps and bounds. *"This company's reputation and success as outfitters was mainly attributable to the guiding talents of Jim and Bill Brewster, but after 1905 neither could afford much time to personally lead parties on the trail."*[10] The *Brewster Brothers* dissolved at the same time that Jasper was coming to life with the prospects of two competing railways—the Canadian Northern Railway and the Grand Trunk Pacific *(GTP)*. The dissolution of the *Brewster Brothers* would make way for a host of new operators in the outfitting industry.

As the railroad pushed west, many young men came with it—like Donald McDonald, John Yates, James Shand-Harvey, Alex Wylie and Tom Groat. Another young man was Fred Kvass who was known to travel with Shand-Harvey. Kvass Creek, Kvass Mountain and Kvass Flats are named after this trapper who had a trapline cabin at Kvass Flats on the Smoky River.

One of the colourful characters that entered the area was a trapper and guide by the name of Donald McDonald. He was a fair-skinned Metis who arrived in the Rockies in 1905. Outfitter, George Kelley stated in an interview on March 18, 2006, *"I know that Donald McDonald was over there* (Willmore) *in 1905—all over that country. He came from the Red River. He wasn't from this country—from Ontario or Manitoba. He was going to school in 1885 when the Riel Rebellion broke out. My grandfather was going to school there at the same time and they both come out with the troops. My grandfather was born in Edmonton, but they sent him to school down there and they came back. That's where Donald McDonald came from."*

Donald McDonald married Louise *(Findlay)* Thappe, sister of Isadore Findlay and a direct descendant of David Thompson's guide, Jacco Findlay. Her first husband was the Beaver Indian called Thappe who was killed in a hunting accident and whose grave can still be found on the Mountain Trail, located at the summit of Rock Creek and the Sulphur River. Louise and Thappe had two children, Joe and Louisa. Joe decided to adopt his stepfather's name and became Joe McDonald. Sister, Louisa married Daniel Wanyandie and took his name.

Donald McDonald traveled extensively, guiding and trapping in what is now Willmore Wilderness Park. He guided a forty-five-day trip from August 26 to October 9, 1926 for Hinton-based outfitter, Nick Nickerson. Other trail hands included guide Jack Wilson, cook Don Empson and big game hunters, Sanford Knaffs and Loring Gale. Several places are named after this exceptional bushman. These include McDonald Flats near Grande Cache, Donald Flats down the Berland River and Donald McDonald Meadows, which are soft, boggy meadows on the Continental Divide near Morkill Pass.

By September 1907, the Canadian Federal Government passed an Order in Council for the creation of "Jasper Forest Park" and this action created many opportunities for guides and outfitters.[11] This, however, had other implications for the indigenous people of the area, as the Canadian Government did not want to have privately-owned land within the Park boundaries.

<hr>

11   Jasper was established by Order in Council under authority of the Dominion Lands Act. It officially became Jasper National Park in 1930 under a new National Parks Act.

Pictured above:

Standing: Louisa *(Wanyandie)* and her brother, Joe McDonald.

Seated: Donald McDonald and
Louise *(Findlay -Thappe)* McDonald *(mother of Louisa and Joe).*

Photo courtesy of Tom Wanyandie,
son of Louisa *(McDonald)* Wanyandie
and Daniel Wanyandie, son of Basa *(Vincent)* Wanyandie.

Pictured above:
James Shand-Harvey at his home in Entrance.

Photo courtesy of
Jacquie Hanington.

James Shand-Harvey was another unique character that was an early trapper and mountain guide. He arrived in the area, spending the rest of his life there. James G. MacGregor shares the story of Shand-Harvey's travel in his book *Packsaddles to Tête Jaune Cache*. Harvey described Jasper as he first saw it in 1909. *"Farther upstream (on the Athabasca River), above the end of Jasper Lake, lay the ranches of John and Ewan Moberly, well-known and respected half-breeds whose residence dated back in the valley at least fifty years. On the west side of the river, in the shadow of the Palisades, was the ranch of Lewis Swift."*[12]

MacGregor's notes stated that, *"Shand met the Moberlys and all of the Iroquois neighbours—the Findlays, Joachims, Caracontes, Gauthiers and Wanyandies—who, scattered along the valley, were faring well on farms similar to (Lewis) Swift's. About a hundred of them lived in the comparative security of a crude white man's type of civilization. Descended from canoe-men and snowshoe-men in the eastern forests, they were now horsemen and mountain climbers. Of them all, Ewan Moberly was the leader. On the left bank of the river, on the flat below Cobblestone Creek, he dwelt in a well-constructed and comfortable house built about 1898—today a landmark in Jasper."*[13] Many families were living in the Park, including Jacco Findlay's great-great grandson, Isadore Findlay who lived with his wife and six children on the south side of the Athabasca River, east of the town of Jasper.

The Native people protested the takeover of their ancestral land—but their voices were not heard. The government deemed Lewis Swift, John Moberly, Adolphus Moberly, Isadore Findlay, Ewan Moberly,

12   Packsaddles to Tête Jaune Cache
           - James G. MacGregor - Page 137
13   Packsaddles to Tête Jaune Cache
           - James G. MacGregor - Page 149

William Moberly and Adam Joachim squatters. They succeeded in pressuring the Native people to take a cash settlement based on the appraised value of *improvements,* which was a small token of what their land was worth; however, Lewis Swift refused to sell his land.[14]

Shand stated, *"Lewis John Swift was a remarkable man, with his ranch no less remarkable. He was one of the breed of men known all over Western States as 'mountain men.'"*[15] Lewis married a Native woman by the name of Suzette Chalifoux in 1897. Prior to her marriage to Lewis, Suzette had a son by the name of Albert Norris who would later play a big role in the guiding and outfitting industry of Jasper and Willmore Wilderness Park. The Swift children included Dean, daughter, Lottie, Jimmie, Willis and John. Willis and John died as infants.

Slowly the families left Jasper. *"John and Ewan and the other heads of families made a trip to Edmonton, where they bought sleighs, wagons and ploughs before starting to build on the new land they had selected. In the spring, John Moberly and his family moved out to Prairie Creek and filed on a quarter section, which to this day (1960s) remains in the family's hands. Ewan Moberly, his sons and Adam Joachim went farther a-field to Grande Cache, a long-time favourite rendezvous of the Indians. Ewan Moberly and his group took their machinery and over two hundred head of stock, mostly horses, over a road, which they cleared out along older hunting trails. Up Solomon Creek they went, up the Wildhay River, past Rock Lake and over the pass to the Sulphur River. By descending that, they came to Grande Cache. Ever since, this way has been called the Moberly road."*[16] This trail is now called the Mountain Trail.

Ed Moberly's wife, Anne detailed the move from Jasper. *"Edward's uncle, Ewan, decided rather than establish himself in the Hinton vicinity,* (it was too crowded) *to move on and cut a trail through the boreal forest north to Grande Cache—where he became quite successful buying and selling furs and raising livestock. Although Ewan had very little education, he was able to figure out his fur prices by jotting them down in Roman numerals. The path Ewan cut, remains known today as the Moberly trail."*[17]

In 1907, Jack Otto and his brothers, Bruce and Closson formed a new outfitting Banff-based business called the *Otto Brothers* and by 1909 were deemed the official outfitters of the Alpine Club of Canada. Without warning, the *Otto Brothers* sold their Banff-based business to Jim Brewster and re-established their operation in Jasper, making them one of the first outfitters of the Jasper area. A new era of outfitting had begun in Jasper and Willmore Wilderness area.

Pictured above:
Bruce Otto.

Photo courtesy
Jasper Yellowhead Museum
& Archives PA 33-79

---

14   The six Métis families in Jasper were offered a cash "compensation" based on an appraised value of their "improvements" such as homes, buildings and fences. They were evidently also promised that they could settle on homesteads outside the Park, which they eventually did.

15   Packsaddles to Tête Jaune Cache - James G. MacGregor - Page 142

16   Packsaddles to Tête Jaune Cache - James G. MacGregor - Page 152

17   History of Hinton by Hazel Hart - Page 54

In 1908, Ewan Moberly's son, Adolphus who was raised in the Jasper area, led outfitter, John Yates in finding a route into Robson Pass. John Yates had been hired by A. P. Coleman, his brother Lucas and Reverend George B. Kinney who were members of the Alpine Club and were interested in an ascent up Mt. Robson. Moberly guided the party up Moose River and over Moose Pass. Adolphus knew Moose Valley, as his family hunted in the area for food. Once the outfit went over the pass, they went onto the headwaters of the Smoky River via Calumet Creek and over Robson Pass. In thanks for his excellent guidance, Adolphus Lake at the headwaters of the Smoky River was named after him. When the party reached the summit of Robson Pass, they could view the beautiful glacial-fed Berg Lake. However, due to the rain and snow, the climbers were unable to ascend Mt. Robson.

Adolphus Moberly was recognized for his superior knowledge, by the alpine lake bearing his name. However, few mountains, rivers or lakes were named after the First People of the Rockies. In fact, the Native people who showed the trails to the first explorers, the Jasper Park wardens, and the outfitters have been generally unrecognized for their eminent skill as mountain men.

With the Native people reluctantly leaving their traditional land base, the Federal Government needed to establish control over the mountain region that it had annexed. The Canadian Commission of Parks organized a Jasper Park Warden Service on March 31, 1909. Many of the men hired by the Federal Government had little knowledge of the rugged Rocky Mountain terrain. The newly appointed Park wardens needed to learn to navigate the old Indian trails, as well as learn to survive in the backcountry. Indigenous guides were the natural choice for the Warden Service as they knew the trail system and how to survive in the wilderness.

One notable trapper and guide was Adam Joachim, a descendant of Colin Fraser who came west for the Hudson's Bay Company in 1827. Adam was born in 1875 near Berland Lake and, at an early age, he was taken from his people by Father Albert Lacombe and sent to a Catholic Mission near Montreal. This young man became fluent in English, French, Latin and his mother tongue, Cree. Upon receiving news of a family matter, Adam decided to return to the Rocky Mountains and settled close to the Moberly homestead. He moved to the Muskeg River after being evicted from Jasper National Park. His education and knowledge played a key role in helping his people. Adam's first wife was Fresine Moberly, daughter of Ewan Moberly. They had eight children; however Fresine died in the 1918 flu epidemic and Adam remarried. His second wife was Caroline McDonald, daughter of Joe McDonald. Caroline bore him nine more children.

Adam Joachim was sought after by the Jasper Warden Service for his expertise as a guide. He also worked for outfitters including Stan Clark, Jack Hargreaves, the *Otto Brothers* and Curly Phillips. Adam was an ideal choice to hire as a mountain guide because of his diverse background, which included being an experienced trapper, prospector, guide and spiritual leader of his people. Adam's up-bringing in the Catholic Church influenced his leadership of the people and he was held in high esteem—soon becoming the unofficial leader of his people, until his death at Muskeg in 1959. Adam's son, Allan Joachim became the unofficial leader until he passed away. *(October 23, 1946 to May 6, 1998).*

In 1909, a young man by the name of Donald *Curly* Phillips entered the guiding and outfitting arena. Curly was born in Dorset, Ontario and learned the arts of hunting, trapping and canoe work from his father. In the winter of 1907-08 he left Ontario in search of adventure and took a job working on the railroad. He worked for the GTP in the winter of 1908-09 and the next spring bought horses and set out for the Yellowhead. On his trip

Pictured above:
Adam Joachim.
Adam became the unofficial leader of this small band of indigenous people of the Rocky Mountains.

Photo courtesy of the
Jasper Yellowhead
Museum & Archives
PA 20-23

west, he ran into Rev. George B. Kinney at John Moberly's homestead near the present day town of Jasper. The Reverend had planned to climb Mt. Robson and had persuaded Phillips to accompany him to the summit. Phillips was a novice to mountaineering and lacked proper climbing gear, however he willingly took up the challenge. Kinney and Phillips claimed to have reached the summit of Robson in a harrowing climb up the icy terrain. Their ascent came into question years later, diminishing the glory of the climb, when Phillips acknowledged that they had climbed slightly short of the summit. Despite the controversy, the fame of climbing Robson with Kinney helped catapult Curly Phillips right into the hub of the guiding and outfitting arena. Phillips was quickly sought after by other mountaineers.

After the completion of their Robson ascent, Kinney and Phillips headed to Ewan Moberly's homestead near Jasper. They met Shand-Harvey and John Yates who were guiding Alpine Club members William Mumm, L.S. Amery, James Priestly, Geoffrey Hastings and Moritz Inderbinen, who hoped to be the first to ascend Mt. Robson. Mumm had attempted to climb Mt. Robson the year before by traveling up the Wildhay River, but this venture proved unsuccessful. Shand-Harvey stated, *"At the Moberly's, the party met the Reverend G.B. Kinney and Donald "Curly" Phillips returning from what both believed to have been a successful assault on Mt. Robson. As a matter of fact, later knowledge of the mountain indicated that the summit scaled by Mr. Kinney was lower by a matter of yards than a nearby peak. Until that came to light, he conscientiously believed that he had been the first man to stand on the summit of the great mountain. While disappointed that someone should have beat him to the top of the mountain, Amery, years later when writing of Kinney's climb, described it as 'one of the most gallant performances in modern mountaineering history.'"*[18]

A striking young man by the name of Tom Groat came west from Edmonton in 1910 as a surveyor for the railroad. Shortly after arriving in the Hinton area, he met and married Clarisse Moberly, one of Ewan Moberly's daughters. He quickly joined the ranks of outfitters in the Jasper and Willmore areas. Tom started his own business. He guided and outfitted for geological survey parties, summer trail riding parties and hunters. Groat became a well-respected outfitter who operated in the Willmore Wilderness area until 1946, when his son Judd Groat purchased the outfit from him. Tom Groat operated professionally for a total of thirty-five years.

In 1910, John Yates, Fred Stephens, Allan McConnochie and George Swain outfitted Arnold Mumm and Dr. Norman J. Collie who were both mountaineers, and guided the party to Berg Lake via the trail that Adolphus Moberly had shown them. The trail, now blazed, was easy to follow and clearly marked all the way; however, the weather was bad and they could not ascend Mt. Robson, so decided to spend their time exploring the Smoky River Valley and its tributaries.

18   Packsaddles to Tête Jaune Cache - James G. MacGregor - Page 137

The party found a good pass over to British Columbia, which Yates called *Bess Pass* after the daughter of Peter Gunn, the Hudson's Bay Factor at Lac Ste. Anne. The pass is on the Continental Divide but also meets the headwaters of the Jackpine River, which is now in Willmore Wilderness Park. Yates knew the country and opted to return home via the Smoky River Valley, to the Stoney *(Snake Indian)* River. The Jasper Natives had told Yates about the pass which led back to Jasper House.

Mumm and Collie decided to return in 1911 to explore the new country. Yates and Stephens combined outfits for a second year and hired McConnochie. The party went up the Stoney River to the pass that Yates had taken them over the previous year. Collie climbed a peak on the east side of the pass and, upon reaching the summit, called it Mt. Hoodoo after Yates' bulldog. From the summit, the climbers had seen mountains that surrounded Mt. Bess and decided to head down the Smoky River to examine the Resthaven Icefield and explore valleys north of there. After climbing Bess Mountain, the party crossed Bess Pass and headed down another old Indian trail before returning to the railhead. The last time that Yates and Stephens co-operated in their outfitting ventures was in 1911, and failing to join forces cost the two of them greatly, as they disappeared from the outfitting scene over the next few years.

By 1911, A.O. Wheeler, a surveyor of the Canadian Rockies, had convinced the Canadian Government that more topographical work needed to be done in the northern Rockies. The GTP was interested in exploring new areas and had contacted Curly Phillips to outfit the party. Phillips hired James Shand-Harvey as one of the packers along with Fred Stephens who agreed to add his horses and expertise to the operation. The party pressed from the railroad up to Kinney Lake. It was a difficult trip as there were no trails—for Phillips had decided to create a new trail into Robson. Phillips arrived at Kinney Lake and ferried his clients across the water with a raft he had constructed and brought them down to a camp on the Grand Fork. Large cliffs had created a problem for Phillips and his crew, which he would have to deal with on future expeditions.

In the winter of 1911/1912 Curly Phillips went trapping on the Smoky River with companion, Conrad Kain, a mountaineer and outfitter. Curly trapped all winter, leaving in early April to meet Jack Otto in Edmonton. They closed a deal with A.O. Wheeler to handle a camp at Mt. Robson Pass in 1912. Curly had a proposition to remedy the problem of the steep cliffs at the Grand Fork when he proposed to fashion some switchbacks up the steep incline and a *Flying Trestle Bridge* around the rocky face to Emperor Falls. Curly's proposal was accepted and his engineering feat allowed people and horses to cross the gorge on the bridge. Curly finished construction in time to join the *Otto Brothers'* outfit, A.O Wheeler's Alpine Club of Canada party. The combined forces of the *Otto Brothers* and Curly Phillips proved to be an excellent combination for large parties. Phillips and the Ottos were kept busy moving members and their gear. One camp was placed six miles down the Smoky River and the other was located near Moose Pass. On July 31, Conrad Kain, Albert H. MacCarthy and William W. Foster successfully climbed Mt. Robson. When they returned to base

Pictured above:
Top: Tom Groat circa 1910.
Photo courtesy of
Emil Moberly,
Victor Lake, Alberta.

Bottom: Flying Trestle
built by Curly Phillips.
Photo courtesy of
Ishbel *(Hargreaves)* Cochrane.

Camp on Calumet Creek, below Moose Pass.

The Mount Robson expedition was guided by Curly Phillips under the auspices of the Canadian Alpine Club. A. O Wheeler was the President. Present in the image are Reverend Kinney, Curly Phillips, H.H. Blagden and J.H. Riley, Shand Harvey, Konrad Kain, C. Walcott, Bob Jones, and A.O Wheeler. Curly Phillips is in front of the tree and James Shand-Harvey is to the far left.

Donald "Curly" Phillips (1884-1938) first came to Jasper in 1909 outfitting for Reverend Kinney's attempt on Mt. Robson and A.O. Wheeler's survey of Mt. Robson (1911). He settled permanently in Jasper in 1912, setting up an outfitting business. Over the years, he worked on many Alpine Club of Canada camps in the area.

Photo courtesy
Jasper Yellowhead Museum & Archives PA 38-42

camp, Curly Phillips had advised them that they were the first to ascend the mountain. This was a surprise to the climbers as Reverend Kinney and Curly Phillips had long maintained that they were the first to ascend Mt. Robson.

Soon after Jasper National Park was established, the Dominion forests on the adjacent foothills were set aside in 1910 as part of the Rocky Mountains Forest Reserve *(RMFR)* that ran from the U.S. border north into Township 61 on the Smoky River watershed. The RMFR was expanded east in 1911 and 1913, and then divided into five Forests, of which the most northerly was called the Athabasca Forest.[19] The Athabasca Forest included, in part, the land base which is now called Willmore Wilderness Park. Stan Clark had entered the employment of the Canadian Forestry Service, becoming the first Superintendent in 1912. He did most of the pioneer work in establishing the Athabasca Forest. After returning from war in 1918, he purchased the Entrance Ranch and began setting up a large horse and cattle ranch. On one occasion, he guided U.S. Army Major Townsend Whelen to the Smoky River country to hunt. Whelen was excited about his expedition and wrote about the success of this hunt in the 1923 and 1924 *Outdoor Life Magazine*. As a result, Stan was inundated with requests to take parties out and, decided to go into the outfitting business.

Stan Clark would take his hunters from Entrance to Rock Lake, over Eagle's Nest, up Rock Creek to the Sulphur River, to Big Grave, up Kvass Creek and down Wolverine Creek, across Smoky River and up to Sheep Creek. There is a legend that Stan Clark had side-packed a collapsible boat to cross the Big Smoky. The area was a difficult ford for foot and horse travelers. In later years, Clark had a permanent boat crossing with a boathouse, which was located upstream from the confluence of Wolverine Creek on the south side of the Smoky River. The site became known as *Clark's Crossing.*

A trapline cabin of Stan Clark's remains standing in Willmore Wilderness Park. It is located on the Smoky River upstream from the mouth of the Muddy Water River and across from his boathouse. Writing on the door of this cabin reads: *1925 Clark's Cash.* The area by the cabin became known as Clark's Cache. The trapline today is owned by Billy and Rachelle McDonald, original descendants of the indigenous people of Jasper. Stan and his wife lived at Entrance Ranch from 1918 to 1948 when they moved to Jasper.

A new outfitting company called *Brewster and Moore* moved to Fitzhugh *(Jasper)* in 1912—where they constructed stables and corrals, and acquired land. Fred, the younger brother of Bill and Jim Brewster, was lured into the outfitting business after the break-up

---

19   The south boundary of the Athabasca Forest ran on the height of land between the Athabasca and McLeod, so it included land on both sides of the Athabasca valley. The next one south was the Brazeau Forest with headquarters at Coalspur.

Pictured above:
Top: Stan Clark standing in the doorway of the
Hinton Ranger Station shack.

Photo courtesy of the
"Dominion Forestry Branch, Alberta Forest Protection Collection."

Bottom: Doorway of Stan's
"1925 Clark's Cash,"
(—referred to as Clark's Cache or *Clark's Crossing, as he crossed the Smoky River in a boat near the cabin)*
located upstream from the Muddy Water River confluence.
Photo by Susan Feddema-Leonard.

of the *Brewster Brothers* in 1905. He decided to throw his hat in the ring and establish his new outfit in Jasper. Fred and seventeen-year-old brother, Jack, along with their brother-in-law, Phil Moore formed a company called *Brewster and Moore*. Phil Moore was an ideal partner as he was married to Fred's sister, Pearl. Initially, the company worked out of the Red Deer area, freighting. In 1911, Fred took a trip to Edson to look at new business prospects, after which he moved the operation to Bickerdike, and later to Prairie Creek. Fred and Jack's younger brothers, Pat and George soon joined forces in their new location at Fitzhugh.

In the summer of 1912, Fred Brewster's new outfit guided one of the more celebrated expeditions for Samuel Prescott Fay. He was interested in hunting and hired Brewster and Moore to handle the trip to the north country. Fred guided, hiring J. Beaumont Gates to accompany him. Fay wanted to explore the north for game and was also interested in solving a question that he had at the time. He wanted to know what variety of sheep inhabited the region north of the Athabasca River. He knew that bighorn sheep ranged south of the Athabasca and that Stone sheep ranged north of the Peace River—and Fay pondered what species of sheep might roam in between. The three set out with seven horses on August 8. The Muddywater, Jackpine Rivers and Sheep Creek were hunted without success and the group struggled through downed timber and treacherous muskegs south of the Muddywater River. They were able to get a good view of Mt. Bess and saw a peak *(Brewster's first sighting of Mt. Sir Alexander)*. It was thirty miles to the northwest and rivalled Mt. Robson. Feeling unsuccessful, by the end of September the group headed home down the Porcupine *(Kakwa)* River through high, snow-covered passes. Brewster believed that he was the first white man to penetrate the country west of the Smoky River for big game hunting. If he was the first, he only beat Curly Phillips by a few weeks, as Curly took a hunting party out the same fall.

In September 1912, Curly's journals detail a hunting trip that he took across the Big Smoky River—the same year and country that Brewster boasted that he explored. Curly's clients included George D. Pratt and Phimister Proctor, both of New York City. Frank Doucette accompanied the party as a packer. Hunting was forbidden in the new Jasper National Park, so Curly took his clients north of the park into what is now known as the Willmore Wilderness area. Curly's journal reports how they traveled to Jackpine Pass where they shot a nice billy goat. They crossed Jackpine Pass and traveled northwest down the Jackpine River three miles where they shot a caribou bull. They packed up and moved down to the Muddy Water River looking for sheep, but were unsuccessful in locating bighorns. During their dry spell, Curly decided to do a little scouting on his own. *"Feeling the need to be alone, Curly took off on a scouting trip. West of their latest camp, which was many miles down the Jackpine River towards its junction with the Smoky River, he climbed a mountain, and from the summit could see the whole country for miles around. About fifteen miles away to the east was the Smoky River, and he could follow its course north where it left the mountains. Farther to the north were three high mountains and numerous valleys.* (Curly's first sighting of Mt. Sir Alexander.) *Just below him was another branch of the Jackpine River flowing out of a beautiful blue-green lake* (Ptarmigan). *Beyond the lake appeared to be a pass through a high range of hills. He made his way across this range, through the thick timber and up steep shale slopes and cliffs. At the summit of the pass were the remains of a white man's camp, which was different than those of Indian teepee poles. Curly felt that this was probably the camp of W.R. Jones, a surveyor for the GTP railroad. Jones had surveyed the area many years before.*[20] (Jones Pass is located between Meadowland Creek and the headwaters of Pauline Creek.)

In 1913, Samuel Fay had undergone a serious medical operation and was unable to travel on an extended trip north of the Smoky. Fred, however, had talked him into taking a shorter trip and Fay spent a few weeks in the vicinity of Mt. Robson and Mt. Bess.

By 1914, Fay was anxious to take another expedition north of the Smoky. Brewster hired Bob Jones, a former railroad worker who later became a Jasper Park warden, and Sack Symes, an ex-North West Mounted Police constable. Fred's brother, Jack guided the party for the first two weeks, however Fred caught up with them and replaced Jack on the Sulphur River. Their party passed through a Native settlement near Grande Cache where the trails were found to be either old or non-existent. It is of interest to note that a vibrant community of indigenous people and trappers were living in the area at that time. They used horses extensively, traveling the old pack trails.

Brewster, Fay and their party fought their way up Sheep Creek. They finally saw the Big Mountain, and as they moved closer, they were distracted by the great size of the mountain. Fred and Fay decided to name it Mount Alexander after the late and famous explorer,g. The 10,700-foot peak was later named Mt. Sir Alexander.

The Samuel Prescott Fay trip reached Hudson's Hope on October 16 after a gruelling sixteen weeks on the trail. Brewster and his staff returned to Jasper on November 21. This five-month trip is the longest recorded pack trip in the Rockies. *"From his observations, (Fay) concluded that there were no sheep between the Peace River and the heads of the northern tributaries of the Smoky River, and that the sheep south of this line were the same species*

Pictured above:
Fred Brewster enjoying a smoke.
Circa 1940.

"CN Photograph Collection"
Courtesy of the
Jasper Yellowhead
Museum & Archives PA 7-52

Pictured above:
Samuel Prescott Fay
was from
Boston, Massachusetts.
He was the leader
of the expedition from
Yellowhead Pass
to Hudson's Hope, B.C.
in 1914.
He hired a newly
established outfitter,
Fred Brewster
to take his party north.

Photo courtesy
of Jasper Yellowhead
Museum & Archives
Image circa 1920
PA 34-5

found between Banff and Jasper; conclusions supported by the reports of Natives and half-breeds met in the course of the journey."[21]

Curly Phillips' outfitting business expanded in 1914 to include his father, Daniel, his brother, Harry and his brother-in-law, Bert Wilkins. Curly also guided a party in 1914 that wished to climb the Big Mountain. Miss Mary Jobe contacted Phillips about a trip, as he was reputed to have been hunting and trapping in the Jackpine Valley, located about forty miles north of Mt. Robson, and he was thought to be the only one to have known the area. In 1914, Curly and his brother-in-law, Bert Wilkins outfitted two women, Mary Jobe and climbing partner, Margaret Springate. These ladies made an unsuccessful attempt to climb the Big Mountain. Mary had named the magnificent rock, Mt. Kitchi, unbeknown to her that it had already been visited and named by Samuel Prescott Fay.

In 1915, Caroline Hinman, a young mountaineer, wrote Curly Phillips requesting a return trip to the Big Mountain. She was to be accompanied by her friend, Mary Jobe. Caroline had met Curly when he was the chief packer on a Mt. Robson climbing camp in 1913, where she had befriended Mary. *Jobie* was the nickname that Caroline liked to call her friend. Both women had a tremendous passion for the mountains and were eager to move into new territory. Curly Phillips was the perfect man to take the mountaineers to the Big Mountain *(Mt. Sir Alexander)* in an attempt to climb it.

Caroline Hinman kept a detailed diary of the expedition called, *An Account of My First Exploring Expedition with Mary L. Jobe of New York City in the Summer of 1915*. A photocopy of this journal was given to the Willmore Wilderness Foundation by the Whyte Museum of Banff.

The outfit left the railhead on July 1. Caroline noted, *"Clear! Up at 6 a.m. to a clear and sparkling day. The day we start on the trail".* Both women were excited about their adventure and the explorers made their first stop at Mt. Robson where the ladies were treated to a raft ride on Berg Lake. Curly had made a raft and decided to take the ladies out on the glacial-fed, icy cold waters. Caroline wrote, *"About 5:30 pm Curly and I went across the flats to his raft of five trees held together with three cross pieces. This we poled into Berg Lake as far as we could—and there Curly rowed out past a huge ice berg which we photographed—then in past the huge Tumbling Glacier which shows its size and huge crevasses—and shows more, the closer you get to it."*

The outfitting crew consisted of guide, Curly Phillips, cook, Joe Sopher, packer, Frank Doucette, and three brothers who were helpers, by the names of John, Walter, and David Tyler. The outfit had twenty-three head of horses and headed down the Smoky drainage, up and over Bess Shoulder, down the Jackpine, over Big Shale Hill to Forget-Me-Not Pass.

Caroline's journal noted that the party frequently saw signs of old abandoned hunting camps of the Grande Cache Indians. The camps included teepee poles and drying racks for meat. Further evidence of Native use of the area is penned by Mrs. Hinman. On July 14 she wrote, *"Three Tylers and I climbed to the top of a ridge and made a cairn there. Very abrupt cliffs separated the real summits on which we stood from a second peak of the mountain a little lower. Got a great view of the Smoky River and its valley. Could also see Jones Peak which the boys had climbed from the camp in the Jackpine* (River)*—and the shoulder which we crossed to our camp on the west branch of the Jackpine* (Pauline Creek)*. To the northwest we could see the lower slopes of the Big Mountain* (Sir Alexander)*, the top being covered with cloud. To the northeast of it we thought we saw the snowy summit of Mt. Ida. From where we had lunch, Frank thought he saw a moose or caribou grazing by a lake to the S.E. Gave Arnold the glasses and Arnold said he saw a teepee! Sure enough it was! The caribou were seven horses. Thought it might be Donald McDonald, the half-breed, or Indians from Grande Cache."*

On July 18, the crew packed up and headed north down Forget-Me-Not Valley. Caroline wrote, *"Our way led into the meadow where* (a grizzly) *had been—then into a thick spruce woods. Here we came upon a well-marked old Indian trail dating back probably 100 years to the time when the Hudson's Bay people were in this country. This we followed in and out through the lovely woods until it brought us out into the broad, open valley of the Sheep Creek. We climbed up to a lovely level bench fifty feet above the river and here we made camp about 3 p.m."*

As the trip progressed, it became more and more apparent there was a blooming romance developing between Mary and Curly, which was noted in Caroline Hinman's journal. Curly endeared Mary with the name *Nitchie. Nichimos* means sweetheart in the Cree language.

The group arrived at Mt. Kitchi *(Sir Alexander)* on July 21st. The party attempted to climb it and was unable to make the summit, so Curly and Arnold took some time to explore the

Pictured above:
"Caroline Hinman & George Camp."
George Camp guided for Curly Phillips on many kids' camps that Caroline Hinman organized. He moved to the Rockies in 1918, making a career as a packer, guide or cook, working for many of the first outfitters based out of Jasper. His first employer was Fred Brewster.

George also spent many winters trapping with Curly on the upper Smoky River, Hardscrabble and Jackpine Valleys.

George ended up finding employment as a Jasper Park Warden in the 1940s.

Photo courtesy of Mary Anne Deagle.

new country for hunting and trapping possibilities. Days later, the men made another attempt to ascend the Big Mountain and climbed to within thirty metres of the top; however, the climb was too dangerous and the men decided to abandon their attempt.

The outfit packed up on August 4 to start their long trip home. On August 17, Caroline noted, *"We passed a fascinating Indian teepee with its chinks filled in with moss and pine needles (a stick teepee). Crossed Sheep Creek where we stopped and camped on its bank at 6 p.m."* The next day the party left Sheep Creek and went up Dry Canyon and passed three or four sulphur lakes. They caught a glimpse of the Muddy Water River far below them and finally hit the valley of the Smoky where the ladies picked delicious plump, red raspberries. They unpacked on the Muddy River and Caroline noted, *"After lunch, Curly and Mary went down to the Smoky into which the Muddy ran a mile below camp. Here they made a raft and went down the Smoky about three miles to see which side of the river the Grande Cache trail was on. They were forced to drive the raft into shore suddenly and jump. Mary missed her footing and slid back into swift water up to her shoulders. Curly grabbed her and pulled her ashore."*

On Friday, August 20, the packtrain crossed the Muddy Water River and found the trail that headed down the Smoky. Around 5 p.m. they came to a little beach in the woods with a thirty-five-foot dugout, which was padlocked to a tree. Beside it was a stake with writing on both sides. Caroline's journal stated, *"One side was in English and the other side was in Cree saying that it would cost anyone using the canoe $10.00—and anyone losing it, $50.00".* Curly

Pictured left:
"As the trip progressed, it became more & more apparent there was a blooming romance developing between Mary & Curly."
- a journal note of Caroline Hinman's.

Curly endeared Mary with the name *Nitchie*. Nichimos means sweetheart in the Cree language. This image is one of Mary & Curly on one of their many walks.

Photo courtesy of Jasper Yellowhead Museum & Archives PA 38-44.

opted to make a raft rather than pay the fee. He built one capable of holding twenty-five hundred pounds and held the raft together with lash ropes. Caroline wrote, *"Frank went off to get the horses and drove them down to the river's edge. When they all assembled, they were chased into the river with everyone yelling and whooping at them. They were soon up to their necks in the swift current and had to swim. One horse got carried downstream but finally made it to shore. It was exciting. Then came the packing up of the raft. Pack saddles on one side, riding saddles on the other. Grub, panniers and dunnage between and all well towards the back. When all was ready, we humans got aboard. Out into the river we swung and down the swift current. We went floating crossways to the opposite shore. It was thrilling! The swift movement of the rushing water swirling up through the logs."* The party arrived on the south side of the Smoky and Curly and the men were off looking for their horses. After lunch the ropes were removed and the fourteen logs were floated into the river.

By 2:25 the group had packed up and crossed the Sulphur River and came across a house with a log fence, big corral, log stable, a little chapel—and knew that they had reached Grande Cache. They also saw a red wagon that belonged to Ewan Moberly. However, all the windows in the house were closed and the door was barred. Curly's outfit had passed other homes that were made of log with moss chinking. It was a deserted village situated by two pretty lakes (*Grande Cache Lake and Victor Lake*).

On August 31, the group packed up for the last time. It was cold and cloudy. Caroline wrote: *"Up at 6:30 am and dressed in time. Freezing cold. Packed up dunnage after breakfast and mounted our steeds for the last time."* The horses were spirited, knowing they were close to the end of the trail, and moved out at a good speed on the packtrail above Berg Lake, heading for home.

At about the same time period, the Hargreaves Brothers were entering into the outfitting industry in the Jasper and Mt. Robson areas. This new outfitting business took hunters and summer trail rides deep into Willmore Wilderness Park. The Hargreaves Brothers would have a profound influence on outfitting over the next seventy-five years. George, Frank, Roy, John *(Jack)* and twin sister, Myrtle Hargreaves moved to Jasper in 1912. By the summer of 1914, Jack Hargreaves had gone to work for the Otto Brothers, and later was also employed by Curly Phillips. A transcript dated 1976 details Mrs. Jack *(Sophia)* Hargreaves' and Mrs. Roy *(Gladys)* Hargreaves' account of an expedition. *"In 1917, Jack went with Curly Phillips and Miss Mary L. Jobe on a trip to the Porcupine* (Kakwa) *River. The purpose of this trip was to build a trapper's cabin for Curly, to take in his winter's supply of food—and to show Miss Jobe the country around the Porcupine River. When this was accomplished, the party started for home. They found very heavy snowfall had occurred, so horses and men moved very slowly. Curly and Jack took turns at breaking trail—the snow being belly deep for the horses. They had little food for either man or beast and they returned through Grande Cache, an Indian village. Jack and Curly were known by some of the Indians and were given fine treatment. Miss Jobe, being a white woman, was of great interest. The party arrived back in Jasper many days overdue."*

Most of the guides and outfitters of the Canadian Rockies were enlisted in the Canadian Armed Forces during World War I. After the war, many of the outfitters returned home resuming their businesses—and the Hargreaves brothers were no exception. Jack and Frank, both war veterans, applied for adjoining homesteads at Mt. Robson. It wasn't long before their brothers, George and Roy joined them to build several log buildings and a small store. Soon the four brothers began outfitting parties using approximately seventy head of horses. Jack decided to pull out of the *Hargreaves Brothers* in 1924 and moved his portion of the outfit to Jasper. Now Jack sent supplies to Devona by freight train and trailed his horses there. He traveled the Snake Indian and over to Willow Creek, out of the National Park to the Willmore Wilderness area, while brothers George and Roy accessed Willmore via Mt. Robson and the upper Smoky River Valley.

Pictured right:
"The Otto Brothers"
From L to R:
Closson, Jack & Bruce Otto.
Unknown man at right.

Photo courtesy
Jasper Yellowhead
Museum & Archives
Circa 1915
997-07-262-54

Next, Jack Brewster decided to open his own company and leave Brewster and Moore. *"As a junior partner in the Brewster and Moore (company), Jack Brewster had never received the recognition he deserved despite the fact that he had single-handedly kept the company afloat during the difficult war years. It was therefore not surprising when he left his brother Fred, bought up much of the Otto Brothers' pack string and equipment, and set up his own business in 1922."*[22]

Jack Brewster's purchase brought an end to the *Otto Brothers'* era as outfitters. The Ottos had started outfitting in 1909 and were in operation thirteen years. The prospects of outfitting changed in 1922 with the introduction of the automobile, and the Otto brothers knew that it would play a big part in tourism in the future. In 1923, they started a new business called Mountain Motors, which was Jasper's first garage. Jack Brewster's outfit operated for the next twenty-four years, until he sold to Larry McGuire and Red Creighton in 1946.

By 1924, Curly was expanding his options. *"Curly diversified and became involved in two other innovative ventures. The first was an irrigated market garden. He was assisted by his brother Harry, packer, Art Allen and (Art's step-father) Joe Saladana, who was a local mountain climbing guide. The second concept Curly had was the creation of a "Dude Trapline."*[23] After World War I, it was apparent that the days of the wealthy tourists were over. Curly put his complaint in writing to a prospective customer. He wrote, *"We have a wonderful country here and I have spent seventeen years building up an outfit and a business only to find when I got to the top there was nothing there and no possible future for the business."*[24] *"Curly Phillips married in 1923, and although he continued to*

22   Diamond Hitch by E.J. Hart - Page 238

23   Diamond Hitch by E.J. Hart - Page 230 - 231

24   Thorington Collection, "Introducing Donald Curly Phillips' Dude Trapline,"
        1924-25: Phillips to Woodward, May 17, 1925

Pictured above:
Norman Willmore 1954.

Courtesy of the
Provincial Archives of
Alberta 1664.2

Norman A. Willmore stated,
"Our forests are a renewable
resource belonging
not only to this but future
generations of Albertans."

A Willmore Park Bill was
introduced to rename
Wilderness Provincial Park
after the Social Credit
cabinet minister
who was killed in a
car crash on
February 3, 1965.

outfit parties, he seldom accompanied them himself."[25] Curly devoted himself to outfitting clients with boat excursions on lakes and rivers. In 1923, Curly Phillips had recruited two Native guides by the names of Adam Joachim and Dave Moberly to guide most of his pack trips. Art Allen also became a regular hunting guide for Phillips. Curly's life was cut short when he died in an avalanche at Elysium Pass in 1938.

Fred Brewster's focus centred on the development of Jasper Park Lodge during the 1920s, and he used this as a headquarters for his outfitting operations. He operated a pony barn out of the lodge and it wasn't long before the *Skyline Trail Rides* to Maligne Lake were popular. He constructed the Medicine Lake Chalet, which was the first of a series of structures that would become known as Fred Brewster's Rocky Mountain camps. These camps included Medicine Lake Chalet, Tonquin Valley Camp, Little and Big Shovel Pass Camps, and Tekarra Basin Camp. By 1935, Fred Brewster had built the main lodge of the *Black Cat Ranch*. It was built for people who felt that Jasper was too developed and who wanted to experience the mountain wilderness. It became a jump-off point for summer pack trips and hunting parties and for venturing into what is now Willmore Wilderness Park. Fred owned the Ranch until World War II, after which it was bought out by Dave Slutker who used the facility for a hunting base. Later, it was sold to Red Creighton.

Slowly, over the next decade, changes were affecting the eastern slopes and by the mid-1940s a visible scar was being perpetrated on the land. *"In 1944, the Imperial Oil Company explored the area north of Hinton, searching for petroleum. Approximately one hundred men were occupied in this search. In 1948, Imperial Oil constructed the 'oil road' to Muskeg* (which is twenty miles east of present-day Grande Cache). *In order to find sites where their seismic crews could drill, Imperial Oil hired various guides and outfitters in the area."*[26] During the 1940s and 1950s, oil and gas leases were awarded in what is now Willmore Wilderness Park. The Hinton and Jasper outfitters and trappers were getting worried about the roads that the oil and gas sector were inflicting on the mountain trails. Outfitter, Tom Vinson stated in a July 19, 2003 interview, *"So we pressured Norman Willmore (MLA) to do something about the oil and gas exploration, and he did. He declared the area a wilderness park where trapping, hunting and fishing would be permitted. That was all—no motor vehicles. That's what we wanted, of course."* Due to the fact that no oil of any consequence was discovered, the pressure from the oil and gas sector subsided when they let their leases expire. In 1959, Norman Willmore was instrumental in getting legislation passed to protect the area. This legislation is now known as the Willmore Wilderness Act.

---

25   Diamond Hitch by E.J. Hart - Page 253
26   History of Hinton by Hazel Hart - Page 344

Pictured right (L to R):
Norman Willmore,
Mrs. Dot Willmore and
Mr. Diefenbaker.

Photo courtesy of
Joyce Hageman, who is
Norman Willmore's niece.

Norman Willmore was a man who believed in the environment and wanted his constituency to have a voice and he encouraged the trappers to organize into a body that could be heard by government.[27] Norman Willmore was also the driving force in the formation of the Alberta Trappers Association. This Member of the Legislative Assembly *listened* and has left a wilderness legacy for future generations.

Ewan Moberly, Adam Joachim, Louis Joachim, Henry Joachim and the McDonald and Wanyandie families continued to live an undisturbed lifestyle in the Smoky, Sheep Creek and Kakwa River Valleys—that is, until the coal mine was developed near Grande Cache. The Native way of life was once again disturbed in 1969 by the establishment of the New Town of Grande Cache. Prior to the building of the town, the small band of indigenous people had to travel to Entrance, Hinton or Grande Prairie twice a year by packtrain. They would sell their furs and trade for provisions, living a traditional lifestyle. Flour, salt, sugar, baking powder, lard and tea were the main goods that they purchased. Sadly, with the establishment of the coal mine, everything changed. Even the newly legislated Willmore Wilderness Park was made smaller from its original size to accommodate the development of the new town. In fact, Willmore Wilderness Park has been reduced in size twice since it was first created by the Provincial Government in 1959.

This story doesn't end without a twist of irony. Quotes from a letter dated March 23, 1922, which is outlined in the *History of Hinton* book, clearly shows the legal entanglement that resulted in the coal found in the Grande Cache area. *"Coal* (in Grande

---

27   Norman Willmore was member for Jasper-Edson, also Minister of Lands and Forests.

Cache) *was discovered in the first place by a half-breed and several other prospectors in the winter of 1909 and 1910, but the leases were not paid in this instance, as the railroad had not reached west of the Pembina River. Later on in 1913, Doctor Hoppe was interested in the matter and was induced to invest money, by paying the rentals of these coal areas.*[28] However, during World War I, money was tight and Dr. Hoppe had asked the government for an extension to make payment. *"Friends of the Government became aware of this and used their influence to have the leases taken away from Hoppe and his associates—Mr. Isenberg and several others—and through advance information which they secured from a clerk and others in the Government—went out and staked these leases before any of the prospectors who were primarily interested in locating this—had any knowledge that Doctor Hoppe had failed in paying his rentals or that his leases had been cancelled. In fact, at this time, one of the parties, the half-breed mentioned, Donald McDonald, was serving overseas with the 218th Regiment from Edmonton. You will, no doubt, remember that an investigation was demanded as to the manner in which these people, friends of the Government, acquired these leases—and the whole situation was so rotten that the Government was compelled, in fear of public opinion, to cancel all the leases—but instead of investigating or giving any consideration to the claims of the original prospectors, or even to Doctor Hoppe and his associates— they immediately threw all this area into a coal reserve, determined that if their friends were unable to get it, they would reserve this until some future date— when some other scheme or plan could be put forward to steal these leases. As a result, Donald McDonald lost all of his interest, along with certain other prospectors, when Dr. Hoppe's interest was wiped out."*[29]

"Donald McDonald, the half-breed, unfortunately can neither read nor write and the Solicitor with whom he had always done his business died during the time he was in France (WWI) and he is unable to find any trace of his papers. His position is that he had nothing to show for his interest in this area except the verbal understanding he had with Dr. Hoppe and the fact that everyone in this country knows he is the man who made the discovery, cut the trail in there (coal seams) and did the work in connection with the property. It seems to me that before any steps are taken by the present Government— they should carefully investigate all these claims, even though some of them are only moral obligations."[30] Sadly, Donald McDonald never saw a penny for his interest in the coal seams he discovered.

28   History of Hinton by Hazel Hart - Page 81
29   History of Hinton by Hazel Hart - Page 81
30   History of Hinton by Hazel Hart - Page 82

The past hundred years have seen a huge transition in the eastern slopes of the Canadian Rockies—and the indigenous people of the area have paid a very heavy price. Their loss of a land base in both the Jasper and Grande Cache areas, and the loss of the coal rights of Donald McDonald have all been bitter pills to swallow. Resource extraction of timber, and oil and gas on the eastern slopes, has ravaged the mountain region, which once attracted Basa Wanyandie, Ewan Moberly and their followers. Despite the betrayal of these indigenous people, it is reassuring to focus on the fact that Norman Willmore had the foresight to have legislation passed which would ensure traditional land use activities in what is now called Willmore Wilderness Park. There is some solace in the fact that future generations will have the right to hunt, trap, fish and use horses—all because of the lobbying in the 1950s from outfitters, trappers, indigenous friends and constituents for what became the Willmore Wilderness Act. Thank you, Norman Willmore!

Pictured above:
Donald McDonald in the foreground sitting with his hunter. Donald was guidng for Nick Nickerson on a forty-five-day trip from August 26 to October 9, 1926.

Photo courtesy of the Nick Nickerson Collection. George Kelley donated this image for this publication.

Today, the Aseniwuche Winewak Nation of Canada *(AWN)* and the Grande Cache Metis Local represent many of the indigenous people that were forced out of Jasper. Dave MacPhee, President of the Aseniwuche Winewak married Yvonne McDonald, a descendant of Louise (Findlay) Thappe who ended up marrying Donald McDonald. Alvin Findlay, President of the Grande Cache Metis local is a direct descendant of Jacco Findlay. Dave MacPhee and Alvin Findlay have been dedicated to bringing a voice to a people who have been displaced and propelled into the twenty-first century. There are other original descendants of Jasper who live in Hinton, Edson and other areas.

The Willmore Wilderness Foundation was founded in 2002 and has been passionate about maintaining and resurrecting badly neglected traditional trails in Willmore Wilderness Park. Then President, Julian Kinisky spent the last years of his life championing the cause of the organization. Today's President, Bazil Leonard has spent close to forty years traveling the old trails of Willmore and the Kakwa regions. He embraced a labour of love in clearing old packtrails with his old friend, Tom Wanyandie, one of Vincent Wanyandie's grandsons. Tom would blaze a tree and shout at the top of his lungs in broken English, *"I'm going to let this trail live again!"* The trails are being cleared for the public to enjoy.

Chapter One references were taken from the following:

A History of Grande Cache by Richard Wuorinen

Caroline B. Hinman - My First Exploring Expedition with Mary Jobe of NY City in the summer of 1915

Diamond Hitch by E.J. Hart

Genealogy of Alvin Findlay of Grande Cache by Mrs. Elizabeth Macpherson

Genealogy of James Wanyandie - descendant of Basa Wanyandie

History of Hinton by Hazel Hart

Jasper Reflections published by Jasper Community History

Journals of Ishbel *(Hargreaves)* Cochrane 1946

Off the Beaten Track by Cindi Smith

Pack Saddles to Tête Jaune Cache by James G. MacGregor

Tracks Across My Trail by William C. Taylor

When Fur Was King by Henry John Moberly and William Bleasdell Cameron

Yellowhead Pass and Its People by Valemount Historical Society 1984

Pictured on right page:
Bighorn Ewes and Lambs - 2006.

Pictured this page:
Alvin Findlay, President of the Grande Cache Metis Local.
David MacPhee, President of the Aseniwuche Winewak Nation *(AWN).*
Bazil Leonard, President of the Willmore Wilderness Foundation.

Photos on both pages by Susan Feddema-Leonard.

CHAPTER TWO:
The Guides & Outfitters

Native guides and their horses were often employed to traverse the rugged country. Most of the packhorses used were Indians' horses known as Cayuses. These indigenous horses had larger feet and were good in crossing muskegs that are common in the Rocky Mountains. Many of the Native men proved to be excellent packers, trackers and guides. Guides included Adolphus Moberly, Bill (William) Moberly, Dave Moberly, Frank Moberly, Ed Moberly, Miles Moberly, Don Moberly, Roddy Moberly, Malcolm Moberly, Paul Moberly, Emil Moberly, Mike Moberly, Donald McDonald, Dave McDonald, Johnny McDonald, Lactap McDonald, Frank McDonald, Dave Findlay, Frank Findlay, Fred Findlay, Henry Joachim, Jimmy Joachim, Felix Joachim, Louis Joachim, Frank Joachim, Milton Joachim, Casey Joachim, Kelly Joachim, Adam Joachim, Harry Wanyandie, Daniel Wanyandie, Tommy Wanyandie, Billy Wanyandie, Robert Wanyandie, James Wanyandie, Tommy Plante, Joe Plante, Fred Plante, Jimmy Plante, Isaac Plante, Walter Delorme, Charlie Delorme, Ernie Delorme, Ronnie Delorme and nephews Lee and Curtis Hallock. The Metis sons of Mrs. Lewis Swift, Albert Norris and Dean Swift, were sought as trail men. Guides also included the sons of Judd Groat—Butch Groat, Manly Groat, Gary Groat and Dusty Groat, as well as Joe Groat and his son, Ken Groat.

Some of the Native men were also anxious to throw their hats into the arena to start their own outfitting businesses. These men were professional entrepreneurs and were highly sought as outfitters. The Hinton area outfitters included: Tommy Groat, Felix Plante, Judd Groat and recently, Johnny Groat. Grande Cache based outfitters included Louis Delorme, his son, Gordon Delorme, Eddie Joachim, Deome Findlay, Fred Wanyandie and since 1997, Lyle Moberly.

There have been many non-Native guides throughout the years. Their names are too numerous to mention. However, some of these skilled mountain men include Allan McConnochie, George Swain, James Shand-Harvey, Frank Doucette, Daniel Phillips, Harry Phillips, George Camp, Pat Smythe, Don Guild, Chuck Chesser, John Chesser, Dick Hargreaves, Gene Merrill, Russell Cooper, Cuff Jameson, Red Ilie, Tom Ross, Mac Elder, John Williams, Cam Taylor, Otto Peterson, Mark Truxler, Jeff Wilson, Charles Berry, Edwin Alstott, Bob Ekroth, Don McMurtry, John Haggblad, Frank Siegfried, Earl Hallett, Alex McDougall, Dan Hallock, Leroy Sharlow, Tom Timperley, and Joe Timperley

Pictured above:
Long-time guide, Albert Norris, courtesy Tom & Yvette Vinson.

Pictured left:
Guides: *(standing),*
Dave and Frank Findlay,
Isaac Plante *(sitting).*
Isaac was a long-time guide
for Roy Hargreaves.
He personally guided
Jack O'Connor on a
bighorn sheep hunt in 1932
while employed by
Hargreaves.
Photo courtesy of
Louis & Elizabeth Joachim.

Over the past century, many outfitters have come and gone in the Jasper and Willmore Wilderness areas. The following represents some of the outfitters from 1900 to 1979 in the approximate order that they entered the profession. We apologize if we missed any of the guides or outfitters, however, some other names will be included in the following chapters and in the subsequent books.

Fred Stephens

Fred Stephens was born in Michigan, U.S.A. in 1868. He moved to Montana and made his living as a hunter, trapper, and a logger. He relocated to Banff in 1896 and was hired by Tom Wilson as a packer and an axe man. By the turn of the century, Fred Stephens ventured out on his own—to become the first outfitter to investigate the Yellowhead country. In 1901 and 1903, he headed north from Lake Louise but was unsuccessful in his endeavours. In 1905, he traveled west from his home in Lacombe to explore the Yellowhead. Not only was he successful but he also visited the area on a regular basis for many years. In later times, Fred Stephens outfitted from a location near Entrance, Alberta. From 1909 to 1913, Fred Stephens worked with outfitter, John Yates, *"...as their clients required more horses and equipment than one outfitter was able to access on short notice. For this reason, temporary partnerships became the most favoured means for compensating for their small (outfit) size."*[1] Stephens disappeared from the outfitting scene, spending much of his time at home during World War I—and left the trail completely, in order to operate a fox farm in Montana, in the 1920s.

---

1   Diamond Hitch by E.J Hart - Page 199

John Yates

John Yates was born in England in 1880, raised in California and moved to Alberta in 1906. He was a partner on a homestead with Allan McConnochie on the west side of Lac Ste. Anne, Alberta. The homestead became known as Hobo Ranch and provided a temporary place for transient young men to stay. Yates made his first pack trip to Prairie Creek near Hinton in 1906 when he packed supplies west for the railroad survey. In 1907, he made a trip to Tête Jaune Cache and met the A.P. Coleman party, mountaineers that had made an unsuccessful attempt to climb Mt. Robson. Coleman's party was exhausted and short of supplies from their expedition—and Yates readily lent Coleman a horse and took him to Edmonton. Coleman was indebted to Yates and hired him to outfit another party in 1908 to attempt the climb of Mt. Robson.

In 1909, 1910, 1911 and 1913, Yates and outfitter, Fred Stephens worked collaboratively, outfitting mountaineering parties. *"While for a time it seemed as though the relationship developed between the two would result in a more lasting partnership—their fierce independence and outside interests gravitated against it. Failing to grasp the opportunity* (to work as partners) *ultimately cost them their chance for the viability—as within a few years both had disappeared from the guiding and outfitting scene."*[2] Yates married in 1910 and took up a homestead in northern Alberta where he raised his family. He retired in Imperial Valley, California in 1920.

Pictured above:
"John Yates
Pack Train Crossing
the McLeod River
on the Ice ."
April 1909. PA 44 -5
Photo courtesy of
Jasper Yellowhead
Museum & Archives.

Pictured on left page:
Top: John Yates
in his camp,
courtesy of the
Whyte Museum of the
Canadian Rockies.
v65-accn.636

2   Diamond Hitch by E.J Hart - Page 203

Alex Wylie

Alex Wylie ventured into Jasper on July 1, 1906. *"Alex came with a packtrain of twenty-five horses, three guides and thirty-four hundred pounds of provisions for the surveyors of the Grand Trunk Pacific who were working through the Yellowhead Pass."*[3] *"In 1918, he settled with his outfit in Jasper, which now was a Federal Park. In winter, he hauled lumber and water for the townsfolk, and in summer, he rented horses. In 1919, he bought a number of horses from Bruce Otto."*[4] *"In the fall of 1939, he sold his outfit, a string of twenty-four horses complete with harness, saddles, bridles and wagons for sixteen hundred dollars to Charlie Matheson."*[5] Alex outfitted tourists for a total of twenty-one years.

---

3   Jasper Reflections - Page 467

4   Jasper Reflections - Page 467

5   Jasper Reflections - Page 467

Tom (Thomas) Groat

Tom Groat was a surveyor for the railroad. *"He was born in Edmonton and came west with the Grand Trunk survey team in 1904."*[6] *"Montana Pete, Tom Groat and Rod McCrimmon were commissioned to deliver twenty-five horses needed by the GTP surveyors in 1906. While they carried some supplies, a large cache had to be made at Prairie Creek, three miles west of present-day Hinton."*[7]

Groat Road in Edmonton was named after Tom Groat's father who worked for the Hudson's Bay Company. He donated a large sector of land to the City of Edmonton as he owned the land from Groat Road to the Parliament Buildings. He also owned land across the Saskatchewan River.

Tom married Clarisse Moberly in 1910 at Prairie Creek. He went into business for himself and became an outfitter in the Jasper area and, what is now, Willmore Wilderness Park. Tom supported his new family by outfitting for various government employees, mineral prospectors and surveyors. In 1912, Tom guided Joe Errington to the Wildhay to stake claims. Errington had controlled the Blue Diamond Coal Company in Brule. Tom built up his business by outfitting geological survey parties, summer trail riding parties, and hunters.

Tom and Clarisse lived in the Brule-Hinton area. The couple had nine children, including Gladys, Judd, Mary, Alberta, Joe, Sara, Alice, Bruce and Freda. Clarisse Moberly was the granddaughter of Henry John Moberly who was a Hudson's Bay Factor at Jasper. Clarisse's father was Ewan Moberly. Clarisse was an original inhabitant of Jasper.

Tom's son, Judd purchased his father's outfit in 1946. Tom operated professionally for a total of thirty-five years. He died in 1949.

Otto Brothers

In 1909, the Otto brothers established their *Otto Brothers* outfitting operation in Jasper. The brothers' names were Jack, Closson and Bruce. They outfitted Alpine Club of Canada parties, summer trail rides and hunting parties. On occasion, they worked in collaboration with Curly Phillips on larger expeditions. Jack Brewster purchased the *Otto Brothers* outfit in 1922. The Otto brothers knew that the newly developed automobile would play a big part in tourism in the future, and in 1923, they started a new business called *Mountain Motors*, which was Jasper's first garage. The Otto brothers operated as outfitters for thirteen years.

Pictured above:
Top: Tom Groat &
a caribou courtesy of
Dusty Groat.

Bottom: Bruce &
Closson Otto,
courtesy of
Jim Babala

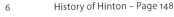

6   History of Hinton – Page 148
7   History of Hinton – Page 65

Curly Phillips

In 1909, Donald "Curly" Phillips entered the guiding and outfitting business. Curly was born in Dorset, Ontario and learned the arts of hunting, trapping and canoe work from his father. In the spring of 1909, he bought horses and set out for the Yellowhead. On his trip west, he ran into Rev. George B. Kinney at John Moberly's homestead near the present-day town of Jasper. The Reverend had planned to climb Mt. Robson and had persuaded Phillips to accompany him. Kinney and Phillips claimed to have successfully made the ascent, but years later Phillips recanted this claim. Despite this, the Kinney-Phillips ascent of Mt. Robson brought Curly's name into the forefront—making him a much sought-after outfitter. He outfitted climbing parties, summer trail rides and hunting parties. During the winter months, he trapped near Obed, Alberta. He also trapped in the Jackpine River, Smoky and Hardscrabble areas. In 1923, Curly Phillips had recruited Native guides by the names of Adam Joachim, Dave Moberly, Ed Moberly, Frank Moberly, Don Moberly and later, Art Allen to guide most of his pack trips—as he primarily devoted himself to outfitting clients for boat excursions on lakes and rivers. Curly's life was cut short when he died in an avalanche at Elysium Pass in 1938.

Fred Brewster

The outfitting business, called *Brewster and Moore*, moved to Fitzhugh *(Jasper)* in 1912, where they constructed stables and corrals, and acquired land. The company consisted of Fred Brewster and seventeen-year-old brother, Jack, along with their brother-in-law, Phil Moore. Phil Moore was an ideal partner as he was married to Fred's sister, Pearl. *Brewster and Moore* outfitted the famous Samuel Prescott Fay expeditions from 1912-1914. During the 1920s, Fred Brewster's focus centered on the development of the *Jasper Park Lodge* pony barn operation, the *Skyline Trail Rides,* the Medicine Lake Chalet and a series of structures that would become known as Fred Brewster's Rocky Mountain Camps. These camps included Medicine Lake Chalet, Tonquin Valley Camp, Little and Big Shovel Pass Camps, and Tekarra Basin Camp. Younger brother, Jack left the business in 1922 and shortly thereafter opened his own outfitting operation. By 1935, Fred Brewster had built the main lodge of the *Black Cat Ranch* near Entrance. He constructed the facility for people who felt that Jasper was too developed and who wanted to experience the mountain wilderness. Fred Brewster operated the Black Cat until the mid-1950s, when he retired, selling off his holdings to some of his staff. Tom Vinson acquired the Brewster's backcountry operations in the Jasper and Willmore areas, while Red Creighton purchased the *Black Cat Ranch.*

Stan Clark

Stan Clark entered the employment of the Canadian Forestry Service, becoming the first Superintendent in 1912. He did most of the pioneer work in establishing the Athabasca Forest Reserve. After returning from war in 1918, he purchased the Entrance Ranch and began setting up a large horse and cattle ranch. He started outfitting hunting parties in the 1920s. After Stan's death, Carl Luger purchased a portion of Clark's outfit in 1947 and Reun Fischer also bought horses and gear.

Bert Wilkins

"Bert Wilkins built a house in Jasper in 1914. He worked for Curly (Phillips) in the summer, and fall in the outfitting business. He also did some trapping. In 1924, he went into partnership with Rufe Neighbor and they stayed together until after World War II when they sold the business." [8] They outfitted big game hunters out of Rock Lake, the Sulphur and Smoky Rivers. For many years, Rufus Neighbor also managed the Entrance and Athabasca Ranches located near Hinton.

Pictured above:

Top: Forestry Office at Hinton.
L to R: Charles Morse, the District Superintendent & Stan Clark Circa 1913, Hinton.
Photographer - Roy Woodley.
Photo courtesy of the
"Dominion Forestry Branch,
Alberta Forest Protection Collection."

Bottom: Bert Wilkins & Rufe Neighbor.
Courtesy Jasper Yellowhead Museum & Archives PA 38-64

Hargreaves Brothers

George, Frank, Roy, Jack and twin sister, Myrtle Hargreaves moved to Jasper in 1912. The boys' father, Edward had lost his wife and remarried—and a half-brother Dick was living with them in Victoria. By the summer of 1914, Jack Hargreaves had gone to work for the Otto Brothers, and later was also employed by Curly Phillips. In 1917 *"Jack Hargreaves went with Curly Phillips and Miss Mary L. Jobe on a trip to the Porcupine (Kakwa) River. The purpose of this trip was to build a trapper's cabin for Curly, to take in his winter's supply of food—and to show Miss Jobe the country around the Porcupine* (Kakwa) *River."*[9]

The brothers enlisted during World War I and were unable to outfit during that period. After 1918, the Hargreaves brothers resumed their outfitting operation. Jack and Frank, both war veterans, applied for adjoining homesteads at Mt. Robson. Roy was under medical care and had to spend a year in hospital in England, convalescing. Once discharged, Roy and George joined them to build several log buildings and a small store on the homesteads. Soon the four brothers began outfitting parties, using approximately seventy head of horses. Jack decided to pull out of the *Hargreaves Brothers* in 1924 and moved his outfitting interest to Jasper.

Chuck Chesser, originally from Edmonton, came to work at the Mt. Robson Dude Ranch in the 1920s where he met his future wife. Chuck married Anne MacLean in 1931. Prior to World War II, *"Anne and Chuck Chesser were partners with Anne's sister, Sophia and her husband, Roy Hargreaves in running Mt. Robson Guest Ranch."*[10] Their business was known as *Hargreaves and Chesser.* Chuck guided with Roy Hargreaves on hunting trips downstream on the Smoky River. One such thirty-day hunting trip took place in 1942, prior to Chuck going

---

9   A transcript dated 1976 by Gladys, Mrs. Jack Hargreaves and Sophia, Mrs. Roy Hargreaves

10   Jasper Reflections - Page 86

to war. Roy, Chuck and Dean Swift guided the party from Mt. Robson Ranch to Sheep Creek Valley. Anne Chesser and Ishbel, Roy's oldest daughter, cooked for the expedition. Shortly after this trip, Chuck Chesser enlisted in the war effort. Upon returning from Europe, he guided until approximately 1950—when he sold out his interest and went to work on the railway.

"Among the many hunters whom Roy Hargreaves guided was Mr. L.S. Chadwick of Cleveland, who enjoyed a successful hunt for bighorn sheep (1935). Next year he asked Roy to join him on a hunt for stone sheep. This trip was arranged with guide and outfitter, Walter Curly Cochrane of Rolla, B.C. Again Mr. Chadwick was successful and took home the world's record stone sheep."[11]

As the years went by, changes were taking place in the Hargreaves' operation. Frank was murdered in his sleep at his home in Jackman B.C. near Valemount B.C. George Hargreaves died on a hunting trip in 1936 and is buried at the headwaters of Sheep Creek. Miss Alice Wright, from the United States, who had been a guest at Mt. Robson Ranch for twenty years, bought the Mt. Robson Ranch when Roy Hargreaves retired in 1959. Miss Wright hired Roy's daughter, Ishbel and her husband, Murray Cochrane to run the ranch. Alice Wright eventually turned the ranch over to Ishbel and Murray who operated Mt. Robson Ranch until the 1990s, when they sold and moved near Valemount B.C.

After Jack left the *Hargreaves Brothers* in the mid-1920s, he continued his guiding and outfitting business based out of Jasper. He operated a first class business, guiding hunters into what is now Willmore Wilderness Park, until he sold his operation to his nephew, Tom McCready.

Pictured above:
Titled: "Our Camp"
at Athabasca Landing
spring 1915.
Hargreaves Brothers' camp.

Pictured on left page (L to R):
Frank Hargreaves;
Roy Hargreaves;
George Hargreaves;
Friend of the brothers;
Jack Hargreaves.
Circa 1915.

Photos courtesy of
Ishbel Cochrane.

11   From a 1976 transcript by Gladys, Mrs. Jack Hargreaves and Sophia, Mrs. Roy Hargreaves

Felix Plante

In 1914, a new player moved into the outfitting circle. Felix Plante, a Metis, was born in 1893 in Lac Ste. Anne. *"Felix's father had come through the area in the winter of 1909-1910, freighting groceries and machinery. His father was familiar with the country and the existing packtrails."*[12]

His father sold their farm at Alberta Beach to the Canadian Northern Railway and the family moved west. It took them one month to travel to Entrance. They moved onto the Big Berland River where they trapped for eight years. Felix married Caroline Moberly, daughter of John and granddaughter of Henry John Moberly. He supported his family by trapping.

Felix relocated to work for Fred Brewster for fifteen years as a guide at the Jasper Park Lodge. He took people on hunting trips that would last from twenty-one to thirty days. Felix guided world-famous geologists, naturalists and doctors. By 1929, he had saved his money and purchased his own outfit, which consisted of fifty horses. His outfit was born in 1930 and he operated out of Entrance. In 1950, Carl Luger took his newly-wed wife, Mildred, who spent her honeymoon cooking, on a forty-four-day sheep hunt, outfitted by Felix Plante.

Felix was known to have a top-notch and striking outfit. He had many pinto horses and his sons wore black and white chaps. Felix's outfit was colour-coordinated and it certainly looked sharp on the trail. He was reputed to have an outstanding string of horses. Felix loved working with his horses and, at one time, he owned two hundred head. He was known far and wide for his handcrafted packsaddles that he made from trees that he cut.

Felix saw many changes as the mountain regions developed over an eighty-year period. He felt that some of the changes were good and some were bad. He saw the first roads built in 1916 and had mixed feelings about the highway. While the new road meant progress, it also meant the end of a way of life. Days before his one hundredth birthday, Felix gave the following interview to the Hinton Parklander Newspaper .

"It's kind of 50-50. It was good for some people, but I didn't like the highway at all. All the people that made a living out of horses, it knocked them out. I used to have four or five hundred horses, and then I had nothing. The highways, they bring tourists, and they bring in the dollars. For a lot of people, it's good, but it wasn't good for me," he said. "We respected the land. We didn't just use stuff once and throw it away—we found ways to use it again. People nowadays don't have respect for the land. They cut down the timber, they throw stuff away," he continued. "Everything is so open now, because they cut down much of the timber. The animals have got to have timber to live in—just like you and me need a house," he said. "In the old days, the wages were small – about two dollars a day, but you made a living on it. You could go to the store with $50, and buy lots of

---

12   History of Hinton by Hazel Hart - Page 58

food and lots of clothes. Now, what can you get for $50? Almost nothing," Plante added with a smile. *"I've been here since 1914, and I'm still here, so I must like it. I like the climate, I like the trapping, I like to be free. There weren't too many people here when I came, and that's why I liked it. There's more people here now, but I guess it's still OK, I guess I'll stay."*[13]

Felix turned one hundred in June 1993. He died in 1994 at one hundred years of age. He was one of the most highly respected mountain men of his day.

---

13   The Hinton Parklander – June 7, 1992 – page B 10

Jack Brewster

Jack Brewster purchased the *Otto Brothers* outfit in 1922. He outfitted hunts in the Willmore area during the 1930s. *"Although he continued to maintain Jasper as his headquarters, he went much further afield in pursuit of his business interests. Jack's reputation as one of western Canada's foremost big game hunting guides kept him constantly on the move in search of new and productive territory, and eventually he developed trips into the Cassiar country of British Columbia for this purpose."[14]* He also helped with the construction of the Banff-Jasper Highway and later offered trail rides and hunting services in the Brazeau country. After World War II, he moved to Banff and operated Brewster's Motel until he died in 1951.

Jack Hargreaves

Jack Hargreaves established his outfitting business in Jasper in 1925—after he left the *Hargreaves Brothers*, which was based out of *Mt. Robson Ranch*. Jack bought out Ralph James, an early outfitter who took guests to the Miette Hot Springs on horseback when there was just a trail there. Ralph James decided to sell a bunch of horses that had Morgan breeding, and Jack decided to purchase them. Ralph James had a place where he ranged his horses at Pocahontas—and Jack ended up with the rights to that area. Jack Hargreaves ran a highly successful outfitting business from Jasper over the next quarter of a century. He outfitted hunting parties, geological survey parties, and summer trail rides into Jasper, Willmore and surrounding areas. He liked to take his sheep hunting parties to Kvass Pass, Winifred Lake and the Hardscrabble area of Willmore Wilderness Park. He was a skilled bear hunter. He took over fifty grizzlies during his guiding years. Jack Hargreaves sold his Jasper-based outfit to his nephew, Tom McCready in the mid-1950s. Jack guided and outfitted in the Jasper-Willmore region for forty years.

Art Allen

Art Allen started trapping coyotes at his homestead near Mt. Robson in 1918, as a twelve-year-old. He continued trapping through the 1920s and, by the winter of 1927, was working with Curly Phillips on his line. He hired on a topographical survey party in 1927 from the first of June until the middle of September. It didn't take long for him to find work as a guide for Curly Phillips, Jack Hargreaves, Roy Hargreaves and George Hargreaves. He eventually started his own outfit and ultimately sold out to Leonard Jeck in the 1960s. Art Allen spent close to forty years guiding, outfitting and trapping in Willmore Wilderness and surrounding areas.

---

14   Diamond Hitch by E.J. Hart - pages 254-255

Pictured right :
Emma & Nick Nickerson.
Courtesy of
Jacquie Hanington.

Pictured on left page:
Top: Jack Brewster
circa 1918.

Middle: Jack Hargreaves.
Photo courtesy
of Fay McCready.

Bottom: Art Allen.
photo courtesy of
Jacquie Hanington.

Emma and Nick Nickerson

"By 1929, Emma and Nick Nickerson started guiding hunters for extended trips. Food costs were nominal: eggs forty cents a dozen; bacon thirty cents a pound; and butter twenty-five cents a pound. They stocked up on outfitting supplies at the Entrance Store. Emma Nickerson held a guide and outfitters license along with her husband. The couple operated their outfit for twenty-nine years."[15]

Ishbel *(Hargreaves)* Cochrane, Roy Hargreaves' daughter wrote about an encounter with the Nickerson outfit. Ishbel's journal, dated Thursday, September 12, 1946 stated, *"Before we turned up the Right Branch* (of Femme Creek) *we met an outfit coming down Femme. They'd just come from the Right Branch—it was the Nickerson outfit from Entrance. We decided to go up* (the creek) *anyway—and when we got up there, I saw a man walking out from a camp. Murray* (Cochrane, Ishbel's husband) *went up to talk to him. He was one of Nickerson's party—the cook. They'd lost two horses—and the cook and the horse wrangler had stayed there, to look for them. We went to our camp, which we had a hard time finding, since there'd been horses in there since August 26th— and there were trails going everywhere. Nickerson's outfit had been there since August 26th but not with the dudes who had flown in to Surprise Lake a couple of weeks ago. Murray brought the two guys up for supper because they had no food or beds. They had one saddle horse which they tethered out."*

In the 1950s, Nickerson guided *Shell Oil* on a ninety-day trip. The Nickersons traveled into the Willmore Wilderness area, north of the Smoky River. Outfitter, George Kelley stated in a March 18, 2006 interview that, *"Nick worked as a packer, a trapper and guide his whole life—it was all he had done. He ended up getting a stroke in the early 1960s working for* (Eben) *Eben-Ebenau somewhere up north of Grande Cache. He had a stroke packing a horse. He spent his whole life doing nothing but that. By the stories you read, the hunters really thought a lot of him. They carried Nick out of the bush after his stroke. He spent his final years in a wheelchair here* (in Hinton).*"* Nickerson Creek that flows into Sheep Creek is named after the Nickersons.

Marvin F. (Red) Creighton

Red was born on October 6, 1902 in Greenhill, Nova Scotia. He moved to Alberta in 1920 and to Jasper in 1924. He worked driving and breaking horses and was known as one of the best teamsters in the business. He could drive four-ups and six-ups. By 1930 he hired on with Jack Brewster, breaking horses and working as a guide. Later on, Red Creighton went into partnership with Stan Kitchen in the outfitting business. Their company was known as *Kitchen and Creighton*. This relationship lasted until 1943 when he sold his interest to Stan Kitchen.

In the mid-1940s, Red Creighton trapped on the Jackpine and Smoky River Valleys with Art Allen. Evidence of his trapping diary can still be found penciled on the walls of a small hand-hewn log cabin that Art Allen constructed. The building is located on the banks of the Jackpine River.

In 1944, Red went into business with Larry McGuire and the pair bought out Jack Brewster's outfitting business. Larry was an ideal partner as he had grown up in Jasper and had helped guide and wrangle and had helped local outfitters in many horse roundups. He also knew how to break horses. Creighton and McGuire started their outfitting partnership in the 1945 season, which resulted in a very successful year.

In the 1946 season, Larry McGuire hired his good friend, John Haggblad as a guide. In 1948, Charles Berry wrangled with guides Red Creighton, Larry McGuire and Ed Moberly. The cook was Betty McGuire. In 1949, Ed Moberly guided a hunter in the Kvass area and bagged an exceptionally good head. The bighorn ram measured out at 41-½ inches. Creighton and McGuire were known to have guided in the Winifred Lakes, Kvass Creek, Berland, Sulphur, and Smoky River basins.

The partners worked together as outfitting partners from 1945 to 1951, when Larry was hired by the Jasper Park Warden Service, and Creighton bought him out. Red Creighton purchased the *Black Cat Ranch* in the mid-1950s from Fred Brewster. Red carried on running a first-class outfit. He retired from outfitting in 1964 when he sold this business and the *Black Cat Ranch* to Dave Slutker of Edmonton.

"At 82 years of age, Red was still of sound mind and his memory could not have been better, however his health was failing. In March of 1985, Red contracted pneumonia and died in the Hinton Hospital—another of Alberta's greatest guides and outfitters gone."[8]

---

18   Notes from Jim Babala – Whitehorse, Yukon

Louis Delorme

One exceptional outfitter was Louis Delorme, who was born in 1904 near the present-day town of Grande Cache. According to his daughter, Helen Hallock, Louis was with his mother at McDonald Flats when she died in the 1918 flu epidemic. His father died the same night—making him an orphan at fourteen years of age. Helen indicated that her father was raised by Pierre Grey for a period of time, during which he received a formal education.

Louis was the grandson of Pierre Delorme who is buried at Big Grave Flats. Pierre was a blind man who became sick while they were traveling on their way home to Grande Cache on a packtrain. He was riding through Rocky Pass and his family decided to make camp at Big Grave Flats. Pierre died that night—so his family buried him there on the Flats before they broke camp. Pierre had two sons, Phillip and Peter. Peter had two children, a son and a daughter. His son, Louis became a highly respected outfitter and trapper. Louis' sister died of pneumonia as a young girl and is buried at Kvass Flats. Her grave is located on a hillside overlooking the Smoky River Valley.

Louis Delorme was one of the first licensed guides in the Province of Alberta. He remained a guide and outfitter for over sixty years. Louis was a first-rate trapper and used this skill to help supplement his family's income. He was very independent and never asked the government for any help. He was also respected far and wide for his skill as a businessman. Mt. Louis, which is located east of Grande Cache, is named after him.

Louis married Flora Joachim, the daughter of Adam Joachim and they had fourteen children. Several of their sons became guides. These included Walter, Charlie, Ernie, Gordon and Ronnie. Daughters, Helen (Hallock) and Eileen were skilled trail cooks. All of Louis' children were accomplished mountain men and women. In later years, Louis' son, Gordon Delorme became an outfitter. Many of Louis' grandchildren have followed in his footsteps, acting as mountain guides—including Lee and Curtis Hallock, who are actively employed as guides.

Pictured left:
Top: Gordon Delorme.
Middle: Helen *(Delorme)* Hallock.
Bottom: (L to R) Eileen Delorme
and Mike Moberly, son of
Adolphus Moberly .
Mike and Eileen were camped
at Lancaster Creek with outfitter Charlie Stricker.
- circa early 1970s.
Photos courtesy of Charlie Stricker.

Pictured right:
Louis Delorme was a
legendary guide & outfitter
of the Willmore Wilderness,
Jasper & Kakwa areas—
his traditional homeland.
Many will recount stories about
Louis throughout their inteviews
in this and the next book.
Louis was a highly respected
outfitter whose knowledge
of the mountain wilderness
was widely renowned.

Photo courtesy of
Fay McCready, taken while
Louis was working for
Tom McCready.

Pictured on bottom (L to R):
Charlie Delorme - guide.
Walter Delorme - guide.
Photos by Susan Feddema-Leonard.
Ernie Delorme - guide.
Photo courtesy
of Rachelle McDonald *(AWN)*.

Pictured above:
Henry was fondly referred to as Big Henry Joachim.
His reputation as an experienced mountain man is well known
in the big game hunting and outfitting worlds.

Photo courtesy of Victoria Moberly.

(Big) Henry Joachim

Henry Joachim was a legendary guide and trapper who was born at the turn of the century. His father was Martin Joachim, the brother of Adam Joachim. Henry's family had roamed the Smoky and Muskeg Rivers for generations. His knowledge of the land and the mountains was unsurpassed. He was an excellent trapper, tracker, horseman and guide. Henry used to call the Smoky River Valley, *My green, green valley*. His wife, Alice was from a reserve at Horse Lake, Alberta. Alice and Henry were known to have raised seventeen children. Some of the outfitters that Henry guided for were Nick Nickerson, Tom McCready, Roy Hargreaves and the Jasper Warden Service.

Henry lived in the Smoky River Valley, near the present-day town of Grande Cache, where his horses grazed on all of the hillsides of Grande Mountain and Flood Mountain. There was a ford on the Smoky River that people of yesteryear would use when crossing this mighty river. There was an island close to Henry's home, which made the crossing easier. Alice, Henry's wife, used to ride a big black stallion when she crossed the Smoky. She never had to worry about the high water when she rode him.

Henry's granddaughter, Audrey *(Moberly)* Printup has worked as a cook and trail hand for most Willmore outfitters over the past thirty years. She is a very competent woman in the mountain terrain. Another one of Henry's descendants is Lyle Moberly. Lyle and his wife, Denise *(Jones)* Moberly operate *JH Horse Services* in Willmore Wilderness Park. They specialize in taking Swiss tourists on extended trips, deep into the remote areas of the Canadian Rockies. One of their notable rides was a fourteen-day summer pack trip from Grande Cache to McBride, along the Continental Divide. The outfit is still actively involved in today's tourism business.

Albert Ceal

Albert George Ceal was born in 1907 and first filed for a homestead in Hinton in 1928, shortly after he arrived in the area. In the mid-1920s, Albert Ceal learned the ropes for wrangling from outfitter, Nick Nickerson. He headed out on sixty-to-ninety-day hunts, working beside competent guides like Donald McDonald and Henry Joachim. Albert eventually ran a small outfit of his own during the 1940s in the area that is now called Willmore Wilderness Park. He primarily took out hunting parties. Albert died on December 31, 1959.

Pictured above:

Top: Lyle Moberly Fall 2005. Outfitter, Lyle Moberly, continues to use Henry Joachim's brand. Photo courtesy of Lyle & Denise Moberly.

Bottom: Albert Ceal, on a 1926 hunt as a wrangler for Nickerson . Photo courtesy of George Kelley from the Nick Nickerson Collection.

Reinhold Eben-Ebenau

Reinhold Eben-Ebenau, called "Eben," was based out of Slave Lake, Alberta. He started guiding in the Willmore and Kakwa areas in the 1930s with trailmen like Leonard Jeck and others. He ran his own outfit after WWII, from 1950 to 1980. His wife, Marie-Luise was a partner and was both a cook and guide. Eben took his outfit of sixty to seventy horses and gear—and loaded them into boxcars and freighted them to Grande Prairie and trailed them to his hunting area. Eben primarily took out Germans on extended trips and hunted the Kakwa River, Sheep Creek and Smoky River valleys. Sometimes he would end his trips in the Hinton area, and would have to take his horses back to Slave Lake by rail. The *Boone and Crockett Record Book* shows Eben's record moose dated as early as 1935. He had the *Boone and Crockett* Canadian number one grizzly.

Eben was a writer and had written several books in German about hunting in the wilds of the Canadian Rockies. This brought him fame in his European homeland. His books and stories were widely sought after and, as a result, he had no shortage of hunters who wanted to try their hand at obtaining trophies in the Canadian wilds. At Llama Mountain, there is a tree on which Eben wrote, "*Got three sheep and three goats in three days.*" Eben was a conservationist, making sure every part of his animals was used. He was given the Order of the Big Horn in 1986 by the Alberta Government.

Harold Anderson

Harold Anderson was bridge engineer with the Canadian Pacific Railway when the railroad was moving west. When he arrived in the Edson-Hinton region, he fell in love with the Hargwen area, instantly putting in for a homestead. Harold's father, Oscar joined him in developing it. Harold eventually acquired a trapline in the Obed district. He also outfitted hunting parties in the Obed vicinity—and in the area now known as Willmore Wilderness Park. Harold had to trail his horses eighty miles in order to hunt in the Rocky Mountains. Two of his sons, Roy Anderson and Jerry Anderson were enlisted to help their dad on the trail.

Harold had a big outfit with lots of horses. *Anderson Outfitting* primarily operated in the '20s, '30s and '40s. Tom Vinson recounted a story of running into Harold Anderson on the trail in the 1940s—when he was camped at the headwaters of the Wildhay River. Harold's outfit had just packed up that morning, and had headed down the trail about a quarter of a mile. His hunters had shot two bears—so they had to stop and set the camp up again. Tom was camped at Eagle's Nest Pass at the head of Rock Creek. He had run into Harold and his hunters while he was out hunting. Vinson was just a young guide starting in the outfitting industry at that time. "*Ed Moberly of Hinton also managed a couple of hunts for outfitter, Harold Anderson—and one season for Roy and Jerry Anderson after their father died. Harold was an outfitter that hunted the Muddy Water River and Femme Creek across the Big Smoky River.*"[26] Harold passed away in the late 1940s.

Charlie Matheson

"Charlie and Mona (Harragin) *Matheson built the Circle M Ranch near Hinton. Charlie and Mona met while working for Fred Brewster at Medicine Lake. In 1930, Charlie started working as a National Park Warden."*[17] However, sometime during the late 1930s, Charlie decided to leave the Warden Service and purchase an outfit. The couple purchased Alex Wylie's outfit in 1939 and by 1940 had started the *Circle M Dude Ranch*. Charlie Matheson was known to take hunting parties into the Willmore Wilderness area from Rock Lake—on thirty-to-forty-day trips. On one trip north of the Smoky River, Charlie's outfit ran into Art Allen, who notes the event in his chapter's transcript. Charlie worked in Willmore until 1949—for approximately ten years.

Pictured above:
"Charlie and the Gang."
September 1928 at
Medicine Lake, Alberta.
Charlie Matheson,
Gwen Pickford,
Charles Golden,
Agnes and Mona Harragin and
Charlie's dog, Dempsey.

Photo by Joe Weiss
courtesy of Jacquie Hanington.

---

17   History of Hinton by Hazel Hart - Page 136 & 137

Leonard Jeck

Leonard Jeck moved to Jasper at the age of sixteen in 1933. He soon found work with Jack Brewster and took tourists to the Columbia Icefields. For many years, he worked for Jack Hargreaves, guiding summer trips and hunting parties. Leonard joined the RCAF during World War II. After the war, he went to work for Fred Brewster at the *Black Cat Ranch* in Brule. He continued guiding hunting parties for Jack Hargreaves, and from '56 to '68, he operated the pony barns at Maligne Lake for owner, Bill Ruddy. In the 1960s, Leonard purchased Art Allen's outfit. He continued to take guests on summer sightseeing trips in the spring and summer. During the fall, he would guide hunting trips in the Willmore Wilderness area. Leonard sold his outfit to John Ward in 1970.

Stan Kitchen

Stan Kitchen came to Jasper in approximately 1937 and outfitted prior to the war. During this period, Kitchen formed a partnership with Art Hughes for a short while. During the war, he worked on the Alaska Highway, and was trucking out of Dawson Creek and Pouce Coupe, B.C. While he was up north, a woman operated his pony barn, which he reclaimed when he returned from the Alaska Highway. Later, Stan went into business with Marvin "Red" Creighton. Their outfit was known as *Kitchen and Creighton*, but their partnership eventually dissolved. Kitchen's most notable trip was in 1947 when he guided the legendary Bing Crosby on a twenty-one-day hunt in what is now Willmore Wilderness Park. Stan retired later that year when he sold the outfit to John Unland, and continued his trucking business. In later years, he worked at Maligne Tours for Bill Ruddy. Stan died in his sleep at Maligne Lake in 1968.

Tom Vinson

Tom Vinson arrived in the area in the 1940s and went guiding for Fred Brewster, before the war broke out. He joined the Canadian Army in 1942 and, once he returned from the war, Tom started guiding bighorn sheep hunts. He took big game hunters from 1945 right up to 1955, when he bought the outfit from Brewster. Tom guided for bighorn sheep until he turned sixty-five years old, making a total of forty years in the profession.

Tom's children purchased his outfitting operation. In 1976, Tom's daughter, Levone and her husband, Wald Olson obtained Tom's operation at the Tonquin Camp. That same year, daughter, Lenore and husband, Ron Moore acquired Tom's operations at Shovel Pass and the Jasper Park Pony Barn. In 1984, Tom Jr. and his wife, Shawn took over the bighorn sheep permits, the big game hunting operations, and the summer trail riding business in Willmore Wilderness Park.

Tom McCready

Tom McCready, who resided in Jasper since birth, guided and outfitted for close to a thirty-year period from 1945 to 1972. Tom was on the trail from an early age, as he was the nephew of Jack Hargreaves—his mother was Jack's twin sister. Tom and his wife, Fay purchased his Uncle Jack's outfit in the mid-1950s. Fay supported her husband by maintaining the homefront, buying groceries for their outfit, and supporting the business end of the operation.

Tom trailed his horses from Jasper into what is now called Willmore Wilderness Park. He had two or three favourite places to guide his hunters' hunts. One of his base hunting camps was on Falls Creek, which comes in just above Big Grave Flats. Falls Creek is south of Whistler Creek. Another special spot was Hardscrabble Pass.

Tom lived in an ideal location that allowed him to outfit in the spring, summer and fall. He stated, *"So lots of times I'd come in from outfitting, take off my cowboy hat and chaps, grab my skis and ski boots and head for Marmot. I love the outfitting and I love to ski and I love the mountains."* Tom's work allowed him to pursue his passions full time.

Due to a heart condition, Tom sold his outfit to Jim Simpson in 1972.

Carl Luger

Carl Luger first worked for a few months for Ed Neighbor in Jasper in 1937. Ed provided Carl with an excellent recommendation and he gained employment with Bert Wilkins and Rufe Neighbor at the *Athabasca Ranch* from 1937 to 1943. Carl obtained his first guide license in 1940, working primarily for Fred Brewster and Jack Hargreaves during the summer months. He bought out a portion of Stan Clark's outfit in 1947.

Carl started outfitting geological survey parties during the late 1940s and 1950s—as well as big game hunters into what is now Willmore Wilderness Park. Carl married Mildred Woodley in 1950 and purchased her grandfather's homestead at Entrance in 1952. In 1960, Carl guided a geological survey party from Entrance to the headwaters of the Wapiti River. This was his last big pack trip, as he needed a steady income to support his growing family—so he went to work at the Hinton Pulp Mill.

Deome Findlay—Louis Joachim—Frank Joachim

Deome Findlay's father was Isadore Findlay, who was one of the Jasper residents who were displaced when the Federal Government created a park. He was a trail man who came by his knowledge naturally, being a descendant of David Thompson's guide, Jacco Findlay. Deome worked many years for outfitter, Carl Luger ending up as one of his main men. During his life, he also worked for outfitters, Glen Kilgour, Dave Simpson and Bazil Leonard.

During the late 1960s, Deome decided to venture into the outfitting business himself. He outfitted hunting parties for a short period of time and his base camp was set up at Kvass Flats in Willmore. The area is often referred to as Findlay Springs, named after Deome. The area is a good source of drinking water. Deome got his start as an outfitter when some hunters that he was guiding for Carl Luger wrote him a letter requesting the use of horses and saddles. At this point, Deome decided to outfit the hunters by himself. Deome and son, Freddie guided hunters from the United States. Youngest son, Alvin was about fourteen or fifteen years old at that time, and worked as a horse wrangler. Rose Findlay, Deome's wife, cooked meals on a wood stove. She even baked bread for the guests who really enjoyed her home baking.

Rose Findlay had two brothers who were legendary guides by the names of Louis and Frank Joachim. Their father was Charlie Joachim, the twin brother of Martin who lived on the Smoky River. Like their dad, Louis and Frank were exceptional trappers, packers, trackers, guides, and trail men. Frank worked for Stan Kitchen, Red Creighton Tom Vinson and Johnny Unland. In fact, Frank guided for outfitter, Stan Kitchen when Bing Crosby, the singer, was on a hunting trip in 1947. Frank drowned in the Wapiti River near Grande Prairie in 1959.

Louis Joachim also worked for Tom Vinson out of Jasper—and for Johnny Unland. Louis had a lot of horses that he kept at McDonald Flats. After he married, he based himself out of Jarvis Lake, which is near Hinton. Louis had three daughters: Blanche, Gladys and Gloria.

Pictured on left page (L to R):
"Packing up"
Carl Luger, outfitter & Deome Findlay, guide
circa early 1950s.
Photo courtesy of Rose Findlay.

Below:
Carl Luger at the Brule Rodeo in 2004.
Photo by Susan Feddema-Leonard.

Pictured from top to bottom:
Top: Deome Findlay.
Photo courtesy of Dusty Groat.
Middle: Louis Joachim.
Photo courtesy of
Jacquie Hanington.
Bottom: Frank Joachim .
Photo courtesy of
Tom & Yvette Vinson.

Judd Groat

Judd *(Walter)* Groat was born in 1913, at Montana Pete's homestead near Entrance. He was the son of Thomas Groat and Clarisse Moberly. In 1928, at the age of fifteen, Judd traveled with his dad on a forty-five-day trip. He quit school in 1930 to go outfitting with his father. Judd bought his father's outfit in 1946. Judd went on to become a reputable outfitter, and his outfitting expanded to include services to oil companies. He also outfitted summer trail rides and big game hunting trips.

Younger bother, Joe *(Malcolm)* was born in 1924 and he, too, followed his father's and brother's footsteps and became a Class A guide. Judd and his wife, Darleen, raised nine children in their outfitting business.

Jim Babala

Jim Babala was born in Edmonton in 1925 and raised in Luscar. He started professionally guiding and outfitting hunting parties in 1946, with brother, Bill. In 1949, Bill sold his share of the outfit to Jim.

In 1949, Jim hired Louis Joachim as a head guide to lead his party to the Hay and Sulphur Rivers—on his first trip into what is now Willmore Wilderness Park. Also, on this thirty-day trip were Bill Bodenchuk and Jim, as guides. George Richmond was the cook and Dave Findlay was the horse wrangler.

Over the years, Jim's guides included George Kelley, Ed Moberly, Miles Moberly, Frank Moberly, Dave Moberly, Fred Plante, Jimmy Plante and Felix Plante. Jim lived in Luscar from 1925 to 1972 when he moved to Whitehorse, Yukon. He left the Willmore area and started outfitting in the Yukon until he retired in 1980.

Glen Kilgour

Glen got his start on a horse outfit in 1945 with Bill Winters of Sundre, Alberta and eventually bought into Bill's operation. Glen moved north and outfitted in Willmore from 1957-1969. He was contracted by an oil company in '57, working from the Athabasca River north—and went through Little Grave, Big Grave, and the Hardscrabble areas. He worked with a geological team of four. Glen liked the area and decided to expand his operation to offer hunts. He hunted in the Willmore for twelve years, taking out big game hunters, and specializing in non-resident bighorn sheep hunts.

The first year or two that Kilgour operated his hunting services, he would fly clients into Cecelia Lake, British Columbia. He had saddle and packhorses ready to pick up his hunters to take them by packtrain into Willmore Wilderness Park. He trailed his string of horses along Cote Creek—then dropped into the Willmore country. Glen and his wife, Claudette moved to northern B.C. to outfit in 1976.

John Unland

John Unland and brother-in-law, Bill Mackenny purchased Stan Kitchen's pony barn and outfit in 1947. *"For sixty-five hundred dollars, they got forty head of horses, equipment and the hopes of attracting fishermen and tourists to the Tonquin Valley. They also took hunters out into what was later known as Willmore Wilderness."* [19] John's wife, Edith was drafted as a trail cook and was reputed to be a good one. Their son, David Ronald traveled with the couple after he turned five years of age. Unland hired the Moberly brothers as hunting guides. These included Miles, Frank, Ed and Dave.

Bill Mackenny remained a silent partner with Johnny Unland until the mid-1950s when Unland bought him out. *"Around 1960, they sold the pony barn to Clint Coleman, but maintained the outfitting business and fishing camp in the Tonquin until 1970 when they sold to John and George Ostashek."* [20] Unland remained an outfitter for twenty-three years.

19   Jasper Reflections - Page 404
20   Jasper Reflections - Page 405

Pictured above:
Top: Jim Babala.
Photo by
Susan Feddema-Leonard.

Middle: Glen Kilgour.
Courtesy of Jim Babala.

Bottom: John Unland.
Courtesy of Fay McCready.

Eddie Joachim

Eddie and Louis Joachim, sons of Felix Joachim and nephews of Felix's brother, Louis Joachim, were two of the men who worked for Eben-Ebenau in 1955. *(Louis the younger was named after his uncle.)* Eddie was guiding while younger brother, Louis was wrangling and helping with the horses. The brothers were living on the Kakwa River at Lynx Creek at that time. There were fifty-four horses that Louis had to look after. They hunted in two areas: one was on Sheep Creek and the other was at Two Lakes. The outfit ended up moving downstream on the Kakwa River. Reinhold Eben-Ebenau sold out to Dave Simpson in 1967. Dave Simpson guided in the Willmore area for more than thirty years.

Eddie Joachim and his brother, Louis were both born on the north bank of the Kakwa River across from Daniel Creek. Eddie married Eliza Plante and Louis married her sister, Elizabeth Plante. Both were the daughters of Isaac Plante who had guided extensively for Roy Hargreaves. In fact, Isaac Plante was reputed to have been the personal guide for the famous Jack O'Connor on a 1943 hunting trip outfitted by Roy Hargreaves.

Eddie and Eliza had three boys: Clarence, Gary and Terry. Eddie guided primarily for George Kelley; however, he also worked for other outfitters including Randy Babala, Larry Delorme, and Gordon Utri. Louis guided for George Ostashek, George Kelley, and his brother, Eddie.

Eddie Joachim also operated his own outfit for many years. He guided hunters from all over the world—including some from Switzerland and the United States. Eddie hired other guides, including his brother, Louis Joachim, Allan Joachim, Casey Joachim, Johnny McDonald, and his sons, Clarence Joachim and Gary Joachim. Clarence was a big help and often cooked for his father or guided if he was needed. They traveled deep into Willmore Wilderness Park where they set up a base camp for hunting. Camps were located at Cowlick Creek, Big Grave, Rocky Pass, Corral Creek, Muddy Water and Sheep Creek. Eddie outfitted from the mid-1960s to the mid-1980s and was in business for a twenty-year period. Eddie had about forty-eight head of horses, which younger brother, Louis would break. Eddie Joachim's business was a family affair.

The Wanyandies

Daniel Creek, which flows into the Kakwa River, is named after the accomplished bushman, Daniel Wanyandie, son of Basa Wanyandie. Daniel guided hunters on occasion, and on one notable trip while working for an outfitter from Hinton, bagged an impressive bighorn ram for his hunter from the United States. Daniel married Louisa, the daughter of Louise *(Findlay-Thappe)* McDonald and a Beaver Indian called Thappe. They had eight children, five boys and three girls, and the family lived at Wanyandie Flats on the Smoky River. The sons were Billy, Harry, Dan, Fred, and Tom. All of these men were accomplished trappers, packers, trackers, guides, and bushmen. Fred, Tom, and one of their sisters' sons, Kelly Joachim would become outfitters—operating separate outfits.

Daniel's son, Fred Wanyandie got his start as a horse wrangler in 1950. In 1965, he and Emil Moberly, son of Adolphus Moberly guided for Glen Kilgour. Emil bagged a ram for his hunter and Fred successfully harvested a thirteen-point elk *(6 x 7)* for his client. On another trip in 1965, he got a nice grizzly for his hunter. Fred worked for other outfitters, which included Felix Plante, Carl Luger, Charlie Stricker, Bazil Leonard, Ron Moore and Tom Vinson Jr. Fred started his own outfitting business around 1968 and ran his company for approximately eight years. His business card featured *Wanyandie Outfitting*. His main camps were located at Kvass Flats, Muddy Water and Cote Creek; however Fred did not limit himself to these camps but traveled all over the mountain region. His outfit offered big game trophy hunts for bighorn sheep, elk, grizzly, black bear and goat. Fred's guides included: Tom Wanyandie, Harry Wanyandie, Casey Joachim, Johnny McDonald, Lactap McDonald, Dave McDonald and Billie Wanyandie. *Wanyandie Outfitting* took out hunters from places such as Detroit, Michigan, as well as Alberta clients from both Calgary and Red Deer.

Fred's younger brother, Tom Wanyandie has guided and trapped Willmore Wilderness Park and the Kakwa River Valleys for close to sixty years—all of his adult life. Over the years, he guided for Fred Wanyandie, Jerry Stojan, Glen Kilgour, Bazil Leonard, Gordon Utri, Larry Delorme, and Montana Mike Barthelmess. Tom also ran his own outfit in the 1960s for a short period.

Pictured right :
Top: Tom Wanyandie with photo by Susan Feddema-Leonard.
Middle: Fred Wanyandie with photo courtesy of Nanette Hamilton Moseley.
Bottom: Harry Wanyandie with photo courtesy of Charlie Stricker.

Rex Logan

Rex Logan, who was originally based out of Sundre, Alberta, guided for geological survey parties. During the late 1950s, Rex guided geologists in, what is now called Willmore Wilderness Park. Dan Hallock of Victor Lake cooked for Rex Logan in 1959. The geologists were from *B.A. Oil Company.* Dan stated in an interview on August 8, 2003, *"In 1959, Rex got a contract to take geological survey parties north of the Athabasca River and over to the Smoky River. He hired me to cook on a one-hundred-day trip that he was outfitting for them. The outfit came up for the whole summer. We arrived on the twenty-third of May and were here until pretty near the end of September. We trucked the horses up from Sundre to Entrance, and then trailed them into the mountains."*

The Kjos

Eric and his wife, Vera Kjos managed the *Black Cat Ranch* at Brule in 1948 and 1949. Eric Kjos and his family were originally from Bearberry, Alberta. Their son, Bobby was an outfitter in the Willmore Wilderness area for a short period and was hired to do geological survey work. Dan Hallock also worked for Bobby Kjos. Dan stated, *"I came back in 1960, and was cooking for Bobby Kjos, another outfitter who was doing geological survey work in the Willmore area at that time. I cooked for Bobby from May until October that year. I don't think that Rex Logan came back after 1959."*

Ken Thompson

Ken Thompson of Rocky Mountain House and later Hinton, catered to geological survey parties north of the Smoky River during the 1950s. His son drowned on one of these trips, while crossing the Smoky River on horseback at Clark's Cache. Ed McKenzie of Rocky Mountain House, pictured left, worked for Ken Thompson as the head man on the trip, as Ken was not on this trip. Ed later operated his own outfit.

Dave Simpson

Dave Simpson started as a horse wrangler for Andy Russell in 1949. Dave met Reinhold Eben-Ebenau at an Alberta Outfitters' meeting in 1962. In 1967, he went up to Slave Lake and bought Eben-Ebenau's outfit, which consisted of horses and equipment, for ten thousand dollars. Eben guided a few years after he sold out to Dave Simpson, but he never returned to the Willmore area.

Dave and Carol Simpson spent a total of twenty-five years operating in the Smoky River and Sheep Creek Valleys. Carol was the camp cook and was reputed to have run a top-notch kitchen. She made scrumptious cinnamon rolls, bread and home-cooked meals and, like other camp cooks, all on a wood stove. Dave sold his permits in the Willmore to his second oldest son, Frank in 1989. Frank operated the business for several years and sold the four bighorn sheep permits to Pete McMahon in 1992.

Otto Peterson

Otto Peterson ran a small outfitting business during the 1960s. He guided bighorn sheep hunters into the Moosehorn area on the south Wildhay River. Kelly Joachim, a Rocky Mountain Cree based out of the Grande Cache area worked for him on at least one occasion. Peterson also operated a guest ranch located in the area now known as the Rock Lake-Solomon Creek Wildland Provincial Park. He ran trail rides from his guest ranch operation into the Moosehorn country. Tom Vinson Jr. acquired the lease that Peterson once held and has been operating his *West Range Cabin Vacations* there since 1996.

Jim Simpson

Jim Simpson of Pincher Creek got his start in the outfitting business with Andy Russell of Waterton National Park. In 1972 he decided to move north and bought out Tom McCready. Jim operated on both sides of the Smoky River during his time in Willmore. He had four bighorn sheep permits, which he sold to George Kelly in 1989. Jim outfitted bighorn sheep hunters and big game hunters in Willmore Wilderness Park for seventeen years.

Bazil Leonard

Bazil Leonard cut his teeth in the guiding and outfitting industry in the summer of 1959. He started as a cook on a one-hundred-day geological survey trip for Nordegg outfitter, Jerry Favero, who had been in operation since 1935. Bazil was rumored to be more interested in horses than cooking. He was known to have quickly baked his pies and meals in order to be with the horses. In the fall of 1959, he obtained his Class A guide license—and guided his first bighorn sheep hunt. Jerry eventually sold his outfit to his son, Ed Favero. Bazil continued to work for the outfit, guiding summer trips and hunting expeditions. Ed sold his horses and equipment to Bazil in 1969. Bazil moved the operation from Nordegg to Grande Cache in 1970—and has since been guiding and outfitting in the Kakwa River Valley and Willmore Wilderness Park.

In 1982, Susan Feddema-Leonard joined Bazil as a trail cook. She has become known far and wide for her home-baked pies and great country-style cooking. The couple raised nine of their blended-family children to become experienced trail hands—along with exposing their grandchildren to the trail way of life. Son, Cody, started on the trail at five weeks of age, and traveled over five-hundred miles on horseback by the time he was six-months old. Sons, Dan Leonard and Cody Leonard work as guides in Willmore Wilderness Park, with Logan Leonard working as a wrangler. Daughters, Jaeda Feddema, Chehala Leonard and Dan's wife, Nadeen *(Vinson)* Leonard are all experienced trail cooks. Sons, Sean, Bill, Jim, Jess *(Feddema),* their wives and children are all experienced trail hands. As of the spring of 2007, Bazil has been guiding and outfitting in the Canadian Rockies for forty-eight years. Today, he continues to operate *High Country Vacations.*

Charlie Stricker

Charlie Stricker started hunting in the Willmore area in '62. He took hunters out in '63 and '64 to the Rock Lake area. Charlie outlined how his outfitting in Willmore progressed, in a May 19, 2004 transcript. *"The first time I saw Bazil* (Leonard) *was going up towards the Sulphur River--I guess over Hayden Ridge, in '69. That was the same year that Grande Cache was built. In '69 I moved my outfit from Rock Lake and brought my hunters into Delorme Flats on Victor Lake. We staged there and headed over Hayden Ridge. We rode over the ridge to the other side and hit Lancaster Creek where I had a base camp. I hunted the Muskeg River and Lancaster Creek."* Charlie purchased an outfit in B.C. in the early 1980s. Stricker stated, *"Frank Simpson ran my Alberta outfit for awhile after I bought the B.C. outfit. He looked after the hunters in '85, and then he ran the operation in '85, '86 and probably '87. Gary Kruger* (of Westlock) *purchased my outfit in '88, I think. I think that my last year in Willmore Wilderness Park was in '84, when we had that big snowstorm."* Charlie Stricker operated for twenty years in the Park.

Pictured above:
Charlie Stricker.
Circa 1970s.

Photo courtesy of
Charlie Sticker.

Pictured on left page:
Bazil Leonard & daughter, Chehala at Big Grave Flats in 2002.
The trip took twenty-five youth from Grande Cache to Rock Lake. There were forty horses on the trip.
Photo by Susan Feddema-Leonard.

George Kelley

George Kelley started working for Jim Babala in 1962 when he was eighteen years old. George described how he got started in his own outfitting business in a March 18, 2006 interview. *"Like anybody else, starting out takes a while. Sometimes I'd have two or three sheep hunters. One year I only had one sheep hunter, a bunch of elk hunters and moose hunters. We had lots of elk then so we could kill them. You could kill all the elk you wanted—but six-point elk—and all the moose, of course. But finally, the sheep were paying better. Then in 1970 or 1971 they started these sheep permits and I was eligible for them."*

George ended up purchasing four more sheep permits from Jim Simpson in 1989. *George Kelley Outfitters* operated eight non-resident sheep tags every year. He continued taking one or two resident sheep hunters as well. During the winter months, George trapped. He became well known for his trapping skills when he live-snared nine wolves in the mid-1990s with his partner, Wade Berry. The wolves were successfully transplanted in Yellowstone National Park in Wyoming, U.S.A.

In the fall of 2006, due to illness, George Kelley signed his sheep permits over to his son, Kipp Kelley. Kipp was born and raised in the outfitting and trapping industries, and will carry on the Kelley tradition.

As of the fall of 2006, George had been in the Willmore area for a total of forty-four years. He had also trapped in and around Willmore Wilderness since he was a young boy. He learned the art of trapping from both his mother and his father—with his mother running her own line. George passed away in February 2007.

Pictured above:
George Kelley.
Photo courtesy of
Nanette Hamilton Moseley.
Photo taken on a
bighorn sheep hunt in 1996.

Pictured on right page
from top to bottom:
Top: Ed Regnier, February 2007 by
Susan Feddema-Leonard.
Second: Jerry Stojan, courtesy of
Chuck Stojan.
Third: John Ward reading a Robert
Service book,
courtesy of John Ward.
Fourth: Randy Babala 2006
courtesy of Susan Feddema-Leonard.

Ed Regnier

Ed Regnier started in the outfitting industry in the early 1960s. As a young lad of fifteen, he went wrangling for Tom McCready. He worked for many outfitters including Charlie Sticker, George Kelley and others. Eventually Ed started *Saracen Head Outfitters* and operates the outfit in both Jasper National Park and in Willmore Wilderness Park. He continues to offer summer trail rides and hunting trips.

Jerry Stojan

Jerry Stojan became a big game guide and outfitter in 1964. Stojan took his hunters to the mountain country south of his home in Sexsmith to an area called Cecelia Lake. The hunters arrived at the lake in a floatplane and Jerry would have the pack and saddle horses ready to take his hunters deep into the mountains. Stojan hunted at the headwaters of Sheep Creek and the Kakwa Rivers, which are tributaries of the Smoky River. Stojan operated from 1964 to 1973 for a total of ten years. He hunted Rocky Mountain goat, bighorn sheep, grizzly bear, black bear, caribou, moose and elk.

John Ward

"In 1967 John (Ward) *bought Leonard Jeck's outfit. It consisted of a license, twenty-five head of horses and all the necessary saddles, pack, etc. There was no limit to the area that he could take parties to, nor was there a limit on the months that he could work. So he took summer riding parties, and fall and winter hunting trips."* [21] John Ward began his operation in 1968. He had employed Ed Moberly of Hinton, Tommy Plante of Marlboro, and Leonard Jeck of Jasper. In 1989 John sold his horses and permits to Cody Dixon. John's son, Gerald Ward, has most of the equipment now. Gerald Ward continues to operate summer trail ride trips and fall hunting services in Willmore Wilderness Park. *Ward Alpine Guiding Services* offers drop camp services for hunters into the mountain wilderness.

Randy Babala

Randy Babala, got his start sheep hunting with his Uncle Jim (Babala) in the mid-1960s. By 1968, he started guiding his own bighorn hunters in the Cadomin area. He ended up with rifle and bow non-resident sheep allocations, as well as offering bear, elk, moose and deer hunts to an international clientele. Randy expanded his business by 1979, operating summer trail rides for Swiss tourists in Willmore Wilderness Park. n 1986, Randy Babala, George Kelley and Malcolm Moberly re-opened the Grande Cache to McBride Trail. This was a historic trail—and his Swiss guests loved traveling along the Continental Divide. In 1993, Randy purchased a hunting area in the Yukon and moved his operation north. He passed on his interest in the Swiss tourism business in 1997 to Lyle Moberly, a descendant of Henry Joachim. Lyle now outfits the Swiss guests throughout the Willmore ranges.

Randy made a name for himself as a bighorn guide, successfully guiding the hunt in which the world's number one bighorn ram was taken. His hunting guides have included Malcolm Moberly, Jimmy Plante, Brian Lalonde, Johnny Groat and Dan Leonard. Cooks include Lenore Vinson, Nadeen *(Vinson)* Leonard, Rene *(Washkanick)* McAllister, and Janice Summerville.

Gordon Delorme

Gordon Delorme, son of Louis Delorme, is based out of Victor Lake near Grande Cache. He is an original descendant of the families forced to relocate from Jasper. Gordon was taught by his father, Louis Delorme, who was s legendary trapper, hunter and mountain guide. All of Louis' sons were very competent trail men. His daughters, Helen Hallock and Eileen Delorme were skilled trail cooks and competent trail hands.

Gordon Delorme was hired by Charlie Stricker, an outfitter who was hunting bighorn sheep in the Smoky Valley. He worked for Charlie during the early 1970s—before striking out on his own. Gordon eventually formed *Diamond G Contracting* and took hunters and guests into Willmore Wilderness Park during the 1980s.

Bill Gosney

Bill Gosney was born in Cadomin near Hinton, Alberta. He was the son of a miner and, while growing up in the Coal Branch area, he kept horses—eventually acquiring approximately thirty head. Bill started guiding American bighorn sheep hunters in the 1970s with his partner, Budd Cook. The pair had a total of six sheep permits in Zone 440. Their business relationship was short lived as Bud got married and moved to Scotland. The permits were in Bud's name and were eventually absorbed by the Alberta government. He continued guiding resident sheep hunters from Calgary, Edmonton and other areas of Alberta. Bill has been outfitting resident hunters in the Kakwa Valley and Willmore Wilderness areas.

John & George Ostashek

George and John Ostashek grew up in Mountain Park, leaving after the town shut down in 1949. They relocated to Mercoal then later to Brule. *Ostashek Outfitting Ltd.* purchased John Unland's outfit in 1967. This new company operated in the Tonquin Valley and the Willmore Wilderness area for a short period of time. John Ostashek then set his sights on the north. He purchased a hunting area in the Yukon in 1975 and moved to Whitehorse. He sold his sheep permits in the mid-1980s to Ferlan Koma, who sold out to Peter Whitlow in 2001. John Ostashek went on to become the Premier of the Yukon Territory for one term.

Wald Olson

Wald started working in the outfitting industry in 1964 at Circle M Guest Ranch west of Hinton—and moved to Jasper in 1967 to work for Tom McCready. Wald met and married Lavone *(Vinson)* Olson, and the couple purchased Tom & Yvette Vinson's Tonquin Valley operation in 1975. Their primary place of operation was Jasper National Park, however their business, *Amethyst Lakes Packtrips Ltd.* offered hunts in Willmore Wilderness Park each fall. Base camps were located on Rock Creek, Wildhay River, Berland, and Sulphur River drainages. Another part of their outfitting business was based at the Overlander Lodge where they operated a pony barn stable from 1977 to 1988. The couple sold their Tonquin operation after twenty-five years, but continued to offer trail rides in Jasper National Park and Willmore Wilderness Park.

Ron Moore

Ron and Lenore *(Vinson)* Moore bought Tom & Yvette Vinson's Jasper Park Lodge Pony Barn operation and the Skyline Camp in 1975. The couple formed a company called *Skyline Trail Rides Ltd.* Their outfit offered moving trips in Willmore Wilderness Park as well as their regular operation near Jasper. This included the famous Skyline Trail from Maligne Lake to Jasper and back through Big and Little Shovel Passes, and over the Wabasso Lake Trail. Ron and Lenore had the distinction of hosting Prince Andrew on a Skyline trip during the time the Royal Family was at the Commonwealth games in 1978.

Ron also took hunting parties into Willmore Wilderness Park each spring and fall. Some of the areas he hunted was at Mile 51 and Mile 58, but he ranged all over Willmore Wilderness Park. He specialized in moose, elk, deer and spring bear hunts.

Tom Vinson Jr.

In 1979, Tom Vinson Jr. formed *Horseback Adventures Ltd.* to offer backcountry pack trips and trail rides into Jasper and Willmore Parks. Tom's father sold him four non-resident sheep permits in 1984. He operated horseback-oriented big game hunts until he sold his permits to Gordon Utri of Evansburg, Alberta in 1995.

Tom and his wife, Shawn diversified their operation to include *West Range Cabin Vacations* in 1996. The cabins are located in the Rock Lake-Solomon Creek Wildland Provincial Park along Jasper National Park's north boundary. *West Range Cabins* offers trail rides in the beautiful backcountry of the Canadian Rockies—with the comforts of home.

Pictured right:
Top: Wald Olson 2007, photo by Susan Feddema-Leonard.
Middle: Ron Moore courtesy of Lenore Vinson.
Bottom: Tom Vinson 2006, photo by Susan Feddema-Leonard.

Larry Delorme

Larry Delorme is from Manitoba. Shortly after arriving in Hinton, he met Joe and Freddie Plante, and started breaking horses for the Plante brothers. He got his Alberta guide license and went with Felix Plante's sons, on the trail. Larry's duties included shoeing horses and guiding. Larry ended up purchasing some of Felix's equipment, and he built up enough tack to have his own outfit. He used to call his business, *Larry's Guiding and Outfitting* and, later called it, *Larry's Riding Stables.* Larry shoes his own horses and provides farrier services for others. He keeps busy breaking his horses to ride. He also breaks horses to harness, and always has a team so that he can offer hay rides and sleigh rides.

Peter McMahon

Pete McMahon started guiding and outfitting in Willmore Wilderness Park in 1978. He called his operation, *Sherwood Guide and Outfitters*, which was a play on words, as his home base was Sherwood Park, Alberta. In 1978 he guided a resident sheep hunter and a non-resident elk hunter and they camped at Clark's Crossing on the Smoky River. His operation quickly expanded by taking summer trail riders in 1980. He was in partnership for the summer rides for a two-year period with Reg Perras, who owned *Wolf Taxidermy* at that time.

Pete obtained non-resident elk tags the first year that they created allocations *(1986)* in Alberta. In 1989 when the allocations were re-assigned, he wound up with more tags. He continued to take out resident bighorn sheep hunters. Pete purchased his first four non-resident sheep permits and other big game trophy tags from Frank Simpson in 1992. In 1997, Pete bought four more non-resident sheep tags from Gordon Utri, who had purchased them two years previously from Tom Vinson Jr.

The heart and soul of *Sherwood Guide and Outfitters* is Lois McMahon, Pete's wife who is the main cook in the base camp at Corral Creek. Many a rider has stopped in to experience her great cinnamon rolls and delicious chocolate chip cookies—which she always serves with great cowboy coffee. Lois always has great meals prepared for guests and staff. The couple operate their business along with their son, Tyler McMahon who started on the outfit at the tender age of three. To date, Tyler has spent over twenty-five years on the trail. Pete McMahon has been in operation in Willmore Wilderness Park for close to thirty years.

Syd Tilbury

Syd outfitted in Willmore Wilderness Park from 1973 to 1990. He took out overnight trail rides and hunting parties. He took clients to Cowlick Creek, the Big Grave Flats area and also to Dry Canyon, Stearn Range and Mt. deVeber. He ran approximately twenty-two head of horses. Syd's guides included Rod Carter, Paul Moberly, Bruce Morrison and Al Keeler. His wife at the time, Pat Tilbury cooked. Lori Carter was also another trail cook. Syd spent his winters trapping in the Copton area.

Dave Manzer

Dave Manzer was originally from the Maritimes. Dave eventually moved to Alberta, and settled in the Peers area. He was a farrier, a blacksmith and trained his own horses. He met and married Rose Fischer, the daughter of Reun Fischer—who owned the *Bar F Ranch* in Hinton. Dave and Rose started *Wild Rose Outfitting* that focused on horseback vacations in the Willmore Wilderness Park from 1979. *Wild Rose Outfitting* was named after Rose and the business offered summer pack trips into the Willmore Wilderness Park.

Dave continued operating *Wild Rose Outfitting* after the pair separated. He traveled throughout the Willmore Wilderness, offering sixty-five to one-hundred-and-sixty-kilometer trips that lasted from twelve to fourteen days. Dave would boast that his handmade saddles would help people who weren't used to riding. He took out clients as young as five years of age and as old as eighty-one years young—and catered the trips to fit each rider's needs. Dave's favourite spot was on the Wildhay River next to Eagle's Nest Pass where he had a permanent base camp set up for the summer months. Manzer offered a variety of summer trail riding packages including 'horse-assisted hiking'—where people hiked and their gear was transported on horses. He sadly passed away in January 2005 and will be missed by friends and former guests. Dave outfitted in Willmore for twenty years.

Pictured above:
Dave Manzer, July 2003

Photo courtesy of Florence Ross.

Pictured on left page:
Top: Larry Delorme, May 2006.
Middle: Pete McMahon, Feb 2006.
Both photos by Susan Feddema-Leonard.

Bottom: Syd Tilbury, courtesy of Syd Tilbury.

Ron Jones

Ron Jones outfitted in the Willmore Wilderness area from the late 1970s to the mid-1980s and was based out of Robb, Alberta. He primarily outfitted grizzly and bighorn sheep hunts, having his base camp in the Big Grave area. During the summer months, Ron also guided trail rides for outfitter, Randy Babala while his wife, Wendy Jones, cooked on these trips. Their only daughter, Denise, grew up in the outfitting world. Denise was in her father's hunting camps in the Big Grave country from the time she was four years old when she used to ride behind her father's saddle in the packtrain. This stood her in good stead, as she knew the ropes when she married outfitter, Lyle Moberly who started his own outfit in 1997. Lyle is a descendant of both Henry John Moberly and Henry Joachim— and uses Henry Joachim's brand to this day.

Ali Yasinowski

Ali Yasinowski operated *Washy Creek Outfitters* during the 1980s. His operation took off when they acquired a lease at Washy Creek, near Grande Cache in 1982. The business offered hunting trips and later, family overnight trips. Ali's wife, Edna, an experienced trail cook was known for her delicious homemade bread and great meals. Their base camp was primarily on the west side of the Muddy Water River. In 1991, the family moved to Edson to a farm where Ali focused on trucking. He sold his horses in 1993.

Conclusion

There are many more outfitters who started after 1980 that could be mentioned—however we will need to write more books—outlining this ever-changing industry.

Pictured left:
Mt. Kvass & the
Smoky River.

Photo by
S. Feddema-Leonard.

71

CHAPTER THREE:
The Hargreaves

The following has been edited for brevity from a transcript by Gladys, Mrs. Jack Hargreaves and Sophia, Mrs. Roy Hargreaves.

Their father was Edward Asquith Hargreaves, their mother, Matilda Susanna Brown. They emigrated from England in 1882, settling in Oregon, and lived there for several years. George, Frank, Roy, John and twin sister, Myrtle were born in Oregon. Two older sisters, Evelyn and Ethel were born in England. The family moved to Canada to be under the British flag, living in various places in British Columbia. Their mother died in 1904 and was buried in Cranbrook, B.C.

George and Roy worked together at construction jobs in many places in Alberta and British Columbia. When their father remarried, his new wife was Evelyn Perron, a teacher with a university degree of B.A. From this second marriage came Bessie and Richard *(Dick)*. One day, Jack asked his new mother what B.A. stood for. She replied, "'Big Ass,' for marrying your father!" She died of the flu in Victoria, B.C., February 1918.

George and Roy worked in the Hedley Mines in the Ashanola, B.C. area, where Frank had taken a homestead. Later on, Jack joined George and Frank working in the Penticton and Princeton, B.C. areas. George and Roy joined the gang of men cutting trail, which led to the building of the Big Bend highway in British Columbia. Later that year, the four brothers went to Athabasca Landing where they spent the winter cutting timber. Their next home was in Jasper in 1912. They lived in a tent, about where the present Jasper High School stands.

Conscription was called in Canada. Jack was on a trail trip and did not get his call-up papers until his return to Jasper. Since he was late answering the call, he was thrown into jail overnight in Edmonton on Dec. 10, 1917, but was released when explanations were given next morning. Frank and Jack entered the expeditionary forces of the 51st Regiment and Roy in the 50th. They saw plenty of action, mostly in France.

Pictured top (L to R):
Jack & Gladys Hargreaves and Don & Myrtle McCready pictured at the CNR cabin that George Hargreaves built near Berg Lake.

Pictured below:
J. Hargreaves Guide & Outfitter

Photos courtesy of Fay McCready

At the time when men were going overseas, George was in hospital in Edmonton with a severe back injury. When he recovered, he went to Tête Jaune, B.C. and opened a camp for the cutting of poles, posts and ties. Jack returned from overseas and he and Frank began work with George at the camp at Tête Jaune. Roy spent over a year in hospital in England before his return home.

While living in Jasper, the Hargreaves brothers built many fine houses, some of which are still standing today. Myrtle became Mrs. D.S. McCready. Roy and Jack took part in many sports, hockey in winter and baseball in summer.

Jack and Frank took adjoining homesteads at Robson in 1921. George, Frank and Jack built log buildings for their homes, saddle shed, barn, store, icehouse, bunkhouse and corrals.

Jack married Gladys Guild, a teacher from Edmonton, June 30, 1922. Roy followed suit the next year and married Sophia MacLean, a teacher in Jasper, May 9, 1923. Jack and Gladys began their married life at Robson. Also from Robson, the Hargreaves began their early outfitting business of big game hunting in the fall and trail trips in the summer, plus tourists to Berg Lake. Curly Phillips and Frank built the first cabin at Berg Lake. This cabin was known as Curly's cabin and was shared by the Hargreaves for overnight stops. It was always left unlocked and many people used it. Built at the foot of Mt. Mumm, it had a fine view of Robson Glacier.

Many hunting parties began from the home ranch at Robson. George and Frank handled one outfit, usually two or more hunters, using extra guides, with Dave Henry as cook. Jack took a second outfit with a single hunter, using Ted Abraham as cook.

George and Dick were guests of Sir Henry Thornton *(1921)*. The meeting was to arrange for the establishment and operation of a camp at Berg Lake, so that Jasper Park Lodge could have an outlet for their guests. George, Frank and Jack built these cabins on contract made with the Canadian National Railway *(CNR)*. Materials such as lumber, windows and furnishings were supplied by the CNR and delivered to Mt. Robson station. All had to be packed on horseback and taken from the ranch to Berg Lake *(a distance of eighteen miles, mostly uphill)*. Jack with Dean Swift of Jasper, and Dick Hargreaves with Don Guild, were the two teams of packers.

New houses were being built in Jasper in order to move the town of Lucerne to Jasper. Roy was working on these houses, carpentering. When construction ended, Roy went to Mt. Robson with his wife, Sophia and became a B.C. guide and outfitter.

The following year, Jack sold his share in the company of *Hargreaves Brothers* at Robson to Roy, and moved to Jasper to begin outfitting from there. Before having his own outfit, Jack had worked with Otto Brothers and Curly Phillips on hunting parties and trail trips. Some of the early outfitters here were: Phillips and Wilkens, *Otto Brothers, Kitchen and Creighton,* Johnnie Unland, Brewster's, etc. Jack's partner was Don Guild who worked with Jack as guide for several years. Don had also worked at Robson as guide for Roy's outfit.

Pictured above:
Sophia & Roy Hargreaves. Sophia was a school teacher & the first high school principal in Jasper.

Photo courtesy of Ishbel Cochrane.

Gordon Edward *(Jack's son)* was born May 17, 1924 and *(daughter)* Evelyn Juanita Hargreaves was born November 15, 1925 in Jasper. *(Evelyn became Mrs. William Ruddy.)*

After Jack moved from Robson, George and Frank each took a homestead and also bought six hundred acres of land near Jackman, B.C.. In 1923, Father took a homestead near Robson. The boys built him a cabin on the banks of the Fraser River.

Roy, at Mt. Robson, carried on with the good help of his wife, Sophia. Roy's daughter, Ishbel was born Feb. 18, 1924. Marguerite *(Margie)*, the younger daughter was born Sept. 26, 1927. When it was difficult, during the Second World War, to hire competent trail staff, Roy's two daughters were always their father's helpers.

Among the many hunters that Roy guided was Mr. L.S. Chadwick of Cleveland, who enjoyed a successful hunt for bighorn sheep *(1935)*. Next year he asked Roy to join him on a hunt for Stone sheep. This trip was arranged with guide and outfitter, Walter Curly Cochrane of Rolla, B.C. Again, Mr. Chadwick was successful and took home the world's record Stone sheep.

Charles Chesser was Roy's partner at Robson and was well known in Jasper through his son, Johnnie Chesser. Roy, from Mt. Robson, took care of many trail parties until his retirement in 1959. At that time, he sold the Robson ranch to Miss Alice Wright who, for almost twenty years, had been a guest each summer. Roy's daughter, Ishbel and husband, Murray Cochrane were hired as managers. Marguerite, the younger daughter, married Buster Duncan of Jasper and farmed at Jackman. They also handled trail trips.

In 1917, Jack went with Curly Phillips and Miss Mary L. Jobe on a trip to the Porcupine (Kakwa) River. The purpose of this trip was to build a trapper's cabin for Curly to take in his winter's supply of food, and to show Miss Jobe the country around the Porcupine River. When this was accomplished, the party started for home. They found a very heavy snowfall had occurred, so horses and men moved very slowly. Curly and Jack took turns at breaking

Jack Hargreaves,
Curly Phillips
& Mary Jobe after a
late packtrip to the Porcupine
(Kakwa) River
in 1917.

Photo courtesy of
Jasper Yellowhead
Museum & Archives.
PA 38-43

trail, the snow being belly-deep for the horses. They had little food for either man or beast and they returned through Grande Cache, an Indian village. Jack and Curly were known by some of the Indians and were given fine treatment. Miss Jobe, being a white woman, was of great interest. The party arrived back in Jasper many days overdue.

Some of the early guides working from either Jasper or Robson were: Art and Ken Allen, Adolphus Moberly, Louis, Jimmie and Henry Joachim, Slim Henry, Manly Rehil, Russell Cooper, Mac Elder, Len Jeck, Isaac Plante, Dick Hargreaves, Red Ilie, Gene Merrill, the McMurtry boys of Sundre, Tom McCready, Oliver Travers, Don Guild and many others. Some guides took wives or sisters along as cooks. Some such teams were Gene and Ellen Merrill, John and Dot Williams, Russell Cooper and sister, Lillian Chesser, Elva McKinnon and brother, Bill McKinnon, Mac Elder and sister, Patsy. Jack always felt a woman cook added good food to a party. There was also another fine trail cook at Robson, Dave Henry. One of Jack's good and faithful workers as cook and wrangler was Pat Smythe, now living at Hinton. Another early member of the outfit was A.B. Webb of Jasper. Here was a man who knew the country and knew horses, as well as being a competent cook. He was a fine one to entertain the party with stories of earlier happenings.

Henry Joachim was one of the early guides who worked for the Hargreaves.

Photo coutesy of Victoria Moberly.

Jack's life as a guide and outfitter for big game hunting parties was an unqualified success. His parties booked early and the entire hunting season would be filled. Jack's outfitting began in 1925 with the Whitcomb and Stowel party. Mabel Stowel shot a goat, which was placed in the book of records of the Boone and Crockett Club. In dealing with hunters over a thirty-year period, several trophies rated recording in the Boone and Crockett Club. Kingsley Birdsall in 1928 placed a bighorn sheep. Mike and Helen Lerner placed a sheep in 1937.

One hunt, which Dick Hargreaves recalls, was with two hunters from Cleveland: Norm Wagner and Carl Borg. Jack and Dick were the guides. They were on Monoghan Creek, a tributary of the Sulphur River. They had been tracking a grizzly bear, only to find it had gone into a cave on the hillside. The bear refused to come out into the open, so Dick, being younger than Jack, was elected to throw a lighted torch into the cave. Upon throwing in the torch, Dick did a hasty retreat. Jack and the hunters took their guns and waited to see what would happen. When the torch landed in the cave, out came not one grizzly but two! There were soon two dead grizzlies and two happy hunters. Jack had a reputation for getting grizzlies for his hunters. In fact, one letter came from a successful hunter addressed to "Grizzly King" Jack Hargreaves, Jasper, Alberta.

Jack had several encounters with grizzlies. The one that gave him the greatest scare happened at Maligne Lake. He was fishing alone in his old rowboat about half a mile from the narrows. As he was tired of sitting and not having any luck, he decided to pull into shore and do a little exploring. After tying the boat to a tree, he climbed the bank to come face-to-face with a large grizzly about fifty feet away. His fishing rod was still in his hand; it being his only weapon, he hit the bear on the nose with the tip of the rod. The bear had never been attacked in this manner before and drew back to think about such a strange occurrence. Each time the bear advanced, the end of the

fishing rod was there, hitting him on the nose. At last the bear turned away. Jack returned to his boat and headed for the boathouse, feeling this time the fish could stay in the lake!

In the spring of 1922, the Hargreaves boys, while out bear hunting, came across two tiny bear cubs whose mother had been shot by some earlier hunters. Each cub was put into a packsack and carried home to the ranch. They were starving hungry. Two large bottles were fitted up with nipples and the little fellows were not long in finding what a bottle of warm milk was for. They would sit up on their haunches while someone held the bottle. The cubs thrived that summer and became quite tame. They were each fitted to a collar with chain attached. Each day, they were taken to meet the passenger trains, which stopped to view Mt. Robson. The porters from the dining car would offer them scraps of food in a dish. One day, the porter took away the dish before the cub was finished. This made the little fellow angry and he made a swipe at the porter, tearing his trouser leg. So that ended the cubs' journey to meet the trains. That fall, a hole several feet deep was dug beside the main house. The cubs hibernated there until April 1st. At that time, melting snow water ran into the hole, and the cubs came out. However, they emerged feeling very cross and would take a swipe at anyone passing, even the person feeding them. The boys felt it was better to return them to the wilds. The Mt. Robson sign on CNR track shows two little bears perched above the top; many pictures were taken of it. Mt. Robson, in 1922, was surveyed to be 13,700 feet (*Mr. A.O. Wheeler in charge*). His measurements were changed to 13,068 feet and later still, 12,972 feet.

Oil survey parties began their search for oil, with horse and pack outfit, in the summer of 1944. They continued this method of travel until 1958, when helicopters took over the job. Many of the oil companies searched for oil and coal, using Jack's outfit of horses and guides. When asked why his outfit was used so successfully, one of the guides replied, "Jack Hargreaves had a reputation for being honest; he gave good service by having good men working for him and good cooks."

Jack gave up the outfitting and hunting business because game was getting scarce. He felt he could no longer book a party, knowing they might come home disappointed. His nephew, Tom McCready had worked with Jack for several years, so when Jack wanted to quit, Tom bought the outfit and continued in business. *(Tom's older brother George was killed as a pilot in WWII.)*

The Hargreaves brothers moved many times in their early years, searching for a place to settle down. They finally found it in Jasper and Mt. Robson, and so were content to stay for their remaining years.

George died at Sheep Creek while with the Hall hunting party in 1936. Art Allen was one of the guides with George, and it was Art's sad duty to phone the wardens at Jasper the news of George's passing. He was buried at Sheep Creek Falls; a copper plaque marks his grave.

Father died at Mt. Robson in June 1939. He was buried on his own property the same year that he and Roy were presented to Their Majesties, King George VI and Queen Elizabeth on their tour of Canada. Roy's death in Ladysmith, B.C. was on March 26, 1971. His ashes were taken to Robson and placed beside his father's gravesite. Jack's death occurred in Jasper Dec. 11, 1971. He is buried in Jasper's cemetery. His last years were spent fishing and hiking through the hills he had loved for so many years.

Among the many tributes paid to Jack at the time of his death was the following from Mr. J.C. Christakos, Superintendent of Jasper National Park: *"Men like Mr. Hargreaves, who have spent almost their entire lives in the region and have not only seen it develop but have, in fact, contributed significantly to such development, become part of the region – they are its history. Certainly, few people can lay claim to the degree of involvement of Jack Hargreaves, who shall live forever in the story of the Jasper-Yellowhead area. Our lives are the richer for their having been here."*

Original Transcript Signed in 1976
by Gladys Hargreaves & Sophia Hargreaves

Pictured above:
George Hargreaves.

Photo courtesy of
Ishbel Cochrane.

Pictured above:
George Hargreaves and friend,
Bruce Otto, in Jasper circa 1917.

Photo courtesy of Ishbel Cochrane.

Interview with Ishbel (Hargreaves) Cochrane

Sue It's May 12, 2005 and I am at Ishbel *(Hargreaves)* Cochrane's home on Stone Road near Valemount B.C. Ishbel is the older daughter of Roy and Sophia. Roy was one of the Hargreaves brothers who operated an internationally known outfit in their day. They outfitted in what is now known as Jasper National Park and Willmore Wilderness Park. Roy enjoyed many notable achievements. For example in 1936, Roy was invited to join L.S. Chadwick on a Stone sheep hunt in which he successfully bagged the now world-famous Chadwick Ram.

Ishbel The *Otto Brothers,* Curly *(Donald)* Phillips and the Hargreaves Brothers were some of the first outfitters in the Jasper area. These men all worked together. Curly Phillips was the first one to build a cabin at Berg Lake, and he built the Flying Trestle, going up the Emperor Falls hill, in order to outfit guests. After World War I, my dad and uncles worked with Curly at Berg Lake. I have a picture of the old saddle shed at the *Mt. Robson Ranch* showing Curly Phillips' outfit—when my father worked with him.

After the war, the Hargreaves brothers homesteaded *Mt. Robson Ranch,* where they ran their outfit. The Hargreaves brothers, who were post-war soldiers, were given three quarters of land. My dad and uncles chose their quarters, which had splendid views of Mt. Robson. They built a big house that is still standing, and two cabins. There was a pack trail that went from the *Mt. Robson Ranch* up to Berg Lake. It was a six-hour trip by horseback to the lake.

Curly Phillips built one of the first cabins at Berg Lake. He built his cabin near the Alberta-B.C. boundary. It looked out on Robson Glacier and Mt. Robson. Curly Phillips was the one who built the Flying Trestle with probably the help of the Hargreaves. It lasted many years until it was blasted out.

The CNR paid the *Hargreaves Brothers* to build four more cabins at Berg Lake. These cabins were even closer to the Alberta-British Columbia border than Curly Phillips' cabin was. One time my Uncle George had to ask CN for more roofing as they had only sent in enough for one cabin. The cabins were there for several years, but CN then abandoned them.

Roy Hargreaves and his brothers were able to get a five-acre lease to build a Chalet at Berg Lake. The Chalet was across from the Tumbling Glacier. The *Hargreaves Brothers* built the Chalet in 1923. Once the Chalet was built, they brought up packhorses of supplies to outfit the cabin. The Chalet had a view of the ice, which was always falling into Berg Lake. It was easy to get ice out of the lake and make ice cream! We had a boat that we used to row across to the side of the glacier. We had to be careful, because if the tumbling ice fell, a person could get

Pictured above:
Berg Lake Chalet.
The main cabin had two
smaller cabins close by.
Photo courtesy of
Ishbel Cochrane.

Pictured on right page:
Top: Jack Hargreaves.
Photo courtesy of
Fay McCready.
Bottom: Dick Hargreaves
circa 1925.
Dick Hargreaves was a
half-brother of
George, Frank, Roy & Jack.

Photo courtesy of
Ishbel Cochrane.

dumped into the icy water. If a big chunk of ice fell, it would create big waves. It could swamp a small rubber boat or any small boat.

Some of the items that were brought to the Chalet were many mirrors, which were stacked against the wall. Eight mirrors were laid carefully against the log wall sides, before they were mounted. Much to the surprise of everyone, the dog went crazy checking himself out at the mirrors. The dog gave the Hargreaves brothers quite a laugh.

The Berg Lake Chalet was a busy place. There were so many guests coming and going that we had to have two staff there all the time. There were usually two women working—one cook and a helper. Many guests returned, as they really liked Berg Lake and Mt. Robson, which is the highest mountain in the Canadian Rockies. Sometimes we used the Berg Lake Chalet as a jump-off point to go on summer pack trips and hunting trips.

One year, one of our guests sent the B.C. government one hundred dollars to re-roof Curly's cabin at Berg Lake. However, Curly Phillips' cabin was torn down by the Mt. Robson Park authorities.

The Park decided to tear down the Hargreaves' Chalet. However one of our guests lobbied the B.C. Provincial Government in Victoria to save the structure. The Mt. Robson authorities tore off the kitchen and bedrooms from the main cabin and left the building as a one-room structure. They did this around 1996. It was a crying shame not to keep the Chalet.

Sue Did the Hargreaves brothers stay together?

Ishbel In the early 1920s, Uncle George said that there was getting to be too many women. My Uncle Jack married Gladys *(Guild)* in 1922 and my dad married my mother in 1923. I guess it was a time for change—and running the *Hargreaves Brothers* was not what they wanted to do anymore.

Sue What happened to each of the brothers?

Ishbel My Uncle Jack and his wife resided in Jasper where he continued outfitting in the Jasper and Willmore Wilderness Park area. His brother, Frank was murdered in Jackman, near Valemount, B.C. in 1940. Frank had been living by himself at Jackman and had stashed some money under his bed mattress. Someone wanted the money, and knew where Frank had hidden it. The would-be thief killed Uncle Frank but didn't throw the mattress back far enough to find it.

My Uncle George Hargreaves was based out of Jackman Flats near Valemount. George died on a hunting trip in Willmore Wilderness Park on September 17, 1936. He is buried at Sheep Creek Falls. He must have died of a heart attack, as he never woke up in the morning. Art Allen and Paddy Ryan were out on the trip with Uncle George.

Paddy worked for Roy Hargreaves on one summer trip to Berg Lake—but decided to go with George on this hunt, as extra help was needed. Paddy was the first to wake and went out for the horses. When he came back with the horse, he called for George—and there was no answer. This was highly unusual as he was always up. Art Allen was also on that trip. He was working as the Alberta guide. They took George's old horse home with his saddle on it. Oh, it was the saddest thing to see George's horse come in with an empty saddle.

When they got back home, my mother paid George's staff and tried to collect from the hunters, one whose name was Mr. Hall. The hunter did not want to pay because he didn't get his thirty days of hunting. We had a lot of guests that came to *Mt. Robson Ranch* and one of them was a lawyer. My mother was so great and everybody liked her. So she wrote a letter to this lawyer in the United States and she got her money back.

Years later, we flew by helicopter to Sheep Creek Falls and put a better fence around the grave. *(This was before there was a restriction on landing a helicopter in Willmore.)* The grave used to be out in the meadow, but now it is obstructed by bush and trees.

Sue I noticed in your journals and pictures that you call the place close to where your Uncle George is buried, Coffin Top Mountain and not Casket Mountain.

Pictured right (L to R):
Hunter, Mr. Hall and
George Hargreaves the day
before George died.
Photo courtesy of
Ishbel Cochrane.

Pictured on right page :
Top: Gravesite of
George Hargreaves
the day they buried him.
Photo courtesy of
Jim Babala.

Middle: Jack O'Connor's ram.
Photo courtesy of
Ishbel Cochrane.

Bottom: Isaac Plante,
Jack Oconnor's guide who
was working for
Roy Hargreaves.
Photo courtesy of
Louis & Elizabeth Joachim.

Ishbel We called it Coffin Top. It looks like a coffin on the top of that mountain. That's what I grew up with. The mountain had a perfectly flat geological formation on the top that resembled a coffin.

Sue You have told me what happened to your uncles. What happened to your dad after the *Hargreaves Brothers* dissolved?

Ishbel After the war my dad hunted in both Alberta and British Columbia and was based at *Mt. Robson Ranch*. Dad usually had a B.C. guide and an Alberta guide working for him. When you went across the border, you had a guide for both sides. Dean Swift of Jasper was one of my dad's Alberta guides. Dean had a glass eye due to a hockey puck accident. We always had an Alberta and a B.C. guide—but then the government officials decided that you had to have an Alberta outfit. That was all because of Jack O'Connor—who went on a hunt with my dad in 1943. Jack O'Connor wrote articles about hunting in B.C. and Alberta that were widely published. Both the B.C. and Alberta outfitters got upset about my father's business and complained. They didn't want B.C. outfitters going to the 'Range'. This made it so we had to keep an extra Alberta outfit.

I went on the O'Connor trip to cook for my dad. Mr. Holliday was Jack's friend and his hunting partner. Isaac Plante, a Grande Cache Native was a guide—and he didn't mind hunting in Alberta or B.C. I guess that's what got dad into trouble. The other outfitters were very disgruntled because my dad was hunting in both provinces. Outfitting in both provinces made sense to us because we were based at Mt. Robson, which was on the Alberta-B.C. border.

Sue Your dad's guide, Isaac Plante, was a Rocky Mountain Cree who was an original descendant from Jasper. He was literally displaced from his ancestral home, which was legislated a National Park in 1907. The Canadian Government declared the land a protected area. Isaac and his people were forced to relocate to the Grande Cache area.

Ishbel Jack O'Connor wanted to come again with us another time, but my dad wrote him and told him to go with Tom McCready, my cousin who was a Jasper outfitter.

When Jack O'Connor was writing his book he said that Margie and I were the best cooks that he ever had on the trail. You see I would make two pies. You would cut the pie in four. My Uncle George would say that it would ruin a pie if you didn't just cut it twice. Mr. O'Connor couldn't believe it because when his wife made a pie—he had several children—there were many pieces.

Sue I understand that your mom rode a lot and that she was a very competent woman in the mountain wilderness, riding with her English saddle.

Ishbel Oh yes, she went on trips all the time.

Sue I heard cowboys talk about your mother crossing the Smoky River on her English saddle.

Ishbel My mother really respected the rivers and never took them for granted. She rode an English saddle all the time. My mother was a guide, excellent cook and had a great sense of humour. She was an extraordinary host and could take everything in stride. In fact, my mother ran the *Mt. Robson Ranch*. She lived there for thirty-five years with no running water in the winter and no electricity. My mother had a long history with the Mt. Robson area. Both my mother and dad were cremated and their ashes were put on the Ranch.

Sue What is your first memory of traveling through the Rockies on horseback?

87

Pictured right:
Roy Hargreaves - 1942 hunt
with caribou near Copton Creek.

Photo courtesy of
Ishbel Cochrane.

Ishbel I first went to Berg Lake on Black Beauty when I was four years old. I have a picture of myself and I had the reins right up to my chin because Black Beauty wasn't going to stand still.

I went to school in Jasper during Grade one and Grade four and stayed with my Aunt Myrtle McCready. I attended Grade nine in Victoria B.C. where I stayed with my Grandfather Hargreaves. My mother was a teacher and she taught me most of my schooling through correspondence. She was really good friends with my Grade nine teacher, so my mother could pull me out of school so that we could go to the Range. That was in 1939, and my teacher passed me in my Grade nine year. My sister and I accompanied my dad and my Uncle Chuck Chesser on Range trips in May of most years, after that. Chuck Chesser was married to my Aunt Anne who was my mother's sister.

The Range was ninety miles north of *Mt. Robson Ranch*. We would travel by trail down the Smoky River to twelve miles south of the present town of Grande Cache. In May, it was time to round up the horses and bring them back to *Mt. Robson Ranch*. My mother and dad had no sons, just Margie and me. My dad taught my mom, sister and I how to haze one hundred head of horses. We could saddle the horses and pack them. We could all cook on the trail. We were good all-around trail hands.

When my uncle, Chuck Chesser went overseas *(World War II)*, I got to ride King horse. Chuck broke him, but he was a *Mt. Robson Ranch* horse. He was a real good horse on the trail but every time we passed a campsite he wanted to turn in—and the packhorses would follow. I loved to ride King, who was a nice sorrel with a white face. King knew every trail in the mountains. He was a smart horse.

Murray *(Cochrane)* and I were married in June 1946. Murray worked for my father as a guide on hunting trips before the war. After Murray came back from World War II, he outfitted in the Willmore area using my dad's outfit. I was there cooking with him in the fall of 1946 right after our marriage—and I was pregnant. I would brush my teeth—and drink some water, and throw up out in the bush. I made an extra sandwich for myself, because by the time they got packed up, I was so hungry. As soon as I got on my horse I had to eat. I ended up having six kids—Margie, Art, Les, Malcolm *(Mac)*, Louise, and Russell. I think my last trip up the Smoky River from *Mt. Robson Ranch* was in 1947. My husband, Murray and I took horses to the Range one fall when my daughter, Margie was a baby. My sister, Margie watched my young daughter that I named after her.

Pictured above:

Top: Ishbel on Black Beauty at the age of four.

Bottom: Chuck Chesser Circa 1942.

Both photos courtesy of Ishbel Cochrane.

Sue I sure can relate to the morning sickness scenario. I too have been cooking breakfast in the cook tent and have had to run out. I remember being at Big Grave camp on a summer trip. I was pregnant with my fourth child and I had my other children with me on the trail. The smell of everything bothered me and would upset my stomach. We had guests in from Germany. I had to hide the fact that I had morning sickness. I haven't met too many other women who experienced this. Ishbel, you are truly a kindred spirit.

Ishbel I cooked for both my dad's and my husband's outfits. I cooked for people from all over the world. I cooked in hunting camps and on summer trail rides. I have some neat pictures of the bread, cookies and pies that I made on the trail. I bottled meat too.

I used to have to use candlelight to see at night when the men came in late and had to be fed in the cook tent. Then things improved when we got a Coleman lantern. One time I did not have to change the mantle on the lantern for thirty days. I packed that lantern on a black horse called Jet. He always made sure to be right behind the lead horse. There was no sashaying around for him.

My daughter, Louise jumped right in behind me and became an excellent cook in the kitchen and on the trail. One summer, Louise cooked for fifty-four days straight while my son, Mac (Malcolm) wrangled during that time. Louise and Mac were both teenagers at the time.

Sue So your husband, Murray's father was Curly *(Arthur)* Cochrane. He worked for your father, Roy Hargreaves.

Ishbel There were two Curly Cochrane brothers. They were look-alike twins. Walter Curly Cochrane of Rolla, B.C. was the guide and outfitter for the Chadwick Stone sheep hunt. My dad was with Mr. L.S. Chadwick of Cleveland, who enjoyed a successful hunt for bighorn sheep *(1935)*. Mr. Chadwick asked my father to join him on a hunt in 1936 where he was successful and took home the world's record Stone sheep.

The other twin was Curly Arthur Cochrane, my husband's father. My father-in-law worked as a cook at Berg Lake and on packing trips for my dad and uncles.

Sue I understand the Range is the area between the Muddy Water River and Eaton Creek—where your horses were wintered. I was wondering if you could tell us about going to the Range?

Pictured above (L to R):
Top: Ishbel and Margie, Roy Hargeaves' daughters ran a top-notch kitchen for the hunting parties. Jack O'Connor once wrote that these two young ladies provided him the best meals he ever had on the trail.

Bottom: Work station in the cook tent.

Pictured on left page: Ishbel & Murray Cochrane's horses at Moose Pass.

Photos courtesy of Ishbel Cochrane.

Ishbel The Range went from the Muddy Water River from Mile 0 to Mile 6. They started the mileage at the Muddy Water River. I remember once when we were going to the Range in the spring—there was my dad, Chuck Chesser, my sister, Margie and I. The Indians were supposed to meet us at Corral Creek—but they didn't come until a whole lot later. We had to jump down into the river and then jump over a log that was in there. I was riding a gelding that wanted his own way. My sister was riding this other horse and he didn't want to jump into the river at all. It was kind of steep—and you had to jump into the water—and immediately go over that log. Finally I had to beat on the back of that horse and he just cleared the whole doggone thing—log and all. There was a big splash. Then my horse slid in there nicely. We were just crossing the Jackpine.

Sue There are two mouths on the Jackpine that drain into the Smoky River. One branch has a very soft muddy bottom and the other has a solid rocky bottom. We crossed the Jackpine upstream before it split into two at the confluence. We avoided the soft muddy crossing that way.

Ishbel Yes, and after you cross the Jackpine you can leave the Smoky Trail and go up a steep hill. Away my father went up there; he was swearing and trying to get the horses to move up that steep hill, which forked off the old Smoky River trail. It was pretty tough going because the horses wanted to stay in the Smoky Valley. We finally got them to move up the steep incline and camped up on the flats. This trail climbed up from the mouth of the Jackpine River and went to Boulder Creek. Murray and I took hunters in there. In September 1946, we forded the mouth of the Jackpine River and went up the vertical rise to Me and Charlie Creek. Then we camped up there quite a while. The

Pictured above:
Roy Hargreaves on the
Smoky River
on a trip from
Mt. Robson
to the 'Range'
near Grande Cache.

Photo courtesy of
Ishbel Cochrane.

camp was on the side of a hill and everything sloped—even the panniers. Anyway, it was a vertical climb up the trail from the Smoky.

Sue   We found your trail and cleared it out. Actually, my son, Cody and our friend by the name of Rod Carter of Darwell, Alberta rode up that steep, well-worn horse path in April of 2000. We were out scouting, trying to re-open the old Smoky trail. I kept a journal of the discovery—and we wondered who would take a pack string up such an extreme climb. The route was well defined. Bazil, my son, Cody and I had found another portion of this trail at Boulder Creek and flagged it down to the confluence of the Jackpine and Smoky River. It took us two years to link the portion that Rod and Cody found to the trail we found on Boulder Creek. In 2003, we took a crew from the Willmore Foundation and cleared the deadfall off the well-worn route. Boy, it was a steep pull off that Jackpine-Smoky junction. I thought there must have been some tough cowboys that had used that route—because it's a five-to-six-hundred-yard pull out of the Smoky Valley. Finding your sign after sixty years was pretty exciting. To complicate our trail clearing, a forest fire had burned the area in 2002. It was tough finding the old blaze marks on the charred trees—but we did it.

Ishbel   We had a couple of wrecks there on that steep hill. It was coming down that was bad.

Sue   I agree. Our horses found it a lot more difficult coming down that precipitous trail than going up.

Ishbel   I have a picture of our camp on the Smoky River just above the confluence of the Jackpine—with some wall tents in it. Usually we would trail down the east side of the Smoky River, from Mt. Robson sometimes, and cross where the two islands are. Then we would travel down the west side of the Smoky, just a short way downstream from the mouth of the Jackpine. We went up that hill and hunted. When we were finished hunting, we had to come down that hill. I was ahead and there was a hornet's nest there. Oh boy, we went down that hill pretty fast!

One time Murray had to take off and look for the missing packhorses—so he took some horses and went from Me and Charlie Creek and up Boulder Creek. Me and Charlie Creek was on a big flat that had creeks running through it.

Sue   From the way you described it, I am sure that Me and Charlie Creek is what came to be called Biffy Creek. Outfitter Dave Simpson advised that they called the creek that flowed into Boulder Creek, Biffy Creek. Most outfits used a tree branch that was nailed up between two trees for their lavatory. Biffy Creek had quite a throne, as someone hand-carved a toilet seat and put it between two rails. The old washroom is still there today and you can see it as you ride along the trail.

Biffy Creek flows into Boulder Creek. Today it has over one hundred beaver dams on it—and the whole valley is flooded with water. There is a long lake that is dammed at the end. Tom Wanyandie, son of Rocky Mountain Cree guide and trapper, Daniel Wanyandie told me that his father went into that area in the 1940s and that there were big meadows there. He said that the old pack trail went across the wide-open meadow, where the lake is now. We have had to re-route the trail along the mountainside. There used to be lots of feed for the horses in days gone by; however, it's a very different story today—and there are slim pickings for any horse outfit. I am guessing that Me and Charlie Creek could be Biffy Creek because Biffy Creek is on a big flat and had a slow running creek through it.

Ishbel It sure sounds like it could be, but I am not absolutely sure.

Your story brings to mind a story. I recall one time when my husband, Murray went down to the Smoky River where Daniel Wanyandie lived *(at the confluence of the Muskeg and Smoky Rivers)*. Murray wanted to buy horses from Daniel. The two were out looking for a horse and came upon a little creek that had a little log over it. Daniel ran over the log like nothing. He looked back to see if Murray could nimbly run across the narrow log. Murray had no trouble at all. We bought a horse off of him and called it Daniel. He was a bay gelding.

Sue I noticed a picture that you have here—and I recognize the lay of the land. You called this other steep part of the Smoky River Trail, Hilda's Hill. It is marked here under this picture. I have heard of that area referred to as The Rock or The Cliffs. I know that outfitter, Dave Simpson referred to the area as The Cliffs, and outfitter, Pete McMahon refers to it as The Rock. Why did you call that incredibly treacherous trail, Hilda's Hill?

Ishbel We called it Hilda's Hill. We were on a hunting trip—and we had this bay horse called Hilda who lost her pack on that hill. Hilda had quite a wreck on the hill that day. So the hill became Hilda's Hill after that.

Pictured above:
Hilda's Hill in 1943.

Photo courtesy
of Ishbel Cochrane.

Sue We should call that place Hilda's Hill. Boy, the trees on Hilda's Hill have really grown up since that picture was taken. That would have been quite a trip up and over those cliffs on your way to and from the Range. Who helped you trail the horses to the Range and back to Mt. Robson?

Ishbel We used to winter our horses on the Range and we would have to round them up each spring, trailing them back to *Mt. Robson Ranch*. Two Native men were supposed to meet us on the Range to help us, because there was just my dad, Margie and myself to round up the horses. That was pretty hard because there were lots of horses—the expected help eventually caught up to us when we were on our way home.

We had a corral at Corral Creek that we rounded up the horses into. We had a big wing on the corral. The old timers knew what we were doing. We would go out there and catch them. All you had to do was have some salt—and you could catch about anything.

One time the water on the Smoky River was too deep and we couldn't move camp from Corral Creek and head back home to Mt. Robson, so we took the horses on the west side of Corral Creek and just let them graze. Three or four of us would be around the horses and wouldn't let them get away. We would return the horses to the corral at night.

When we reached the range each spring, the horses would be scattered across the mountainside. One group would be way up on an open rise—and Popcorn, for example would have a big pile of horses with her.

On a trip one time, my father was riding across all these open hillsides. His horse stepped on a rock and slipped and bumped Dad's ankle but he kept riding—and he didn't take off his boot. He just slept with that boot on, in his eiderdown. Several days later, the outfit arrived back at *Mt. Robson Ranch* at ten o'clock at night—it was almost dark. I went outside because I could hear the horses. He was there first and he told me to come over to him. Dad's hand went down on me when he got off his horse and his weight almost crumpled me. He needed help to get off, brace himself and hop around. My dad had to take the train to Jasper to the hospital the next day.

Every fall after the hunts were over, we would trail our horses from Mt. Robson to the Range. Each spring we would have to round the horses up again and bring them home. Not all of our horses would stay at the Range. We had Jackman horses that were raised here close to Valemount that would come back home from the Range in spring by themselves, looking for some hay. Uncle George had a farm at Jackman Flats. Uncle Frank looked after the place after George died. My sister, Margie and her husband, Buster Duncan ended up with the place after Uncle Frank was murdered. It has been since passed on to their son, Rex Duncan.

Sue Can you tell me about the route that you took up the Smoky River?

Ishbel We always started our summer trail riding trips from *Mt. Robson Ranch* and lunched at Kinney Lake, which was about halfway from the Ranch to Berg Lake. Mostly we would stay at the Berg Lake Chalet.

One time Uncle Dick took out a party and we camped at Kinney Lake. This lake was not usually used as a stopover, however we were unusually late in getting away, so we camped there. Uncle Dick was going out on a hunting trip. Normally when we took guests out, Kinney Lake was a great place to have a short lunch break. After you left Kinney Lake, there was a winter cabin below Emperor Falls that the wardens used.

Once we left Berg Lake, we would ride to what we called Mile 9 on the Smoky River and set up camp there. (Mile Zero was the Alberta / B.C. Boundary). The first warden's cabin was below Adolphus Lake just across the border on the Alberta side. They also had another warden's cabin halfway down the trail just before Short River. There were little cabins in between the larger cabins—so the wardens had several warm places to stay in the winter.

Sometimes we left the Ranch and went to Mile 9. There used to be a sign at Mile 9 a long time ago —before my time—but then they changed and started the mileage from the Muddy Water River—and did it backwards. Next we would camp at Short River and then move downstream to the Jackpine River. We would finally reach the Range and would camp at Corral Creek. Then it was back to Mt. Robson. Dad had left the old stoves stashed along the way at each campsite so we had base camps that we would stay in.

It would take us four days from Mt. Robson to trail to our camp at Corral Creek. The Range was ninety miles and there were dangerous river crossings. Both the Smoky River and the Muddy Water River could be treacherous. We preferred to stay on the east side of the Smoky River. Sometimes we would cross the Smoky upstream from the mouth of the Jackpine River. The other alternative was to chase the horses across the Smoky at Clark's Crossing. We would use a yellow rubber boat to cross the river at Clark's Crossing *(a boat crossing).* We had to blow the raft up by mouth when we first started going up to the Range—but then we got a pump. We would pack our rubber boat on a packhorse from Mt. Robson and float our supplies across the river. Then we would swim the horses across. Crossing the Smoky River was something that we took seriously—packing the gear and people in the boat and pushing the horses into the cold, deep river. In fact, I have some movies of it.

Miss Wright was from the United States and she bought the *Mt. Robson Ranch* when my father retired in 1959. She was supposed to take over in September and she hired Murray and me to manage it. Miss Wright didn't have a clue how to run a ranch. One time we told her that we needed oats for the horses and she bought a little package of rolled oats. Murray and I bought the ranch from her—and later sold it.

One time Murray and I took the horses to the Range by ourselves. We chased them from Mt. Robson to the Range. The horses would move out pretty fast when they knew they were going to their winter home. Once in a while, when we were at Berg Lake, the horses thought they should go back to the Range, so we had to hobble them.

One time the horses pulled out when Murray and I were on a hunting trip, camped at Berg Lake. Murray had hurt himself, and was crippled up. Luckily he had kept one horse in the pen and had to ride many

Pictured left (L to R):
Miss Alice Wright &
Roy Hargreaves at Berg Lake
with Rose horse.

Photo courtesy of
Ishbel *(Hargreaves)* Cochrane.

miles to find the rest of the horses that had pulled out and gone downstream on the Smoky. My dad did that one time too. He had to find horses that had pulled out—but he rode that trip with no saddle. He rode bareback. He was rounding up the horses to go to work. Those horses had moseyed off. Sometimes they would go the other way into Mt. Robson Park. It was easier when we hobbled the horses—and they didn't go so far.

There was only one time that the Smoky was high that we didn't cross at Clark's crossing. We stayed on the northwest side of the river and headed upstream, crossing above the mouth of the Jackpine River. We could get all the way to the Range that way. Murray and I did that the last time we went to the Range from Mt. Robson to Corral Creek. We stayed on the northwest side of the Smoky River. The horses were up in the high country. There were more trails there than you could shake a stick at. There were no elk, just deer.

Sue That is exactly what Emil Moberly said. The first elk that he ever saw in the Smoky River Valley was in 1949 and Emil and his people didn't know what it was. Emil Moberly is a Rocky Mountain Cree Elder who had a trapline, which was located on the Range from 1950 to 1995. *(See Glen Kilgour's interview for a direct quote from Emil Moberly regarding this.)*

Did you ever run into any trappers?

Ishbel Daniel Wanyandie used to trap at Wolverine Creek and Art Allen was out there all the time. Murray bought some horses from Daniel.

Art Allen was both a trapper and an outfitter. Art went out from Mt. Robson each fall. When it was time to trail the horses to the Range for the winter, he would have all his gear at *Mt. Robson Ranch* and my dad would pack his winter supplies into his trapline cabin. We would pack in his supplies and grub for the winter with the horses, which were moving downstream on the Smoky River. They put the bell straps at Art Allen's cabin. They dug a hole and buried the bell straps—to be used again next spring. Sometimes my dad buried the bell straps, as Art had a lot of "goodies" in his cabin running around. The packrats, squirrels and mice liked to chew on the bell strap leather, so it was safer to bury them and dig them up the next spring.

After my dad and Art pushed the horses across the Smoky River, the horses would wander down to their winter range. Art would spend the winter trapping. He used to be sure to get back to *Mt. Robson Ranch* before his birthday with his load of fur from the trapline. February 2nd was his birthday so mother always had a birthday cake for him. Then he'd show us all the furs he'd trapped over the winter. Art and Dad were good friends.

Sue   Boy, life is full of coincidences. You mentioned running into two trappers, Daniel Wanyandie and Art Allen. Daniel Wanyandie was a Rocky Mountain Cree and is my daughter, Chehala's grandfather—and my husband, Bazil bought Art Allen's trapline and I have the trapline on the Range at Kvass Flats. Art was in the Jackpine country when hardly anybody was in there. We heard that sometimes he would take his furs and walk out to Mt. Robson.

Tom Vinson told me that he packed in supplies for Art in 1947. Tom Vinson took his outfit from Brule to Eagle's Nest up the West Sulphur, down the Hardscrabble, across the two islands on the Smoky River, and up to Art Allen's cabin, which was located downstream about a half-mile from Pauline Creek.

Ishbel   That was after we stopped outfitting in that area. Our last year was 1946.

Sue   So Art Allen learned the trails and the country from your father.

Ishbel   Art Allen worked at *Mt. Robson Ranch* when he was pretty young. He was on the trip when Uncle George died in1936. Art was on the trail with my dad and uncles, so he would have learned the trails from them.

Sue   I noticed in some of your pictures and in your journal that you refer to staying at McDonald's. Can you tell me where McDonald's camp was?

Ishbel   It was called Donald McDonald—it was in B.C. I think there is another McDonald Flats close to Grande Cache too.

Sue Donald McDonald was a Métis trapper. Donald originally had a place at Lake Isle, Alberta. He moved to Jasper and married Louise *(Findlay)* Thappe in 1891. Louise was an original descendant of Jasper. She was married to a Beaver Indian called Thappe who was killed in a hunting accident. His grave is located in Willmore Wilderness Park on the Mountain Trail west of the Summit cabin. Louise and Thappe had two children by the names of Joe and Louise. The children adopted McDonald as their surname after their mother's marriage to Donald. When Jasper became a National Park in 1907, the Federal Government did not take kindly to the Rocky Mountain People who lived in the Athabasca Valley. The small band of people was told to move from there to the Rocky Mountain Forest Reserve—despite their protests. Today there are many McDonald descendants living in the Cooperatives around Grande Cache. Louise and their children moved to the Grande Cache area at McDonald Flats, which is named after him. Donald Flats on the Berland River was also named after Donald McDonald.

In your 1942 to 1946 journals you were camped at Forget-Me-Not Pass on the Continental Divide. Next, the journal states that you were at McDonald's. In Art

Pictured above:

Margie *(Hargreaves)* Duncan fording the Short River. Margie was Roy and Sophia Hargeaves' younger daughter.

Margie was on a trip from Mt. Robson Ranch to Corral Creek with Ishbel, Roy Hargreaves, Isaac Plante, Jack O'Connor and his hunting partner, Mr. Haliday in 1943.

Photographer Ishbel *(Hargreaves)* Cochrane.

Allen's trapline cabin on the Jackpine River there is reference made to the McDonald line. I have been wondering where this trapline was.

Ishbel   Yes, you could go in one day from there—up and over Shale Mountain. With this hunter, we got up there but there was so much snow that we just went back and stayed at McDonald Meadows at the foot of the hill *(Shale Mountain).*

I think that Donald McDonald was at Tête Jaune, too. I also believe that Curly Phillips trapped around the head of the Jackpine River. Ross Cochrane, my cousin, used to go out there too. Curly Cochrane also went out to the upper Jackpine. On a summer trip, my husband, Murray found an old cabin with traps in it. The dude *(guest)* found a trap and so he kept it. It was over Bess's Shoulder, on the Jackpine—on a hillside.

Sue   There is drainage off the muskeg meadows between Mt. deVeber and Mt. Talbot, which we have dubbed Bazil Creek. Past the summit of the head of Bazil Creek are the headwaters of the Muddy Water River. We cut a trail up Bazil Creek to the upper meadows that are between Mt. Talbot and Mt. deVeber, in 2003. The confluence of this drainage is one creek downstream from Pauline Creek with its mouth at the Jackpine River. The re-opened trail opens up into beautiful alpine meadows that are soft and muskeggy. We were at the headwaters of the Muddy Water River and I drank the water there, thinking of how wild and dirty the Muddy Water can get downstream. From looking at your pictures, we rode to within a half-mile of your camp. You can ride up this old pack trail that we cleared on Bazil Creek right to the Continental Divide, Morkill Pass and Forget-Me-Not Pass. What was the country like when you traveled it?

Ishbel   There were pretty good trails. Sometimes when we stayed at Donald McDonald's we would go across the meadow and down the Muddy Water River. We went on the McDonald Meadow and followed the headwaters of the Muddy downstream. Some say that Donald McDonald had a place at Tête Jaune.

Sue   Your 1944 journal also mentioned that you went up to Winifred Lakes from the Smoky River. I know that you can also access the trail to Winifred Lakes if you go to Big Grave Cabin and travel west up Kvass Creek. You would find the lakes about a four-hour ride up that creek.

Ishbel   We used to camp at the moose lick on the east side of the Smoky River. We would go up the trail to Winifred Lakes from there. When we were camped at Winifred Lakes one time, I just stayed in camp. I wanted something behind the cook stove, so I had one of the men build a table. Ted Blackman, a wrangler built a husky table, so that I would have a place to put stuff. When we went back there the next year, we had to put the cook tent over that table. I bet that table is still there.

Pictured above:

Top: Sleepy mare and her foal and Pepper with Margie. Going up Shale Mountain.

Bottom: Top of Shale Mountain.

Pictured on left page:
Murray Cochrane.

Photos courtesy of Ishbel Cochrane

Pictured above:
Ishbel Hargreaves before she was married—
pictured at Winifred Lakes In 1944.
Murray Cochrane, was fighting in WWII at the time.
The brand that Roy Hargreaves used on his horses
is on the lower right hand corner of the image.

Photo courtesy of Ishbel Cochrane.

On a typical hunting trip, we would stay at Winifred Lakes a week to ten days. It was good hunting in that area. After we finished hunting, we returned to the Moose Lick camp on the Smoky River. Our next stop would be Bess Creek and then our last camp would be Berg Lake.

Sue Do you have any other stories that you would want to share with us?

Ishbel One time my dad found this perfectly round black rock that looked like a bowling ball, at the Muddy Water River. One of the hunters wanted to cut it in half—but I told him not to. I gave the rock to my son, Mac. There were small bumps on each side of the round rock. It looked like you could spin the rock from the bumps.

Sue We too have found the round black bowling balls. I know that Dave and Carol Simpson who outfitted in the Smoky River and Sheep Creek Valley found some round black balls as well. They outfitted in the Smoky River area from 1967 to the early 1990s. They kept the black balls and didn't know what caused the phenomena. We have kept our round black bowling ball as well and it's pretty cool.

Ishbel I would like to tell you a story about my dad and the grizzly bears. They used to call my Uncle Jack Hargreaves, Grizzly Jack. My dad also had a special relationship with the grizzly. Twice my dad arrived in camp with the outfit. He didn't unpack or tie up a horse—he just took the hunter—and away they went—they came back with a grizzly bear. On one trip we had stopped at Berg Lake and the packhorses went into the corral. One hunter did not have a grizzly. Dad walked out on the lakeshore and looked up into the basin. It was a clear basin and he saw a grizzly bear up there—so up they went. When he got up on the hill—there is this big grizzly—and the hunter shot. I think that he nicked it or something. The grizzly bear was coming down the hill and the hunter was standing there pulling the shells out of his gun—he got so excited. Dad was trying to get around his hunter—but he was in the way. Luckily, Dad had his rifle and he killed the bear right in front of them. The hunter panicked and he was just like a kid, he got so excited. A lot of hunters get excited when they see game. There were only two times that he abruptly up and left the outfit on a hunting trip—but that's what happened.

Sue Your dad retired in 1959. I understand that the Forestry wanted to clear your father's horses out of the Smoky Valley around 1962. I believe that a man by the name of Ed Benny went in and rounded up your dad's horses in 1963, eight years before your father passed away in 1971.

Ishbel They put somebody in there on the Smoky Valley to round up all of our horses. The authorities called them wild horses—but there were still some of the Hargreaves' brands on the horses. The officials told us that they had Dad's horses—as they knew what our brand was. My husband, Murray went up to see what horses he would bring home—but he didn't want to bring any of them home because they were all scarred. They had tied a rope around their foot and had tied them to a tree or something. Whoever it was that rounded our horses up sure hurt them—so Murray said that he would not take any of them—so the horses were shipped.

Sue How do you feel about the creation of Willmore Wilderness Park?

Ishbel When the government creates parks—they don't know what they are taking away. We just had a fight to take the horses into Berg Lake. They did a big study to see if the horses hurt the trail. My gosh, it was the outfitters who built and maintained the trails. My dad used to keep the trails in shape.

Sue The reason I started writing the book was because I hoped to educate people on the reality of outfitters and trappers in Willmore Wilderness Park and how they were an integral part of the Park's ecosystem.

Ishbel I don't think you can educate people who have gone to school and university—and think that they know a whole lot better. I will tell you about one warden that was on the north boundary of Jasper National Park. Russell, my son was out to get horses. The warden called him in, so Russell went to see what he wanted. The warden was going to shoe his horse because he had lost a front shoe. The warden had put the shoe on the ground and the horses hoof on top of the shoe. He was planning on driving the nail down from the top of the horse's hoof. Russell was alarmed with this operation, so he told the warden to take the horse over to the Chalet and he would fix the shoe for him. Russell had his horses ready to hit the trail—but he took some time and shod the warden's horse. *(You drive a nail into the horse's hoof through the shoe and through the bottom of the hoof upwards, then clinch it.)*

Pictured above:
Ishbel, the mighty fisherman for one day, at Sheep Creek Falls in 1945.

Photo courtesy of Ishbel Cochrane.

Brian Wallace was a warden who used to live at Mt. Robson. This was before a new Head Warden from Jasper Park came and changed everything. He said that there would be no wardens in Mt. Robson Park—so Brian had to move to Jasper. Brian Wallace just retired from the Warden Service this year and he told me the last time I talked to him that there probably wouldn't be wardens going in the backcountry now.

We rode up to the Smoky River after the Alberta Government had closed the horse area down to us. We were not allowed to graze our horses there due to the creation of Willmore Wilderness Park. When we went back to see the country, it had grown up so much. There were deer and elk in there. The elk must have moved in the valley. There was no elk when we had our horses in there. I think the elk were brought into the valley by truck.

Sue   The Alberta Government transplanted some of the elk in the Smoky Valley in the late 1970s.

Ishbel   There was always deer in the Smoky Valley. Everything at Kvass Flats was grown up. The trails were still there. There used to be a little child's grave on a bench at Kvass Flats. There was no name on the grave. There was a little spirit house on the grave.

Sue   I believe the grave belonged to Louis Delorme's sister. She died of pneumonia at a young age. The spirit house has gone, but we have erected a wooden fence around the grave. There is a little cross there, but the elk seem to push the fence down every year.

Ishbel When we camped on the Smoky, we had a corral on Corral Creek. We had a smaller fence on this creek but we put an addition on it. There were times when we left that Smoky drainage with as many as one hundred and five horses. We didn't always get home with them all.

Sue Emil Moberly, a Rocky Mountain Cree Elder told me that with your dad's horses and the Natives' horses, there were over four hundred head of horses in the Smoky River Valley.

Ishbel In 1923, Walter *(Curly)* Cochrane trailed his horses to the Range with Dad's horses. In the spring he took his horses north to Charlie Lake, B.C. Walter trailed his outfit through to Grande Prairie via the Smoky and on to B.C. Come to think of it, the Range certainly supported a lot of horses. In fact, George Dennison also had a range beyond ours. He was linked to Mt. Robson. He was an outfitter. He did some hunting and summer trips.

We went back to the Range with my nephew, Tom McCready, Bill Ruddy, my cousin's husband, Murray and I. Things sure changed a lot. It was really grown up and Corral Creek had changed channels. There was a bit of our corral left. I wouldn't want to go from Mt. Robson down to the Range now, because a lot of the trail would be washed out. I believe that a lot of the trail from the Jasper Park boundary to the mouth of the Jackpine River would need to be cleared out.

Sue Now the government won't let outfitters camp in Jasper Park without permits and there is a very limited number of permits issued. The only way to get around it would be to camp at Rock Creek on the Willmore boundary and travel up and over Bess Pass and back to the headwaters of the Jackpine River on a long day-move.

Ishbel Well, Bess Pass is quite a climb when you are going up. You know one time we were camped over the hill from Bess Creek on the shoulder of Bess Mountain. We were camped on the other side, down below. Our cook tent was close to the trail. In the morning there were grizzly tracks right by our camp, up and over Bess's Shoulder. We had a dog and it never barked. The grizzly bear never bothered us.

Sue Working on the trail can be tough work, especially if you have deadfall and winter blow-down to contend with. Did you have to cut most of the trail by hand?

Ishbel Cutting trail by hand was pretty hard work and we used axes and Swede saws for many years. It was nice when we finally bought a small power saw. We had it in a box that we top-packed—so we didn't have to fight for it when we needed it. My father, uncles and husband kept the trails open. It was done each year so that there was good access into the mountains.

Sue I don't think anyone has maintained the trails up the Smoky, Hardscrabble, and Jackpine rivers since your dad's time. It has certainly been a challenge trying to find and restore them. Bazil Leonard, Tom Wanyandie and I have been the driving forces since 1992 to re-open your dad's long-forgotten trails. In 2002, the Willmore Wilderness Foundation was formed and one of its primary mandates is to find, restore and record the old pack trails so that future generations can enjoy one of the most beautiful places on this planet. I can see that your dad's horses were key in keeping the mountain trail systems open—and they were essential in keeping the meadows grazed off. Your family wintered horses in the Smoky Valley—and these horses were a part of the Rocky Mountain ecosystem.

Ishbel My dad used to say that you could winter horses where sheep wintered.

Sue Thank you for your interview. You are a kindred spirit.

CHAPTER FOUR:

1936 Season Hunting Report by Jack Brewster

❧ Authors Note ❧

The following 'Hunting Report' of Jack W. Brewster, guide and outfitter was provided to the Willmore Wildneress Foundation by Tom Vinson. The 'Hunting Report' is for the 1936 season and was written personally by Jack Brewster who was hunting in what is now called Willmore Wilderness Park..

For me, it is a much more difficult task to settle down and write the little story of my hunting activities in the country north of Jasper during the fall of 1936, than it was for me to trail back four days into the mountains and hunt the trophies that I will tell about further on in these pages.

My first party was made up of four sportsmen from California: Clarence Turner, Verne Johnson, Bob Gardiner and H.L. Ricks. With the exception of Mr. Turner, who was a normal-sized man, they were all big fellows. Messrs. Johnson and Gardiner were both over six feet and while Toppy Ricks was not all that tall, he more than made up for it in other dimensions. During this hunting trip, which was their first into this section, they proved to be good sports. When not hunting, they spent most of their time kidding one another.

Our two-and-a-half day's travel from Devona to the Park boundary was uneventful. The fact that we saw but little game made these gentlemen feel that they were doomed for disappointment. However, after we crossed the Park boundary and entered the hunting country *(Willmore Wilderness Park)* on the afternoon of August 30th, their hopes were raised. Riding for the last three hours of this day's trip through the open meadows of Rock Creek, which would lead us to our first hunting camp at the head of the Sulphur River, we saw an abundance of game. First we saw a bunch of deer, then a cow caribou, further on, a cow moose and calf, and at each half-mile, other moose would emerge from the timber to take their evening meals. Above timberline, small herds of sheep and goat could be seen feeding on the slopes, and as the last rays of the setting sun bathed the higher peaks with golden splendor, a magnificent white-necked caribou bull came down to the trail to watch the party ride by.

Pictured on left page:
Jack Brewster with bighorn sheep trophy horns.

Jasper Yellowhead Museum & Archives
PA 7 - 25

We had one full-day to spend at this camp before the hunting season opened, September 1st, so the other three guides went out to see what game was nearby. Ed Moberly went to look over the basins west of camp, while Ernie Stenton and Otto Anderson covered the mountain range to the east of camp. When they returned that evening, Ed had located eleven rams, including two good ones in the mountains to the west. Ernie and Otto had seen plenty of game but no rams.

When we looked out of our tents next morning, it was raining and the clouds hung very low. In spite of the weather, Ed and Ernie took both Messrs. Turner and Gardiner into the basin where Ed had seen the eleven rams the day before. When Gardiner got there, they located the rams alright, but the bunch had split into two bands, with one of the big rams in each.

The party divided at this point. Ed and Mr. Turner stalked the three rams that were on a ridge to the right, while Ernie and Mr. Gardiner went after the other rams that were bedded down in a rockslide some distance to the south. As Ed and Mr. Turner followed up the ridge in the direction of their rams, a heavy fog settled and cut off their view of the sheep. After proceeding a short distance through the drifting fog, they could see the outline of the big ram. They estimated the distance to be about three hundred yards. Mr. Turner fixed his rifle sights for that distance and fired three shots at the ram, but when the fog disappeared a moment or so later, they found that the sheep had vanished with it. Ernie and Mr. Gardiner had better luck. As they worked along a ridge hoping to get above the sheep that were lying in the rock slide, they looked into the basin below them and there, to their surprise, they saw two rams coming straight towards them. They studied these two rams carefully and decided they had better heads than those they were stalking. The hunters, back-tracking about two hundred yards down the ridge, found comfortable positions in the rocks and sat waiting until the oncoming rams were near enough to kill; their first bighorn sheep. That same day, Otto and Mr. Johnson went out to hunt moose but just got very wet and came back to camp. Toppy Ricks and I sat in camp most of the day telling stories to Mac, the cook, and Jeff, the horse wrangler, but around five o'clock, we went out and killed a deer.

Determined to do better the next day, Ed and Mr. Turner took horses and went back down the valley to examine more closely seven rams that we had seen two days previously when we had moved in with the outfit. Ernie and Mr. Gardner stayed in camp to photograph and skin out their sheep head. Otto and Mr. Johnson went back into the mountains west of camp where more rams had been located. Mr. Ricks and I puffed our way to the top of a ridge that would give us a good view of a large sheep basin beyond. On the way up this slope, I encouraged Toppy *(Mr. Ricks)* by telling him that for many years past, a ram with a very large pair of horns had inhabited this and other nearby basins and that during that time, this ram had been shot at by at least a dozen eager sportsmen but none of them had connected

Pictured left (L to R): Jack Brewster and Bill Oliver.

Jasper Yellowhead Museum & Archives. PA 34-67

with him. In order to give my hunter further encouragement to make the last one hundred yards of this climb, I assured him that we were going to get that ram before the sun set that day. From the top of the ridge, we looked over the basin and sure enough, there was the big ram I had been telling him about. Eight smaller rams were with him. Unfortunately, about the time we discovered them, they discovered us and pulled out. The sheep went south along the face of the mountain and, from the course they took, I figured they did not intend to go over the top and that there was still a chance to circle on them. From this point on, Toppy needed no more encouragement. In fact, my greatest difficulty was in keeping up with him. We climbed straight up the mountain to the top, about two thousand feet. When we reached the top, we turned south along the ridge searching the basin on both sides of the mountain as we went. At 1:30 in the afternoon, I located four rams lying on a shale slope about a mile ahead of us, and about one thousand feet below our level. There being only four in the bunch, led me to believe that these were not our rams. While eating lunch at this spot, I made out four more rams feeding on the slope about five hundred yards below the others. Then, I was sure these were the rams we were after. All these sheep were in a most difficult spot to approach. It seemed there were miles of loose shale on all sides of them. The wind was favourable, so we decided that our course should be in a straight line towards the sheep. The going was bad and the noise terrific. In fact, the shale was so noisy that for the last two hundred yards of our stalk, we moved only when the wind blew strong enough to carry the sound up the mountain, away from the sheep. I never had a sportsman make a better stalk than Mr. Ricks did that day. Eventually, we raised our heads over a small mound of shale and, to our great joy, the four big rams were still lying in the same place and now, only about seventy yards below us. It was only a matter of seconds however, before they were all on their feet. Mr. Ricks took a hurried shot at the big fellow but missed him. By the time he had re-loaded for a second shot, another ram had taken up a position between us and the big sheep, which prevented further shooting. In this order, they galloped into a canyon and out of sight. I picked out a large rock on the other side of the canyon and told Mr. Ricks that that was where the sheep would come out but, when they did come out, nine-and-a-half feet below this rock, Mr. Ricks missed again. However, the big fellow did not get away this time. The third shot hit the rocks about ten feet behind the sheep that was now running straight away from us. The fourth shot hit right at his heels and the fifth shot broke his back right behind his shoulders. This was, indeed, a magnificent trophy. His horns were not heavy but his great curl came one-and-a-half inches past his base and was well rubbed at the points.

When we returned to camp that evening, we found that Ed and Mr. Turner had not come in yet. Late that night they had not shown up. They were still missing the next morning. At 10:30 in the forenoon, they returned to camp, bringing with them a very fine sheep head as well as a magnificent caribou. According to their story, they had located the seven rams we had seen before the season opened, and were stalking them when they saw two larger rams in another place. This meant another stalk. After they had secured one of these rams and were on their way back to their horses, they saw this big bull caribou in a bunch of thirty-six in all. By the time they had stalked and killed this caribou, it was dark, so they spent the night under a tree eating caribou steaks with no salt.

During the next four days spent at this camp, each of the other hunters secured a caribou, and Mr. Turner and Mr. Gardiner got a moose each.

Our next hunting camp was down the Sulphur a few miles. Here, we expected to get a goat and moose. The first day here, Otto and I took Mr. Johnson and Mr. Ricks back in the mountains where they shot a goat each—some very good shooting on the part of Mr. Johnson. On the return to camp, we found that Ernie and Mr. Gardiner had killed a goat, and when Ed and Mr. Turner came in, they said they had a lot of sport shooting at goats but did not hit any. The next day, Ed and Mr. Turner went after goats again and had about the same luck. Ernie and Mr. Turner went after five big billies that we had seen the day before. They got right into the bunch. After killing one, they cornered another one in the rocks, and took more than a hundred feet of movie film of him. This was Mr. Gardiner's big day and, in spite of the long hard trip he had, he was filled with joy that evening. Mr. Ricks and I climbed to timberline on the mountain east of camp to try to find a really big moose that had been there for a couple of days. We had reached the point we were heading for and, upon looking across the valley, we saw two bull moose in the dead timber about three miles away. Soon we heard a terrific bombardment over in that neighborhood and, in a few seconds, the whole mountainside was alive with moose running in all directions. Presently, we saw Otto and Mr. Johnson emerge from the brush and walk over to a magnificent bull moose that Mr. Johnson had killed. At this moment, we saw a very large goat walk out on to a point straight above them and look down. Having convinced himself that all was well below, he lay down. We had no idea that the moose hunters had seen the goat but, a few minutes later when we saw Mr. Johnson start up the mountain, we were sure they had seen him. After a considerable time, the distance between Mr. Johnson and the goat greatly reduced, and we saw him get ready to shoot. After the first shot, the goat got up. After the second shot, he moved further up the mountain. Hearing no more shots he lay down again. Mr. Johnson went up on the mountain to where the goat had been; decided that he had missed him and came back down. Mr. Ricks and I had spent so much time watching the play across the valley that we did not get our moose.

From this camp, we moved down to Big Grave Flats where we had hoped that Mr. Johnson would get a sheep and Mr. Ricks, a moose. On the way down the Sulphur River, I spotted a very large bull moose on a brush-covered side hill directly across the river from us. This moose had, by far, the largest set of horns we had seen yet. As there was no chance of getting nearer to him and at any moment he might look in our direction and see the packtrain, I suggested to Mr. Ricks that he shoot from where we were. It was a long shot but, at the first crack of the rifle, a large limb fell off a tree directly over the moose's shoulder. The next six shots cut limbs off other trees all around the moose but, when the eighth shot struck the moose in the right horn, he went out of there so fast that the rest of the bullets could not catch up to him.

Just before we reached camp that afternoon, we ran into a terrific snowstorm, the first we had had on the trip. It continued to snow and rain for the next four days, which made sheep hunting impossible. However, Mr. Ricks went out in the storm one afternoon and killed a moose; the horns had a fifty-three-inch spread.

From Big Grave Flats, we pulled right back to the railway without further layover. Mr. Johnson had not killed his sheep yet, so I planned our return trip so that we would pass some good sheep basins that I knew had not been hunted. Mr. Johnson and his guide left camp early on the second morning and went on ahead to hunt these basins, while the rest of the party moved camp. When they caught up to us that evening, they said they had found nine good rams in the first basin but, after getting within one hundred and twenty-five yards of them, Mr. Johnson was unable to hit the one he wanted.

Clarence Turner kept a record of the game seen by the party in the seventeen days we were in the hunting country, and his figures were as follow:

> 21 deer
> 86 caribou
> 200 moose
> 139 goats
> 84 rams
> —————————
> 530
> 1 wolverine
> 4 coyotes
> 2 silver fox

Pictured above:

Jack Brewster, taken on the Glacier Trail, Jasper to Lake Louise. Part of the photographic record of Joan Robson's packhorse trip with Jack Brewster over the Glacier Trail, July 3 to 23, 1927, before the road was built.

On the trip were Mr. and Mrs. Edmonds, Otto Schulz Jr., George Schulz, Joan Robson, Carl Madsen *(cook)*, Dorrel Shovar *(guide)*, Felix Plante *(guide)*, Sunshine and Blizzard *(Jack Brewster's husky pups)*.

Photo courtesy of Jasper Yellowhead Museum & Archives 93-37-18-9

Pictured right:
Art Allen.

Courtesy of
Jacquie Hanington.

CHAPTER FIVE:
Art Allen

Pictured above:
Art Allen.

Courtesy of
Linda Hokanson.

❧ *Authors Note* ❧

I personally found doing this chapter very rewarding, as my husband, Bazil Leonard had the good fortune to acquire Art's trapline. The line was purchased from Laurier Adams of Grande Cache in 1992. Since that time, Bazil and I have been in the process of finding and clearing the old pack trails that Art so loved.

As fate would have it, I ended up editing this transcript in a hunting camp in "Art's trapping and hunting territory." As I re-read his words while in the camp's cook tent, I could feel his love of the land, wildlife and the universe. I was blessed with long days alone to work on this chapter. I also had a wonderful opportunity to photograph the area using a camcorder and digital SLR.

There is "no time" in Art's world or in the mountain wilderness. Rain, snow or shine, Willmore Wilderness Park is truly a magnificent part of 'Mother Earth'. The world that Art lived, hunted and trapped in remains unchanged. I am sure if he were to traverse the time-line, he would ride into our camp and be totally in his element. One can never tire of the incredible beauty of the Canadian Rockies or the simple way of life that living in an outfitting camp affords.

I would love to have known Art Allen, and wish I could have spoken with him in person. I am very grateful that his daughter, Linda and her husband, Lynn Hokanson had the foresight to tape-record Art in 1992. Linda and Lynn interviewed Art at his home in Hinton, Alberta.

Art was born 1906 in London, England and came to Canada in 1908. His father had been smitten by the Caribou Gold Rush and was working in the mines two years prior to his family's arrival. Art's mother and father worked at various camps but separated when Art was four or five years old. His mother married Joseph Saladana, a climbing guide, and the new family moved to Louis Creek, British Columbia (B.C.). They relocated to Mt. Robson B.C. on a homestead where Art began learning the art of hunting, trapping and guiding. While on their homestead at Mt. Robson, Art got to know the Hargreaves family. Sadly, the Saladana home burnt down and

Pictured above:
Art Allen.

Courtesy of
Jacquie Hanington.

the family moved to Edmonton. Later, they went back to Jasper, where Art's step-dad and mom worked for Curly Phillips at his market garden. Curly was a well-known trapper, guide and one of the foremost outfitters who worked in the Jasper, Mt. Robson and Willmore areas.

At the age of fifteen, Art got a job putting up the poles and wire on the telegraph line. After the telegraph job was completed, he moved to Jasper, Alberta and guided and trapped from the town as a base.

Linda What year did you first start trapping and how old were you?

Art I was about twelve years old *(1918)*. I first trapped coyotes when I was eleven years old, I guess. We had a sandpit down by the Fraser River. We used to play in the sand down there, on the homestead at Mt. Robson. I seen some tracks in the sand and they looked like dog tracks. I wondered whose dogs had been around. I got a funny feeling and a chill run down my back and I looked around and saw this big coyote staring at me. I picked up a rock and threw it to scare him, and the rock hit him—and down he went. So I picked up a stick that we used for shingles and I beat him on the head. I was hollering and screaming. Mother and my brother, Ken came over with a shotgun but he was already dead. I was sitting on this coyote. I took him home and skinned him out and stretched him out as best as I could. I took him up to the store at Moose Creek, B.C. and he gave me eight or ten bucks for it. He said, "I'll have to show you how to skin. You need to skin down the back of the legs and not the front of the legs." My brother, Ken was only eight years old at the time.

In 1926, when I was twenty, Fred Noble went up to the Coal Branch to see the Forest Ranger because they opened traplines. He said that there was one down the Embarras River and the guy that owned it was in jail. So we put our stuff on the raft and went down the Embarras River. There was a sawmill that had a boom across the river. We had quite a time getting past the boom. We went down Rodney Creek and built our cabin there. We trapped there all winter, left after Christmas, and went to Elk Point. Ken came and joined me to put in the rest of the winter. We were down in the bush, shooting squirrels around the end of the season. We were hollering back and forth to each other, and then this strange voice piped up and said, "Ha!"

Linda Who was that?

Art The guy that owned the line—he got out of jail. His name was Ray Winters. We went up to the cabin and had coffee—and shook hands. He said, "Well you built me a good cabin anyways." I said, "I guess we did." It was just about the end of the season. He said I was doggone nice to pick this place for a line and build such a nice cabin for him. Back then, they

weren't registered lines. It was outside the Athabasca Forest Reserve. You'd pick up a line wherever you could. You'd have to chase a guy off your line sometimes.

Actually, I got my own line in '26. I trapped other lines before that. I was trapping in '23 and '24, and in '24 and '25. There were three of us. One winter, we trapped one hundred and sixty-nine *(marten)* and the next year, one hundred and forty.

I think that it would be '27 that I worked for Curly Phillips. We went out on his trapline in September. We picked up his horses at Brule and went down the Hay River and, later in the winter, to the Old Man River near Obed *(Alberta)*. I trapped with Curly Phillips in '28 and '29. It was his trapline. We took his horses in there to winter them. We were out on Curly Phillips' trapline on the second winter in '28. In '27, '28 and '29, we spent time out on the Old Man River.

In '27 I started packing for the Federal Government on a survey trip. The cook on that trip was Al Lamont. He came from Valemount. After that, he went up and homesteaded in the Fort St. John area on the Peace River.

Lynn How long did you work on the topographical survey? *(In later years, Art told his friend, Mac Elder who was a packer, guide and later, a Jasper Park warden, that in 1927 and 1928, he was packing for a survey crew. These surveys were to establish the north boundary of Jasper National Park. Art was one of the climbers who built many of the cairns and markers on the mountain tops.)*

Art First in '27, I worked doing the topographical surveys from the first of June until the middle of September. In '28 I worked from July until August or September. It was thirty days at a time.

Lynn Did you take enough supplies for the whole trip or did you have to go back to Jasper to stock up?

Art The Jasper Park warden brought quite a bit of supplies out to us. In fact, I remember making one trip for supplies into Jasper. We had some extra horses we didn't need. I brought them in and took one packhorse load back. Anyway, I had a saddle horse and a packhorse. I had one case of eggs with thirty-eight dozen on one side for a side pack. I was walking up this hill on the Snake Indian River leading my saddle horse. I had the packhorse looped over the horn. Going around a switchback, the packhorse decided to go around one side of the tree and the saddle horse, around the other. He pulled back and broke my cinch and the saddle. My horse went over backwards down the hill. I had bottle of gin tied to the back of my saddle and it broke. And the eggs—there was eggs running out of the crate and I was scared to look. I didn't know if there were any left or not. Anyway, I re-packed the horse and took off again.

Next day, I caught up to my outfit. So the cook and I looked to see if there were any eggs left. I told him what had happened. We looked in the crate and took them all out and separated them. I didn't do too badly— I only broke six. It was only six eggs out of thirty-eight dozen! Juicy stuff was running out of four or five eggs.

Lynn How long of a trip could you pack supplies for?

Art Thirty days—but it all depended. If you went for forty days, you took more horses. It depended on how many days you were going, and how many horses you took.

Lynn How many people did you take?

Art You had a cook and a guide, at least. There were anywhere from three to ten.

Lynn What does a complete outfit consist of?

Art Horses, saddles, blankets, halters and bridles, pack panniers *(or packboxes)*, ropes and lash ropes and basket ropes, tents, beds, stoves, cook stove for the cook tent, heater stoves for the other guys' tents, folding tables.

Lynn What kind of food did you take?

Art We took mostly dried stuff. We had fresh fried potatoes—except in the fall, they would freeze. In the summertime, we took fresh vegetables.

Lynn This was when you were on your Jasper Park boundary surveys, I guess. Would you hunt for fresh meat as you went?

Art We were allowed one animal for the whole summer. We got meat in the hunting season. One hunting season, we were camped at Rock Lake and along came Alex Nelles *(father of Larry Nelles)*, a Jasper Park warden. Alex was stationed at Willow Creek; he came over and helped me hunt for grizzlies. Funny thing was, he was using his boss's rifle. Alex and I went down toward the Jasper Park boundary— hunting in there. We were sitting down discussing the gun. We opened up the assembly and, at the same time, we heard a crack and there was a goldarn bull moose standing there. He was looking at us. Alex shot and missed him. We went a little further down into a draw and saw a cow moose standing there. By golly, Alex up and missed that too. We went down into the shintangle and by golly he missed. We took off going down through this old burn and second-growth pine and windfall. We'd gone a little way and came to this little creek. It got too bad a-going and there was an opening between the creek and the second-growth pine. We were walking along, and out of the creek bottom came a bull moose, out onto the bank. So we hit him in the guts. The moose went into second growth windfall and lay down, so we waited there for a while. Finally, we got a long pole and I tied my hunting knife onto it. I snuck up to the moose and I jabbed him in the neck. That old bastard wasn't dead. There he was, a knife hanging from his neck—and that was it. So I had an axe on the packhorse.

A tree had fallen down just in front of the moose. I said, "Alex, you go around behind the windfall and keep his attention. I'll go around from behind him and see if I can sneak up." I thought, "OK, we can try this once." By golly, he was standing his ground, wiggling and making me move for him. I had to step over the hind legs of the moose and in behind his antlers, and reach for the pole with my knife in it. We were standing about three or four feet away from him. The moose jumped over the edge of the riverbank and I jumped six feet in the air! I got thinking afterward that only damn fools would try this. There was no protection there whatsoever!

In '27 Grant Hare went out on a topographical survey party with me. He had his wife and kids staying in Jasper.

Pictured above:
Art Allen and a grizzly bear.

Photo courtesy of
Jacquie Hanington.

Pictured right (L to R)
"North Boundary Survey Crew."

Standing: Hank Hansen,
Grant Hare, Al Lamonte *(cook)* .
Sitting: Art Allen, Ken Allen,
Frank Burstrom.
Jimmy Lamb was also a
member of the survey party.

Jasper Yellowhead
Museum & Archives PA 3-2

Lynn Did you have your own outfit then?

Art No, we used Brewster's horses. Grant Hare and I looked after the horses and packed them. We set up camp and the horses took off down the Snake Indian River about six miles—there were slides and feed down there. We were waiting for the weather to change so that we could move. We had one mountain left to climb and survey for the Jasper Park boundary. The weather was bad and it rained every day and it was foggy. We were camped there eating whistlers—groundhogs mostly. I found this old trap and I trapped groundhogs to eat. We had grub down at Blue Creek Cabin, as the warden had brought grub there for us. We were supposed to be down there but, instead of that, we were upstream on Blue Creek waiting for the weather to clear.

This one evening, Alex Nelles came into camp. It seems to me that he walked right through that day. That would be about thirty-eight miles. He had a message for Grant. His kids had polio and one of them was dead and the other one wasn't expected to live. It was just before dark when Alex got to camp.

Grant lost no time. He got a few things together. He couldn't pack his gear. We had to go down to where these horses were, about three miles down from camp. We had to try to find and catch the horses in the dark and we needed another flashlight. We took off with a bridle apiece. I was going to catch a horse and go with him as far as Blue Creek to the first warden's cabin. I was going to wait there while he went onto Willow Creek. The next day, I was going to come back and pick the horses up and bring them back to camp so we could move. We took off and it was plenty dark by the time we left camp.

We got down to where the horses were and I asked Alex if he saw any of them when he rode up. He said yes, that they were on the side hills. We got down there and could hear the bells in the dark. We saw one in the ditch. Good old Stony, you could do anything with him—skid, harness, saddle or pack. I figured that was good enough for me, but Grant wanted to ride Bob, my horse. He was the toughest one of the bunch and the hardest one to catch. So I found a bay standing up on the hillside in the dark. I couldn't make out which one he was. If you had a piece of bread—sometimes you could catch Bob in the corral with a piece of bread. I went up there with this bread calling him by name. He never moved. He never came for the bread or anything. He just stood there. I said, "I don't know who the hell you are, but I'll put the bridle on you anyway." I picked up my line and led him back down, lit a match and, by gosh, it was Bob. He was hard to catch in the corral. He must have known I was coming up. He just stood there like he was frozen.

So then, we went on down to Blue Creek cabin and made some supper in the warden's cabin. Of course, I had no saddle. You kind of get sore when you ride that far bareback. So I told Grant to phone me in the morning when he got to Willow Creek because I wanted to know he made it, before I went back to our camp. *(Jasper Park warden's cabins were all equipped with phones.)*

I was up pretty early the next morning. By golly, Grant didn't phone until about eight o'clock in the morning. He just got to the Willow Creek cabin. He told me about trying to get out of the yard. There was just so much fog, he couldn't see anything. He just couldn't see where the trail started. He went up to the bush and found the drift fence. He tied his horse up to the fence and followed it along until he found the barn. He went back and got his horse. You couldn't tell a hole from a hump. He thought his horse was going to step up—instead of that, he went down in a hole. He got off and walked a-way. He said it was hard to walk because you couldn't see anything. It was really tough going. Anyway, he got to Willow Creek and this warden lent him a saddle. He saddled up Bob and away he went to Devona. That was fifty miles that he travelled. It was tough, I know. *(Blue Creek to Willow Creek is twenty-four miles. Willow Creek to Devona is twenty-four miles. The fifty miles referred to, is from six miles upstream on Blue Creek to Devona.)*

Grant got to Devona just in time to catch the train to Jasper. He got home and one girl had died and the other girl was going to make it. She was getting over her polio.

Later on, Grant pulled out and left the marriage, as he was disappointed with his wife. He figured the girl was going to be like her–so he just pulled out. He changed his name and he moved to Quesnel, B.C. Eventually, he and Dr. Baker's wife got married. They had a farm down there. He worked construction and mines and different things. I hadn't seen him for years. That was in '27.

In 1939, I located my brother that I hadn't seen in twenty years. So I went down to Quesnel to see George and his wife. So we went to town for a New Year's dance. George introduced me to Grant Bryant and his wife. We talked for a while and Grant asked me to come to his house for New Year's Day. I said, "Sure." Grant and his wife got in the front of the car and I got in the back. Grant handed me this bottle and said, "Here, Art, to the old surveys in 1927!" I said, "You're not Grant Hare are you?" He said, "That's who I am." He was a nice guy and we got along pretty good. A few years after that, he passed away. I had no idea it was Grant. I thought I should know the face but I just couldn't place the name.

Lynn What did you do in 1928?

Art In 1928, I also built the chalet at Medicine Lake—south end of Medicine Lake. I packed a bunch of stuff into Maligne *(Lake)* to the boathouse. I was packing siding on two horses—fifteen-foot lengths. There was a *(stove)* chimney on one horse and another one on the other. It's hard to remember exactly what year. *(The Medicine Lake Chalet was in use until the road was built around Medicine Lake in 1963-64. The building was not in use for a few years and sat empty. In 1966 or 1967 Tom Vinson bought the building, took it apart, log-by-log, and moved it to Brule. It is the log house that Tom and Yvette Vinson now live in.)*

In the fall of 1928, we built a new trestle up to Berg Lake. We tore the old one out that Curly Phillips had built years ago. We put in a new one. Now they have torn that one out and blown the rocks all out and made a solid one. I worked for the B.C. Government and went out trapping on the Old Man River *(near Obed, Alberta)*.

Linda Who did you work for in '29?

Art In '29 we took a summer party to Mt. Sir Alexander Mackenzie, B.C. for Curly Phillips. We had five dudes, some of which were mountain climbers. We had some older people that were not mountain climbers. There was this guy that was seventy-four years old who had never been on a horse. That was a long trip, back then. It was a forty-day trip. There were three in the party that were mountain climbers. The others went along to see the country. A woman called Mary Porter was in her seventies and I'm not sure if she'd rode before or not. A man called Lyle Waffle was in charge of the party and he was from New Jersey. Waffle, Dr. Gilmore and Helen Brook, a young woman, climbed Mt. Sir Alexander. We came home and came out at Mt. Robson. It was surprising how well the old people could travel. The old people got off and walked and the young people rode the horses.

Lyle Waffle came back the next year in 1930 and he wanted to climb Mt. Robson by the west ridge. He tried to get someone to come with him, but no one would go with him. There were two Swiss guides going up and he wanted to go with them, but they didn't want to take him. He wanted me to go with him, but there was no way I wanted to go up that mountain. I took him down to the lake with a boat and turned him loose by himself and wished him luck. He went up Mt. Robson and never came back. Some guides went to look for him and found his jacket with his alpine badge on it. They never found his rope or packsack. Down in a hole, they thought that they could see a watch, but never saw him. He might have gone down on a snow bank. He bought me a leather coat the first year I went out with him. It was the first time I ever had a leather coat.

I had climbed Mt. Resplendent the year before. Waffle, Allan Barker, and I climbed up Resplendent, which is just east of Mt. Robson. It's practically the same range. We were camped up at the Park boundary. We left at three in the morning and came back at three the next morning. When we hit the top, we ran into a snowstorm and coming back was icy. On our return trip at night and in the dark, we had to be careful. We came to a big crevasse and didn't know how to cross it because it was wide and deep. We walked down it for a-ways and saw a big piece of ice stuck in the crack about six feet down from the top. Allan and I held the rope and Lyle went down and crossed on this chunk of ice. He got across and pulled me across. It was scary in the dark.

Linda   When did you start guiding?

Art   I started guiding hunts in '29 after we came back off of that Mackenzie trip. Dave Moberly was in charge of the party. *(Dave Moberly was an original descendant of the Jasper area and Athabasca Valley.)* Dave Moberly would do the guiding and send me fishing. Well, that was my first hunting trip. Dave Moberly was in charge and we were both working for Curly Phillips. We had Mr. Brown, his wife, his son, Tommy and his friend called Jackie. That would be the Brown party in '29. Jackie was about twelve years old.

We went up Mumm Creek by Rock Lake and we camped there on Mumm, halfway up to the pass. We had to do some scouting before the season opened. I think it was a Friday night, and Saturday morning Dave said, "I'm going up to the head of the creek to check up and see how many sheep I can find." He didn't tell me what I was supposed to do. I told him that I would go on the hill around the camp and check up there for sheep. On Saturday morning he took off and I went up and spotted a bunch of rams up in the basin. I spotted two real good ones in the bunch. There were some other rams further down, from a good size to small. All together, there must have been at least five trophy heads in the bunch. I think there were nine all together. I watched them for a half an hour or so and went

Pictured above:
Art Allen.

Photo courtesy of
Jacquie Hanington.

back to camp. Dave came in just before dark after his scouting. I asked him how he made out. He said, "Not very good". All that he could find was ewes and lambs. He said he saw two small rams and that was all. He told us that we would have to move the next day. I said, "No, we won't. I spotted a bunch of rams above camp."

So on Sunday, I went up to check the bighorns. There were two guys coming down the drainage with a deer head. There was fog and you couldn't see anything. I was sitting below the mist. When you tried to see up into the clouds, it was just a blank. I caught some movement down in the creek with my eye. Here are these two guys coming down the creek from the basin where my sheep were. I thought, "Boy, they got one of my sheep!" I looked with my binocular and no, it didn't look like a sheep head. It looked like a deer head. So I went down and intercepted them. I knew the guide quite well but didn't know the hunter. I asked John what the heck he was doing hunting before the season opened. The season opened on Monday morning. Well, he said, "It's hard to keep track of the days when you're out here." He said he thought it was Monday. I said, "Yeah, I guess so." I told him that he had scared my sheep as he had come out of the basin where my rams were. I was pretty mad. He said he was sorry and that he didn't see anything. I said, "Of course you didn't see anything in the thick cloud like that!" The pair had come up from the other side and had walked up over the top. They got the deer below the fog. Anyways, I went up and waited and waited but the fog didn't lift.

On Monday morning, Dave said I had to go back up and see if I could find the sheep. He said that they were probably scared out all right, with those guys coming through there. He said that he would wait and if I found them, we would go after them. So I climbed the mountain and got up on top. It was a nice clear Monday. I could see all over and there wasn't a sign of a sheep in the basin. I looked up on the highest peak and there were my two big ones. I glassed left, over into some other basins and I picked up the other seven big rams laying just at tree line. I went back and told Dave that there was no use getting our hunter up to the two big ones because we had no way of stalking them. The bighorn sheep were way up the mountainside where they could see everything. No matter what way you went they'd see you coming. I told him we could pick some out of the other bunch. Dave took the lead and went up the creek to the basin where the sheep were. We had to go through this little short canyon and, in doing so, were in plain sight of the sheep. We decided to go through one at a time on our hand and knees, very slowly. One would watch with binoculars and the other would go through. As soon as we got out of the canyon, we were out of sight again. So that's what we did. By golly, we didn't disturb them! They were laying there chewing their cuds and quite happy.

We went up on a little ridge below the sheep site. We had to get around this ridge the rams were on, come over the top and down the mountain. Dave said it would be a lot of work to go up and over the top. I told him I thought it would be the safest way. We stopped and had a smoke. Dave took his hunter, Tom in order to let him have the first shot. Dave was the head guide, so what could I do? Tom and Dave took off and there was just the old man and I left.

I told the old man to watch the sheep, as the rams could take off before the other guys even got a shot. I told Mr. Brown that we could shoot from right where we were watching. Just as I predicted, we saw the sheep jump up. The sheep got the wind of them coming. A bunch of rams went into the bush where there was shintangle and small trees. The bighorns jumped up and took off. I told the old man to shoot, that he could probably shoot one from where we were located. He said No, that we had better give his son a chance.

Pretty soon we saw the rams come out. Dave and Tommy started following the sheep, which were going up and down these little gullies. They were heading to a big mountain to the left of the ridge. Once the sheep got up on the rocks, they didn't seem to be in too much of a hurry to get out of there. I stood up there and watched. Finally, Dave and Tommy got within shooting range of them. The kid shot two rams. One was for him and one was for his dad.

The next day, we moved over onto the head of Mumm Creek and made a base there. There was a goat that tried to jump some ice and came tumbling down the mountain and killed himself. He smashed his horns all to heck and we couldn't even get him for a trophy. I said to Dave, "I don't know what you're going to do tomorrow, but I'd like to take Tommy and head up to the big ridge there at Pope Creek and see if we could pick up a caribou or something." Dave said No, because that was what he was going to do. He took Tom hunting and told me to take Jackie and the old man fishing at Mumm Creek. There were Dolly Vardens and it was good fishing.

While we were fishing, I spotted this goat just across from us. I asked Jackie if he would like to get that goat up there and he said that would be good, so I told him that I would take him there tomorrow. Tommy and Dave came back that evening with a forty-point caribou. I told him about the goat and that I wanted to take Jackie hunting tomorrow. Dave said No, that he would take Jackie for the goat and I should take the guys fishing. They went out and sure enough, they got the goat and on the way back they got a deer.

That's when I approached Mr. and Mrs. Brown to take Tommy fly camping. Tommy thought it would be great because we were close to the same age. In 1929, I'd be twenty-three. Old Brown thought that would be great and Dave could take care of them. Old Dave gave in on that. I thought he'd object, but he said OK. Once his mind was made up, I knew we'd better go. We agreed where to meet on a certain date. Tommy and I took off.

We were going to look for moose, goat and a bear if we could. We did get a nice moose and a goat, but we didn't get a bear. Tommy got what he wanted except the bear—but that's

Pictured above:
Art Allen on a summer trip to the Tonquin Valley. Circa 1926.

Photo courtesy of Jim Babala.

something special anyways. After we were done hunting, we came back and joined up with the main camp. We broke camp the next day and headed for home. We stopped at Devona and Curly Phillips came across the Athabasca River in a boat to pick everyone up and take us to Jasper. We were out in the boat and Mrs. Brown yelled, "My, Curly, that Dave is sure a good hunter!"

Linda Did you have to start as Second Class and work your way up to First Class?

Art Yes.

Linda When did you become a First Class Guide?

Art In the summer time when you weren't hunting, all the hands were guides. You were all working together. There was a head guide, but everyone generally all got the same weight—First Class or Second Class. I became a First Class Guide on my second summer out in 1929. It wasn't long before I was taking parties out for different guys. Most people didn't even have to work up to a license in the first place. By horse wrangling for so many years, a guy would easily work his way into a First Class Guide. Curly Phillips gave me my first license. I worked for him. I had been packing before I worked with Curly—working for the Government.

Lynn Can you tell me about the time you guided the movie stars? I know that movie producer, Darryl Zanuck, John Dalcour, Wayne Wright and Bill Wellman went out on a hunt in October of 1929. (*Darryl Zanuck was one of the kingpins of Hollywood's studio system. Bill Wellman was the producer of an aviation drama called "Wings," set during World War I by Paramount Pictures.*)

There were four hunters and that was quite a trip too. The outfit's staff included outfitter, Roy Hargreaves with Chuck Chesser, Don Guild and me who were guides. (*Chuck Chesser was Roy Hargreaves' brother-in-law.*) The cooks were Albert Jervis, Dave Henry and Oliver Travers. We went down from Mt. Robson Ranch to Bess Creek and Roy decided to split the party up. Roy Hargreaves and I took the two younger hunters and cook, Oliver Travers. Old Dave Henry cooked for the other half of the party. Anyway, we were supposed to meet up at Femme Creek across the Smoky River. We figured that there would be sheep spotted for us by the time we got there.

Roy, our hunters and I went around the headwaters of the Jackpine, downstream on the Jackpine River and over Shale Mountain to Donald McDonald Meadow. We went all through that country to the head of Sheep Creek and to Forget-Me-Not Lake. We were camped at Forget-Me-Not Lake and had to move to the next camp—the rivers had so much ice on them and it was a cold October. In the morning, we packed up at Forget-Me-Not. Roy was on one side of the horse and I was on the other and by gosh we couldn't see each other it was snowing so hard. We were anxious to get down to where the other guys were supposed to meet us because Bill Wellman had sore feet. Bill was a film director. He directed a picture called *Wings*, years ago. I don't remember if I ever saw that picture.

Anyways, Bill's feet were sore and we wanted to get back to the main camp to get the medical kit. We were out of ammunition and we wanted to get to the Femme Creek camp. When we got to main camp, there were only two guides—Don Guild and another guy. Of course, there was no liquor left. The rest of the hunters had all gone home with Chuck Chesser. One hunter who was an actor was newly married and he had wanted to go. He had talked the other guys into going home. One hunter had successfully bagged a moose. He took solace in getting a moose and thought that he wouldn't do better than that. We asked Don Guild where the rest of the party was. He told us they went back to Mt. Robson and were going to stay there, waiting for us.

I told the other guides that I knew that they had set up camp before the snowstorm because the tents were all dry inside. I asked Don Guild and the other guy if they had some sheep spotted for us—and they said No, they hadn't been out spotting.

We asked them about the medical kit. Don Guild told us that there was no medical kit, that they took it back with them. We asked about the ammunition. He said, "No, no ammunition." They took the ammunition back, too. The only ammunition was what they had, some 30.06 shells that the hunter had given them. Both those guys had been given a new gun a-piece and ammunition. The hunters and I asked for a shot of liquor, as I like a snort before supper. They said, "No, no, they took that back with them too."

The next day, Darryl Zanuck went out with Roy and spotted this big moose. Darryl shot the moose. In the meantime, John Dalcour and I went up trying to spot some sheep.

Pictured above:
Art Allen & Chuck Chesser.

Photo courtesy of
Jacquie Hanington.

The following day, Roy and Darryl went back to get the moose. He was 61 inches and was a pretty big moose. Later Roy took John sheep hunting. I took Zanuck and went up Femme Creek. There's a basin there where I got a sheep. When we got back, the other party of men had shot a goat, but he had rolled down the mountain and they didn't go down after it. They went back the next day and took the cook with them. They skinned this goat out and brought it back. They also went hunting and finally got a sheep, too.

We decided to finish the hunt, which we did and got a pretty big bag of game. We went through our bad weather. We went on and finished hunting the game.

Anyway, we were packing up to leave and Don Guild and the other guide went into the bush and got two sheep heads. They had gone out and shot two sheep before we got there. By golly, they sold those sheep heads to the hunters. Zanuck gave one hundred dollars for each sheep head. In those days guides had licenses and they could shoot. Later on, they cut this out and changed the law, which was a good idea.

Don Guild and the other guy who had stayed in camp all the time had also shot a wolf and they sold the wolf, too. So the two guides did pretty good. They had two brand new rifles with ammunition. They sold two sheep and a wolf. They made more than Roy and I—and we went through all that rough weather and everything. I think we got two hundred dollars in tips.

Linda When did you start guiding for the Hargreaves?

Art I started working for the Hargreaves on the 1929 Zanuck hunt and again in 1930. I went to work for Roy Hargreaves all summer in 1930 at Mt. Robson. They went by the name the *Hargreaves Brothers* at Mt. Robson. At one time, they were all together but then they split. Jack started up an outfit in Jasper. Dick never did anything on his own, but he did some guiding. George had an outfit. He was actually the best of the bunch. He outfitted out of Jackman, half way between Tête Jaune and Valemount. Roy Hargreaves' younger daughter is living on the place yet—Buster Duncan and Margie. *(Buster and Margie Duncan have both passed away since this interview.)*

Lynn So what did you do in 1930?

Art Darryl Zanuck returned for a spring bear hunt in 1930 after he heard Roy Hargreaves talking about the bears on the Columbia River during the '29 fall hunting trip. John Godfrey accompanied Zanuck and died of a heart attack on that fall trip. Floyd Bacon, Ray Enright and a photographer were also on the trip. *(A transcript of this trip is available from the Willmore Wilderness Foundation.)*

I stayed home that winter *(1930/31)*. It was such a beautiful winter—it was too warm. It was too tough for trapping as it was too warm. My friend, Harvey Crate and I decided in March *(1931)* to go down to the Range where the Hargreaves put their horses—down below my trapline on the Smoky. It was real nice out. The only place that we used snowshoes was on Berg Lake, in going across the pass. It was good traveling as there was ice on the river and everything—it was beautiful. We got to the warden's cabin on the lower Smoky and stayed there overnight. The next day, went on down the river. We got about half way and we ran into a big snowstorm. There was an old trapper's cabin on Short River. We stopped there overnight and when we got up the next morning, it was still snowing. So we broke trail to the warden's cabin and stayed there. It snowed for three days. There was three feet of snow on the ground when we left the warden's lower cabin. I tell you, it was hard breaking trail. It was heartbreaking—all that trip for nothing. One, two, three, four—four days each way—eight days. We didn't get any pictures. We were going to get some pictures of some rams on the horse range. Sheep wintered down there too with the horses. Then a snowstorm chased us out of there. It's hard breaking trail with snowshoes when it snows like that.

Pictured above:
Roy Hargreaves.

Photo courtesy of Ishbel Cochrane.

In 1931, I worked for George Hargreaves. I took a party out for him, a summer trip. I think I worked a little bit for Roy Hargreaves too, out of Berg Lake—and then I went out with Hargreaves in the fall with the King party. Mr. and Mrs. Charles King, a doctor and a taxidermist, were collecting museum specimens, besides hunting. A taxidermist was taking care of the trophies. It was a good trip for them—it was a thirty-day trip. My brother was with us, and Mrs. Jack Hargreaves' brother, Don Guild. At Sheep Creek they brought Dr. King back to town. They took a bunch of bones back and stuff for the museum with them.

In the fall, I went partnerships with Frank Owens down the Smoky—on a trapline down the Smoky River. I trapped on the Smoky, Jackpine, Hardscrabble Creek, Rockslide Creek and Short River at that time, before they extended the Jasper Park boundary.

I trapped all winter in '31 and '32. In the fall of '31, I went back out on the trapline with Frank before Christmas, when I bought his share of the trapline—his half. He was having a little trouble with his wife in Jasper so he quit trapping. That was the winter of '31/'32. Frank and his wife were nice people. I went back on the line alone because I bought him out. I kept the line until 1958 and that was the last year that I spent on the Smoky trapping. *(Art spent twenty-eight years trapping on the Smoky, Jackpine, Hardscrabble, Rockslide and Short River areas.)*

After 1958, I bought the line on the Big Horn. *(The trapline was up the Big Horn Mountain south of Hinton. It was located east of what is now known as Highway 40. He sold the trapline to Bill Kulyek in the '70s and it now belongs to Ted Armstrong.)*

The summer of '32 I worked with Fred Brewster at Maligne Lake. We took parties to the Tonquin Valley. We took summer trips, taking pictures and fishing trips. I took quite a few hunting trips for Jack Hargreaves, in the falls of different years. It's hard to remember the dates.

In '33 there were Depression days and you jumped around and took jobs wherever you could get them. I worked on what they called Relief, in Jasper, working on roads and stuff like that. I worked in a market garden where *(Lewis)* Swifts had their place. I think that's where I camped. I ran a market garden down there for old Swift. *(Lewis Swift owned land in Jasper National Park. He refused to move when the National Park was created in 1909.)*

Ken, my brother and Ted Shevie from Edmonton, Ken's brother-in-law went back trapping on the Smoky that winter. The three of us went out that winter. That was '33. *(Ken Allen lived in Jasper and worked for the Canadian National Railway during the 1940s and 1950s.)*

In '34, I worked for Fred Brewster some more, taking parties into the Tonquin Valley. In 1934, I was also on a summer trip with Stan Kitchen and Red Creighton.

Pictured left:
Art Allen.

Photo courtesy of
Jacquie Hanington.

In the fall of '34, I went out with Jack Brewster on a hunting trip. I had the head mucky-mucks from Sears Roebuck by the names of General Darryl Woods, Colonel Humphrey and his sixteen-year-old son. General Woods was the manager of Sears Roebuck in the United States and Colonel was his assistant. This other fellow who worked with them came, also.

Jack Brewster gave me the boy to guide. We went up to Mile 52 and camped. I got a goat for the boy and he got a caribou there too. We went to Mile 58 to the Ranger's Cabin and camped beside the cabin. *(Mile 52 and Mile 58 are on the Mountain Trail from Entrance to Sheep Creek. There is an Alberta Forestry Ranger cabin at the headwaters of Rock Creek.)*

We spotted a bunch of rams, way up on the side of the mountain. They lay there all day and never came down until evening to eat and drink. Jack Brewster asked me if I'd climb the opposite mountain and watch them and keep out of sight. They'd take the dude up on a knoll and wait there until they got my signal. I was supposed to wave my hat when the rams got up to come down. So we did that. He was guiding General Woods. Red Creighton was guiding the Colonel. *(Red Creighton worked for Jack Brewster and eventually bought his outfit.)*

Anyways, I climbed way up into the snow—it was quite a climb to get up into that corner of the mountain. About 4:30 the sheep got up and started to come down and so I waved my hat. Boy, they came a long ways to the creek to get a drink. So the hunters were cached behind a little ridge. The sheep went down and had a drink, but instead of coming back to the basin again, they went up a side hill across the creek. Red Creighton and the Colonel jumped up to shoot and the sheep went in all directions and they figured that they missed everything. I was watching with glasses. I saw this big sheep drop into the creek. So I took off, as there was no point in my staying up there any longer. I got down there and they were all on their horses ready to go home. I asked Jack Brewster where the guys were going and he told me that they were going home. I asked them if they were leaving the big sheep. Jack asked me, "What big sheep?" I told them about the big sheep that was lying in the creek. They figured he missed him completely. I don't know why they didn't watch when they crossed the creek to see if the big one was with them or not. If I hadn't been on the mountain, they would have left it there. Damn nice sheep too—but we got it.

Later that same trip, we were going down to Monoghan Creek to hunt moose. Red and the Colonel were hunting what they called the Moose Farm. They spent just about a week trying to find a big enough moose. *(The Moose Farm is an area between Little Grave and Monoghan Creek.)*

The young boy hunter and I went up behind the ridge and got another sheep. We went all the way up the mountain behind the ridge. These sheep were lying under a little ledge in the basin on the other side. We couldn't walk on top of the ridge, as they would see us. We had to walk along side and away up, so we got out of sight. We crossed the creek and came down the side of the ledge they were on. We peeked over and all you could see was the horns. They were lying behind a little cliff. So I said, "We should drop a rock down there and scare them out. There was one good enough to shoot." So I tossed a rock down and I hit the damn sheep right on the horns. Boy, did they ever come out of there! He swung in front of us and we dinged him. Down went a ram! So he fell in the creek, dead. So all we needed then was a moose.

We had one more day left to hunt moose. I said to Jack Brewster, "Where in the heck am I going to go?" I said that the only place to hunt moose here is the Moose Farm and Red and the Colonel are there. Red told me to go up the trail to Grizzly Pass. He said wait until they start shooting, then we could go in and hunt. And we did that—hunting, going up the creek and waiting and waiting. About four o'clock I heard them shoot. We had to leave the next day to go home. I said that we would cross the creek and go up to the Moose Farm and see what we could find before we got to Little Grave Flats. We went on down and we got pretty near to the end of it, and it was getting dark a little bit. I saw this moose and we knocked him down—first shot. So we had to skin him in the dark. I sent the boy hunter back for the saddle horses, as I had left them tied up. I built a fire in order to have a light to skin the head out. So I put the head on my saddle horse and I walked from there to Monoghan Creek. That was about six miles.

It was quite late by the time we got back to camp. The boy's dad was getting kind of worried. They came out of the tent when they saw us coming. Jack Brewster was out of there first. He saw that I had the moose head on the horse. The old man yelled, "Where the heck have you been?" I yelled back, "Getting a moose and we got one too!" Of course, we took the moose off the horse. Fred got a moose that day. I said,

"Holy smokes, Fred, ours is an inch bigger than yours!" The moose were in the 50-inch range—56-inch or 57-inch—something like that.

I worked at the Jasper Park Lodge in '34 and '35. I must have worked for George Hargreaves on a summer trip. In '36, I worked at the Palisades all summer. An Englishman bought the Palisades from Lewis Swift. He wanted to make a dude ranch. I was building barns and houses; digging ditches putting in sewers and water—all by hand.

I think I went out for George Hargreaves in '36 on a summer trip. I can't remember what year that road went into Banff—it's called the Jasper-Banff Highway. I spent one summer up there. *(The construction of the Jasper-Banff Highway was from 1931 to 1939. The Highway officially opened in 1940.)* They had a lot of camps and it took years before they opened the road. The new road now is blacktop. It cuts a lot of corners off the old road. It was quite a climb coming out of the Saskatchewan River over the Icefields.

Two years, '36 and '38—George Hargreaves died in one year and Curly Phillips in the other year. I think it was '36 that George Hargreaves died. We buried him in the hills up at Sheep Creek. *(Art was guiding on a hunting trip in the fall of 1936 for George Hargreaves. According to Art, all was well when everyone had gone to bed. They had sat around the campfire telling stories as they usually did. George was always the first to rise in the morning, but on this day he did not. They became worried and Art checked and found that George had passed away in his sleep during the night. They buried him in the country he loved, believing he had chosen where he wished to be. George Hargreaves is buried close to where Casket Creek runs into Sheep Creek.)*

In '38, Curly Phillips was buried in a snow slide and I was one of the men who helped recover his body. *(Please contact the Willmore Wilderness Foundation for Art's story of Curly Phillips avalanche recovery.)*

Pictured above:
George Hargreaves & Art Allen.

Photo courtesy of
Jim Babala.

Pictured above:
Mark Truxler, guide
Art Allen, guide.

Photo courtesy of
Jacquie Hanington.

Lynn You recovered him in the spring of '38. What did you do for the fall?

Art In '38, I know I worked for Jack Hargreaves guiding a hunting trip because I had Tom Bunion out. There were three other guys. Two older guys came and a younger guy by the name of Bullock.

Tom Bunion, he still writes to me, lives in New Jersey. Well anyway, we went out. We'd been out on a trip before that one, which was a short twenty-one-day trip. When we came out, we had left at least one packhorse full of grub in camp in a cache. There was a cook tent with a stove in it. We came out to Jasper and Mrs. Gladys Hargreaves met these guys at the train. She thought it was a twenty-one-day hunting trip, but we never talked about the *(length of)* time. Jack Hargreaves was out in the hills and we couldn't ask him. So I took supplies for twenty-one days. There were ten of us altogether in the party, counting the guides, the cook and hands. Mrs. Hargreaves asked if I had enough horses to handle the party. I said twenty-one days, yes. We had left a packhorse full of food out there in camp. I could pack a little heavy and not go so far each day and make it up. It would save more money—save hiring more horses. We got out to the main camp and we were the last day in Jasper Park *(traveling into Willmore Wilderness territory)*. The hunters were talking to the other guides and they were talking about going across the Smoky, so the guides came and asked me about it. I said sure we can hunt across the Smoky. It was my favourite hunting ground, however we couldn't make it in twenty-one days. The hunters asked who the heck said anything about twenty-one days and that they had specifically told Jack Hargreaves in the letter that they wanted an open trip. This trip should be the last trip in October and last as long as the weather stayed good. They would stay and hunt.

Well, I said that I wished I'd known that before I left Jasper and that we only had enough grub for twenty-one days. Well, they said, let's go anyways. They said that they could tighten their belts. I felt if they wanted to take a chance, I couldn't very well say, No. I told them I didn't want any squabbling. Well, they all promised that they wouldn't say anything.

Well, I packed my saddle horse with everything I could and just walked. We kept on going and we finally got out to the mouth of Femme Creek and Sheep Creek. We set up our main camp there. Pat Smythe was horse wrangling. He stayed looking after the main camp, looking after the horses. *(Pat Smythe arrived in Hinton in 1936 and over the years he worked as a packer, wrangler and blacksmith. He worked at the Athabasca Ranch in the 1940s and the 1950s.)*

I told everyone that they had to go out and try and get some meat. We'd have some bear bait when we came back from sheep hunting. Tom Bunion and I were the only ones that got a moose. We came back to camp with a moose head and nobody else had bagged anything.

The next day was the day we were supposed to go sheep hunting, so we went down to the basin. It's a good place to hunt. If the sheep weren't there one day, they'd be in the basin the next. The sheep were coming and going all the time. When we got to the basin, Tom, my hunter told me that he wanted a certain sized sheep. He wanted a lot longer horns that would come up beside the head. He wanted to backpack for a week, if I agreed. I told him sure I would be willing, but we had to think about the other guys too. We couldn't leave him wandering around for a week. He told me that they weren't after something special like he wanted. They were just after a trophy.

So I talked to the guides and I told them that Tom Bunion wanted to go and backpack and hunt some sheep. They said that there were a lot of sheep around here good enough for these younger hunters who weren't particular. They just wanted a trophy. I had already spotted twenty rams up in the pass. They weren't real big, but they were trophies. There could have been an extra large ram and over forty inches but it couldn't come up to the ram Tom wanted. Anyways, I told my guides to try and get some rams out of that bunch. There are always herds of sheep coming back into the basins and if they didn't have a ram by the time I got finished backpacking, I would come and help them.

So we went out on the first day of the backpack. We got a nice goat the first day—7 ½ inches. We camped that night. The next day is when we saw the big ram. He sure was nice. I sure would have loved to get that one but Bunion didn't want it. Tom didn't want him. Boy, I sure wish I had one of the other guys with me. He was sure a nice sheep though.

We got back to camp and saw more sheep, two more. Sheep were all over the place. We got back to camp and the other guys hadn't got a sheep. I told them not to get discouraged, as there were sheep all over the place.

The next day, we went out and were stalking sheep in the basin that we had seen the day before—and they were on our high trail where we wanted them. So we camped all night down in a creek bottom. The next morning, we went up and over the ridge and stalked and shot the bighorn ram. He thought he was going to get a record. Tom bellowed, "We're gonna get a record! We're gonna get a record!" I said, "You're not going to get a record, Tom. The measurements won't be that good!" The ram had a 36-inch curl.

It was raining and cold. So I skinned the old head out and took the hindquarters and tied them on my pack. Tom carried the head. Anyway it was quite a climb to get up into this pass. By the time I got up to the top, was I ever sweating, and getting wet! I got to the top and took the pack off. There were no bells. When I didn't hear bells, I knew that the horses had pulled out and left us. I said, "Well, there's no way that I can carry that meat back to the main camp. It's just too far. We'll have to climb back of the basin on the other side and get up over the top." Anyway, we took off and left the meat. I forded Sheep Creek near the canyon. It was about knee deep, full of water. When I went down the west side of the mountain, after sweating like that, I cooled down too quickly. By the time I got to the bottom I was chilly and I wasn't feeling that good. I figured that I had a touch of pneumonia and I was pretty sick.

We went up this creek with water up to our knees. We had to walk in water up to our waists in Sheep Creek. Then we came out onto shore. There was a trail there and right on top of the horse tracks was some fresh game tracks. I said to Tom, "Well I think we have a grizzly in the bag." He asked what I meant. I said, "Those tracks mean grizzly hides." Our horses had gone opposite to where a dead carcass was. Sure enough the horses got past us. It was too late in the day and I told Tom that we would come back tomorrow.

When we got back to camp, I asked Pat where in the heck the other hunters were. I thought they'd be back in camp and would have had a sheep. He said they were up Femme Creek and bear hunting.

The other hunters and their guides were in a fly camp, so we went back the next day and got a grizzly. We couldn't go where we wanted to go to stalk him because the wind changed. The wind was coming from the east instead of the west—so we had to go through the thick brush to stalk him. There was no way we were going to get up on a bear eating a carcass, so we kept up high above the remains. We finally came out on this muskeg that opened up. Something caught my eye through a little opening in the thick shintangle. It was feet sticking in the air. It was the doggone bear. I told Tom to lean up against a tree and when the bear gets up, let him have 'er. Tom dropped him first shot. I got a picture of that bear.

Anyways, we came down the mountain and back to camp. The next morning I was really sick. I had pneumonia now. I had a couple of days of rest and on the third day, I told Tom that we could resume our hunt and that I didn't feel that badly anymore. I asked him, "What do you want to do? Join those other guys or should we go up Sheep Creek after caribou?" He said, "Let's go up Sheep Creek. They left us—so to hell with them."

Tom Bunion and I went up Sheep Creek by ourselves and got the caribou and a bear that was fooling around there. We went up and camped on one of our favourite spots, Rolling Hills, which was a good place for caribou on the north fork of Sheep Creek. We only had three horses with us: a packhorse and two saddle horses. I made camp with a lean-to. I tethered two of the horses and let the other one loose. I didn't think he'd leave the area. About midnight, Tom got sick and he was really ill. I didn't know what to do, so I made some hot tea to give him. I didn't have a medical kit with me. While he was drinking that, I went out to check the horses. The loose one was gone. No sight of him anywhere.

I went back in and told Tom that one of the horses was missing. I asked him if he thought he would be all right for an hour or two. I didn't know how long it would take me to catch up to him. I told Tom he might be in the main camp right now for all we knew. Tom said he thought he would be all right. He said he was starting to feel a little better already with that tea. I thought it would be OK because there was lots of tea there, so I told him to take care. I saddled my horse and took off. I couldn't tell until I got down the valley about two miles that the tracks were not on the trail. They were on the grass and traveling. There was one place where he went through Sheep Creek and he left a pretty clear trail through the creek. I came down to the

lick and got off of my horse and lit a match. Sure enough, there were his tracks going back. So I got on my horse and away I went back in the dark and I saw something off to the side of the trail. It was an animal of some kind. I rode up toward it and I heard a kind of a "grrrump-grrrump" sound. It was a bull moose. I told the moose that I was going to put my halter on him!

Anyway, I kept on going on the trail through some big, long muskeg. It was terrible—and a game trail! Finally, it cleared and with the moon, I could see an object way ahead of me. It was standing still. It was surely an animal. The closer I got, the more sure I was that it was my horse. He was standing looking ahead of him down the valley. He never turned and looked at me when I pulled up behind him. I spoke to him and he just froze. He must have seen something—a grizzly or some damn thing. I had my horse and my halter. I walked around him and put the halter on him. I turned around and started for home. I got back to camp at three o'clock in the morning. Tom Bunion did pretty well the whole time. I think what made him sick was a spruce hen that I had cooked up just before we left camp. That might have been what made him sick, but it didn't make me sick.

So the next day we decided what to do. I said that we'd do a little scouting and glassing. I started glassing; there were many caribou cows and calves. Right next to where we were looking, there were the bulls, adjacent to the cows. There were a lot of bulls there. There must have been a lot of cows. I said, "Well Tom, that's the way we'll go. We will go around there and pick up a caribou and keep on going." We packed up our stuff and took off. Sheep Creek came down there and joined in a 'V'. In between the 'V', was a bunch of caribou. We couldn't stop and glass because some of them would be bound to see us. I told Tom that we would try and bag one in the first bunch, as it was a pretty good place to stop the caribou. Tom Bunion tied his horse up in the timber close to Sheep Creek. We were up the left-hand branch of the creek. We climbed up and over the top and peeked over—and holy smokes, the rest were there! There was one big one right there and he was good enough. Before he got too far away, Tom shot him. We skinned his head out and went down and got the horses across the creek. I took the head and put it on the pack horse and away we went, over the south of the range and down to camp.

We got down to camp and just the cook was there. I asked where the other hunters were and he told me they were out hunting caribou. There was a bull up there in the timber they were trying to get out. They'd been trying to get him out for a few days now. I couldn't understand that. I never heard a story like that before in my life! Surely one guy could have gone in and chased it out and the other guys could have shot him. Pat said that there were just four of them. There was just Harvey Crate, Harry Tofield and the two old hunters. Merv, a guide and his hunter were gone. They were going through to the Smoky *(River)*, backpacking further down, looking for sheep. They said that they would meet us at the Smoky.

So Tom Bunion and I went across the creek to where Harry, Harvey, the two old boys and the caribou were. They had bagged one goat and not too big of a moose head. They had been in the area for a week at least. I said that we had to pull out in the morning and go back to the main camp on Corral Creek. We had to pack up. The old guy there—he was a nice old fellow and was a little disappointed. I guess he should be, as Tom had bagged everything. The next day we packed up. We went down to Corral Creek where Merv and his hunter were to meet us at the Smoky and rode right through to the camp.

It was pretty early when we got to camp. I said that I was going to climb up a ridge and see if I could see some sheep, as they generally show up about this time of night. Tom said that he'd go with me. He said we always see some darn thing and it would be better than sitting around camp. We took some saddle horses and took off. We crossed the creek, tied the horses up and climbed up onto a knoll and glassed the side of the hill that the camp was on. Pretty soon we spotted three sheep, and to the left on another slope, there were seven more. We came back and told the others that we had spotted these sheep. I told them that one of the guides could come with me in the morning and that I would take the two old guys hunting. The other guide could stay and help Pat cook and pack up the gear for the move next day. I asked which one wanted to go—Harry or Harvey Crate. Harry said that there was no need to draw straws, that Harvey knew more about hunting sheep than he did. Harry wanted me to take Harvey. I said OK, and in the morning we took off. We had three saddle horses and a packhorse. So we went past the seven rams. They were closer to camp than the other three were. We kept going around this meadow and headed up the creek into the basin. There were three sheep on the side hill. We tied our horses up and stalked these sheep. We got into the basin but they weren't in the basin. They were on the side hill, at the top end of it. There were two great big rams right together. I knew that there was no chance at getting both of them. I told Harvey to take his hunter over to the patch of shintangle and shoot from there. So he shot and missed. The sheep went around a corner to a creek and they were on the run. I said to my hunter, "Come on, let's get out of here!" Away we went down into the creek bottom. I picked up a chunk of shale from the edge. I told my hunter to lie down and put his gun over a rock. We could see a few of them there

Pictured right:
Art Allen.

Photo courtesy of
Jaccquie Hanington.

every once in a while at the top of the pass and they must have been four or five hundred yards at the most. And my hunter had a .35 Remington.

So Tom got down and put a gun over the rock. I told my hunter to shoot over the ram. He shot. It went bang and he hit a sheep. The sheep turned right around and started coming back down the creek. By this time, Harvey and the other hunter were around the edge of the mountain. The sheep was coming right down to us! We didn't do anything. By golly, we just sat there. The darn thing came down just across the creek from us. We skinned him out and got the meat off.

I told Harvey, while we were cleaning the sheep up and getting ready to pack, "You go up the mountain and go around the top and get past the other sheep. We'll come up, and when I get to where I want you to shoot, I'll wave my hat and you shoot down alongside of them. The sheep will come barrelling out that way."

I waved my hat to Harvey and over the top came the sheep. They were going so fast and they were all bunched up. It was pretty hard to tell one from another. As they were going past us I yelled, "Shoot him!" BANG—down he went! We had our two sheep. I got the hams off the old sheep. We packed the meat on the horses.

Back to camp we went. I yelled, "Well guys, we had quite a day! We got the sheep and we got the meat." I never felt so good in all my life! We got back to camp and the boys unpacked the game. We had a picnic table outside of the cook tent and sitting on top of the table were the sheep heads. They got their rams. Pretty close to where that town *(Grande Cache)* is. It was just over the ridge.

You know, it's a funny thing. Two of the longest shots I'd ever seen a dude make, was on that trip: one was made by a .35 Remington, and the other was made by a Mossberg. By golly, one hunter got sheep with a .35 Remington and a big black bear with the Mossberg—all with long shots. There were guys there with 30.06 rifles, shooting too. Guys with smaller guns were a way more accurate. They had bush guns, mountain guns. Anyway, we got that bear and he was eight feet six inches. The grizzly bear was eight foot eight inches.

Tightening their belts going out—well we did have meat and flour anyways. It was about all we had. By thirty-one days, we were all out—and it was pretty tough. It was hard not to say anything. Tom Bunion and the other hunters had promised no squabbling. Tom has been in touch with me ever since '38. It's been fifty some years or so.

So we got to Shale Banks the first day out from Devona and I phoned Jack Hargreaves. He was supposed to meet us at Rocky River, at the campground that used to be there. And a truck was supposed to pick up the stuff. The horses would be kicked out and turned loose for the winter. I told Jack to bring lots of lunches because we had nothing to eat—and we hadn't had for quite a while.

In the fall of '39 we went out for Jack Hargreaves with a hunter. My older brother, George was with me. We headed across the Smoky on a thirty-day hunt with old Jack Roach from Houston, Texas. He had a big garage there in Houston. We got across the Smoky and ran into Charlie Matheson coming out with a party. He didn't have much stuff. *(Charlie Matheson was a Jasper Park warden who left the Warden Service to become an outfitter. He started the Circle M Ranch on the east side of Jasper Park's gate. Charlie Matheson's wife, Mona was the sister of Agnes Harragin who married Mark Truxler. All four were mountain guides. Mona and Agnes cooked and guided trail rides in Jasper National Park for Fred Brewster. Mark Truxler and Charlie Matheson guided trail riders in Jasper National Park and big game hunters in what is now Willmore Wilderness Park.)*

Terry Boone was one of Charlie Matheson's guides and I knew him quite well and we got talking. He said he tried to tell Charlie that they were going too far afield. He said, "We rode right out of the sheep country." I agreed with him and told them that they rode out of caribou and bear country too.

Matheson and company had a small caribou and a small moose. Charlie asked me where he could pick up a sheep on his way out. I told where he could get one, nothing real big—just trophy sheep. They are old rams, but they're broomed off.

Matheson's hunters went into our cook tent where our cook was with my dude, Jack Roach. We were helping the Matheson party get across the *(Smoky)* river. Charlie's hunters said, "I don't know why you're coming here to hunt, there's certainly nothing here." These guys had just come out from hunting the same area. Jack Roach told the Matheson hunters, "Jack Hargreaves stated that according to Art Allen it was a pretty good hunting area. Art knows the country pretty well. Hargreaves told me Art practically had a ram tied up. According to my correspondence with Jack, he said Art Allen was going to take me out and that he trapped the area and knew it. I'm not worried."

So the next morning they packed up and pulled out and we went up the Muddy *(Water)* River. We got up to where Chocolate Creek came into the Muddy. We tied our horses up and walked up the gravel bars. There was an opening in the timber on the side hill and there stood a big ram. I pointed to Jack and said, "Shoot." He took the gun out and put it on his shoulder and–BANG. He said, "What did I get?" I said he got a big sheep. Just then the others came out of the timber and took off up this ridge. There was one quite a bit bigger than him. He was a dandy, but how did we know what was behind the timber? So we got this 39-inch ram without even climbing. We skinned him out and packed him back to where the horses were and came home. We were back by dinnertime. One of the Forest Rangers was there on the Smoky. He had a little cabin across the river. When we came back, he was talking to the cook. He said, "Where did you get that. My, oh my, oh my!" I told him we got him up the river there. He said that he would like to get one for himself, as he was such a dandy.

The next day the Forest Ranger pulled out, and darned if he didn't catch up to Charlie's outfit. Instead of keeping his mouth shut—the first thing they asked him was how we made out yesterday and he said we got a 39-inch ram, which was a beauty. He shouldn't have done that because that news made them feel real bad. I guess these guys that Charlie had were millionaires because Charlie wanted to borrow some money from the bank to get an outfitter's license. The bank manager asked who he was taking—and he told Charlie he could have the whole bank! The hunters never came back though.

On our way back to Jasper we caught up with *(outfitter)* Stan Clark's party on Kvass Creek. We were going out and they were halfway through a sixty-day hunt and were going north of the Smoky. I told Clark and his hunters about the war breaking out *(in 1939)*. One of the hunters' faces turned white. He said, "Holy Smokes, take me home tomorrow!" Stan Clark asked why and the hunter told him that he had property in Germany. He said that he had to get back to take care of things. They had to drop thirty days. This German hunter paid Clark and all the men for the entire sixty days. They got in an extra month's wages. The poor old guy; I've often wondered how he made out. I think he was from Germany.

So that was my brother, George's first trip. He didn't guide on the trail—just horse wrangled. We did pretty well. We got everything other than a bear.

We went out on the trapline that winter of '39 and '40. My brother, George went with me trapping. On the trapline, if anybody said anything, he was just working for me. I didn't have a license for him. I just took him along for company.

(End of transcript)

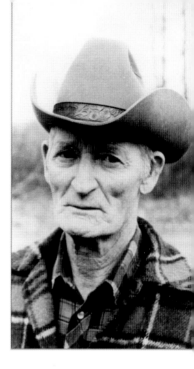

Pictured above:
Art Allen
circa early 1990s.

Photo courtesy
of Jim Babala.

Postscript

In 1942, Art married Clara (Rawling-Prosser) at Cottonwood House, B.C. Clara was a widow with two sons. Art and Clara had five children. Keith and Les Prosser were Art's stepsons from Clara's first marriage to Conrad Prosser. Art thought of Keith and Les as his own children. They also had Carole, Linda and Brenda. Art and his family lived in Quesnel, B.C., Prince George, B.C. and Jasper. In 1946, the family moved to Hinton and eventually bought a quarter section of land south of the town where he ran a trapline as well as a logging business. He also operated his own outfitting business until the pulp mill came to Hinton in 1960. He lost his grazing leases, making it difficult to keep horses for an outfit and decided to go back to Jasper to work for the National Park on a full-time basis.

In December 1952, Art was trapping on the Jackpine River and was staying at his hand-hewn log cabin. Art had received word that his wife, Clara was going into the Jasper Hospital to have a baby. He strapped on his snowshoes, packed some supplies and headed for Jasper. He made the ninety-mile trip in about twenty-four hours non-stop—which astounded everyone. Linda, his new daughter was born on December 11, a scrawny, five-pound baby girl. Art returned to the trapline later to pull his sets.

If one ever set out and walked with Art, they would not have a problem believing this extraordinary trip. Art would set a pace that he could maintain for hours and hours. Art was considered a tough mountain man. He was a long, lanky man who was very kind and tender hearted. He taught his family to respect the land and all the things on it. He didn't much care for the wolves, but respected that they did have their place in the whole scheme of things.

In 1957, Art Allen came to Jasper National Park to be the log foreman on a project to build two new log patrol cabins for the Warden Service. Mr. F.J. *(Mickey)* McGuire was the Chief Park Warden of Jasper during that era. He knew Art very well as he had been the District Warden at Mt. Robson and the upper Smoky Watershed for several years. This was during the time when Art had a trapline on the lower Smoky River Watershed, north of the Park boundary.

Art also worked in 1957 with Mac Elder who was a guide, packer and *(later)* a Jasper Park warden. They were both hired to work on a cabin project on Adolphus Lake, at the headwaters of the Smoky River. The second cabin was constructed at Twintree Lake, further down on the Smoky Watershed. Art was the 'log man' while Mac worked as a 'packer.' Mac packed more than seven thousand feet of lumber on packhorses for the two cabins and the two small fire equipment sheds.

Art and his crew re-built the Hoodoo Cabin at the headwaters of the Snake Indian River on the Blue Creek District in 1958. In 1959, he built a new warden's cabin at Welbourn Creek, in the Blue Creek District. In 1959, Mac Elder and Art worked on a cabin project in the Willow Creek District. Mac packed in lumber and supplies to Art and his crew. The pair also worked on a headquarters cabin at Blue Creek in 1960. In the next four or five years, Art and his crew built a cabin in the Tonquin Valley, one on the Rocky River and two in the Brazeau Lake District.

Art also worked with Miles Moberly, whose family was one of the original inhabitants of Jasper National Park. Miles was also a highly skilled 'log man.' The pair built the Jasper Park wardens' log cabins, and the Blue Lakes Lodge and cabins north of Hinton. Miles and Art worked together for many years and were good friends. The cabins they built had cement foundations, tongue-and-groove floors, windows with shutters, rafters and shiplap on the roof. Some of the cabins had aluminium on the eves so the snow would side off. Some had cement block chimneys.

In the mid-1960s, Art took one last ride to the Jackpine, Smoky and Hardscrabble Valleys to pick up his traps and some items left in the cabins he built. The rivers were high for that time of year, which was September. Art noticed that much more underbrush had grown up in the area and the trails had changed. Art brought back a box of Jersey Milk chocolate

Pictured above:
Various views of Art Allen's Jackpine trapline cabin and surrounding area.

Photos taken by Susan Feddema-Leonard in 2005.

bars that somehow had never been discovered by any rodents. They were still good to eat. One other item he brought back was a 30.06 rifle. The porcupines had managed to chew some of the stock off, which Art easily repaired. Art's daughter, Linda and her husband, Lynn Hokanson still have the rifle as a keepsake.

In the 1960s, Art Allen sold his outfit to Jasper guide, Leonard Jeck. Art and his wife, Clara retired in 1970 in Hinton, Alberta. They moved to Quesnel, B.C. in 1976 and back to Hinton in 1985. The couple had an amazing relationship with the horse. They had remarkable horsemanship skills. Art Allen died on April 10, 1994 followed by his wife in March 1996.

Art Allen's belief can simply be described by Psalm 121, verses 1 and 2. *"I will lift up mine eyes unto the hills from whence cometh my help. My help cometh from the Lord, which made heaven and earth."*

Pictured right:
A hand-hewn trapline cabin found on the banks of the Jackpine River. Art Allen & Red Creighton's signatures were found on the structure dated 1945. Art Allen is generally considered the master logman and used an adze to build it. The walls were flattened on the inside— truly the work of a highly skilled craftsman.

Photo courtesy of Marc Salesse.

CHAPTER SIX:
Nick Nickerson

CO Authors Note CO

We can gain a glimpse into Nick Nickerson's world as early as 1926, through the eyes of his hunter, Loring Gale. In 1926, Loring and his partner, Sanford Knaffs had booked a forty-five day hunt. Nick Nickerson had left the the two hunters in the care of his capable guides, Jeff Wilson and Donald McDonald, with cook Don Empson. Running more than one party of hunters is common place with bigger operations, however, despite a successful hunt and good cooking, Loring Gale was unhappy about the fact that Nick decided to personally guide another hunting party. Loring writes his memoirs thirty years after his three hunts with Nickerson in 1926 and 1938.

Loring Gale has provided a detailed description of some photos he took, along with a brief description of the 1926 and 1938 hunts. A short exposé of pictures and notes that follows this intoduction, certainly provides one with a window into Nickerson's outfitting career.

A creek that flows into the north side of Sheep Creek is named after Nick and Emma Nickerson. Nickerson Creek's confluence is close to the present day *Sheep Creek Back Country Lodge & Cabins,* which is owned and operated by Brian and Deana Bildson of Grande Prairie. Brian Bildson is the current Executive Director of the Willmore Wilderness Foundation.

The Willmore Wilderness Foundation is grateful to George Kelley who gave the images and notes of Nick Nickerson for publication. Nick, George's neighbour, provided him this collection of photos and notes. Nick was a big influence in George's life.

Hunter, Loring R. Gale was from Bala-Cynwyd, Pennsylvania, U.S.A. He wrote Nick stating, *"With Respect and Friendship, for that wonderful guy 'Nick the King,' on the 26th anniversary of our greatest day together Sept 12, 1938."* The following are quotes from Loring Gale's notes describing the 1926 and 1938 hunts.

Pictured above:
Nick Nickerson on the same 1926 hunting trip.

Pictured on left page: (L to R):
Loring Gale &
outfitter Nick Nickerson
on a 1926 hunt.

Photos from the Nick Nickerson Collection that were passed on to George Kelley who donated these images for this publication.

✦ *Loring Gale's Notes* ✦

First 45-day Hunting Trip
August 26 to October 9, 1926

Nick Nickerson - Outfitter;
Jack Wilson - guide;
Donald McDonald - guide;
Don Empson - cook;
Sanford Knaffs - sports hunter;
Loring Gale - sports hunter.

Sanford and Loring were supposed to start the trip from Entrance with Captain Paul A. Curtis of New York. Nick was persuaded to start the hunt with Curtis (*another hunter*) the day before Sanford and Loring arrived at Entrance with the expectation of joining forces later, however we never met. Nick left Jack Wilson, a fine guide, a real man, and a great friend of ours, who we will never forget. He was in charge of our party. Donald McDonald was Sanford's guide and Don Empson was the cook, and a dandy.

We had fifteen days of snow in September which greatly hampered our hunting and traveling; but we enjoyed the hunt and Jack Wilson guided Loring to a truly tremendous moose with a pair of boards that looked like sails. The head hangs on the wall in Riverdale (*Loring's home*), and the picture of Jack and the moose is one of Loring's happiest and most prized souvenirs of hunting.

Curtis and Nick arrived at Entrance a (ahead of us, and the former lost no time taking off for New York. Nick came back to look for us. Sanford and Loring talked things over between themselves and decided to ask Nick to take us on another hunt right away.

Nick said he would be glad to do this – with Sanford and Loring to pay for the grub only.

Nick and Loring got this magnificent buck in October 1926. He was huge, even for a mule deer, and has by far the best set of horns of any we saw in Alberta. Nick spotted him, sneaking along on our right, in some woods nearly at the top of timberline. He pointed him out to Loring, who had a hell of a time making him out. Remember that there were no scopes in 1926.

We hit him the first shot, and he crept along, well hidden all the time in the woods—up, across, and down to our left. Nick picked him up again, and we let drive. He rolled downhill into the open. He was done for, but we walked up close, and gave him one in the neck. The picture does not do him justice as he is so hidden in the snow. The deer is a great trophy and hangs on the wall in Loring's (*my*) room in Riverdale, near the Ram.

We went on the second hunt with Nick, a very good one, but could not take advantage of the generosity of his offer. Sanford and Loring later received some sort of a letter of apology or "explanation" from Curtis, to which we did not bother to reply. We haven't laid eyes on the Good Captain to this day.

Nick Nickerson -
Outfitter, Guide and Captain in Chief;
Henry Joachim - guide;
Dickie - cook;
Sanford Knaff - sports hunter;
Loring Gale - sports hunter.

Jeff Wilson, because of a previous commitment, was unable to go with us. He was a mighty good man, and we hated to lose him. Dickie was cook and an all-around guy, good at everything, and such great light-hearted company. Henry Joachim was Sanford's guide, and a damn good one. We had great weather, a fine bag of trophies and a hunt that left nothing to be desired.

God only knows why Nick is not in one of these moose pictures. Nor can Loring find any picture of you and our first trophy of 1938—the fine billy which warbled over dead as a door nail with Loring's first shot at anything with a scope—nor of you and the equally splendid Billy which we downed over the iron sights at very long range in 1926. (Lucky, Lucky). Nor can Loring find any picture of Emma or Dickie.

Pity the poor old guide especially! He just gets all the work, including headwork; none of the glory, and a kick in the ass for his pains!

Anyway ---- That's what it looked like to you sometimes, eh kid?

Nick Nickerson – TheHeadman;
His wife Emma - the cook...
and the best one we ever had.
Al Ceal - horse wrangler... as fine as hell and as good company as they come.
Loring Gale - Hunter

We brought home the bacon, all real great trophies: moose, deer, ram, two goats that were legal that year and caribou, all collected by September 12. After that we relaxed and did some fishing, enjoyed life and just had one hell of a good time.

This picture is of you *(Nick Nickerson)* and me *(Loring Gale)* and Al Ceal. We went back to camp and got Al and the horses, the same day we got the buck and goat. We returned to get the works, including the whole buck. Here we are, at the scene of the buck kill, happy as crickets, roasting the venison on sticks over a fire. Jesus, that meat tasted good!

We're sitting on a log, with somebody's hat on a bush, and a saddle, I guess on a log at the right. If you use enough imagination it looks just like a big bears head pointing right.

Another great day with you, kid!

Another salute to Nick the King!

Alberta and all our friends! This is our idea of the legendary happy hunting ground. Maybe we'll all meet again there

Pictured above (L to R):
Top: "Three Men by a Camp Fire," Nick Nickerson, Al Ceal & Loring Gale.
Bottom: Albert Ceal & Loring Gale
Photos from the Nick Nickerson Collection courtesy of George Kelley.

Pictured left:
Henry Joachim.
on a 45-day hunt in 1926.
Outfitter, Nick Nickerson.
The caribou was bagged
by Loring's hunting
partner, Sanford Knaff of
California. Henry was
Sanford's guide.

Pictured right:
Mark & Agnes Truxler
on their wedding day
October 6, 1930.

Photo courtesy of
Jacquie Hanington

CHAPTER SEVEN:
Mark Truxler

❧ Authors Note ❧

Mark Truxler was a packer and a guide in the Jasper Park and Willmore Wilderness area who guided many hunting trips in what is now known as Willmore. He was born in Vernon, B.C. and worked on the O'Keefe Ranch, which was a working ranch.

Mark left B.C. and moved to Banff in 1922, spending four years working there. He moved to Jasper in 1926 and hired on with Fred Brewster. Later he found employment with Hughes and *(Stan)* Kitchen. Mark's family moved to Entrance, Alberta in 1936 and he commenced working for outfitters in that area.

In the 1930s, hunters were outfitted from the Entrance store, where the horses were packed up in preparation for long trips into the wilderness. Horses were trailed to where the outfits needed to go. Mark Truxler was known as a good hand with the horses.

Agnes *(Harragin)* Truxler and her sister, Mona were cooks for Fred Brewster. They both worked at a tent camp at Medicine Lake where the girls had to wash the sheets in the lake. Agnes and Mona wanted to work with the horses and told Brewster that they wouldn't come back the next year unless they could guide. Mrs. Brewster influenced her husband, Fred to hire the two girls, as she felt that some of the women customers would prefer a woman guide. The sisters worked for Brewster for three years as guides.

One year, Agnes shot a bear that was terrorizing her camp. The warden came by and Agnes had to hide the bear for fear the Jasper Park Warden would see it. The warden did not mention a thing, although he probably knew that the bear was there. Agnes skinned the bear out and kept the hide.

Agnes and Mark met each other when they were working for Brewster and married in the autumn of 1930. Agnes gave up guiding after that, while Mark continued his work packing and guiding for geological survey parties and hunting trips.

Pictured above:
Mark Truxler.

Photo courtesy of
Jacquie Hanington.

Pictured above:
Charlie and Mona Matheson.
Mona is a sister to Agnes Truxler.

Photos courtesy of
Jacquie Hanington.

Agnes's sister, Mona married Charlie Matheson. In the late 1930s Charlie decided to leave the Jasper Warden Service and purchase an outfit. The couple purchased Alex Wylie's outfit in 1939 and by 1940 had started the *Circle M Dude Ranch*. Charlie Matheson was known to take hunting parties into the Willmore Wilderness area from Rock Lake—on thirty-to-forty-day trips. Charlie outfitted in Willmore until 1949—for approximately ten years.

Good guides and packers were always in demand in the 1930s and there were many rich Americans that wanted to hunt trophies. Mark Truxler saw no shortage of work and was hired on by Roy Hargreaves out of *Mt. Robson Ranch*. Over the years, Felix Plante, Art Allen, and Tom Vinson put Truxler on their payrolls. He also worked for Ralph Rink from Banff. On one notable trip, Mark guided a ninety-nine-day trip with Professor Huntington who was mapping the watersheds of the Canadian Rockies. Truxler also worked with Coyote Cliff *(Faulk)* of Entrance who was a trail cook and who was great at making pies.

Mark remained a guide and packer until he was hurt while building the road to Miette Hot Springs near Jasper. A log flipped up, giving him a compound facture. The injury did not set properly, giving him a limp for the rest of his life. Mark could not guide any more, but decided to take up trail cooking. Mark had some awesome recipes, which he penned for his trips into the mountains. Mark finished working on the trail in the early 1950s. He worked more than thirty years in the mountains.

Mark Truxler kept journals of his life on the trail. The following represents four of his journals from 1934 to 1937. The journals are unedited and provide a clear picture of life in the Willmore Wilderness area during the Great Depression.

Mark Truxler's Journal from 1934

Hunting Trip: Outfitter Felix Plante; Guide Mark Truxler

August 17:   Left Entrance with Felix Plante, guide and two dudes by the names of Sam Knight and "Pem" Lincoln. Had fifteen horses—with eleven packhorses and four riding horses. Camped at Mile 12 on Solomon Creek at 9:00 p.m. It was dark.

August 18:   Went to Rock Lake and camped at the cabin. We arrived at 6:30 p.m.

August 19:   Went through Eagle's Nest Pass and camped at Mile 52 on Rock Creek. We arrived at 6:50 p.m.

August 20:   Went to Little Grave Flats. Left one horse behind.

August 21:   We laid over. There was lots of moose.

August 22:   Moved to Big Graves. It was a wet day. We camped across the river at 4:00 p.m.

August 23:   Laid over. Mile 77.

August 24:   Laid over.

August 25:   Went up Kvass Creek and over pass and camped on the Smoky River. Trail bad on the Smoky *(River)* side.

August 26:   Crossed the Smoky. Camped at Clark's Cache. Target practice.

August 27:   Laid over, warm weather. Felix was sick. Mile 93. Crossed horses *(Smoky River)*.

August 28:   Left the Smoky and went up the Muddy Water River and then to Sheep Creek to Mile 14. Crossed Sheep Creek and camped about two miles at Femme Creek. It was a rough trail between the Smoky and the Sheep. We made a new campground.

August 29:   We laid over. Jack Glen *(an Alberta Forest Officer)* arrived with the mail. Jack stayed with us overnight.

August 30:   Jack left for the Smoky and for town *(Entrance)*. All hands write home.

Pictured above:
Felix Plante.
Photo courtesy of Jim Babala.

August 31:   Still at Femme Creek. Baked bread.

September 1:   Boys hunted and got two goats that were eight inches and nine-and-a-half inches. Pem broke ejector on his rifle in the morning. We went out after sheep at 11:30 a.m. and got two nice rams. We didn't get back to camp until 9:00 a.m. the next morning. The sheep heads had a 15-inch base. One curl was 36 inches and the other 38-½ inches. One sheep was sixteen years and the other was twelve years old.

September 2:   Cleaned heads the rest of the day.

September 3:   Rode out to spot game.

September 4:   Moved camp over right branch of Femme Creek to head of Bachelor Creek. We got a deer and a moose. We met two marmot hunters from Grande Cache.

September 5:   Hunted caribou but got nothing. Weather was good.

September 6:   Sam got a grizzly. A B.C. outfit hunting sheep tried to steal the grizzly. We got two caribou in the evening and watched two silver-tipped grizzlies for hours playing half a mile from camp.

September 7:   We skinned heads. It was raining.

September 8:   Pem and Felix hunted bear, but no luck.

September 9:   Snowing. Left camp at the Pass and went back toward the Smoky. The weather was not bad. Camped at Mile One—the Muddy River at 5:00 p.m.

September 10:   Rain and snow, very dirty weather. We laid over and everybody slept.

September 11:   Left the Muddy. It was still snowing. We picked up a cache at the Smoky and camped at Mile 11 down the Smoky from Clark's cache. We arrived at 8:30 p.m.

September 12:   Forded the Smoky a half-mile above the upper ford. Went through Grande Cache and camped at Grave Creek. It was still snowing.

September 13:   Felix and Pem got an early start. Pem left the outfit to chase a grizzly. Camped at Tepee Creek. One foot of snow.

September 14: Made Big Berland. Pem got a 52-inch moose.
It took him twenty-nine shots. We had more snow.

September 15: Move eleven miles to Pinto Creek. Pem and Felix left the outfit again.

September 16: Camped on the Hay River out of the snow.

September 17: We pulled into Entrance at 9:00 p.m.

Party of five: Mr. and Mrs. Bullock and son; Warren Castle and Bell Lillard. Crew included Dick Hargreaves, Harold McKenzie, Abe Reimer and M.T. *(Mark Truxler)* for guides. We had Dave Henry as cook and Frank Glover as our wrangler. We left Mt. Robson on August 23 and camped at Kinney Lake.

August 24:   Moved to the cabin on the Smoky River. *(The party would have gone past Berg Lake, and Adolphus Lake and down the Smoky River.)* It rained all day.

August 25: Moved to the south side of *(Mt.)* Bess Shoulder—good camp. It took six hours.

August 26:   Moved to the first slide on the Jackpine River—six hours. *(The trail goes up Bess Creek over the shoulder to the headwaters of the Jackpine River.)*

August 27:   Moved down *(-stream on)* the Jackpine to above the Jackpine knoll— seven-and-a-half hours.

August 28:   Moved over Big Shale Mountain. Camped at a cache. Four-and-a-half hours. Bad trail but good horse feed.

August 29:   Lay over. Weather good.

August 30:   Camped at Coffin Top Mountain *(Casket Mountain).* Long day.

August 31:   Made Fox Pass and over Surprise Pass and saw a good caribou.

September 1:   Lay over and hunted. No luck.

September 2:   Moved to Wolf Pass. It was a bad trail and moose country. It was a long day.

September 3:   Moved into base camp at Twin Lakes and very bad going.

September 4:   Went over to Windy Camp on a fly trip. Met Osbourne of Wembley. Hunted with no luck.

September 5:   Hunted again—still no luck.

September 6: Went back to main camp.

September 7: Moved to Wolf Pass—seven hours.

September 8: Hunted and got a moose.

September 9: Moved to Fox Pass and met Stan Clark *(outfitter)*.

September 10: Hunted in a snowstorm with no luck.

September 11: Moved to Forget-Me-Not Lake—snowing.

September 12: Hunted part of the day.

September 13: Hunted again—three caribou.

September 14: Moved to McDonald Camp—lots of snow.
(McDonald Camp is near Morkill Pass.)

September 15: Started for railroad and moved steady until we landed back at Mt. Robson on September 20th.

Pictured above:
Camp at
Donald McDonald Flats.

Photo courtesy of
Jacquie Hanington .

Mark Truxler's Journal from 1937: 28-day trip

Started out from Mt. Robson on August 26 with the three Cutter Brothers *(Ted, Bob and Fred Cutter owned pharmaceutical labora-tories in Berkley, California).* Chuck Chesser, Art Allen and myself as guides. H. Parkins was the cook and Murray Cochrane was the wrangler. Moved eight hours to a camp six miles from Berg Lake on the Smoky. It was raining. Murray and one of the hunters had to sleep out overnight because they couldn't get to camp.

August 27:   Moved down the Smoky seven hours to Rockslide Creek. Good Camp. Snowed.

August 28:   Moved to the mouth of the Jackpine (River)— seven hours. Good Camp.

August 29:   Moved to Muddy Crossing - seven hours.

August 30:   Short move to Femme Creek. Rain.

August 31:   Left base camp and took in a fly camp to sheep hills. Weather good. Four hours. No trail. Poor camp.

September 1:   Climbed after sheep and got three good rams: a 39-inch, a 37-inch and a 36-inch.
Good Sheep Country.

September 2:   Moved back to base camp. Weather was bad.

September 3:   Hunted moose. Got one 51-¼. Weather bad. Moose scarce.

September 4:   Still cold. Hunted moose. No luck. Lots of bulls—too small.

September 5:   Weather fine. Hunted moose on Sheep Creek burn. No luck.

September 6:   Moved to the middle fork of Femme Creek. Good place for horses and camp.

September 7:   Hunted big basin for caribou. None, but got two goats—Fred.

September 8:   Laid over and did nothing.

September 9:   Moved through big basin over pass to Sheep Creek and up to Forget-Me-Not Lake— six hours. Good camp and good feed.

September 10:   Fred got caribou. Bob got caribou. Ted got goat. Game not rutting yet.

September 11:   Hunted again. Fred got a coyote. Ted a caribou. Bob got a goat. Weather still good.

September 12:   Hunted burn for moose on Sheep Creek at mouth of Casket Creek. No luck again. Jimmy Smith pulled in with a party of five hunters.

September 13:   Moved to (Donald) McDonald (Meadows). Weather fine.

Pictured above:
Left: Art Allen, Mark Truxler & Murray Cochrane.
Right: Fred Cutter with a caribou.

Pictured left page (L to R):
Mark Truxler.

The Cutter Brothers, Ted, Fred & Bob.

Photos courtesy of Jacquie Hanington .

Pictured right (L to R):

Top:
"The Dog Faced Bear."
Art Allen, Ted Cutter
amd Mark Truxler.

Bottom:
Mark Truxler and
Fred Cutter.

Photos courtesy of
Jacquie Hanington .

September 14:   Hunted toward Gun Sight Pass. No luck. Weather too good for hunting. Met half of Roy's *(Hargreaves)* party going in. Ted got a bear.

September 15:   Hunted burn for moose. Saw only one small bull.

September 16:   Pulled out. Went over Shale Mountain. Crossed west fork of Jackpine *(Pauline Creek)* over Little Shale and camped in burn. Seven hours.

September 17:   Moved to Moose Lick on Jackpine—six hours. Fred got a moose.

September 18:   Made short pull to hole between Jackpine Pass and Bess Shoulder. Weather fine.

September 19:   All hands went to high country west of Jackpine for bear. Fred and Doc each got one grizzly, making a full bag for all three hunters. Got into camp about 9:00 p.m.

September 20:   Skinned out bear and made short move to mouth of Bess Creek.

September 21:   Moved to Berg Lake. Snow and Cold.

September 22:   Moved to railroad *(Mt. Robson Ranch)*. Game was scarce all through except bear, which were plentiful.

Pictured right:
Top: Mark Truxler 1926.
Bottom: Mark Truxler 1942.

Photos courtesy of
Jacquie Hanington .

167

Mark Truxler's Second Journal from 1937: 21-day trip

Dick Hargreaves, Fred Vale, Chas *(Charlie)* McMurtry and two hunters, Jim Hyland and Dave Knoll left Devona on September 26. Camped at Shale Banks. Met Harry Phillips on way in. Red *(Creighton)* and Ken also at Shale Banks.

September 27: Lost three horses and didn't get away till 2:00 p.m. Made Willow Creek in six hours.

September 28: Moved to camp half-way between Little Heaven summit and Spruce Camp. Very cold and snowing—seven hours.

September 29: Moved to Brewster's Wall—six hours. Clearing up. Saw quite a little game. Still quite cold. Good camp.

September 30: Hunted sheep. Saw twenty-five but all too small. Cold.

October 1: Laid over—horses lost.

October 2: Moved to head of south fork of Sulphur River. Good camp—horse feed and sheep and goats.

October 3: Sunday no hunt.

October 4: Hunted goat. No luck.

October 5: Hunted goat. Jim got big Billy. Weather fine.

October 6: Moved to Jack's *(Hargreaves)* camp on Hardscrabble Creek. Very rough trail. Dave got goat.

October 7: Laid over for rain. Hunted P.M. Jim got bear.

October 8: Moved to Winifred Camp—six hours. Poor Trail. Met Ken and Red *(Creighton)* who also camped there.

October 9: Hunted sheep—got two rams.

October 10: Hunted deer. No luck. Jack *(Hargreaves)* pulled in.

October 11: Hunted goat. No luck.

October 12: Moved to Kvass Creek—five miles above Big Graves. No trail, going bad. Got moose.

October 13: Moved camp two miles above Monoghan Creek.

October 14: Moved to Mile 52—six hours. Good Weather.
Got one moose and two caribou.

October 15: Laid over and skinned heads all day.

October 16: Started for railroad via Rock Creek and Willow Creek.
Arrived Devona 12:45, October 18th.

Pictured above:
Mark Truxler and
the packstring.

Photo courtesy of
Jacquie Hanington .

CHAPTER EIGHT:
Carl Luger

Sue It is July 6, 2003 and we are at Tom and Yvette Vinson's house in Brule, Alberta with Carl Luger and his daughter, Mary Luger. Bazil Leonard is also present. We're discussing *(Coyote)* Cliff Faulk *(pronounced Folk),* an old trapper who trapped the Smoky River and Boulder Creek area in the 1940s and 1950s. His home was in Entrance, Alberta.

Bazil and I located some old abandoned cabins on Boulder Creek. We found several old cabins in the area. A *(Rocky Mountain)* Cree Elder by the name of Tom Wanyandie believed at least one of these structures belonged to Coyote Cliff.

Carl Ol' Cliff, he trapped on the Smoky—*(it's a)* long trip out there *(on foot from Entrance).* And his cabin no doubt is still standing right there. You use Clark's *(boat)* Crossing and ol' Cliff was just down to your right. Clark's boathouse is on this side of the River. I know Cliff's cabin is just down below Clark's establishment. *(Cliff had a cabin on the north side of the Smoky across from Stan Clark's boathouse.)*

(There are also remnants of Coyote Cliff's trapline cabin on Biffy Creek, which flows into Boulder Creek at Many Faces Camp.)

Mary I remember Coyote Cliff at Entrance—as an old man in the 1960s. He was a slim man but fairly tall. We were a bit afraid of him as kids. We'd go up to his dark, low-roofed, ramshackle cabin at Halloween and he'd give us foil-wrapped Oxo cubes as a treat.

Sue Tom Wanyandie told Bazil and me a legend about Coyote Cliff. A friend of Coyote Cliff was crossing the Smoky with a string of horses and was drowned in the river. Some time after that, Cliff saw Tom's older brother, Daniel Wanyandie and said that he could take all of his traps and could trap that area. He walked out towards Entrance and never came back. Tom Wanyandie figured that old Coyote Cliff might have seen the ghost of his friend, which scared him off.

Pictured above:
Carl Luger 2003.
Photo by
Susan Feddema-Leonard.

Pictured on left page:
Top: Carl Luger at
Eagle's Nest.
Photo courtesy
of Dan Berry.

Carl   And Cliff took up playin' the fiddle, and ol' Harold *(Lake, another trapper)* come down and was gonna spend Christmas with him. Harold Lake was also trappin' and had a cabin on Sheep Creek about ten miles from Clark's Crossing. Cliff's cabin was at Clark's Crossing. Harold arrived and he did wait 'til he got dinner, but Cliff wouldn't quit playing the fiddle, *(so)* Harold took off, by golly! The ol' trapper wasn't gonna listen to ol' Cliff practice on the fiddle all night. Harold went back home to his cabin on Sheep Creek, in the dark.

Mary   Dad, you trapped out there *(Jackpine)* with Art Allen too, didn't you? You were out on the Smoky at least one winter.

Carl   Oh boy, yes on the Jackpine, yeah. See, Art Allen took over all of Curly Phillips' trappin' area. Curly was the only one in the country. He had a big trappin' area. He traveled so fast *(on foot or by snowshoe)* he needed a big area. Curly Philips and George Camp were trappin' on the Smoky and Jackpine Rivers when I came here in '37. Curly lived in Jasper. He had a start of a place at Maligne Lake and his boathouse was there on the lake. Curly died in an avalanche in 1938 up above Geike *(in Elysium Pass)* in Jasper.

Sue   So when you trapped with Art Allen, where did you stay?

Carl   We were up on Curly's line and stayed in one of his cabins. I walked with Art Allen *(from Entrance)* to trap up to the headwaters of the Smoky River and we trapped up to the *(Jasper)* Park boundary. Art and I trapped separately.

Tom   The trapper cabins are about eight or nine miles apart. That's about what you'd like to snowshoe in the wintertime. Carl, there's two cabins on this side *(east)* of the Smoky River. One is at the mouth of Hardscrabble Crick and the other one is at the mouth of Rock Slide Crick. There's a cabin on each one of them. I packed grub into them. They're both on this side of the river. There is another cabin downstream below the mouth of the Jackpine River.

Carl   Yeah, there was.

Sue   You trapped the Smoky River. Were you also in the Ptarmigan Lake area?

Carl   Not much grass *(there)*! Starvation! Get out of there as quick as you could! Oh yeah, I was outfitting there. *(Carl took geologists to this area with his packhorse outfit.)*

Pictured left:
Curly Phillips' cabin.
Located on the Jackpine River,
a twenty-minute horseback ride
from Ptarmigan Lake,
taken in 2005.

Photo by
Susan Feddema-Leonard.

Sue   We found the pack trail last week *(July 2003),* the blaze marks are very old. You can tell by the deep axe cuts in the trees. On the Jackpine River there's a dilapidated cabin a twenty-minute ride from Ptarmigan Lake. My son, Cody *(Leonard)* found the structure while looking for the old pack trail to Ptarmigan Lake. Once we cleared the original trail, it only took twenty minutes to ride from the Jackpine River over to the lake.

Tom   That's up the river—a long ways, though. You're talking about being away heck and gone up the Jackpine. You go up there to Ptarmigan Lake—it must have been damn close to it—within a mile *(of the cabin).* It's trappin' country, forest country… and short on grass.

Sue   When I said it took twenty minutes to get to Ptarmigan Lake from Curly Phillips' cabin, I should have noted that it is a three-day horseback ride from the Sulphur Gate Staging area near Grande Cache to the newly-found cabin.

There is another cabin downstream from Curly Phillips' Ptarmigan Lake cabin. Red Creighton, Art Allen and Tom Ross had their signatures on the wall of this structure, dated 1945. I believe that Art Allen was the log cabin man who was the driving force behind the construction of this well-built log structure. Tom, you packed the groceries to this cabin that is located one creek below Pauline Creek.

Tom   Were they dovetail corners *(in the cabin)*?

Bazil   No, they weren't dovetail, they were saddle-notch but the inside of the logs is hand-hewed flat.

Sue   Then Curly must have been trapping on the Jackpine as well. He trapped the Jackpine and the Smoky Rivers?

Carl   Curly was trappin' in the Jackpine Valley. Art Allen would have a huntin' trip out and he'd turn around and go up to Curly's cabin at the mouth of Hardscrabble Crick with a packstring of horses. He had a good solid cabin and he'd just drop the grub there. He would cache supplies for winter trappin'. After huntin' season, Art started early each trappin' season, yeah. Art, he'd take off, walked straight the way through, *(from Entrance to the Smoky and Jackpine).* I walked in with him. Oh yeah, *(Red)* Creighton went *(trapping)*, I remember that.

Sue   Carl, when you went to Ptarmigan Lake, how did you get there, which way did you go?

Carl   Right up from the river, from the Jackpine—from right up the side of the mountain. I crossed it *(Jackpine River)* where Curly Phillips' cabin was.

Sue   So Curly Phillips must have built the cabin that Cody found. Maybe the structure is Curly's cabin, as the old pack trail went right to the lake *(Ptarmigan).*

Tom   If the first cabins are really old buildings, then they would be Curly's— before Coyote Cliff even got there.

Sue   Curly Phillips' cabin was much older than that other one we found downstream from Pauline Creek that Art Allen built.

Mary   On one trip, Mary Jobe accompanied Curly Phillips. Then they built a cabin somewhere on the Jackpine. They spent two weeks and built a cabin, and then floundered through the snow for two weeks or more and then came out near Mt. Sir Alexander. *(They headed north to the Wapiti River)* and there the grass was green and the willows still had the leaves on them.

Bazil   Yes, in October of 1917, Mary Jobe accompanied Curly Phillips and Jack Hargreaves on a packhorse trip to the Wapiti River. Their goal was to build a shelter and cache supplies to be used for trapping later that winter. This cabin is upstream from where Meadowland Creek flows into the Jackpine River. The trail from the cabin that Cody *(Leonard)* found to the cabin that Hargreaves, Jobe and Phillips built, still needs to be cleared. The Willmore Wilderness Foundation will clear that trail at a later date.

Sue   Tom, you packed groceries on a packtrain out to the Jackpine in the 1940s. The trapper's cabin there is not very big. Three grown men were trapping there.

*Pictured left
(L to R):
Joe Songerie,
Judd Groat,
Carl Luger
in 1942
at Maligne Lake.*

Photo courtesy
of Mary Luger.

Tom   But some of those cabins you were looking at were made for overnight cabins for one guy traveling. So he could snowshoe. Just a place to stay overnight, you know. The shelters were better than a tent or under a tree. Get there, build a fire and get rested up for the next day. Up Kvass Crick there's Jimmy Joachim's trapline. Dave and Miles and Frank Moberly used to work for me a lot. And we went down there and there'd be a little place there—a tree where you could see there was a little fire underneath. And there was a blaze on a tree and some Cree writing on it. I used to get old Dave and Frank to read to me what it said. He said, most of them were written something like this, *'Jimmy Joachim'* he left the date on there, *'December 27th'* or something, *'Cold day, camped here the night. And he was very hungry and he was very lonesome.'* I'll bet he was lonesome. He would be, underneath that Christmas tree. But those trees were marked all the way up Kvass Crick.

(Henry John Moberly (1835-1931) was the chief factor of the Hudson's Bay Company in charge of Jasper House from 1855 to 1861. Henry married Suzanne Karakuntie and they had two sons, Ewan and John. Both brothers had homesteads, which were close to the present town of Jasper. Ewan and John and their people were forced out of the Jasper area when the Canadian Federal Government decreed what is now known as Jasper National Park. Ewan and his descendants ended up in the Smoky River and Victor Lake areas near the present town of Grande Cache. John stayed in the Hinton area. Dave, Donald, Ed, Miles and Frank Moberly were the sons of John Moberly and were raised in the Hinton area. They were considered some of the best guides and packers in the district. Dave, Miles and Frank Moberly worked for Carl Luger considerably.)

Before Curly Philips' time, the Indians were trappin' when the fur trade was on. In fact, I know they were because the Plains Indians were the ones that chased these Indians back up to the mountains. They were just small groups of Indians, these Mountain Indians.

They were all Eastern Indians. Well, like ol' Charlie Joachim, he could speak three languages. That's Louis's dad, old Louis Joachim and Rosie Findlay's dad. He could speak three languages.—Cree, Shuswap and English. English was his poorest language.

Carl The natives of Grande Cache, they'd get together at Lac Ste. Anne and they'd all gather at Entrance getting ready to go. Well, they had a little old cabin up there behind the *(general)* store but there was nowhere near room for them there. They had to camp out at different places. And they even got Big Henry Joachim to build them a cabin.

Sue So they'd come down from Grande Cache on the packtrain, stay at the store, and then catch the train to Lac Ste. Anne?

Mary Years before, they'd come to my grandfather's, the store at Old Entrance. When they'd come down, usually for a few weeks, they would camp near Jarvis Lake in the Red Willow Flats where a good water spring comes up. Roy Woodley's store, *Woodley Bros. General Merchants* operated between 1914 and 1927 at Entrance, now known as Old Entrance. During these years, Roy Woodley also packed out supplies to a log cache on Bean's Creek *(now known as Sterne Creek)* where it flows into Susa Creek, to trade with the area trappers for their furs. Roy had a camera and developed his own photos in his store in the dark of night. Many of his photos were made up as post cards, presumably for sale at his Post Office.

Tom They *(Rocky Mountain Cree)* used to have a teepee camp there at Red Willow Flats.

Mary That was until the oil road was pushed through in 1947 on the old pack trail to the Muskeg. There are pictures taken during the war in the 1940s that I've seen, when they were still camping in teepees there.

Tom I was up there one time—you could drive up there—I think there were sixteen teepees and horses all over the flats.

Mary They'd come down from the Grande Cache area; they'd fish the lakes and get their winter supplies off the train at Entrance.

Sue Now, there weren't really a whole lot of guys going back deep in the Park were there?

Tom Not many people were on the Jackpine very much, but Carl Luger was there. Carl put a lot of time in there, you know. George Hargreaves was in that vicinity. He is buried at the headwaters of Sheep Creek.

Carl Roy Hargreaves used to take horses and winter them on the Smoky. This went on for years and years. They were always trying to tag *(charge)* him for it but, of course, they never caught him. By the time the Rangers got out there, he'd have his horses gone.

Pictured right:
Top: Alex McDougall, Carl Luger & Tom Vinson.
Alex McDougall knew the trails & history
both inside & outside the park.
Photo courtesy of Tom Vinson.

Bottom: Carl Luger courtesy of Mary Luger.

Tom Well, I think Roy Hargreaves paid dues there *(a fee)*. When the pulp mill moved in here and we had meetings, Roy Hargreaves and his wife were over here for those meetings in regard to what was going to happen to the open grazing here in Alberta. That was right here at the pulp mill meetings *(in Hinton, Alberta)*. They were over here because they were paying dues on the horses. But you see, ol' Roy hunted sheep in Alberta. He had to hunt sheep in Alberta because there are none in B.C. And he had to hire Alberta guides.

Carl He had an Alberta resident for a guide and he happened to be blind, but that didn't count, he was still an Alberta guide—Dean Swift *(son of Lewis Swift who kept his homestead in Jasper despite the formation of Jasper Park and the coming of the railroad)*.

Tom Well he used to hire old Dean and he was blinded in both eyes during the 1940s. He had a guide's license. They didn't know how blind he was, so ol' Roy would get him 'cause he didn't really guide and he done the guiding himself. Then the B.C. Government got tough with their regulations and they wouldn't let an Alberta outfitter in there to hunt grizzly. And in turn, the Alberta Government got tough and wouldn't let him come over here and hunt sheep, which finished him.

Roy used to winter his horses down there on the Smoky. I know, 'cause Art Allen one time came up there to trap and there was a bunch of ol' Roy Hargreaves' horses hung up on an island just above the Jackpine, in the middle of the Smoky. The Smoky was iced up on both sides of them and he tried to chase them the hell off of there and he couldn't get them off because he was on foot, of course. The horses wouldn't hit that ice and I guess they died right there.

The Hargreaves used to just bring those horses up the Smoky River. Then they'd go right back down to their own winter range downstream on the Smoky River. They had studs down there, and were raising colts and everything.

Bazil The horses were all the way down to where Grande Cache is now.

Tom Well they went down as far as the Muddy anyway.

Bazil They went further downstream because there is more grass downstream from the Muddy *(Water River)*.

Tom But they used to get old Louis *(Delorme)* and Henry Joachim down there to gather the horses for them when the rivers opened up and start them back towards Mt. Robson. They'd trail them back in the spring.

Pictured left (L to R):
Carl Luger, Miss Suska
& Deome Findlay.

Photo courtesy of
Rose Findlay.

Sue The other outfitter that I heard had spent a lot of time in the Jackpine and western portion of Willmore Wilderness Park is Leonard Jeck. He spent a lot of time back in the same country you were in?

Carl I became an outfitter in 1947. It was right after the war. After a year or two, Leonard Jeck wanted to know if I could take a party out for him. Well, I told him I could, but I told Leonard to get his own outfitter's license. Leonard was worried that he might not get any business. He said, "You've got to remember I just got married." I told Leonard, "Well, all the better, you don't need to spend any money on cookin'." And I'll be damned, since I turned him down and wouldn't take him out, he went and got an outfitter's license. And he never looked back. *(Leonard Jeck bought his outfit from Art Allen.)*

See, Leonard worked for ol' Jack Brewster. I worked for Fred Brewster. Believe me it was more saving *(easier)* working for Fred. To get long trips in *(deep into the mountains)*, you had to go with Jack. It was good *(easier work)* at the pony barns at Jasper Park Lodge *(Fred's business)*, eh.

Mary Dad bought Stan Clark's outfit but he bought it from a man named Allan Innes-Taylor who had owned it for about a year.

Carl I bought it *(Stan Clark's outfit)* off of Allan Innes-Taylor, *'the Colonel'* who had bought it the year before. Then Allan went broke. I knew he was gonna go broke. But I was still workin' for him and I had eight hundred dollars comin' for wages when he went broke. I caught a ride up to Jasper and got all my savings out, came down and turned it over to him. Two thousand dollars was handed over to Taylor and he paid a few of his debts. He left and went to Edson. I bought a third of the outfit and I had the pick of everything. And *(Reun)* Fischer was just comin' into this country, but I had the first pick of the horses. Reun was left with the quiet but older horses from Stan Clark's outfit.

Pictured above:
Top: Carl Luger at the
Athabasca Ranch 1941.
Bottom: Carl crossing the
Athabasca Bridge 1956
with the packstring.

Photos courtesy of Mary Luger.

During the 1950s, I was in the Jackpine, Smoky and Muddy Water River areas with the geologists. By the 1960s, geology was over with. I took the geologists wherever the guys wanted to go, if we could camp close enough. We didn't need to take them to work, but if we got too far away, we had to travel with the horses. The only way to be sure to get the geologists there was to go mind their horses till they came back down the mountain, even if it was midnight. Finally we told them, "You son of a gun, you ride up that mountain, so you can get down in time for supper!" That would frighten them geologists. "Well, what are we gonna eat?" "You guys get in earlier and we'll eat. If you don't come back to camp before dark, you're not gonna eat!"

Mary Where did you have the geologist lady out?

Carl Oh, Miss Suska. She came to England from Poland and became a geologist. She was only twenty-seven years old. She was out here doing geology and was contracting from different people in 1953. *(Note from Mary: Dad has always referred to her as Mrs. Suska, he now is uncertain as to her marital status or her first name. Born in Poland, she had been held in a concentration camp during the war. Following the war, she had gone to school in England.)*

Well, I took her *(outfitting)* with Deome Findlay *(a Cree guide from Grande Cache)*. It would be easier to say where we didn't go with Suska. Deome, well he cooked for a week and I'd take Suska. And then Deome would take over and he'd go for a week until he was pooped out. Oh, she was a traveler. She could really hike. No use having a saddle horse for her.

Deome, he was soon talkin' like Miss Suska, and she was talkin' like Deome. Well, of course that happens. Oh boy, did they ever carry on a conversation. She wanted to get up this side of that mountain. I told her, "You can't go there." "Why not?" "Well we haven't got time." So she asked Deome, "Can we get up this side of that mountain *(or as she would say, 'dis side of dot mountain')*?" "Well sure," he said. "You young, me young. Lot's of time."

Mrs. Suska was forever leaving her maps *(which she referred to as "me meps")* and we would have to figure out where she had been. That's why we couldn't turn her loose alone because we were losin' too much time backtrackin' to find out where she had left her maps.

She used to squirrel away food in her sleeping bag. We would have to shake it out and there would be all this stuff from off the table. She'd take anything, even

Pictured left:
Carl Luger.
Photo courtesy of
Tom Vinson.

potatoes. We had to take over rolling up her bed before packin' it up, because she never had time. She was busy reading her maps and making notes.

Miss Suska was out for one summer. It was pretty near every day for a hundred days. Oh boy! And of course she, being a 'holy' woman *(prim and proper),* she always used to have to air everything out *(implying 'under garments').* I really paid special attention to her.

Yeah, I was pretty lucky *(for work).* The only thing that kept me going was them oil *(company)* parties, you know.

I went up to see Rosie Findlay *(Deome's wife).* She's a good lady. I had a visit with Rosie *(recently).* I rapped on the door and I rapped again and I started to walk away and the door flew open. "Hey you, Carl!" Well, how she recognized me after all those years, while walkin' away, is beyond me. She sat down right there where the stairs come down and we had quite a visit, went over all the old times with Rosie. And Alvin *(Findlay who is Rose and Deome's son)* is named after our boy.

Deome was workin' for me and he took a horse and went in *(to town).* Rosie was right there on time *(giving birth to her baby).* And Deome came back, "I think we call that boy All-vin." " Not quite an Indian name," I said. "No, that's a really good Indian name," Deome said. Our boy, Alvin was all of two years old and he gets a baby named after him.

Sue What is the farthest north and west you have ever been in the Willmore?

Carl In 1960 we worked *(outfitted geological survey parties)* clear up to Porcupine Lake *(Kakwa Lake)*. Then we moved down towards the Kakwa Falls, as it is called now, and around the corner of the lake to Big Jarvis Lakes, which lay just behind the Kakwa Lake in B.C. From there we went up to a big alpine area. You can ride from there to the headwaters of the Wapiti River. That ended my travels north, except to go around the other way when I went through Fort St. John. Once I went over Nose Mountain just out from Hythe *(Alberta)*.

Another time, we landed in B.C. and made a deal there with a geology company to trail the horses back to Entrance. That was better. The geology company paid for all the grub and the horse wranglers got their wages. Horse wranglers didn't like to work for only half a season.

Sue So you did the geological work from about 1950 to 1960?

Carl I had outfitted Mannix *(a geological survey party)* in 1948. You measure outcrops and take your notes and you take a little sample. I don't know what Mannix did with those samples, but after a while, the samples ran into a lot of weight that had to be packed out. Mannix had open mines at the Crowsnest Pass at that time. One of their geologists was Lee Slind and another was Homer Johnson who worked for Home Oil. When you were workin' on the geological surveys, you could only get paid by the horse. You got compensated for rent of the horses and so much for a wage. You had to pay compensation and purchase a few licenses and you hoped you could get by until you got your first pay cheque.

I outfitted for geologists who were doing surveys from 1950 right up to the 1960s. After Leduc *(oil)* came in, well there was quite a rush on to get out here and get the geology of this country. And I was sittin' there, right in the road. We left on the geological survey trips around the beginning of June and came out in September. We needed to wait for grass for the horses. The oil companies paid for the groceries. Ol' Joe Groat was cookin' for me in 1958 until he got mad at me and quit. I sure didn't have to figure the grub when Joe was there. Joe was very sharp.

In 1960, we didn't have to come for grub. We had *(air)* drops every thirty days. The boys were flyin' out of Prince George. The brothers' name was Tremblay. They'd coast right over us. We had a radio to get in touch with them. The airplane flew in close and gave us a drop.

That was my geology work from 1950 to 1960. I was also trappin' in the Jackpine and Smoky River country in the winter with Art Allen. One time, I was comin' from the Smoky and we got into Rock Lake. We were traveling long days with good snowshoeing. We stayed in ol' Huff's cabin *(trapper Ludwig Hoff),* at Rock Lake. Course there's no grub, just stacks and stacks of magazines—Allen just stopped to read. From Mile 32 we cut it right through. We thought we'd make a fly camp on the way but Art just kept a-goin'. So I trailed along behind. We come into Old Entrance. Holy smokes, the Truxlers *(Mark and Agnes Truxler of Entrance)* got a light on at seven o'clock at night, and so in we went. Of course, she jumped right up and in just a matter of minutes the feed was on. Boy, we had a great big feed! Then we went on up to the old place *(now Entrance Ranch)* where I had a cabin. I was kind of living there, squatting there *(on Stan Clark's homestead, then owned by the Athabasca Ranch).* The next day, Art took off. He was right back in soon; he traveled light. He had a full load of marten. Oh, marten were somethin' wonderful up there *(plentiful)!*

Sue It's good marten country.

Carl Oh yeah, gee leave your traps overnight and the next day you could go through and pick up the marten; go along and set up another line and do the same there.

Tom How many marten did you get that winter, Carl?

Carl Over fifty--I think it was fifty-four--and they were selling. We were pretty stakey! *(An expression used for having plenty of cash.)*

Tom A lot of them were bringing in a hundred bucks.

Carl Well, sixty dollars anyhow. They were nice martens, pretty—all big black ones.

Mary I remember 'Mr. Huff' had a neat little house in Entrance in the 1960s. He loved visiting people, playing cards and he was always joking and laughing.

Tom Entrance was full of these old trappers, like ol' Andy Slatten, quiet-spoken old guy, and he ended up shooting it out. He took a couple of *(gun)* shots at ol' Gordon Watt. *(Gordon was formerly a mountain Ranger and later the storekeeper at Entrance.)* But they finally had the police there all that day, 'cause Gordon told 'em, "He'll come out and go to the woodpile at quarter to three." He walked out, but he shot through the door a couple of times first.

Mary When he finally walked out and saw the police, he said he was glad to see them because somebody had been harassing him all day. He pointed up to the water bucket on top of his

stovepipe and told them someone tried to smoke him out. But they took him off to Oliver *(a mental institute)*—our "Mad Trapper of Entrance."

Tom "Sure glad to see you guys," he said. "I've been harassed all day here."

Carl He said to the cops, "Oh, am I ever glad to see you guys; they have been just bothering me all night. I didn't dare go to sleep."

Tom And they took the poor old guy and I never saw him again. They had the Journal truck sittin' there—a guy from the Edmonton Journal—it was quite a write-up.

Tom Is Miss Suska the woman that fainted on the side of the mountain and rolled off the mountain on you?

Carl Oh, no.

Tom That was a different one?

Carl That was a hunting trip. That was terrible.

Mary Where was it that Dorothy Kean fell off the mountain, do you remember? She was hunting sheep on your forty-four-day trip outfitted by Felix Plante *(immediately after Carl and Mildred's marriage in August 1950).*

Carl That was across the Smoky *(northwest)*—big country across the Smoky. My wife, Mildred was cookin'. We were camped right on the Smoky and we went up the Muddy Water. The weather turned cold and it snowed. She hit her head open. She took a terrible tumble. She really got hurt.

Mary Mother stitched up her head with a sewing kit.

Carl We were watchin' these sheep and oh, it was tough weather. I was just going out and oh yes, she stayed there. I never thought about her getting too cold to sit there 'cause she had all the clothes, the best in the world. I never even thought about her getting cold. But she got cold, and when she got up, she fell down, and she went sliding feet first. Then she went a-tumbling and rolled right into the trees down below. I thought she was dead. I picked her up and oh the blood was runnin' all over. I gave her an hour or two and then we got her back to camp. And for two or three days she just laid there. Then she was up and at it again.

Mary So how cold did it get? It was minus thirty or something after that and snow. It was so cold the dog lay underneath the stove and burned his hair off its back.

Carl Well it was so cold, it wasn't fit for man or dog to be in.

Mary You got a real fine caribou for her, didn't you?

Carl Yeah, but gee that was almost in Grande Cache. Go up to Dry Canyon and cut up to your right and you hit that big rolling country and that's the caribou country. When you travel across the Smoky and up the Muddy Water and the headwaters of Sheep Creek and over into Big Shale Mountain and the Jackpine River, there's where you see caribou.

I really have no one to check with about the trails across the Smoky. You people *(Bazil Leonard and Susan Feddema-Leonard)* have to keep this work up. I suppose I should mosey on. Well, you have a good trip up the Jackpine and good luck!

ꕔ *Authors Note* ꕔ

Carl Luger passed away on January 3, 2007. We are very grateful to have obtained the interview from this skilled trailman. His knowledge of the area and detailed maps helped piece together the trail systems in the western portion of Willmore Wilderness Park. The dialogue with Carl helped us identify Curly Phillips' cabin, located a twenty-minute ride from Ptarmigan Lake on the Jackpine River.

Pictured above:
Carl Luger on the
Wildhay River in 1958.

Pictured on left page:
Top: Dorothy Kean's caribou mounted.
This caribou had 44-points total.
Middle: Dorothy Kean with Carl Luger.
Bottom left: Carl & Mildred Luger.
Carl is wearing a buckskin jacket
made by Alice Joachim.
Alice was married to
'Big' Henry Joachim.
Bottom right: Carl & Mildred Luger - 1950
on the Smoky River.

Photos courtesy of
Mary Luger.

CHAPTER NINE:
Interview with Rose Findlay

On her life, the trail, her husband Deome Findlay
and brothers, Frank and Louis Joachim.

Sue I'm with Rose Findlay at her home in Grande Cache and it is May 21, 2004. Rose is the sister of Louis and Frank Joachim, who were exceptional mountain guides, and is the wife of Deome Findlay who guided for Carl Luger, Glen Kilgour and other outfitters. Deome and Rose also operated their own outfit for a short time.

Rose I was born in Grande Prairie and my mother was Marian Campbell, but she died when I was six years old. My dad, Charlie Joachim was a farmer. His twin brother, Martin lived in the Smoky River and traveled with a packtrain of horses to a Grande Prairie rodeo in 1929. He traveled a hundred and twenty miles north to get my dad to move to the Smoky River Valley.

My whole family was at the rodeo—my sister and two brothers, Louis and Frank. My dad told me that he was going to move—so I asked my father to take me with him, but he said No, that I had to stay in Grande Prairie. I grabbed hold of my sister's hand as she wanted me to stay—but I started crying and my dad changed his mind and said it was okay, I could come. So I came with him to the Smoky Valley and I was glad to make the move.

I was born in 1917—and I was twelve years old when I arrived at Gustavs Flats. *(The Flats are six kilometers north of the Blue Bridge near Grande Cache.)* There was nothing there but a big open meadow. There were lots of horses in the valley and on Grande Mountain. It was all open country and there were no trees in between the two creeks *(Malcolm Creek and Roddy Creeks).* Henry and Alice Joachim were living there on the Flats. Henry was a well-known guide who worked for Roy Hargreaves and many other outfitters. He was my cousin and both of our dads were twins. My father moved on to Muskeg shortly after we arrived on the Smoky River.

Pictured right:
Alice & Henry Joachim,
with the black stallion
that took Alice safely
across the Smoky River.
Photo courtesy of
Nanette Hamilton Moseley.

Pictured below:
Flora Delorme,
Vicky Joachim (Henry's mother),
and Jeremy Joachim,
courtesy of
Helen Hallock.

(Muskeg River is a Native settlement twenty miles east of Grande Cache). I stayed with my Uncle Martin and Aunt Victoria at Gustavs Flats.

A barn was constructed for cows on the east side of the meadow, after I had lived at the Flats for a while. The barns were towards the river and belonged to Bill Moberly who was married to Virginia, Henry Joachim's sister. It was after I settled at the Flats that Bill built the barns and brought the cattle in. He had a lot of cows and we had a great garden in the field. We raised barley and we made soup out of it. I still make soup with barley.

We used to travel by horse to Victor Lake to where the Delormes used to live. Flora had just married Louis *(Delorme)* when I first came to this area. I traveled to visit with Flora—who had a little boy named Walter *(Delorme).*

(Flora was the daughter of Adam Joachim. Adam had attended a seminary in Montreal and knew how to speak Latin, Cree, English and French. He was also a good trapper, guide and spiritual man, which made him the leader of the small band of Rocky Mountain Cree. Adam worked as a guide for Stan Clark, Jack Hargreaves, the Otto Brothers and Curly Phillips. He died at Muskeg in 1959.)

Sue Can you describe what your life was like back then?

Rose When I grew up, we used to go to Entrance, with about ten packhorses. My dad, Henry, my Uncle Martin and me—four of us used to go on the trip.

We had hundred-pound bags to pack up and bring back, along with our supplies. We would side pack the hundred-pound bags on the packhorses.

We would leave Gustavs Flats and cross the Smoky River in a boat, while the horses swam. We had to pack the horses up on the north side before we departed. The string of horses followed the pack trail on the Smoky that went along the side of Grande Mountain and over to Susa Creek. You can still see that trail on the hill if you look for it. When we came back from Entrance, we'd go down that same hill and somebody would be waiting across the river with a great big boat. We would unpack the horses at the river. We let the horses swim back across while we hauled the groceries back on the boat. I went on many of the trips, and we would bring back lots of supplies.

It took four days to go to Entrance, which was on the Athabasca River and close to a hundred miles— and it took four days to come back. I used to go on this trip, even in the winter. There was no road, just a horse trail.

Sue   So when you were a teenager, what kind of activities did you do?

Rose   They used to have tea dances and pow-wows and there would be singing with the drums. There would also be dancing—round dancing. Sometimes they had dances, when somebody played the violin or mouth organ. We used to have a good time.

Sue   How did you meet Deome?

Rose   Deome used to come up here a long time ago. He grew up in Shining Bank and Long Lake *(Alberta)*. He came to the Smoky on the Forestry Trunk Road. The first time I met him was over where we lived *(at Gustavs Flats)*. I was staying with my Uncle Martin when he first came for a visit.

(Deome's family was forced from Jasper in 1910 after the Federal Government relocated the aboriginal peoples from the Park. Jasper National Park was legislated a National Park in 1907, but the original inhabitants did not leave for some time later. Once evicted, Deome's parents moved to Rat Lake near Hinton where Deome was born one year later, in 1911. The family moved later to Shining Bank near Edson, Alberta. They also lived in Long Lake, Alberta.)

Pictured right:
Top: Bill Moberly courtesy of Emil Moberly.
Bottom: Virginia Moberly, *(Henry Joachim's daughter)*
courtesy of Audrey *(Moberly)* Printup.

Pictured above:
Top: Fred Findlay.
Bottom: Deome &
Rose Findlay
and son Alvin Findlay.

Photos courtesy of
Rose Findlay.

Sue So what made you decide to leave this beautiful Smoky Valley?

Rose My dad and my brother, Frank lived in Muskeg. I didn't want to stay at the Flats any more and I told my brother that I wanted to move—so I moved to Muskeg. It was great because my dad had time to trap with me—so I trapped squirrels. When I lived at the Flats *(Gustavs)*, we trapped coyotes and weasels too. We all skinned the animals we trapped—my uncles, auntie, Dad, brothers, and me. We would take our fur to the Entrance Store and sell them. We didn't get much for our fur. We only got ten cents for a squirrel, but things were cheaper at that time. You could get lots of stuff for five dollars.

After I left Muskeg, I moved to Jarvis Lake, which is near Hinton where my brother, Louis lived. Louis was based out of that area after he married. He had three daughters: Blanche, Gladys and Gloria.

When I first met Deome, he was married—and then I never saw him for a long time. Deome had a son by the name of Fred *(Findlay)*. I moved to Hinton in 1951 and I met Deome again—we got married that year. We had our son, Alvin (Findlay). I also had a daughter called Irene that died of pneumonia when she was five years old.

We moved back to Muskeg River after the railroad construction started from Hinton to Grande Prairie. Alvin was five years old. We lived in a cabin in a settlement at Muskeg and I stayed there until the early 1970s when Billy Belcourt came to Grande Cache to help Native people. He told me he would help me rent a trailer in town. It was getting hard for me to haul wood and water, to keep my cabin going. Billy got me a trailer and I moved to Grande Cache.

(The Town of Grande Cache was established in 1969. Billy Belcourt worked for the Alberta Government under a Civil Servant called John Birch. The Government had given Billy a Jeep and equipment to work with the aboriginal people. He was hired to help the Rocky Mountain Cree make the transition to the new town.)

Sue Deome was a guide for geological survey crews and hunting parties. Frank and Louis Joachim, your brothers were also well-known guides in the mountains.

Rose Frank worked for Stan Kitchen, Johnny Unland, Red Creighton and Tom Vinson. Frank guided Bing Crosby, the singer, before he died. I heard that Bing Crosby took a nice ram on the trip in 1947. Frank, he drowned in the Wapiti River near Grande Prairie while guiding there one August. My other brother, Louis worked for Tom Vinson out of Jasper every year—and also worked for Johnny Unland.

Deome also guided for Glen Kilgour when we were still living in Entrance. Danny Hallock worked for Glen Kilgour, as a cook. Glen Kilgour used to stop at our place, when Deome went guiding for him. Glen used to wear a black cowboy hat and was tall. Deome also worked for Charlie Stricker who brought us some porcupine to eat. He also worked for Tom Vinson, Red Creighton and guided big game hunters for Carl Luger. We lived by Carl Luger's house in Entrance for a time. Deome worked quite a time for Carl.

Deome and I outfitted a hunting party. We had a camp set up on Kvass Flats *(now in Willmore Wilderness Park)*. Deome met hunters who sent a letter to see if he could get horses and saddles and we ended up taking out the hunters as a result. Deome and his son, Freddie guided. Alvin was about fourteen or fifteen years old at that time and he was the horse wrangler. We camped where the springs are on Kvass Flats. There is a good source of water that's great to drink. *(The area is now called Findlay Springs after Deome Findlay.)* I cooked everything on a wood stove for the hunting party. The stove would fold up so we could pack it. I even baked bread for the hunters who really liked my homemade bread. These men were from the United States.

Sue   I know that you made your own hides and became well known for your beadwork and you have won awards.

Rose   Deome and I would make lots of smoke-tanned hides. We used to get five to seven dollars for a hide—that's all. Now we get up to five hundred dollars for a hide. A bunch of us used to work at Victor Lake making hides. My first cousin, Flora and her husband, Louis (Delorme) worked with us as a team. Everyone would bring hides and help each other. We would tan twenty hides or more. Everyone liked to make smoke-tanned hides.

I learned to bead from my Aunt Victoria, my Uncle Martin's wife. She showed me shortly after I moved to Gustavs Flats. I made jackets, moccasins, gloves and we used to make pants with hides. Hide pants were warmer and my cousin, Henry used them for trapping in the wintertime.

I also made horsehair moccasins. I sent a pair of horsehair moccasins to Edmonton one time and some people picked my moccasins and sent them away to a North American competition. One day I was sitting in my kitchen and the phone rang and someone told me that I was a lucky person—because I had won second prize for my moccasins. At first they sent me one hundred dollars for my work. Later, a woman told me that she was going to send six hundred more for the moccasins. I got seven hundred dollars all together.

Pictured above:
Deome Findlay.

Photo courtesy of
Rose Findlay.

It is hard to explain how we applied the horsehair to the moccasins. First you had to dye the horsehair any colour you want—blue, pink, red, green. You need white horse hair to dye and I usually could find the dye in the drug store. You had white hair on the bottom, about five of them. Then you take the coloured hair and twist them, and stitch them down as you go. You had to twist the horsehair to get it on the moccasins.

Sue There have been many changes since you first came here until now. What do you think of these changes?

Rose Everything is so easy now. A long time ago, people were strong and could do everything. They were working, hauling water and wood. Now it's easy. I sure miss my wood cook stove. I used to bake bread on it all the time—when we lived in Muskeg.

There used to be a lot of open meadows a long time ago and there were no trees at all. Now, it's all trees and there is no open country. A long time ago the people would burn the meadows in the spring so the grass would grow. There used to be lots of wild horses on the Smoky Valley—from the Muddy Water to Kvass Flats—and there were horses on Grande Mountain. There were also horses at McDonald Flats and all along the Muskeg River. The horses were all over. My dad used to go chase them and whatever he could catch, he could keep. My brother,

Pictured above:
Deome Findlay
& Judd Groat.

Photo courtesy of
Dusty Groat.

Louis used to have horses at McDonald Flats. Horses grazed freely and there was no charge. There was lots of grass back then—but now there is a lot of brush.

We used to go camping over by Copton Creek in the fall. We would go moose hunting and make dried meat. In the summer we would garden and in the summer and fall we would collect wild berries. There used to be a lot of strawberries in the field at the flats. There were raspberries, saskatoon berries, chokecherries, high-bush blueberries, huckleberries—all kinds of berries. We dried the saskatoons. You would put a tarp outside in the sun—and put a whole bunch of saskatoons on it to dry. After they dried, we would put them away and cook them in the winter—with sugar.

Sue One time I went to Granny's *(Alice Joachim)* place and she made me pounded-up dried meat with berries and fat. It must have had sugar in the mixture because it was sweet.

Rose The berries were chokecherries.

Sue Another time she served me beaver tail and I found it very fatty. It was like pork.

Rose My brothers, Louis and Frank used to eat beaver tail, but I didn't like it—and I don't like moose nose either.

Sue We ate porcupine on the trail—and gopher too.

Rose I'll eat porcupine anytime—and eat gopher too. When I was a kid, I would put some snares out for gophers and, when they came out of their holes, we would catch them. We also used traps to catch them. We would snare rabbits too—and would catch a whole bunch and smoke them.

There have been many changes and it is hard to talk about them all. The people used to have their traplines around here, then the loggers came and started clear-cutting—and we could not stop them. I miss the old way of life. All my relations are gone now. Deome, Alice, Henry, Flora, Louis—they are all gone.

☙ *Authors Note* ❧

Deome Findlay was the son of Isadore Findlay and a descendant of Jacco Findlay. Deome and Roses' son, Alvin Findlay is now the President of the Metis Nation of Alberta Local Council *(1994)* Grande Cache. Alvin, as President, is a strong voice for the traditional use of the Willmore Wilderness Park and Kakwa Wildlands Park areas. Hunting, trapping, fishing and horse use of the mountain region have long been historical activities, which are important to manage for future generations.

Rose Findlay passed away on February 6, 2007 at 89 years of age. She will be sadly missed by her family and friends.

Pictured above:

It is common knowledge that the elk and horses graze together—and have historically cohabited the mountain valleys for survival reasons. Horses protect the elk calves from predators. The elk also follow the horses during the winter and eat the grasses that the horses paw up. This image was taken in 2005 Willmore Wilderness Park at Findlay Flats. This area is named after Deome and Rose Findlay, for one of their old outfitting camps.

Pictured left:

Cody Leonard and Deome Findlay circa 1987.

Both photos by Susan Feddema-Leonard.

CHAPTER TEN:
The Groats

Tom Groat - Judd Groat - Joe Groat

Pictured above:
Clarisse (Moberly) Groat, daughter of Ewan Moberly and wife of Tom Groat.

Photo courtesy of Jasper Yellowhead Museum & Archives. 89.36.240

Pictured on lert page: Tom Groat

Photo courtesy of Ken Groat.

༄ *Authors Note* ༄

The interview with Judd Groat (Walter Thomas Groat) *outfitter, packer and trapper was conducted by Peter J. Murphy and Bob Stevenson, and recorded in Brule, Alberta on August 12, 1998. This interview was carried out as part of the Service & Weldwood Forest History Projects 1997-99. The Willmore Wilderness Foundation wishes to express thanks to them and to Peter Murphy and Bob Stevenson for allowing us to use portions of the transcript in this chapter. Please note that the transcript in its original form is much longer. The interview was edited by Susan Feddema-Leonard with the help of Judd's youngest son, Dusty Groat who resides in Brule, Alberta. Dusty was able to provide important information and the Willmore Wilderness Foundation is grateful for his assistance. Much of the information provided by Dusty is added in parentheses. We have separated Judd's thoughts with distinctive symbols to make the interview easier to follow.*

Part One: Interview with Judd Groat

My dad was Tom Groat and my mother was Clarisse Moberly. *(Tom Groat, a Metis, came to the area in 1910 from Edmonton. He was a surveyor for the railroad. Groat Road in Edmonton was named after Tom Groat's father who worked for the Hudson's Bay Company. He donated land to the City of Edmonton. He owned the land from Groat Road to the Parliament Buildings. He also owned land across the Saskatchewan River. Clarisse Moberly was the granddaughter of Henry John Moberly who was a Hudson's Bay Factor at Jasper. Clarisse's father was Ewan Moberly. Clarisse was an original inhabitant of Jasper.)*

Well, Ewan Moberly in 1910—when they run him out of Jasper Park, they told him they could go live some place else where they could hunt and trap. You see, they were going to make a park in Jasper. At that time, the park was only about seven miles on each side of the

Athabasca.[1] Then, of course, they extended it out and now there is over four thousand square miles of parkland. After the Moberlys left Jasper, they *(Federal Government)* called the area Moberly Flats. Ewan, William and Adolphus Moberly moved to Grande Cache as they apparently had seen that country and hunted it. *(John Moberly went to the Hinton area, as did Judd's mother Clarisse.)* Ewan and those who went to Grande Cache took some cattle in there with them and they hauled a mowing machine and a rake. They took the rake apart and packed the wheels, and pulled the rest of the rake on a travois behind a packhorse. They cut a trail up there and that trail went up what they called Moberly Creek and over to Little Berland and the Big Berland. They cut that road out.

I was born in 1913, April 1 at Montana Pete's homestead down there at Entrance. *(Montana Pete had a homestead located just after you turn off the Grande Cache Highway onto the Brule road, on the right hand side. Tom Groat moved into Montana Pete's homestead and just stayed there. Tom Groat started outfitting from there.)* My dad moved into Brule about 1917 because I had a sister who was older and it was time we were getting to school—and that is the sole reason for moving to Brule. I went to school here too.

---

1   In 1911 the Jasper Park area had been reduced to a narrow strip measuring ten miles on each side of the Grand Trunk Pacific Railway. It was increased in size again in 1914 and went through several boundary changes to 1930 when the present boundary was set.

Pictured left:
Tom Groat &
his daughter, Alice.

Photo courtesy
Jacquie Hanington.

My dad trapped, and was an outfitter and a guide. He ran a business right up to the time he died—guiding and outfitting big game hunters—but it was completely all horse work, you know. My dad guided north of Brule and in between—and around the Smoky River and across the Smoky. My first trip I took with him was about 1928 *(at age fifteen)*. We traveled and seen a lot of country that year. We had an old hunter that had hunted with my dad previous to this. His health was going and he didn't have too much time to live, but he wanted to come back and spend it in the mountains. So he came out for forty-five days in the mountains, by himself to do as he wanted. He had a hunting license but he didn't shoot anything. He had hunted before and he just wanted to be out and reminisce about old times and places where he had been—like up north hunting.

It was in 1928 that I went on that trip with the old hunter, but I didn't quit school until 1930. I missed the month of September in 1928 because we took off from here in August with this trip with my dad. I missed a month of school but I learned a hell of a lot more in that month than I did in the rest of the nine months. We packed right out from Brule here. We went up to Kakwa Lake and down that, over to Sherman Meadows. That was named after an old Forest Ranger. I forget his first name, but Sherman was his last name, and he trapped over in that country.

Well, later in years, I met him *(Sherman)* again down here and he was working for the Forestry during the war. In them days, Forest Rangers worked six months of the year for the government and six months of the winter doing whatever they could get for a job. It was quite an outing for them. They all patrolled on horseback with a packhorse. They took a saddle horse and a packhorse and

Pictured above:
Judd Groat.
Photo courtesy of
Dusty Groat.

were out a month at a time. But they kept a diary because they had no communication whatsoever with the Forestry. They were just out patrolling in the area and they came in at the end of the month. I think they were allowed about two days in town to buy their grub and re-pack it. They would get their horses re-shod, and then they were gone for another thirty days. They had no communication at all, until later years when they got these radios. Well, then they had to have another packhorse to pack this radio and the battery! They were cumbersome deals you know, not like any modern things we have today. But you had to carry a lot of batteries with you to last a month on these two-way radios.

Jack Glen was responsible for some of the forestry cabins they built—the first one they built north of here at Rock Lake. That went up at Mile 58 *(Summit cabin)*. He built that cabin in there. Some of the cabins have cement foundations under them but they had to whipsaw that lumber. Well, they built that cabin up there—and sawed lumber in there for the roof and the floor, and the rest was log building. Jack was a good cabin builder. But I remember Jack done real good. He used to be a policeman, apparently, before he joined the Alberta Forest Service. Jack Glen and the Forestry patrols built lots of trails. They used to send out road gangs. Trail gangs, they called them.

There was an old Ranger—his name was Louis Holmes. He used to be in charge of maintaining some of these old roads, putting in corduroy on them where they were mostly muskegs, and stuff like that. They cut a lot of trails in the Willmore area.

Stan Clark came from Ontario. He was, I guess, a University of Toronto man. He got to be the first Ranger that they had in the Athabasca Forest at Hinton. That was the end of the railroad because they had to put in the Athabasca Bridge and the bridge over that Maskuta Creek. So they were held up there for a couple of years. That is when Stan came to Hinton around 1911 or 1912. My dad and mother got married in Hinton in 1910, and that was the end of the railroad at that time.

Stan homesteaded on the north side of the Athabasca. He sold out his place to the Davidson family who still got it. This happened in the early 1930s. Stan was married but he had no family. He went up to Rock Lake and he built a cabin. Stan wanted to get a foothold in there, so he bought this trapline from old Hoff *(a trapper from Entrance)*. Hoff was a fellow that trapped in there for years and years. He built a cabin, which was a modern house and he got a permit to build a barn and a pasture. He was going to outfit out of there. Stan Clark took out summer parties and some hunters. He was in that operation when he died. It was Tommy McCready that got the lease at Rock Lake. Mrs. Clark had a sale and sold his horses and packsaddles and all his rigging. *(Carl Luger bought half the outfit and Ruen Fisher bought the other half.)* And that is how I got this trapline. Old Stan died—by God he did!

When I finished school in 1930, I stuck around here and worked for some outfitters at Jasper—packing on the trails and guiding. I did that pretty well. But my dad had an outfit and I helped him every fall in his hunting trips. He passed away in 1949 but I bought his outfit in 1946 off him. We had this hunter who owned a brewery. Dad wanted to sell—he was going to sell out—he was all crippled up. He had five strokes before he died and he died in 1949. So this hunter that we had out, who owned the brewery said, "Why don't you buy it?" I said, "Where the hell would I get the money to buy it?" Money was pretty hard to come by, but today it would be no problem. But he said, "I will tell you what I will do. I will buy your dad's outfit for you. I will pay him cash and I will see if you can make a good go of it. I am going hunting myself every year as long as I can. I will take my trips when you are not tied up with other hunters, so I won't leave you short. I will take care of the expenses of the trip and everything. You can pay me off that way, and I will send friends up to hunt with you, to help you pay up." Jesus Christ—fine and dandy! It took me two years and we were square! So I got the outfit. He still hunted with me after that—so that is how I come to get the outfit.

I trapped mostly in the wintertime. Christ, I raised nine kids *(with wife Darleen, raising four sons and five daughters)*. But I had this outfit. Then I got hooked up with some oil companies, so I did a lot of exploration work for these oil companies, like the *Gulf Oil* and different outfits. Then there was *Standard* from Indiana, and *Shell*. I worked for different outfits and they were a good deal. I used to get about one hundred and twenty days of work a year, just going up through the mountains doing exploration work. That paid off pretty good. Then I did the hunting in the fall after I got through with the geologists. When I got through with that, I went trapping for the winter.

Pictured above:
Judd & Darleen Groat.

Photo courtesy of
Dusty Groat.

I would work from Brule and sometimes from Rock Lake. It depended on where they needed to work. I started at Rock Lake usually, which was the end of the road. But if we had to start at Grande Cache, that is where I had to take my horses. They wouldn't pay you for transporting them there, but for one hundred and twenty days worth of work with twenty-five head of horses—it was a good deal. And I seen a lot of country that I wouldn't have seen otherwise. And some damn tough trails, I will tell you. That one year, we followed all the mountain streams from the mountains to where they run into the Athabasca—like the Berland, Hay River, and the Simonette—and followed the streams from one end to the other. There were no trails or nothing, so I walked through the bush.

Once you got tied onto an oil company, and you got acquainted with them, like for *Gulf Oil* and *Standard* of Indiana and outfits like that, if they decided they needed a pack outfit in this area, they came to me directly. They didn't look around for anybody else, you know. We could handle about twenty-five head of horses. There was one hundred and twenty days and they used to give me three dollars a packhorse. That was pretty good money—if you had twenty-five head, that was seventy-five dollars a day!

The oil company paid the wages of the cooks and wranglers. They hired the cook and they hired the assistant packer and they hired me. They paid me wages as well as my horses.

I saw a lot of country with a helicopter when I worked for the *Gulf Oil* one time. We were stationed at Grande Cache for thirty-four days. I had twenty-five head of horses on that job and they never used my horses once in thirty-four days there. The pilot could take two geologists in the helicopter. They could take two passengers because they carried gas on these side ramps. So the pilot would take two geologists over to this location, and two over to that location, and there were five of us. The party chief used to go on the last trip so there was room for an extra passenger, so I used to ride up with him. Anyway, I used to go up on this last flight. They used to take these geologists out in the morning and pick them up in the evening. I never even checked my horses. I used to ride up on this helicopter when they took this geologist out. I would fly over the country and we would come back. We would circle around and see where the hell my horses were. We could see if they were getting too far from camp. Well they were bound to move around in thirty-four days. I let them wander sometimes for two or three days. The pilot would get me up there in a helicopter and he would set me down and I'd catch one horse. I'd ride bare back and chase the others back to camp. I put in a good summer—and seen a lot of country.

I can remember the time when the caribou ran in hundreds—like even in the high elevations at Jasper. Up through the mountains there were hundreds of caribou, but they are all gone now.

There weren't many wolves at that time. Oh, I suppose there was some, but not as many as there are today. It's a crying shame that the government don't do something about the wolf population. Over at the mines, here at Luscar and Cadomin where they replanted that grass, the sheep moved in there. I've got some nephews working over there and a couple of boys. They will tell you they see them wolves every day. Those wolves are killing sheep. I will tell you why I know—because if you found a *(sheep)* head and a wolf killed it and if you worked for the mines, you could have that head. But just in the last two years the Fish and Wildlife said, "No more." They *(sheep horns)* get sent over to the Fish and Wildlife. It is a crying shame that they are not doing something about these wolves because they are going to clean everything out.

◦|◦　◦|◦　◦|◦　◦|◦　◦|◦　◦|◦　◦|◦

In the 1930s we went in one time with a movie outfit that filmed movies of caribou when we went to the Tonquin Valley. I guess they filmed in Jasper at Amethyst Lake. There was caribou all over and, by God, they are gone today! The same thing is happening around the north country here. It is a shame that they *(wolves)* are killing the game and they *(government)* are not doing nothing about it. I would like to see them making an attempt to get them *(wolves)* anyhow.

Billie McGee, an Entrance trapper, got sixty-some-odd wolves and I forget how many cougars he got. They let him use his own methods and he poisoned them. And that's a sure bet now. I know the government one time decided they wanted to take over predator control. I forget what year it was. I don't think it was twenty years ago but it might have been about that time. They got a wolf hunter up here and they were using these cyanide guns. What he did was carried an auger and drilled a hole into a tree and then he shoved this stick out there with a platform on it. That is where he put these cyanide guns. He travelled up and down the Mountain Trail *(in Willmore Wilderness Park)* to kill these wolves.

Now this old Adam Joachim—you have probably heard of Adam. He was an old timer in this country. He actually talked to this guy that the government sent up to kill these wolves. This government guy got twenty-some-odd lynx down on the Sulphur River on Adam's trapline. So that was a bad mistake! Well, you take twenty lynx off a trapline—they *(government)* should have done something better than that.

There was an old trapper I know and Cliff Faulk is his name. *(Coyote Cliff Faulk was a trapper from Entrance.)* He trapped on the Smoky at the mouth

Pictured above:
Top: Judd Groat.
Bottom: Darleen Groat.

Photos courtesy of
Dusty Groat.

Pictured right:
Judd Groat.

Photo courtesy of
Dusty Groat.

of the Muddywater. He used to go up there in the fall about October, and he wintered there. He never came out at all. He would stay there until spring to trap beaver. At that particular time, the government did pay a bounty on wolves and cougars. I forget the sum that the bounty was—somewhere around ten dollars or fifteen dollars. The trappers were allowed to cut down their *(predators)* numbers and would get them any way they could. Cliff was telling me that there was an old horse that was grazing along the river there. The horse wintered on the river. I guess the horse must have got out on the ford and he got stranded. He was between the two streams of the river and it was iced in. The horse couldn't get out and died there. Cliff said he was up there one day looking around to see how the river was opening up in order to start trapping beaver. These wolves had found this old horse. It wasn't far from this cabin so he went up there with some poison and he got nineteen wolves off that horse. I don't know how many females there were, but his kid got the pups and there were forty-five in all. Like, the pups were sticking their heads out of the females. He skinned them bastards out too and sent them in. He had twenty-six pups and nineteen wolves—and that was off that dead horse. Now Cliff did a lot of good there, you know. That is nineteen mature wolves, and he got them pups too—because in tough winters they would feed on these moose, too.

There was a bounty paid at one time—and there used to be a twenty-dollar bounty on cougars. That is about the time Billy McGee was trapping for the government. Billy was on the north side of the Athabasca. And Billy trapped all around Hinton there. He used to have a trapline close to the little Berland. But I think Billy said he got sixty-some-odd wolves all together and I forget how many cougar he got. He done a lot of good, but he knew what he was doing. If they got a man with a little experience like Billy McGee who was a trapper, why he'd make out a lot better than that government guy that had that little pan shoved into the tree.

There were not as many wolves then, as there are today. Hell, you can hear them right from here in the wintertime—out running on these hills. Well, they're going to take over. I'll tell you what I think the difference is between the wolves today and the wolves back in the 1920s. The trappers trapped them and it was a lot of hard work skinning them. So when they dropped the price of wolves, the trappers said, "I wouldn't bother skinning the buggers for what all we get out of them." But I wouldn't say that was all of the reasons. A lot of wolves grew up in places where there was lots of country, like between here and Grande Prairie. I know wolves are down in low country, like down in the Berland and on Hay River and along the Athabasca Valley. There are lots of wolves in there. There is lots of game too. Wolves cover a lot of country and do a lot of traveling.

I knew a trapper there at Susa Creek. His name was Danny Wanyandie (Daniel Wanyanidie's son). A young fellow at that time—I would say about twenty-five years old—he told me this story. He had some pack dogs that he used to use on his trapline, rather than a toboggan. He had four dogs at his cabin, and one morning about daylight, his dog was barking. That dog barely ever barked. So he knew there was something out there. He went out and he said there were five wolves running down past the flat just in front of his cabin. The wolves loped on down the valley. Danny said there was about four inches of snow. He said they were heading down Susa Creek where there is a big bald hill. There is quite a series of bald hills there. There was lots of deer in that poplar country. Dan said with that many deer, the wolves wouldn't be long finding them. He said that they would stop to eat and then he would be able to get a shot at them. So he took his gun and took after them on foot. The wolves only had maybe twenty minutes start—just the time it took to get his moccasins on and laced up. He said he followed them until noon, and in the course of that time, they killed five deer and they never stopped to eat! If they just happened to see deer, why they killed and left it. He said that they never ate one of them, but killed five when he quit following them. He said he followed them until noon but never got a shot at them.

At one time they used to shoot wolves in Jasper Park. But then they *(government)* decided the wolves should stay free. They said that the wolves would take the sick and the poor, as they were weak. But I know that the wolves just took the first one they saw!

There is an area we used to call Henry House Flats. Everybody ran their horses between there and the Rocky River. The elk stayed in there year round. But you take back in the 1930s—god, there were hundreds of elk! At that time we had a hunting party from the States and they wanted elk, but we had to go to where the Cardinal River ran into the Brazeau. That was the

only place that you could hunt elk—between the Cardinal and the Brazeau. But there were so many elk at Henry House Flats; they were like hunting cattle with bells on! You hear one bugle and go over and see him. Well hell, he isn't big enough. They would sit there and hear another and go over and look at him. Now this one is not big enough. They were four and five points, you know. But the elk are not there today. Like even around Jasper, there is nothing compared to what there used to be. But these elk have migrated from here clean up above Fort Nelson. There is a place called Toad River that is one hundred and twenty miles north of Fort Nelson. I have a daughter that lives up there. She is married to a consultant for an oil company. There are lots of elk there now and there are lots of hunters hunting them. One time there wasn't an elk back in that country. I think where those elk started *(from)* was here in Jasper Park—when they shipped two hundred head of elk into Jasper and turned them loose. That is where the elk all come from around here. There were no elk around here before then. That was the first elk I ever seen, when they shipped them in. A lot of people looked at them, because they had never seen an elk. The big herds are all gone now.

•┆• •┆• •┆• •┆• •┆• •┆• •┆•

Well, there were lots of buffalo skulls scattered out through the north country here. Somebody was talking about that just the other day. Down at the mouth of Mumm Creek just up between here and Rock Lake, there is kind of a mountain cliff and it has open bald hills back behind it. The Indians in the early days used to run buffalo and they would stampede and go over the bank. The Indians go along and pick up what was killed and crippled.

I have heard that several times about that spot there. But you take this hill here at Solomon Creek or any hills north of Rock Lake; you can see the old buffalo trails yet. You know where they have been traveling on the side of the mountain and you can see the skulls. It wasn't too long ago that I found a

Pictured left:
Judd Groat.

Photo courtesy of
Dusty Groat.

skull just over at the foot of that big hill where the old buffalo trails are. This was in soft ground and the horns were still on it. The shells were still on the horns. I gave it to a fellow at Hinton. He was a friend of mine and he wanted it. I said, "You can have it. I sure as hell got no use for it." He told me that he would hang it up in front of his fireplace. There is one place across the Smoky that we found a skull one time. It was at Kvass Flats and that was an old skull. You can find skulls all through the mountains.

Oh, I had a run-in with bears in my travels. I had a lot of experiences with them buggers. That mark I got on my forehead; that is a bear track. I have some scars on my fingers too. I got kind of chewed up one time by a black bear. We had this spring bear hunt. That was the year my dad died in 1949. This hunter had killed a grizzly, so we were up looking for black bear and we found one on a hill. He was a big bear—and he looked bigger when he got on top of me. The bear was facing us when we went up to him. This guy was a pretty good shot. The bear was looking at us and the hunter said, "Where will I shoot him?" I said, "That white spot on his throat." So he up with the gun and shot. The bear dropped and rolled down this open side hill right past us. The last time I saw him, he went into a strip of jackpine. But it wasn't the bottom of the hill; it was kind of a bench on the hill and then the mountain dropped down some more. So the hunter had shot him and knocked him down.

"Well," I said, "that finishes your hunting." So we sat down and had a smoke, and then we went down to skin out this bear. We got down to where I last saw him where he had just rolled a little ways in the timber and had hung up in some jackpine. There was a little blood there—well, quite a bit of blood—but the bear wasn't there.

Pictured above:
Judd Groat crossing
the Smoky River near
Henry & Alice Joachim's
home at the flats.

Photo courtesy of
Dusty Groat.

"Well," I said, "he hung up here for a while. He's bleeding pretty good." So we just went through this timber to where it went downhill again. The bear was at the edge of it—and there he lay. So we walked up to him. I got up closer to the bear and I backed up. I had a Mannlicher gun, myself, and I only had two shells in it. I had some more in my saddle pocket. I had thought, "Hell, that's all I will need." Because I wasn't going to shoot the bear, I just had the extra shells for an emergency.

So when I walked up to the bear, he was laying there with his eyes shut—and I backed the hell away from him! I told this old hunter, "That bear ain't dead." He said, "How can you tell?"

"He has got his eyes shut," I said. "Those buggers don't die with their eyes shut." So we walked back to him a little closer and I said, "Shoot him." He had a .357 magnum and so I said, "Shoot him again!"

"God," he said, "if I shoot him I'll blow a hole in him that you could throw a dog through. You shoot him with that little pea-shooter that you've got there." So we stood there talking, with the damn bear laying there and us paying no attention to him. I said to the hunter, "I was going to shoot the bear in the head. Are you are going to have this bear rug mounted with a head mount?" He said, "I think I will have him mounted with his mouth open."

"Well," I said, "I won't bust the skull off. I won't shoot him in the head. I'll shoot him behind the shoulder." I stepped to one side, where I was going to get a shot, right up next to his front leg. Goddamn, the bear jumped up and he come at me! I had this gun and I had a shell in it and he grabbed the gun in his mouth. The stock was made of hardwood. That bugger sunk his teeth in that hardwood and we had a tug-of-war! It kind of bent the barrel like a bar. I was going to try and pull the barrel through his mouth and shoot him in his big head. I tried it, but he wouldn't let go of that gun. Finally the bear did let go and he bit at my face. That's when I got my hand up *(to protect my face)* and he got these three fingers down across here. A part of the gunstock was hung up in his teeth and that's when he hauled off and hit me—but he didn't claw me. He just hit me with the palm of his mitt and he pushed all the hide off my forehead. Of course this knocked me down and I fell backwards down this hill. I lost my gun when I hit the goddamn ground. I didn't roll over too much as I was more or less sliding. I got stopped and I was grabbing for earth. He come down after me and he run over me after I got stopped. The bear went twenty feet or more below me before he got tangled up in some timber and stopped.

I thought I'd better find my gun. The goddamn blood was running into both of my eyes from his pushing all the hide off my forehead. So I wiped the blood away on my shirt, started back up the hill and found my gun. It's funny the goddamn gun didn't go off when I fell with it. So the bear was standing down below me and not too far. I gave him a shot with this gun and he flinched. So I give him the other shot—I only had the two shells. I seen him flinch again and it never knocked him down.

Christ, then I heard this hollering! The hunter hollered. He was about five hundred yards up the side of the mountain. He was getting the hell out of there! He had a .357 magnum in his hand and he said, "Kill him!!" I said, "You better come down and kill him before he eats me up!"

So he come on down and then he had to shoot the bugger again to kill him. But I never said anything to him about running away when he had a gun in his hand. Goddamn, when a bear takes after a fellow—why, I think the hunter should have come and helped me out! But I didn't say nothing. I didn't blame him. That was quite a deal there with him!

You can see the tooth mark on one finger. He bit down but he didn't break any bones. He hit me on the hand but he didn't take any fingers. I know a lot of guys that have been chewed by those black bears.

There were big fires long before my time. There had been some big timber in this country at one time because when the trees burned off at the roots, they fell over like windfall. I remember when I was a kid up the Solomon Valley, the logs were still sound when I first remember them. There were some logs that were so big you couldn't ride across them. If one of them fell across the trail, you couldn't cross it with a pack string. There was big timber. Jesus, there were huge timber and there was a lot of it in that Solomon Valley! At one time in Solomon Valley it was so thick along the trail, they had to cut a trail through there. The Rangers or the outfitters or whoever would just make a set of bars *(rails)* and you could bar that trail and you had your horse in a fence. *(The bars made a corral for the horses.)* The logs were so big that those horses couldn't jump out of there. There have been some big fires here and a lot of big timber. But that big timber never came back.

Pictured above:
Judd Groat

Photo courtesy of
Dusty Groat.

We went down the Simonette *(River Valley)* with an oil company and I was down there about four or five days travel. I seen a big burn there and the logs were still sound. That was big timber. I'll tell you, if you rode up to one of those logs you couldn't jump it. You had to go around it. We went down through it with the pack outfit, and there was nothing but fireweed and windfall in there. The area is north of Deep Valley Creek. It was west of Deep Valley Creek where it runs into Simonette. There has been some big timber in there—some huge timber. But you don't see that kind of timber any more. I have never seen one.

Lots of the flats like Willow Creek have grown in *(with willows and buck brush)*. Around Grande Cache, they had a landing strip there. It used to belong to old Bill Moberly. He was one of the Natives that come from Jasper. *(He was also Judd Groat's uncle.)* There was a natural field, and they put up hay there. So, when he passed away, he left it to the kids but they didn't cut hay. The poplars were starting to come, but they were small. A man could have gone in there and thrashed them down if he had the rigging. Then the mines started up there. US Steel came up there doing some exploration work around them coal mines. They made a landing field out of this fellow's hay field. They gave that kid three hundred dollars for his field so they could land their planes on it. The last time I was down there, there were poplar trees and probably the whole flat is gone. That used to be an open meadow. They used to cut hay off it. It was a natural field—like, old Bill Moberly didn't clear anything on it. He just went ahead and cut the Wildhay off it. He used to keep the cows off it, but then they'd hay it and the cows would have hay in the wintertime. That was all fields—right through to the mountains and clear to the river. I remember that trip I made through there in 1928. I was down through there and you could see this big field and there was nothing on it, so we camped there for a while. There was nothing but pure grass flats, but now it is all grown into poplar. *(This is at #1 Mine Flats a few miles north of Grande Cache.)*

I will tell you about some old corrals that were at the Willow Creek Ranger Station. At one time, all the outfitters in Jasper had to move their horses out of the Athabasca Valley because that was elk habitat. There had been packhorses there *(at Willow Creek)* a long time before they brought elk to Jasper. They used to winter the horses at Willow Creek. Rufe Neighbor had his horses there. Rufe used to manage the Athabasca Ranch that Stan Clark sold to these people *(Davidsons)*. Rufe left his horses out there at Willow Creek and they run there quite a while.

So we went up there in 1944 to round up these horses. We brought out forty-some-odd head. There were five or six *(horses)* that we left in there. We couldn't corral them, and we had no place to hold them. We had no place to keep them at nights. We couldn't keep the horses tied up. By the time we had the forty horses hobbled, there was no time to go after the others, so we left them. There was only five or six head left—not too many. Nobody ever bothered these horses until somebody tried to get them in later years. By god, they couldn't corral them! There was a grey mare in the outfit and she would be about a two or three year old. We had seen her and the other four with the bunch. She was a wild little mare. She could run faster than the others, and that is how she led the outfit. So then they tried to get them and couldn't catch them.

Bob Ekroth used to go up there and look after the government horses at Willow Creek. *(Bob was the Barn Boss for Parks Canada at Jasper National Park.)* Bob had nothing else to do. He thought, "I'll catch some horses." So he built those corrals there. I forget just what year that was. He built them corrals and he caught those horses. The government used to haul hay part of the way and then Bob hauled the last seven miles with his team and horses. So he baited them with some hay, and he got them. They weren't actually wild horses, but that is how come the corrals have been there. But Bob got them.

(According to Mac Elder, a guide at that time, they caught the horses in the winter 1952 and 1953. Mac stated that Ekroth salted the horses and got them in the trap. He caught five geldings, however the two mares evaded him. A brown mare and grey/white mare stayed in the area for many years after that. All the horses were branded except the two mares.)

I had one horse in that outfit that I traded Rufe. There was a good-looking bay horse in that outfit. I remember because I chased him. The geological survey was looking to buy some horses. They wanted a saddle horse then, and Rufe didn't have one handy. I had a brown mare that I had there. I was going to get her bred. She was a good old saddle horse. This geological survey needed a saddle horse so Rufe said, "What will you take for that old mare of yours?" I said, "I will trade you something for her. Go ahead and sell her." When it come to settle up, I took a little horse that we left up there at Willow Creek—we brought him out and sold old Badger for a bucking horse! This was in 1944—because that is the last time that I worked at the ranch was in 1944. I was breaking horses down there, so I went up with Rufe to bring the horses out from Willow Creek.

•|• •|• •|• •|• •|• •|• •|•

There is a steam boiler up on Pope-Thoreau trail. The Blue Diamond Coal Company had some coal claims up there on Carson Creek and up Pope- Thoreau Creek trail. They had to do some improvements on that, so they had this diamond drill. The fellow that owned the diamond drill was Bush. They took that drill in with horses and drilled. They took coal samples from the diamond drill to see what they had there. And they had some miners in there too. They dug tunnels in different places to find out how big the seam was or how much coal was there, because this mine in Brule was going to peter out. It did peter out in 1928. But the coal was there. There was lots of coal there left in the mines apparently, but there was something in the coal that created more ash than it should have. I imagine that they could overcome that today. The coal was dirty because there were other ingredients in it, so they gave it up.

They packed that steam boiler into Pope-Thoreau. That is where they got that power for the diamond drills. I imagine that they would have put it right on a sleigh runner. You couldn't take it up there in the summer time. You would have to wait until the muskegs and creeks froze up.

I saw the operation there. They got the coal out of the mine for the fuel. They dug it right out of the coal seam and burned it in that old steam boiler, which they used to operate the diamond drills. They had wagons up there to haul coal. It wouldn't take too much coal to run that steam boiler.

There would have been no problem building a *(railroad)* line up there. I guess a lot of this coal now comes mostly from the Smoky River mines. You know they were a long time getting that road through there *(Grande Cache)*. If it wasn't for the government, I guess they never would have had a road in there. But I remember talk about the coal claims on the Smoky. That was previous to 1920 that they had coal claims on the Smoky. It eventually turned out all right and they mined coal out of there.

••• ••• ••• ••• ••• ••• •••

I seen a lot of creeks and one thing or another named after a lot of the old time Forest Rangers. They got the names of different outfits like old Hendrickson Creek—that was named after old Fred Hendrickson. *(Fred worked for Alberta Forest Service. He was first employed to cut trail from Entrance to the Big Smoky for Forestry.)* There was a Rowe Creek, which was named after Percy Rowe who was a Ranger out there. Then at Lone Teepee Creek back in the 1920s, there was a fellow who was a guide, packer, cowboy, trapper—and he worked for the Forestry as a Ranger. He went to Grande Prairie for supplies. He lived somewhere across the Smoky and he met this girl. He went back the following year and he married her and brought her back out on his area. So he made camp at Lone Teepee Creek. There was damn good fishing in the creek and lots of horse feed, so he set up a teepee there. He and his bride was the only one there. That is why they called it Lone Teepee Creek because that is where old Calvert Nixon had his base. There were old teepee pits up there. He worked for the Forestry and came into Entrance once a month to get his supplies, then turned around and went back to Teepee Creek.

••• ••• ••• ••• ••• ••• •••

I was trapping every damn year. I sold some of the fur that I trapped to Gordon Watt and he done all right. *(In 1951, Gordon Watt bought the Entrance Store from Stan Clark who had operated it since 1941. Watt and Clark both worked for Alberta Forest Service in earlier years.)* Gordon would give you a fair deal on the fur. I remember one time we had some lynx. Red Creighton was trapping between here and where my trapline was on Mumm Creek. He had twenty-some-odd marten. He was going to ship to the fur auction in Edmonton. I had five lynx and sixteen martens. Red had twenty-two martens and he shipped his to the fur auction sale in Edmonton. That sale was either in December or January.

Gordon Watt was buying fur and marten at a pretty good price. The lynx wasn't up too well. Gordon Watt gave me fifty dollars a hide straight through for my marten. He gave me eight hundred dollars for the sixteen marten. These lynx, he said, "I don't know about them kits." I had a couple of yearlings that were small. It wasn't really big mature lynx, you know. He said, "I don't think I can give you too much for them." I knew that these lynx pelts were pretty good, yet I didn't know the price of fur. So Gordon said, "I will give you so much for them kits. I don't think I will get that back." He got his returns back after he shipped the

Pictured above:
Judd Groat.

Photo courtesy of
Victoria Moberly.

lynx and he was right. He didn't get what he expected for the lynx kits but he fared out a little better than fifty dollars a-piece on the marten.

So when Red Creighton got his return from the auction sale, they'd graded his fur. They'd give him thirty-seven dollars for this one, and diddled back and forth—and by hell, he never got fifty dollars for any one of them! I got Gordon to give me fifty dollars straight through for mine—and Gordon made money on them! So Gordon told me, "I fared out good enough on the marten." I said, "I will split that difference with you on them two *(lynx)* kits. You gave me a pretty good price." But I didn't tell Gordon that Red didn't get that fifty dollars a-piece for his though.

You see, Red Creighton trapped in there, I forget what year it was, but it was after the lumber company closed here. They closed it up here in 1956—so it was later than that. Red got some tin off some of the old sawmill buildings on the Hay River. Then he got some timber too. It would be after 1956. It was at Mile 12. Bensons have it now. My dad used to have that trapline, and he sold it to Otto Peterson and Otto got a miscellaneous lease there.

•¦• •¦• •¦• •¦• •¦• •¦• •¦•

I didn't know anything else but guiding and outfitting. I guided sheep mostly. Sheep was the number one trophy in this country. A lot of fellows prefer bear. One time you were allowed five trophies on a tag, which included a black bear and a grizzly. Now they are mostly just hunting sheep as the number one trophy. Everybody is trying for the *grand slam*. I had a lot of American hunters. I knew the country like the back of my hand. I just had an idea of where the sheep would be and we went right into there. We often went where we had luck before. I knew where the bighorn sheep were around.

Brule is my favourite place! There is no place I would rather live that I have seen.

(Judd Groat was an accomplished horseman, guide, outfitter, trapper and tracker. Judd used to work up at Fort St. John, B.C. area where he met and married Darleen Lundeen of Fort St. John in 1946. Darleen spent time on the trail with her husband. She cooked for Judd as well as for other outfitters. The couple raised nine children in Brule, Alberta. Their names are Butch, Linda, Sharon, Manley, Cecilia, Sherry, John, Wendy and Dusty. Judd Groat died on January 3, 1999, four months after he was interviewed by Peter J. Murphy and Bob Stevenson.)

Pictured above:
Judd Groat.

Photo courtesy of
Dusty Groat.

Part Two: Joe Groat

Interview On Joe *(Malcolm)* Groat

Sue   I am at the home of Ken Groat's, oldest son of Joe Groat. Ken's mother, Maxine Thompson, who was the wife of Joe Groat is also present. Shelli Orava, Ken's fiancée and Dan Hallock of Grande Cache who traveled with me to Brule are also here at the interview. It is March 18, 2006.

Maxine, can you tell me about your husband, Joe Groat and how you two came to meet each other?

Maxine   Joe was born in 1922. He was nine or ten years younger than his brother, Judd. Joe grew up in Brule, but attended school in Hinton. He learned to be a skilled hunter, tracker, packer, trapper and guide from his father, Tom Groat and his older brother, Judd. He followed in his father's and brother's footsteps, becoming an accomplished guide. Joe was a colourful character who spent a lot of time in the hills.

I *(Maxine nee Collins)* am from Bearberry, Alberta. I grew up there with Tom Vinson and was best friends with his sister. I came to the Tonquin Valley for a summer to work for Eric and Vera Kjos who were working for Brewster. The next summer the Kjoses ran the *Black Cat Ranch* at Brule. I came back for a second year to work for them. That's how I met Joe.

Joe and I married in December 1948. Joe was guiding at the time of our marriage. Joe's dad *(Tom Groat)* died the spring after we were married. I met Tom Groat—I never got to know him. I never met Joe's mother. She died in 1943 and was buried up here *(Brule)* in the cemetery. Tom died in 1949 and was buried in Edmonton. Joe and I had seven children. We lost our first one, Joanne in 1975. Their names are: Joanne, Ken, Gordon, Sherril, Gary, Donny and Ronny.

Dan Hallock   I don't remember Joe having any kids.

Maxine   Maybe he told you he was single. We had the youngest in 1958.

Dan   I worked with him in '59 when he worked for Rex Logan *(an outfitter based out of Sundre, Alberta)*. We were out there in the hills taking some geologists out for a geological survey. They were geologists from *B.A. Oil Company*. We were on the trail from the first part of May right up to hunting season. I was cooking there. Joe told me that you were teaching at the time.

Pictured above:
Maxine & Joe Groat.
Photo courtesy
of Dusty Groat

Pictured on left page:
Joe Groat.

Photo courtesy of
Ken Groat.

Pictrured right:
Louis Joachim &
Joe Groat.

Pictured on right page:
'Boundary Trip.'
Top: Packed up and ready
to go.
Middle: Joe Groat and son,
Ken Groat.
Bottom: On the trail to
Berg Lake.

Photos courtesy of
Ken Groat.

Maxine   I was substitute teaching at the school here *(in Brule)* for a short time. That must have been the year. One of the teachers had a baby.

Dan   That was the year that Rex Logan got really sick. He had ulcers. He came out for medical treatment and got Joe to take his place. I was cooking on that trip.

Maxine   Joe was a good cook on the trail too.

Dan   Joe was leading us out there. He took Rex's place for about two months. Ollie Sorenson from Sundre was out there too. Both Ollie and Joe were guides and packers. Joe was a good hand and he knew the country. He ran a good outfit. Joe was sure a good storyteller. There was never a dull moment.

Rex Logan was out there for a month before he got sick. Joe was out there for the rest of the time.

Sue   Maxine, did you ever go out on the trail with Joe?

Maxine   I went out on a bear hunt the spring after we got married and that's the only time. I was cooking for the grizzly hunt. The guys went out hunting and I went part-way with them. I was on my way back to camp and I met a grizzly. It crossed the trail in front of me. That was the year that Judd was in contact with a bear and it chewed his hand.

My oldest son, Ken went out on the trail with his father. He was born in 1952. He also guided up north *(in British Columbia)* for Kjos. *(The Kjoses moved from Bearberry, Alberta to Toad River, B.C.)* Ken learned to pack from his father. He's my only one that took to the trail.

Sue Ken, when did you start on the trail with your father?

Ken I went on the first trip when I was nine years old. My dad was working for the Warden Service. He was working for Parks *(Canada)* and we left from Mt. Robson. We went into Berg Lake, Adolphus Flats and Twintree Lakes. My dad was on the Berg Lake Patrol and he was patrolling the north boundary *(of Jasper National Park)*. We had five or six packhorses and we went up there for two weeks, I think. It was the first time that I ever swam a horse. That's because I couldn't hear him hollering at me where the best place was to cross the river. We were crossing just below Emperor Falls. I had some chaps on that trip. I still have them. They were my dad's chaps and my grandfather's *(Tom Groat's)* chaps before that.

There were a lot of "firsts" on that trip. I was chased by a cow moose. I rode up too close to her calf and she scared the hell out of me. We were moving from one camp to another *(warden's)* cabin. There were five or six packhorses between me and my dad. I must have been pulling slack when we packed up because my dad and I were alone. When we moved—it was just him and I.

One day when we were on patrol, we came around a corner and there was a sow grizzly bear with her cub. Dad always packed a lariat. He took off chasing that bear with that lariat. I thought he was going to rope her. I was screaming and hollering at my dad to leave her alone. He was just trying to scare her off the trail. Dad was always chasing bears.

There is a bear story about my dad that I'd like to tell you. A train hit a horse on the track down here *(in Brule)*. There was a black bear feeding on that horse. Dad was supposedly pretty good with a rope. So he and his older brother, Judd went down to the tracks, both riding their horses. Judd was going to spook this bear

Pictured above:
Joe Groat singing &
picking his guitar at the
Jasper Park Lodge.

Photo courtesy of
Ken Groat.

out into this field and Dad was going to rope him with his lariat. I don't know what he was going to do with the bear after he roped him though. So Dad hid behind some trees and Judd snuck down with a .22 *(rifle)* and crossed the tracks from the lake side. He said that this old bear was lying on top of this horse sleeping. Judd thought that he would shoot in front of the bear and spook him into the field. He shot and hit him on the end of the nose and killed him. The bear never even got up. It's probably just as well, because if the bear went out in that field, I don't know what would have happened.

Dad was a good horseman. He shod horses. He taught me how to shoe horses. I remember my dad and me shoeing a horse at the same time. You'd have to hold him up a little bit, but you could shoe a horse in a short time. I was on the front foot and he was on the opposite back foot. Later, I took a corrective shoeing course in Dawson Creek when I was working for Bob Kjos *(outfitter)*.

Maxine   Joe used to shoe all the mill's horses *(Hinton Pulp Mill)*. These were workhorses that would work out in the bush. They didn't have machines then. He was the mill's farrier.

Ken   Dad shod the mill's horse in the 1960s. The mill was using horses at that time.

Sue   Did Joe run his own outfitting business?

Maxine   No, Judd got the outfit from his dad with the help of a hunter. Joe worked for Judd on the trail for quite a while. Joe also worked for Johnny Unland who was based out of Jasper. I know that Joe worked for him during the summer months.

Pictured above:
Tom Groat & daughter
Freda (Groat) Angers.

Photo courtesy of
Dusty Groat.

Ken   Dad worked for Johnny Unland on summer trips. He also worked with Carl Luger when they took geologists out on the geological survey trips during the summer months. They had some long trips. They'd go out for the whole summer. My dad knew the country pretty well. Carl and my dad had been darn near to Grande Prairie with a pack outfit. There was a lot of geological activity in those days. Dad also spent quite a bit of time working for Jim Babala, guiding on hunting trips.

Sue   Can you tell me a little about your grandfather, Tom Groat and your grandmother, Clarisse *(Moberly)* Groat?

Ken   My grandfather, Tom Groat came to this area *(Hinton)* in 1910 with a survey team for the railroad. He decided to stay in this area and became one of the best outfitters in his day. He was probably one of the first outfitters in the province of Alberta along with the *Otto Brothers,* the *Hargreaves Brothers* and the Brewsters. I think a lot of my grandmother's family *(the Moberlys)* who moved to Grande Cache guided for him.

My grandfather, Tom Groat quit outfitting because he had a stroke, and Judd took over. Judd and Dad worked together for quite a few years. I know that they went out on geological survey trips as well.

My grandmother's name was Clarisse Moberly. She was Ewan Moberly's daughter. Ewan was the son of Henry John Moberly and Suzanne Karakunte. Suzanne's family was

indigenous to the area. Henry John Moberly was a Hudson's Bay Factor at Jasper. Clarisse and her family lived in Jasper on the Celestine Lake road.

(In 1907, the Canadian Federal Government nationalized Jasper National Park. They forced the indigenous people to leave the area by seizing their guns. The indigenous people were unable to hunt without their weapons. They were only given back their rifles when they left the park. Despite the fact that legislation was passed in 1907, most people did not leave the Jasper area until 1910.)

After my grandmother's family left Jasper, they moved into Entrance *(Alberta)* at Montana Pete's homestead. My grandfather married Clarisse in 1910 and they settled down. They moved in and squatted on a school quarter. In the early 1900s you could do that. Later, they moved into Brule, over the hill toward the lake. My grandparents did have a ninety-nine-year lease there. Nobody kept the taxes up, so it is gone. I'm not sure where the lease was. My grandparents had eleven children and their names were Gladys, Judd, Mary, Alberta, Joe, Sara, Alice, Bruce, Freda, Dorothy and Billy.

Sue I understand that your father went on a trip on the old Grande Prairie Trail. Can you tell me about that trip?

Ken In 1966, some Edson Kinsmen wanted to travel the old Grande Prairie Trail with a pack outfit. The trail hadn't been traveled much since 1916 when the railroad was put through to Grande Prairie. Only two of the Kinsmen had ever ridden horses before the trip. They were Tony Grant, Mel Soltys, Tom Brown, Nino Chiesa, Lorne Kroetch, Dick Topott and Bob Joy. The trip would take these travelers two hundred and forty miles through muskegs, rivers and deadfall. The Kinsmen wanted to take the thirteen-day trip in order to attend the Alberta Kinsmen Convention being held in Grande Prairie on June 2nd.

It was a bad time of year for a pack trip as the rivers are highest at the end of May with the spring run-off. The trek was planned in two phases. The first phase would take them from Edson to the Athabasca River *(fifty-two miles north)*. They used a Bombardier vehicle to haul the equipment and personal items to the trailhead there. The group left from Edson on May 21st on a cold and rainy day. It was rough going and the guys even awoke to frozen water one morning. To make matters worse, the men lost a case of whisky when it slipped off the vehicle. The gear and men were freighted across by boat when they arrived at the Athabasca River. Dr. Crawford and a friend of his flew a case of whiskey into a Forestry airstrip nearby. One bottle was missing when their case was delivered, which they believed the pilot took in payment for his hard work.

The second phase of the expedition would take the group from the Athabasca River to Grande Prairie. It was during this portion of the journey that they met John Ostashek, an outfitter out of Brule, and my dad. John supplied the horses for the party. My dad was the trail boss and cook for the trip. Butch Groat *(Judd's son)* and Chuck Wright were the wranglers. Dad and the boys had trailed twenty-six horses from Brule to the Athabasca River Crossing. John Ostashek left outfitting and entered politics. He eventually became the Government Leader *(Premier)* of the Yukon from 1992-1996.

Butch, Chuck and Dad picked the party up at the Athabasca River, north of Edson. The trail hadn't been used in many years and it was grown in. Dad had been on it years earlier, so he had an idea where the trail was. He said that there were times during the trip when they didn't have a clue where they were, as it had grown in so much. There were lots of beaver dams and muskeg. It was a pretty wet spring and when they got to the Smoky River, it was quite high.

The high water forced the party to re-assess the situation. They laid over a day and scouted a trail to cross the Smoky River, as it had grown in so bad. They were thinking of trying the river to see if they could get across. Butch had a little horse called Rimrock and he was supposed to be pretty good in the water. They got up there and my dad told Butch, "You go ahead; you've got no kids." Butch wouldn't go. They ended up building a raft. They rafted the Smoky and swam the horses across the river.

During the adventure, one horse fell in the mud on the Smoky River. He lunged on a *(sharpened)* beaver stump and punctured his belly. They lost him. One mare had a newborn colt on the trail. The foal was a complete surprise to everyone. They didn't even know that she was going to have it. The colt survived and they got it safely up to Grande Prairie. So they ended up even—they lost one horse and gained one.

There was lots of excitement on the trip. Dad taught the Kinsmen how to tie a diamond hitch on a packhorse. These guys were pretty proud of their accomplishments. Towards the end

of the trip, the party stopped at some watering holes. The Valleyview Kinsmen met the group at Sturgeon Lake for a dinner and party. The trip only took ten days, resulting in the guys spending two days at the Debolt Bar, where my dad disappeared for a few hours. He showed up later in a brand new shirt and white cowboy hat for his ride to the Grande Prairie Parade.

The party arrived in Grande Prairie just in time for the Kinsmen parade. They unpacked the horses in front of the York Hotel. The City of Grande Prairie had even erected a hitching post in honour of the arriving travelers. The group attended a dinner that included Harvey Switzer who, with two other men, had originally cut at least sixty miles of the trail in 1911.

Sue Did you ever take any other trips with your father into Willmore Wilderness Park?

Ken One time my dad and I took a trip into Willmore. There was a family from Iowa who had three kids. They were going on a fishing trip into Rock Creek. We were going to camp at Eagle's Nest pass.

I wasn't that old, either. Before the trip, we had to trail the horses from Brule to Rock Lake. I took off from Brule and took the horses to Rock Lake by myself. About three-quarters of the way up there, Dad was supposed to catch up with me. You could drive up from Brule to Rock Lake then. I rode all day and it was getting dark. All you could see was the sparks flying off the horses' shoes every once in a while, when the horse shoes hit a rock. I was riding behind the horses and

chasing them up the road. The horses knew where they were going. At midnight, I was just about to Rock Lake and finally I saw some headlights coming. If I was big enough, I would have tried to ihup my dad, I was so mad at him! I took the horses all the way there by myself!

When Dad caught up to me, we tied up the horses, fed them and went back to Brule. We got up early the next morning, and went back to Rock Lake. We packed up that day and headed into Eagle's Nest with our guests. Dad cooked and I helped him haul wood, water and pack up the horses. When we were leaving there and were packing, I grabbed the wrong rope when I was pulling slack. He hollered at me and I turned around and walked away from the horse. I got about ten feet away from that horse and he booted my butt. I went right back to the horse and asked, "What rope do I pull?" That's the way to learn. You don't forget that. I learned a lot from him.

My favourite areas in Willmore Wilderness Park are the Starlight Range and the Rock Creek Valley. I remember years ago, the willows were pretty small. There was a lot more game there then. The willows have grown so much now. I think there were more moose then and that kept the willows grazed off.

My dad was a super cook. I remember in his later years, he would jump up and make cinnamon buns. That was a favorite thing—he liked baking. Everybody liked his cinnamon buns. Dad was a good trail hand and he was really good with horses.

Maxine   Joe died of cancer in November of 1977. When Joe died, I actually found out how old he was. We said that he was fifty-three when he died, but he was actually fifty-five years old. During his life, Joe worked for the railroad for nine years from 1967 to 1976. He also worked at the mine and shod horses for the pulp mill. Joe started to work at Cardinal River Mine in 1976 and he made good money there. You don't make much money as a guide or the CN *(railroad)*, so the salary increase was welcomed. He didn't live to enjoy it. Joe liked any job he had but I think that his favorite work was being on the trail and working with the horses. Joe really loved his kids and he loved his horses. He loved being in the mountains.

CHAPTER ELEVEN:
Tom Vinson

Sue This is July 19, 2003. I'm sitting here with Tom and Yvette Vinson and Bazil Leonard. Tom, what year did you start outfitting in Willmore Wilderness Park? What brought you here and how did you get involved in the very beginning?

Tom I rode horseback all the way here from Sundre *(Alberta)* and trailed up a bunch of horses with Dave McMurtry. Dave McMurtry was a rancher from west of Sundre, where I grew up. He worked in Jasper in the 1920s for Fred Brewster at the pony barns.

Once we arrived with the horses, Fred Brewster bought twenty-two head. Nick Nickerson took sixteen head. Nick and Emma Nickerson were outfitters who lived in Hinton *(Alberta)*.

Sue I understand that Emma and Nick Nickerson started guiding in 1929 and operated their outfit for twenty-nine years. In fact, Emma Nickerson held both a guide and outfitter license. There's a creek called Nickerson that is a tributary of Sheep Creek that is named after them. I have heard that Emma was quite a competent mountain woman.

So after you arrived in this country—who did you work for?

Tom After that, I went to work for Fred Brewster wrangling horses. Later, I had shares in his company. Fred and Jack Brewster were Jasper outfitters. They unloaded horses in Edson when it was the end of the steel *(railway)* and packed up to the British Collieries, and established the coal mine there. That was in .....I don't know what year it was—it was the end of the railroad then.

Yvette That would be about 1908.

Tom Fred wintered horses in Jasper Park for years. He started to winter his horses here in Brule in 1933. He always had someone to look after them. Fred built the Black Cat Ranch in 1936. I bought Fred's horse business out of Jasper Park in 1955.

Pictured above:
Top: Yvette Vinson 1944.
Middle: old Vinson ranch.
Bottom: Old Homestead dairy farm circa 1912.

Pictured on left page:
Tom Vinson on location for "The Far Country" movie 1953, at the Columbia Ice Fields.

Photos courtesy of Tom & Yvette Vinson

Sue   Can you tell me a little bit about the areas you started outfitting in Willmore?

Tom   We never had areas. Except we did have some honor between outfitters at one time. That has just about disappeared now. Alex McDougall was chief guide for Fred Brewster, and he wouldn't even camp in another outfitter's campground when he knew they weren't going to be there. He'd go up the creek another mile and build a campground of his own. That's the way they used to treat each other—the outfitters. But that kind of honour fell by the wayside.

Sue   Can you tell about your involvement with bighorn sheep hunting?

Tom   I guided for Fred Brewster before the war, then joined the army in 1942. After the army, I went back to work for Fred and took out hunting parties. We hunted bighorn sheep in 1945 right up to 1955 when I bought the outfit from Brewster. I guided for bighorn sheep until I turned sixty-five years old and altogether, I guided hunting parties for forty years. I've seen a lot of country and built a lot of campgrounds. I did all my hunting in Willmore.

The best sheep hunting in the country is Femme Creek and Corral Creek. Hargreaves told me that. The west side of the Sulphur is rough but Jack Hargreaves said it was good sheep country. Blue Grouse Pass up to Whistler Pass is good country. Ed Regnier (outfitter) takes sheep hunters up there for George Kelly *(outfitter)*.

Sue   When you started in the Park, who would have been outfitting?

Tom   There was *(Stan)* Kitchen and *(Red)* Creighton, and then it got to be Creighton and *(Larry)* McGuire, and Jack Brewster with Jack Hargreaves. They ran two outfits, generally in the Park. When Stan Kitchen quit outfittin', Creighton got McGuire as a partner. Four other outfitters who worked in the Willmore Wilderness Park included Harold Anderson, Nick Nickerson, Albert Ceal and Art Allen. Harold Anderson was from Hargwen. This was a railway station thirty-one miles west of Edson *(Alberta)*.

Sue   So Art Allen was both a trapper and outfitter?

Tom   Art Allen outfitted until Leonard Jeck bought him out. Art was with George Hargreaves when he died at the head of Sheep Creek. They were traveling ten to twelve days on a trip when Hargreaves died. The two men were sharing the same wall tent. Art woke up and went to the cook tent and made fire. When he went back to wake George up, he was dead. George Hargreaves is the only white man that I know of that is buried in Willmore Wilderness Park.

Sue   What guides from the Grande Cache area guided for you?

Tom There weren't too many guys from Grande Cache down here. But the Moberlys here were renowned sheep hunters and they became famous in the *(United)* States—Frank, Miles, Dave, and Eddie. They lived at John's *(Moberly)* place. The Natives were in the Willmore area long before any white man. There are Indian graves all over Willmore. Louis Delorme's grandfather is buried at Big Grave.

It's funny how things change. Mt. Russell used to be called Big Grave Mountain. I don't know who 'Russell' is or why they changed the name of the mountain. There used to be a lot of stick teepees in the Big Grave area. These wicky-ups were used for shelters when a guy was out trapping.

Many other graves exist like Little Grave and the grave at Dead Man Creek *(Thappe's grave)*. In fact his skull is still there today. I was told that he was killed in a hunting accident in a snow slide.

Adam Joachim's mother is buried on the Berland River. There is another grave at Sunset Meadows, but I don't know who it belongs to.

Frank and Dave McDonald worked for me. Joe Karakuntie, Gordon Delorme, Walter Delorme and Charlie Delorme also guided on my outfit. We also had Kelly Joachim, Casey Joachim, Milton Joachim and Eddie Joachim. Malcolm Moberly, Walter Moberly and Collin *(Jasper)* Moberly also guided. Jasper got this nickname because he worked for me in Jasper. All of these guys were pretty good men. They were all exceptional hunters.

Sue Did you ever hear the old timers talk about the buffalo in this area?

Tom Joe McDonald once told me that he killed a buffalo and ate it. Joe McDonald was Johnny and Dave McDonald's father. There was some buffalo in this area. Joe is the only guy that I talked to who remembered eating buffalo meat. Walter Moberly was the one who found a buffalo bone. I found an old buffalo skull on the Berland one time. Old-time trappers and the

Natives ate the meat they trapped. They ate muskrat and beaver, anything that was vegetarian.

There are beautiful areas and good trails in Willmore Wilderness Park. Willmore is 'game country.' There were beautiful passes like Glacier Pass, Rocky Pass, Desolation Pass, Kvass Pass and Hardscrabble Pass. Desolation Pass is at the head of Rock Creek. This is a kind of area that tourists can come to see game and the scenic mountains. Rocky Pass, Eagle's Nest Pass and Jack Knife Pass are good places to take guests into the park. Jack Knife Pass is more open than Rocky Pass and not as far.

The Natives used to travel from Jasper by pack train to Muskeg by the Indian Trail. The Indian Trail goes over three or four passes until it reaches Muskeg. The Forestry put in the Mountain Trail, but today Forestry has cut back and there is little or no maintenance or patrolling of that trail.

The mileage from Entrance resulted in the naming of the trail system. For example Big Grave Cabin is Mile 76 from Entrance. There is another cabin at Mile 58 and Dead Man Creek is at Mile 62.

Sue Can you tell me about some of the trappers who worked the Jackpine Valley, Boulder Creek Valley and upper Smoky Valley?

Tom 'Coyote' Cliff Faulk and Harold Lake were the first two trappers in that area after trapper Curly Phillip's time.

Pictured above:
Guide, Frank McDonald and hunter, Lucille McConnaughey 1968.

Photo courtesy of Tom & Yvette Vinson.

Coyote Cliff also had a cabin at the head of Kvass Creek. I know that Jimmy Joachim had a trapline cabin on Brandy Creek. They don't call it Brandy Creek today, but it used to be called by that name. The drainage is called Brandy Creek on all the old maps. Red Creighton, Art Allan and Tom Ross also trapped marten in the Jackpine Valley.

Art Allen always went up to the Jackpine Valley through the *(Mt.) Robson* way. He walked in from there. Yeah, it was Art's trapline then. Art Allen built that cabin in there— it's a good one. Those guys used to stay there all winter and trap. When spring was getting around and there was still a lot of snow, those guys would go up and stay at that cabin at Rockslide Creek. There were cabins at the mouth of Rockslide Creek and also at the mouth of Hardscrabble Creek that the trappers used. That would be their shortest way out. They went back down *(the Jackpine River)*, up the Smoky and down into B.C. They snowshoed over to *(Mt.) Robson*. It was too far to come out this way *(back to Brule)*.

Tom Ross spent the winters trapping with Red *(Creighton)* and Art Allen before he became a Jasper Park Warden. He also worked as a trail hand for Red Creighton. He worked as cook for the hunting parties.

Sue   What route did you take to pack in the groceries and supplies?

Tom   Outfitters from Jasper would send their supplies to Devona by freight train. They would trail their horses there to pick up their groceries and gear. They'd go up the Snake Indian and over to Willow Creek, out of the National Park to the Willmore Wilderness area. I packed groceries out there *(Jackpine River)* for them with Creighton's horses and Brewster's horses in the mid-1940s.

We started at Devona—Don McMurtry *(Dave's brother)* and I, and we rode right through. Devona is twenty-five miles east of Jasper directly across from Disaster Point and Rocky River. There used to be a warden station and a railroad section there.

We went up to the Sulphur *(River)*, then up the west fork of the Sulphur on Hardscrabble, and then down Hardscrabble Creek. Just before you get to that trail that goes into Winifred Basin, off of Hardscrabble, you go up over Jackpine Ridge. There are canyons down below on Hardscrabble Creek. You go over Jackpine Ridge and drop down onto the Smoky *(River)* to where the moose licks are. There is a campground there of Hargreaves.

Pictured above:
Top: Art Allen PA 3 3
Bottom: Red Creighton is standing with his work horse team. Mr. Joyce is squatting and he was the secretary to Mr. Wilby who purchased Lewis Swift's homestead. PA 46 116

Both photos courtesy of the
Jasper Yellowhead Museum & Archives

Winifred Basin is one of the most beautiful places I ever saw in my life. Larry McGuire once said it was like being on the moon. It's a different world in this basin. There are three beautiful lakes there. Caribou and goats live in this magnificent place, but I don't think there are many bighorn sheep.

Roy Hargreaves used to run his horses down the Smoky years ago. Then they'd trail them back and forth. At that time, if he hired an Alberta guide, he could hunt sheep in Alberta. Roy Hargreaves did all the time. Jack *(Hargreaves)* didn't have to hire *(an Albertan)* as he lived in Alberta. Both brothers outfitted in the park, but Roy used to hunt north of the Smoky, pretty near all of the time. Then the British Columbia government got tough policies. First it was on Alberta outfitters hunting grizzlies in B.C. Then somehow or other, the Alberta Government retaliated and said if you weren't a resident of Alberta you couldn't outfit in here, regardless of whether you hired an Alberta guide or not. That's what put the crimp on Roy because he lived in B.C. This upset Jack, because they didn't get along. The brothers fought like cats and dogs.

It was Roy Hargreaves that built the corral at Corral Creek. When he wintered his horses in the Smoky Valley and rounded them up each spring, he used the corrals to entrap his horses. That's why the corral was there. That's why they call it Corral Creek.

I don't think any hunters ever went into the Jackpine and Upper Smoky Valleys, because what the heck were they going to hunt? But Carl Luger spent a hell of a pile of time in there. He knows that country better than anybody I know. He lives in Entrance, but you have to holler at him, he can't hear. I haven't been north of the Smoky for a long time. Carl Luger was telling me that you don't have to travel through the muskegs on the Jackpine *(River)*. He said you don't have to travel on the soft ground. There's a pine ridge there where Carl blazed a trail. He said that the trail wasn't in thick timber on that ridge. His trail followed right along the ridge, dropped down .... would it be on the Pauline Creek? But Carl says you don't have to go near that muskeg at all. But other outfitters have never found Luger's trail.

Yvette   What did Carl Luger do up there?

Pictured above:
Top: Tom Vinson 1980.
Middle: Tom Vinson 1945.
Bottom: Tom Vinson
& Merv Cooper 1956.
Photos courtesy of Tom & Yvette Vinson.

235

Tom   He was up there with geological survey parties. He's got a camp on Ptarmigan Lake. He camped there with some geologists but he said he ran out of horse feed—with no grass there.

Sue   What was the game like in the Willmore when you started outfitting?

Tom   Jack Brewster wrote a report about a 1936 hunting trip in the Willmore area. He described the large amount of game they saw. In 1939 the abundant population of game was the same as when I was wrangling horses in that area. *(See Chapter Three, Page 111, for the "Hunting Report by Jack Brewster," which Tom Vinson provided the Willmore Wilderness Foundation.)*

I blame the wolves for the antlered population decline. The wolves have eaten the moose. Now the willows are as high as the ceiling and there's no moose to eat them, and no caribou either. The willows have grown up and you can't even ride through them. The willows are killing off all the grass. These are things that could have been prevented. Now you can ride all day or all week and never see a moose. You used to see lots of them.

There was enough moose in the Willmore that kept the valleys free of willows. It was like the willows had been cut with a scythe. And of course there were new shoots coming up. It was perfect moose feed. The moose kept the valleys leveled right off. There were hundreds of moose out there. When I wrangled horses, it was nothing to get up at daylight and hike down the valley and see forty, fifty moose. Lots of them— there were moose all over. It didn't matter if you were on the Sulphur, or Rock Creek—anywhere you went there were moose. The Berland *(River)* you know had lots of moose. You were nearly scared to walk down the valley in September because there were so many moose in the rut.

I just don't understand why the government was so afraid of the environmentalists. Every time we propositioned the government to do something about the predators, they would make a start on it. But as soon as the news got out that something was going to be done about the wolves, the environmentalists would protest and the authorities would drop the issue. They didn't have predator control, but they sent two biologists out to do a survey on how many caribou were left. I told the biologists that they were too late. They should have started on controlling the wolves years before. There still is hardly any caribou left.

I talked to some of the environmentalists who felt the wolf was a great noble animal. I said to them, "Have you ever seen a bunch of them pull down an old cow moose—the guts hanging out? That's the way they kill them." They get their guts hanging out so then they *(the moose)* lose control of their hindquarters. They sit there on their ass and spin around while the wolves jump back and forth to keep pulling on their guts until they die. That's what they call being a noble animal? I can't see it. We need to manage the wolves like we have done historically. They have been trapped and hunted for generations.

Pictured above:

Top: Tom Vinson and Charlie Bolen 1946.

Middle: Hunter and Tom Vinson circa late 1940s.

Bottom: Milton Joachim, Joe Plante, Butch Groat, Tom Vinson & Hellena Morehouse.

Photos courtesy of Tom & Yvette Vinson.

Pictured above (L to R)
Jim and Tilly Richards,
Cecelia Piff (hunter),
Frank Kukitz (hunter),
Alex McDougal (guide),
Carl Luger & Tom Vinson.

Photo courtesy
of Tom Vinson.

I have a picture of Carl Luger and me with some trophies *(game)*. The picture was from a Phillip Neweller hunting expedition. Philip was from Croppy, Pennsylvania and he owned a brewery there. He was the main hunter on that trip. He was a good photographer. The photo is of hunters who were on a twenty-one-day trip. Back in those days you were expected to come out with a full bag *(of game)*. You can see from the picture that there was no shortage of game.

I asked environmentalists what they were talking about. I asked them to consider if they were a wolf or a bear, would they tackle the biggest animal on the creek or would they kill the smaller calf? Wolves have killed more calves than anything, because it is the easiest. I told the environmentalist they would do the same thing, if they were wolves. That's what happens to the antlered population. The wolves killed the little ones first, which resulted in leaving few animals to reproduce. In 1939 you could count forty or fifty moose every morning, and now there is none. They affected the sheep some; the goats were not affected as much.

We were out there and watched the wolves eat up all the moose and caribou. We told the biologists about our observations. The government would not do anything about it because the environmentalists had too much influence. When we finally got the government involved with predator control, they decided to get some biologist to go out and make another survey because the environmentalists were demanding another survey on the caribou. They came out here with their stun guns and nets. They killed a couple of caribou before they finished. I don't even like to talk about things like that.

The biologists phoned up and came out here to have a meeting before they started. They wanted to see if I could get somebody involved that knew about the wildlife patterns. I had Red Creighton, Gordon Watt, a Ranger in the mountain area in Willmore, Judd Groat and myself and two biologists. They wanted to find out where the caribou were crossing Highway 40. We told them where the caribou migrated to. The biologists told us that they wanted to save the last few caribou. We suggested that they start some predator control. One biologist told us if he told the government that, they would cut their budget off and they would not be able to carry on what they were doing. I asked them if they thought they were going to do any good. The biologist told us that they were going to collar the caribou and find out where they were going. I told them they did not have to and that we could tell them where the caribou migrated. The caribou go up the mountain in the spring and come back down in the fall at about the same time each year, where they cross the highway.

Anyway, the biologists went out there and used their stun gun and nets. They got some collars on some of them. The next fall I was camped out on the west fork of the Sulphur River and two biologists rode into camp. They were camping at a campground close to ours. The pair kept their horses picketed there, where there was little grass. Someone had been in there before them and grazed the area off.

Every day the biologists would ride up to Hardscrabble Pass and listen with their beepers for the caribou. After a day of work they would stop into our camp for a coffee. The biologists told us that the caribou were over there past Blue Lake. I told them that they were always over

Pictured above:
Billie McGee
& his winter catch.
Billie McGee is pictured
here at a trapper's cabin
on Donald Flats, which is
ten miles downstream
from highway 40 on the
Berland River. The cabin
was located half-way
between the highway &
Chases Flats.

Photo courtesy of
Jim Babala.

there but that they won't always be there because it was getting late in the season. One night the biologists stopped in for coffee and told us that the 'beep' was gone—been gone for two days. I told them this was normal. They asked me where they went. I told them that the caribou holed up on the Berland or Pope Creek for a week or two before they pull on down into the timber. I told them to look there. It would be a two-day move with a pack outfit, if one knew where to go. The biologists told us that the caribou would not move that far in just two days. I told them that a caribou could go twenty miles in one-and-a half hours if they wanted to. That is what the government spends their money on: they just keep making another survey.

Billie McGee was on predator control, when they had that big scare about rabies. He collected a bounty on over one hundred wolves. Billie McGee was an old timer in the Hinton-Brule area. He used to own a piece of old Entrance. Billie worked for Mrs. Davidson at the Athabasca Dude Ranch. He also worked for other outfitters. McGee was a trapper.

Billie McGee told me before he died that he thought there were more wolves than when he was on predator control. Every time we talk about predator control, the environmentalists get up on their hind legs and say that wolves are noble animals and we can't do predator control.

When I was trapping out there, I used to watch certain groups of moose wintering here and there. Later in the winter, I returned to the area and there were three out of the four left and sometimes only two left. The wolves were taking a lot of moose. You would see a pack of fifteen wolves traveling around together. They would eat one moose every day. I remember once I saw a fresh moose kill. I came back the next morning and there was nothing left but a big patch of blood and his feet. The wolves even peeled the skin off of his skull. They chewed his entire nose.

Pictured left:
Top: Tom Vinson, September 1943.
Middle (L to R): Leroy Sharlow, Edwin Alstott, & Tom Vinson 1956.
Bottom: Tom Vinson takes the Bell party out in the Tonquin Valley—in 1948 while working for Fred Brewster.
Photos courtesy of Tom & Yvette Vinson.

We had two sessions of wolves. The first one was with that scare of rabies in the 1940s and 1950s. The Willmore Wilderness Park had a predator control on as well. They issued everyone with cyanide guns. All the trappers had them. I had some. They had a second predator control program that carried well into the 1950s. The government put bounties on wolves and cougars.

Sue What do you think about the grizzly bears in the mountain region?

Tom I don't think the government is paying too much attention to the grizzly matter. Premier Ralph Klein's bureaucrats took away some of the resident grizzly permits. We should have had seventy permits this year, but we will have fifty now. Out of fifty permits, only eight or nine grizzly get shot. I think that they should leave the seventy permits for residents because these grizzlies need to show a little respect. When the grizzly is hunted he respects man more. You know a grizzly is a lot harder to hunt than a sheep. When they saw you they

took off over the mountain. You didn't see them on the trail, when we could hunt them. Now you meet them on the trail and have a heck of a time to get them off the trail. The grizzly knows that he has no natural enemies.

There is no way that you can convince an environmentalist that they might be wrong. They think they know everything. You try and tell them but they say these wolves just kill the old animals that are going to die anyways— and the same with the bears.

Sue   What do you think about the biologists putting collars on the wolves and bears?

Tom   It is the worst thing that they can do. Every time they collared the bears in the park, there were more people that got hurt. Those old grizzlies don't think like a regular animal. They got it figured out. When the bear lies there after they are tranquilized, with their eyes blinkin' and they pull a tooth, earmark him and put a collar on his neck. When he gets up he's still thinking. You better look out when they meet you. He'll get even. I think it's the worst thing that they can do.

These bears have been going in their dens for generations and for centuries. I don't believe that we need to know where the bears den up, but the biologists really want to know. They can follow the bears with their receivers.

There was this biologist in Yellowstone, Wyoming. He collared up a bunch of grizzly bears. He maintained that the bears went into their caves the same day. The title of his paper was, The Day the Bears Go To Bed. He maintained that all the bears went to bed the same day. Just before the bears went to bed, that night a blizzard came and it snowed two feet. I didn't dispute his claim because he might be right. I know that our grizzlies don't go to bed all at the same time. I've seen bears stomping around here in January. I've seen their tracks in the snow.

Sue   You were in some tough country in some tough times, like in the 1940s. That's amazing that there just wasn't any development in this area. You say there were good trails from Jasper Park into the Willmore Wilderness area back then?

Yvette   The wardens used to cut trail, you know, years ago.

Tom   Guys like Alex Nelles *(father of Larry Nelles)*, Frank Wells, Frank Burstrom, Frank Camp, George Camp and Bob Jones had an area each *(these men were Jasper Park wardens)*. They'd stay out on that area. These old-time wardens would keep the trails clean by maintaining them. Once a month they would come into the town of Jasper. They kept the area in shape. They kept the culverts up and the phone lines *(from patrol cabin to patrol cabin)*. They had phone lines all over the Park. They kept the trails in top condition.

Pictured above:
Top: Tom & Yvette Vinson 2004.
Photo by
Susan Feddema-Leonard.
Bottom: Mining cabins at
Thoreau Creek.
Photo courtesy of Helny Jeck.

Pictured on left page (L to R):
Leroy Sharlow & Tom Vinson
Packin' up a caribou in 1956.
Photo courtesy of
Tom & Yvette Vinson

Yvette   All the Park wardens are unionized now and they have job descriptions.

Tom   They get the high salary—they don't do that kind of work anymore.

Sue   Can you tell me about the coal mine at Thoreau Creek?

Tom   There was a coal mine at Thoreau Creek on the east side of Willmore Wilderness Park. There is an old steam engine that is still there today. There's also a hole on the side of the mountain and a mine-car track across from Carson Creek. There used to be an old cabin at Carson Creek. The Blue Diamond Coal Company of Brule explored Thoreau Creek Mine. There are many shafts and coal seams. There was prospecting in that area.

The steam engine was small. Tom Groat hauled the steam engine in with a team of horses and runners. They ran the train up there on its own steam as well.

Sue   Willmore Wilderness is one of the last wilderness frontiers left in North America. I know that you knew Norman Willmore personally. Can you tell me about him?

Tom   He was Minister of Lands and Forests from 1955 till 1965. He was Minister of Labor from 1953 till 1955. But it was when he was Minister of Lands and Forests when he lobbied to protect the Willmore Wilderness area.

Before he was elected, Norman Willmore had a clothing store in Edson. He ran on the Social Credit ticket. He was in before the Social Creditors were defeated, and was well-liked in this country, really well liked. He could have run on any *(political)* ticket and would have got elected in this area. You could go and talk with him and he'd do something for you if he thought you were right. When all these outfitters came up here from all over hell and some from here, they had that Willmore country plugged with outfitters packing for oil companies. If you looked on some of the trapline cabin doors, you'd see names there of so-and-so and so-and-so for Shell Oil from Indiana .... and stuff like that.

We were realizing that the outfitters from Sundre and Rocky Mountain House didn't give a damn what happened up here. The southern outfitters would bid on the geological contracts and ended up with contracts in the Willmore area. But the locals were worried because we had never handled the geological parties. We were the summer business; the tourist business, and we were hoping there would be a place left to take clientele. So we were pressuring Norman Willmore to do something about the oil and gas exploration pressure, and he did. He declared the area a wilderness park where trapping, and hunting, and fishing, would be permitted. That was all—no motor vehicles. That's what we wanted, of course.

The only thing Norman didn't do was he didn't look into the situation as strongly as he should have—because they finally quit the geological work and went into seismic exploration. That's what we were afraid of. And sure as hell, they came up here with cats and bulldozers. We had 'em stopped at the park boundary. We held 'em up—Norman Willmore did, until he found out that there wasn't a thing he could do. The government had already leased the whole country. They had a lease on the whole damn country and the seismologists demanded to do their seismograph work. He had to let them in.

I was up there in Jasper where a lot of local people were backing the idea of creating a wilderness park. There were guys who were pretty important people in the Jasper and Edson areas. They were backing Norman Willmore up on this Park thing. I was in Jasper one time when they had these guys *(oil companies)* stopped. They had cats *(bulldozers)* sitting there and they were pretty damned mean. These oil companies were getting pretty 'owly'.

I was in Jasper and I was telling Oran Olson about it. He had the drug store there. His daughter still runs that Jasper Camera and Gifts. Oran grabbed the phone and he called up Norman right there and said, "Now Norman, you know you promised us that you'd never let those guys go in there with equipment." Norman told Oran that he couldn't stop them because they had a lease on the area. The government leased the whole damn country to them, unbeknown to him. This was done before his time, when somebody else was Minister. But he didn't go into that because he did promise us. So then he said, "They'll be glorified pack trails." And I said, "Yeah, they will be alright." The pack trails would be ruined—and they were too—all of them.

Ernest Manning was like that; he was the Premier—anything for industry! Those people went in there and they had no sense of reclamation. There are places in the Park where the whole flats were washed out where the bulldozers had crossed. Down the south branch of the Berland River, they damned near washed that whole meadow out—a big meadow. They'd take the topsoil off and run across there. The creeks would jam up and come down and wash out all the soil. There'd be cuts they'd make on the trails that are still there today—twenty feet deep. Some of the ditches are in Eagle's Nest Pass and lots of other places.

Pictured above (L to R):
Tom Vinson,
Victoria Moberly,
Audrey *(Moberly)* Printup, 2003.
Victoria & Audrey are the
granddaughters of
Henry Joachim.

Photo by
Susan Feddema-Leonard.

Pictured on left page:
Top: Tom Vinson at
Cathedral Mountain.
Middle: Tom Vinson on a
trail ride in the Tonquin Valley.
Bottom (L to R): Laura Vinson,
Nadeen *(Vinson)* Leonard,
Yvette Vinson & Fred Brewster,
circa mid 1960s.

Photos by
Tom & Yvette Vinson.

Sue   We couldn't believe it last year when we went through Eagle's Nest. The cat trail went right up and over Eagle's Nest and then up the west branch of the Sulphur River, all the way up to the head of Hardscrabble Creek. How much farther did the seismic exploration road go from there?

Tom   To the Jasper Park boundary, yeah, up Glacier Pass, up Hardscrabble Pass, to south fork of the Sulphur River.

Yvette   When did they stop the industry going in there?

Tom   Well, they didn't stop. They went up Kvass Creek. They went up every creek, Whistler Creek, every creek. If they could go up with a cat, they went up it and seismographed it all the way. They blew holes in the ground, you know.

Yvette   Then they had to get out of there at some point?

Tom   When they found out there was nothing, they pulled out. And as soon as they dropped the lease, well then the government held onto it. And it was lucky they didn't find something.

Sue   Did Norman Willmore lobby to make tighter legislation for the Park?

Tom   No, he was killed in 1965. He was coming up the highway, west of Niton Junction. A wheel come off a big truck and hit his car and killed him.

It's funny how these people find out these things. I was just thinking about that. It took about ten years (before) the people found out that it wasn't really legislated. Meanwhile, others were trying to crowd in with their Jeeps, or four-wheel drives. There were no quads then. I would tell them that they were breaking the law here. They would respond and tell me they were not breaking the law. They told me that there's no law made yet. Then we had to go back to the government and get them to legislate the area to protect it. We had to make a law so that people could not go into Willmore Wilderness with motorized vehicles.

Yeah, it was a bad situation. It was all politics. But it's funny how people like to destroy things. As long as they had a vehicle they could go in the Willmore *(Park)*. And they did too. Quads ended up in there and lots of them. I don't know that they would ever have saved Willmore as a wilderness if there had been as many quads then as there are now.

I went to a meeting and there were sixty guys. Every one of 'em had two or three quads, and four-wheel drives. And they told the government that they wouldn't stand for any restrictions at all. You know, they'd get up and make a big long spiel that they didn't have to do this and

they didn't have to do that. And they weren't doing any harm. I got up there and I said," I don't think you guys have got the right to go up there with all your four-wheel drives and quads and destroy all the Alpine flowers."

Sue   Did you guys put Norman Willmore's name forward for the Park then? How did that happen?

Tom   Well, I think they named the Park after him after he was killed. But that's the way it started—the outfitters pressuring Norman Willmore. He was a guy that would listen to you. He tried to do the best he could. Well, he was busy as a Cabinet Minister when I got to know him. He went on a holiday with Brewster and went into the Tonquin Valley. Fred was a personal friend of Willmore.

I was freighting *(supplies)* into the Tonquin with snow machines. Norman Willmore went in there with us and cross-country skied out. He had a hell of a trip in there. I asked Fred, I said, "I don't know Norman that good. What the hell does a man talk to a politician about?" Like he was going to be there a couple of nights or so. Brewster said, "Just talk about anything but politics. When you want to talk politics to a politician go to his office, but don't invite him out to go on a trip and talk politics."

Norman Willmore set up the Alberta Trappers Association. The first meeting was held in Edson, Alberta. I still have the button that Norman Willmore gave us at that meeting. We formed the Alberta Trappers Association in order that trappers would have a voice and that government would listen to our concerns.

Sue   Well, I'm really glad you guys lobbied Norman Willmore. Who helped you?

Tom   Well, all the outfitters, like Hargreaves, Kitchen and Creighton and Larry McGuire and even a lot of the town people. We got everyone behind us and everybody in this area knew Norman Willmore and knew he was a guy you could talk to.

Sue   What happened to the outfitters that came from southern Alberta?

Tom   Once the helicopters came in, it put an end to the geological survey parties. Many of the southern outfitters who came into this country were out of business, so they went into the business of guiding hunters.

Sue   Norman Willmore has helped preserve a legacy for future generations. Have your children been influenced by the Willmore Wilderness area? Have they followed your footsteps in any way?

Tom All my children worked in the outfitting business. Laura started working on the desk at Jasper Park Lodge first. She also helped me in the hunting camps. I have a picture of her skinning out bear feet in one of our hunting camps.

Lavone, Lenore and Nona *(Tom's daughters)* ran the pony barn in Jasper. They had sixty head of horses there and were renting them out. I bought the pony barns from Fred Brewster, and operated them out of Jasper, the Tonquin Valley, Skyline and Shovel Pass. I had horses at Maligne and ran the backcountry trips too. We had over one hundred head of horses out there. I also outfitted hunting trips in the fall. My daughters worked in the mountains with me and on the trail, and also helped me when I outfitted summer trips. In fact, the girls were on the trail with ol' Albert Norris. *(Albert Norris was half-brother to Dean Swift and Lotti Swift of Jasper. Larry Nelles' father, Alex Nelles' first wife was Lotti Swift. When she died, Larry's dad married again.)*

I decided to turn part of the business over to Lenore and her husband, Ron (Moore). I also turned part over to Lavone and her husband, Wald (Olson). Wald and Lavone ran the Tonquin Valley. Ron and Lenore ran the pony barns and Skyline.

Tom, my son started working at the pony barns for me when he was nine years old. He started when he was big enough to carry a scoop shovel of horse turds.

Yvette Robert Kroch wrote stories regarding Alberta. At that time, he was writing in regards to the 1967 Centennial. Robert authored an article about our operation on the Skyline in Jasper Park after he came with us on a trail ride. He took pictures of the alpine flowers and wildlife. My young Tommy was only nine years old at the time. Robert wrote about him in his article.

Tom Tom took over my bighorn sheep permits. Tom and his wife, Shawn are in the summer tourist business now. He runs summer trail rides for the tourism industry.

Sue Tom is the President of the Alberta Outfitters Association now.

Tom The AOA is still recognized by the government.

Yvette   Lenore is working with Randy Babala in the Yukon. She is still in the outfitting business.

Tom   Wald and Lavone still take the odd trip out in Willmore Wilderness Park. Nadeen and her husband, Dan *(Leonard, son of Bazil Leonard)* work in the hunting end of it with Dave Wiens. Dave runs a hunting outfit in northern British Columbia called Stone Mountain Safaris. Dan and Deenie have worked for him close to fifteen years. Danny guides and Deenie cooks. Yes, they are still in the business.

Yvette   Nona enjoys her first love—art. Because she has lived in many places, her art subjects are varied: western, native and wildlife. She is self-taught and creates from her heart. She paints the mountains, horses, wildlife, people and her experiences.

Tom   Nona still makes a trip into the mountains every once in awhile. She married Keith Foster, a park warden.

Yvette   Laura initially sang country and western music. Now she sings contemporary music. She's had five Juno nominations. My favorite song is Rocky Mountain Skyline. She now works at the Ben Calf Robe School *(a school in Edmonton for Native and Metis children)*.

Sue   All your children have carried on the tradition of the Rocky Mountains. What do you see as the future for Willmore Wilderness Park?

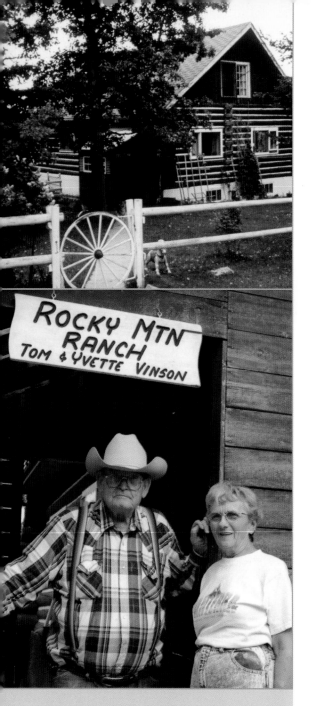

Tom The government needs to burn off some of the willows. There is a big need for controlled burns. I said this forty years ago. There is also a big need for predator control. The biologists listen but they don't pay any attention to what you're saying. You are supposed to go along with the way they are thinking. There were five of us who were experienced mountain men, speaking to the biologists. We all told them the same thing. They came too late and completed a survey on what caribou was left in the mountainous areas, because the wolves had taken most of them. The thing to do was to get after the predators to save the few caribou that were left. The biologists couldn't do that because the bureaucracy would cut their budget off. So they spent their money snaring and tranquilizing the caribou and from that, two caribou were killed—one in the net and one with a tranquilizer gun.

Sue Tom, you've been one of the longest operating outfitters during the twentieth century. You've had years of experience and a great deal of knowledge to impart to our readers. I want to thank you very much for the time you gave me for this interview. I know that your children are carrying on the tradition of outfitting and that your family name is certainly one of the biggest in the industry.

Tom You're welcome.

Pictured above:
Top: Vinson homeplace 2003.
Photo courtesy of
Tom & Yvette Vinson.

Bottom: Tom & Yvette Vinson 2003.
Photo by Susan Feddema-Leonard.

Pictured right page:
Tom Vinson on a movie set in 1946.
Tom is standing by the white horse.

Photo courtesy of Tom & Yvette Vinson

CHAPTER TWELVE:
Tom McCready

(This transcript is an excerpt from an interview that Vickie Wallace had with Tom McCready on May 2, 1995. Vickie completed the interview for the Jasper Historical Society.)

My dad, originally from Ontario, came to Jasper in 1910 and met my mother who was working as a cook for her brothers. My mother, Myrtle was the twin sister of outfitter, Jack Hargreaves. My mom loved horses, hiking, and picnics. I was born in Jasper on October 15, 1923 in the house that my dad and Uncle Roy Hargreaves built. My mother was a good gardener and always had a big garden.

When I grew up in Jasper there were no elk. I remember seeing the first elk when they shipped elk into this area by railway. Everyone was in awe, because it was a strange animal. We were used to the deer and moose.

I have always loved horses. My first horseback trip over the Icefield Parkway was when I wasn't very old. I took the last horse that the *Otto Brothers* had from their outfitting days. I rode that horse from the Athabasca Falls to the Columbia Fields. I turned that horse over to a fellow by the name of Gordon Galvin. He and two or three of his friends were going to take the horse to pack into Fortress Lake because they were going to prospect for gold that fall and spend the winter trapping.

My first paying job, after running a paper route over at the Jasper Park Lodge, was to work for Fred Brewster grazing seventy head of horses from the confluence of the Maligne River and the Athabasca River. There's a picnic area there now. There used to be a little shack and a set of corrals and I used to keep seventy head of horses in there all summer long. Charlie Bolan was the barn boss working for Fred Brewster, running the pony barns at Jasper Park Lodge. Every Friday I'd have to graze the horses over to the lodge and these horses would be exchanged for the horses that were in the pony barns. I would bring those other horses over to the Maligne range.

During the summer, my mother and my dad would come out periodically with a picnic lunch and I would meet them at Lake Annette and have a real nice home-cooked meal that my mother made. Through the summer, there were a few people that lived around Lake Edith that had children. There wouldn't be a family that moved into Lake Edith that I didn't know about. If there were any kids there, I would always show up around dinnertime and I'd give the kids a ride. Invariably they would come out with some lemonade and some sandwiches and stuff. I kind of rode the grub line there for part of the summer. My own food, the food that was supplied to me by Fred, was pretty meagre. I had oatmeal porridge; I had rice and raisins; I had sardines and bully beef but no fresh potatoes or carrots, except for what my mother would give me. I'd catch a fish every once in awhile out of Maligne or the Athabasca River. I was a pretty good fisherman then, so that would be a change from sardines and bully beef. The biggest change was when Mother would bring out a picnic lunch and we would meet at Lake Annette. I worked all summer long for Fred. I worked sixty-four days total and I made sixty-four dollars that summer.

I remember taking a friend of mine out. He came and got me one evening, so we took in the late show. I bought him a ticket to the show and I bought him a milkshake. When I left, I bought a package of gum and a comic book. I hadn't spent more than a dollar that evening. I was a rich man. That was the first time I was able to buy Christmas presents for the family. I had sixty-four dollars to spend and I bought my second set of skis, boots and poles too with my earnings. I was thirteen years old when I worked for Fred. I was born and brought up with horses, so it wasn't a big job for me, it was just a job. I found Fred very good to work for. He always treated me well. He wasn't too strong in the grocery department, but I lived.

My uncles were outfitters. My Uncle George Hargreaves had an outfit at Jackman near Valemount *(B.C)*. When Uncle George died *(1936),* he gave us seven horses and that was the nucleus of my start in outfitting.

I worked for the Ski Patrol for eleven years, which gave me winter employment. The ski hill was generally closed by April of each year and it would be time to go outfitting. The outfitting business kept me busy all summer and fall. One business would overlap the other. I would be hunting to the fifteenth of November and the ski school started the same day. So lots of times I'd come in from outfitting, take off my cowboy hat and chaps, grab my skis and ski boots and head for Marmot. I love the outfitting and I love to ski and I love the mountains.

Frank Owens worked for the government for years and years. He was originally a trapper and trapped on the Smoky River. He would go out to Mt. Robson, put his snowshoes on and go to Berg Lake, eventually find his way down the Smoky, and trap the Jackpine and Hardscrabble Creek. During the Depression, he and another fellow got caught trapping in the Park *(Jasper).* They were trapping on Jack Creek on the Rocky River. They trapped whatever they could

catch—marten and lynx. Jack Otto drove them down to their trapline and dropped them off. Jack was a meticulous fellow. He had recorded taking them down in a taxi and what he charged them. When an accountant was doing Jack's books, he asked what this trip was regarding—in the winter down to Rocky River. This accountant also did some work for the government and he let it slip out. Two of the wardens from here *(Jasper)*, Frank Bryant and Frank Wells went down and caught them. Poaching was quite a problem back in those days. People had to make money some way. However, poaching stopped after the Dirty Thirties.

The biggest change that I've seen in Jasper is that when I was a kid it was all horses. The roadwork was done with horses. Everybody traveled with horses—then the automobile came. Today, Jasper is a modern town. That's the biggest change.

In the backcountry and wilderness areas, there have been changes with the upgrading of the trail systems. The government has bigger and better-bred horses. Jasper Park trail crews keep the trails open throughout the Park. They are wonderful trails. In my outfitting day, we had to cut a lot of the trails and we always had an axe on our saddles. We never went anywhere without an axe. You had to cut trail whenever you left the Park *(Jasper).*

I outfitted in Willmore Wilderness Park from 1945 right through to 1972. I had two or three favorite places. Falls Creek was one of my base hunting camps and it has a lot of fond memories. Falls Creek is the creek that comes in just above Big Grave Flats. It's the creek south of Whistler Creek. Anyone who has been in Willmore knows where Whistler Creek runs. It was a pretty good creek, where you could take horses up. Falls Creek was in kind of an out-of-the-way place that was up a little bit higher. Camp was up at tree line. There was good horse feed and a good basin for your horses to run in. You never had to worry about your horses. There was always good hunting and it was away from everybody else. It was only good on the early hunts because the snow hit there pretty early.

Hardscrabble Pass has a lot of fond memories and Blue Grouse camp. I had another camp down at Big Grave where I always had fine hunting—that's always been a fond place.

I always tried to limit my hunts to two hunters because I found any more than that, the competition was too great. So I limited my hunts to two hunters, two guides, a cook and a horse wrangler. There would be a crew of four. Sometimes I would be forced to take out another hunter but I didn't like it. There were a lot of 'threes' that liked to come together. We were committed to take them, but I found I had greater success if I took two hunters.

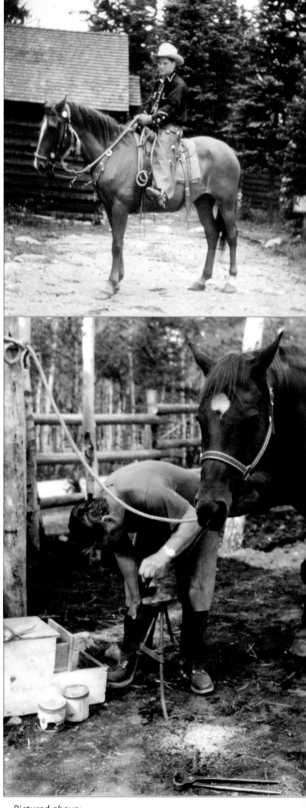

Pictured above:
Top: Tom McCready on a horse in his early 20s.
Bottom: Tom McCready shoeing.
Photos courtesy of Fay McCready.

I was trophy hunting and I never wasted anything. We always kept the meat. We would hunt sheep, goat, big timberline bucks, mule deer bucks, moose, caribou, grizzly bear and black bear. When I first started outfitting, we would go for thirty days. We would take two hunts out in the fall and they would be a month long. Later, right after the war, people didn't seem to have the time that the earlier hunters had. So I had to limit the hunts to twenty-one days; a lot of them wanted ten-day hunts and two-week hunts. I was quite successful because I would explain to the hunter that it was too short. You had to travel a minimum of two days to get to the hunting country. So that's four days off of a fourteen-day hunt which only left him ten days to hunt. So I said by the time you get out there and get back it shortens your hunt— take an extra week—you'll do much better and get better trophies. That's the way it worked out. When I first started, I took hunters out for $25 dollars per day. When I ended up, I charged $85 dollars per day.

Fay Jervis of McBride, B.C. and I got married in 1953. Fay cooked some of the time on the summer trips. I had another cook for the fall hunts. Fay had to be home because of the children being in school. It was good for her to be home because there were always phone calls and letters to write. She looked after things when I was away. She kept the business end of things going when I was on the trail.

Picutred above:
Tom McCready's outfit
on Hardscrabble Pass.

Photo courtesy of
Fay McCready

I think living in Jasper National Park helped me over the years because a lot of people come here in the summer time. I booked a lot of people to go fishing in the Tonquin. People that just came here right off the street. People would read our brochure and the next thing you know the phone would ring, and we were going out with a party. I had a camp up in the Tonquin from 1946 to the time I retired in 1972. Brewsters camped there originally. Fred Brewster camped at one end of the lake but then he moved up to the middle of the lake into the 'Narrows.' The first time I was there was in 1943 with my brother, George. The next time I went to the Tonquin was in 1946. I had taken a fishing party in from the States, which consisted of three doctors and their wives. They were from Cincinnati, Ohio and were wonderful people. It just progressed from there. I had a cookhouse and a series of cabins in there. They were tent frames.

In order to get some boats into the Tonquin for my fishermen, I tinned the bottom of three boats and took them in by skis in the wintertime. That was a pretty tough trip. I had another fellow help me. I made a harness and one fellow pulled and the other fellow pushed. We made a trip for each boat. We took three boats in one year and two in another year.

I worked for seven years during the late 1970s and 1980s on cabin maintenance for Parks Canada. I worked on a lot of cabins on the south boundary and the north boundary *(between Jasper Park and*

Willmore Wilderness Park). We completely rebuilt the Willow Creek District cabin and shed. We also did work at Wilbur and Blue Creek. We gutted the cabin at Blue Creek and had to put in new floor joists. We also did a lot of work on the cabins on the south boundary of the Park. I had two fellows working with me. I had my son, Todd work with me a couple of years. He was my right hand man, a hard worker, and very good with horses. For the first couple of years, we did everything with horses. We used helicopters after we got into the major construction.

Two of my favourite spots in Jasper Park were the Willow Creek area and Little Heaven Summit. You could travel on the north boundary trail into Willmore Wilderness Park via Little Heaven and Glacier Pass. I always preferred the north boundary of the park. It is nicer country than the south boundary. There are more meadows and much better horse feed in the north. My horses wintered in the Willow Creek area for ten years. We didn't pay for the winter range but did pay for our summer range. We had a winter range down at Pocahontas that we paid a little grazing fee on. When Parks Canada moved all of the outfitters from along the highway up into Willow Creek, we didn't have to pay a fee. With all the government horses, there were two hundred and fifty head of horses running at Willow Creek. There were quite a number of elk, so the horses and elk would intermix. You'd find the elk coming in after the horses worked over an area. Horses will paw up a lot of grass that they don't eat. The elk would come in and forage after the horses had been pawing. It definitely helped the elk when they grazed with the horses.

The last time I gathered my horses up at Willow Creek was in 1972. We had to round them up. There was a holding pen and a double set of corrals at Mud Creek Flats. We could gather the horses

Pictured left:
Tom McCready at
Blue Grouse Camp.

Photo courtesy of
Fay McCready.

from three different directions into the corrals at Mud Creek until it was full. Then we would trail them down and put them through the bars just between Willow Creek and Seldom Inn. The bar was a drift fence that came down off the hill. There was a gate that was close to Willow Creek, a set of bars at Seldom Inn. You would just let the bars down and let the horses go, so you could trail them back to Jasper. The corral was a godsend—otherwise you'd have to gather one bunch of horses, take them all the way down to the bars, then come all the way back to hunt horses again. So that was a very central location.

Since the horses have been banned from Willow Creek, the elk population has really dropped. This was occurring when I was on the cabin maintenance *(late 1970s–'80s.)* You'd see fewer and fewer elk. I was in the north country for four years, working on the cabins and every year there would be less and less elk. When the horses moved out, the brush took over in the meadow. The brush took over the grassland and forced the elk out of there. I believe the predators had an effect on them too. There were lots of wolves in the area and a few cougars. It used to be easier for elk to winter down in the main valley than it was up at Willow Creek. There was more snow on Willow Creek and winter was a month longer.

I have a story that I want to tell about something that I found when I was out hunting in Willmore Wilderness Park. I was surrounded by some arctic willow. It was coarse willow and nothing really eats it. I was looking for a place to sit down to glass a basin for bighorn sheep. *(It is common practice to use binoculars and spotting scopes to 'glass' for game.)* I finally pulled some willow out, made a place to sit and put my packsack down. But I couldn't get my feet comfortable so I started kicking my heel in. Every time I kicked my heel in, something moved about three feet away from me. So I finally pulled a bunch more brush out and kicked more dust off and I picked up a big bull buffalo skull. Part of the eye sockets were there, however it was pretty well decomposed. It was kind of brown looking because it had been under the dust so long. To me, it was a real trophy. This was just up on the head of Rock Creek between Mile 58 and Mile 59 on the old Forestry Trail. It was on the right hand side of the trail, on a little knob there. That's the Old Indian Trail. I found this skull in the 1960s.

I found another skull—part of a skull at Little Heaven Summit—right in the creek. We were looking for gravel to put in the tower for the radio. We were chasing around these gopher holes that had white rocks on them. We couldn't find any gravel so I started up and down the creek. I said there has got to be gravel somewhere on this creek. I went to step across the creek and, lo and behold, there was a buffalo horn sticking out. So I wrenched this buffalo head out of the creek and washed it off.

The biggest find was when they were putting the road around Medicine Lake. They had a 'borrow' pit a couple of miles below Medicine Lake. They were hauling gravel out of

there—just pit run gravel—and they uncovered a whole herd of buffalo there. They were buried under tons of rock, so they probably had been killed by an avalanche in the spring or winter. They uncovered all the skulls when they started to haul gravel out of there.

When we were kids traveling around, we found buffalo skulls on the government range over on Buffalo Prairie through the Valley of Five. There weren't a great amount of them but we'd see them occasionally. We even found them up on the Pyramid Bench. There were buffalo scattered throughout this country.

I was happy when Parks Canada tried to re-introduce bison in the north part of the Park. I was hoping that the buffalo would take and stay. They would be an added attraction. The buffalo were here years ago. Adam Joachim remembered when the buffalo died. Adam was an old Indian from Grande Cache. He was just a young boy and it was a very, very severe winter—a deep snow winter. The buffalo died that winter. Adam was living at Grande Cache. *(Adam Joachim was born in 1875 and was a guide, spiritual leader and political leader of the Aseniwuche Winewak or Rocky Mountain People. Adam worked as a guide for outfitters namely, the Otto Brothers, Stan Clark, Curly Phillips and Jack Hargreaves. He was well educated, speaking four languages. He died at Muskeg in 1959.)*

Pictured above:
Wade Berry, Todd, Fay, Tom & Chris McCready.
Photo courtesy of Fay McCready.

Interview with Fay McCready

Sue It is May 12, 2005 and I am at the home of Fay McCready, in Jasper, Alberta. I came to visit Fay at the urging of Larry Nelles, a close friend of the McCready family, to find out about the McCready guide and outfitting business, firsthand.

Fay, I know that you worked alongside your husband, supporting his outfitting business both off and on the trail. Most outfitting wives are the heart and soul of the outfit. The evidence of your love for the mountains and your family is shown in the short excerpt that Tom penned in 1996 for the book, *Jasper Reflections*. "Not long ago, Fay and I took two grandchildren out to Mt. Robson where we set up the cook tent, stove and tables in a traditional fashion. Fay could not wait to start cooking. The nostalgia was something else." In 1997, shortly after writing this passage, Tom passed away. I know that your husband, Tom was a well-known guide and outfitter. Can you tell me about him?

Fay When Tom was only eight years old, he went out on an eighteen-day trip, and by the time he was ten years of age, he was able to pack a horse. Tom knew full well that everyone was expected to do their share of work.

When I first met Tom, he didn't have an outfit. He was working for his uncle. As a teenager, he wrangled horses for his uncle, Jack Hargreaves. Jack was his mother's twin brother. Tom's mother's family was in the outfitting business, which was known at one time as the *Hargreaves Brothers*. Tom got his apprenticeship with his uncles, but Tom's hero was his uncle, George Hargreaves. His Uncle George had an outfitting operation in Valemount, B.C. Tom worked his summers as a horse wrangler. He got up early every morning and went out and looked for the horses. After he brought them into camp, he got them ready for the day's work. George died in 1936 and is buried at the headwaters of Sheep Creek.

When Tom was a young adult and after the Second World War in 1945, he became a licensed guide and began leading packhorse expeditions. Tom wrote the following excerpt in *Jasper Reflections*. "My horse outfitting business was starting to take off with many enquiries for summer and fishing trips, with big game hunters wishing to book in September and October for hunting. Young colts that were yearlings and two-year-olds when I left for the Navy were now four, five and six—much needed for the string. Springtime would find me riding and training these colts. There were the usual blow-ups and wrecks when breaking horses. I suffered a broken wrist, broken legs, three times, and a broken neck—all horse related—and each a story of its own."

Pictured above:
Fay & Tom McCready
in 1953 at Rock Creek
in what is now known as
Willmore Wilderness Park.

Photo courtesy of
Fay McCready.

Tom led organized pack trips into the mountains from our base in Jasper. He took out tourists and fishermen during the summer months. In the fall, he took out big game hunters and never had a shortage of business. Tom guided a lot of Americans and some Canadians. He would correspond with his customers before they arrived in the area, to get to know the person before they went on the trail with him. Tom would send Christmas cards years later to his customers, who became his friends.

There was one good story about Tom's good friend, Tom Ross, which I would like to share, in Tom's own words in *Jasper Reflections*. "My good friend, Tom Ross, had been running a landing barge during the Normandy Landing. As the war was winding down, Tom was back on the west coast. Before being discharged from the Canadian Navy, we were granted a one-month leave. This found Tom and me on the banks of the Athabasca River, below the confluence of Rocky River across from Devona. *(Devona is twenty-five miles east of Jasper directly across from Disaster Point and Rocky River.)* Our worldly possessions consisted of a small duffle bag each and two riding saddles. We borrowed bedrolls. A rowboat was coming across to pick us up and take us to camp at Devona. We were both going out on a thirty-day hunting trip—Tom Ross with Red Creighton, and I with my Uncle Jack Hargreaves, two brand-new horse wranglers eager to be back riding again. The winters of 1945-1946, I ran the Jasper skating rink, while summer and fall would find me working out on the trail. That fall, I had my first big game hunters on two thirty-day hunting trips, using mostly my own horses."

Sue I found Tom Ross' writing on a trapline cabin in the Jackpine Valley. I believe the cabin was built by Art Allen. There is evidence of Red Creighton being there as well. The writing dates back to November 1945. I know that these guys were trapping the Jackpine Valley. They left notes on the cabin wall describing the weather conditions and how they were doing trapping. The only mention that I can find about Tom Ross is in the book by Frank Camp called *Roots of the Rockies*. In there it states, "That winter *(1948-49)* a new *(Jasper Park)* warden was hired, Tom Ross, a Navy veteran. When he arrived home, he went to work for Red Creighton as a trail cook for hunting parties. He had spent the winters as a trapper with Red and Art Allen on the Jackpine River, a tributary of the Smoky River, before becoming a park warden. Tom's qualifications to be a warden were excellent, having lived in Jasper most of his life. He knew the country and the Park. His interest was in the outdoors—and he had the ability of a back-country traveler."

The writings that I found on the wall clearly show that Tom, Art and Red were on the Jackpine in 1945 and 1946 from November to the end of January. Art Allen's writing in the cabin continued to 1950. Apparently Tom Ross got hired as a Jasper Park warden in 1948 and he did not go back to that country to trap.

Fay Tom Ross and my Tom were very close friends. They were like brothers. It is interesting that you found the writing on that old cabin in the Jackpine Valley.

Sue Can you tell me a little about your life with Tom on a personal level?

Fay I was born in Drumheller, Alberta in 1934. My family moved to McBride in 1945. I moved four years later to Jasper, Alberta to work and to complete my high school grades. Tom and I were married in 1953 and we had three children: Tess, Todd and Chris. Tom made a short excerpt about our family in the same book. He wrote, "Our children loved the great outdoors and accompanied Fay and me on many pack trips." Our family had a great love of the mountains and the outdoor life.

Tom eventually bought his Uncle Jack's horses and outfit off him. Sometimes Tom staged out of Rock Lake. Other times, it would take Tom and his Uncle Jack three days to ride through Jasper Park to get to their hunting area *(in Willmore Park)*. He would trail the horses from Jasper to Seldom Inn, which is about fifty miles north of Jasper. They would have to trail three days before they got into the hunting territory.

Sue Who bought the outfit off of Tom McCready?

Pictured above:
Top: Fay McCready.
Middle: Tom McCready 'The Cook.'
Bottom: Tom McCready on the North Boundary of Jasper National Park.
Photos courtesy of Fay McCready.

Fay He sold his outfit to Jim Simpson *(a first cousin of Dave Simpson)*. Tom also described his leaving outfitting in *Jasper Reflections*. "In 1972, I had to give up outfitting because of a heart condition—I underwent open heart surgery. Within two months, I was working for the *(Jasper)* Warden Service running the cabin crew, with my son, Todd and Floyd Coleman as helpers. We built some new cabins and repaired many existing ones. At first, we packed all our material on horses, but soon we were using Gary Forman of Yellowhead Helicopters."

Cody Dixon bought the trail-riding portion of the business, which was based out of Jasper Park. He bought the Jasper Park permit to give him the right to offer trail rides in the National Park. Jim Simpson bought the hunting area that was in Willmore Wilderness Park.

Sue I remember that George Kelley bought the permits from Jim Simpson in 1988 or 1989. Jim Simpson must have had the permits for fifteen years.

Fay When Tom sold the outfit, he worked with Jim for a year. So, 1973 would have been Tom's last year.

Tom had many good men working for him. Eddie Regnier worked for us when he was a very young guy and he stayed with us for a long time. Ed married Margaret Wilkins. Her father was a Jasper Park warden. Eddie's brother, Richard *(Dick)* Regnier was also a guide and handled a part of the 'outfit' for one summer.

Another cowboy that worked for us was Wald Olson and he was eighteen or nineteen at the time. He married Tom Vinson's daughter, Levone. Bill McKinnon worked for us for a long time. He lives in Houston, B.C. Bob Barker worked for us for quite a few years before he became a Jasper Park warden. Tom Timperly also worked as a wrangler, packer and guide.

Louis Joachim, Louis Delorme and Dave McDonald were from Grande Cache and they also worked for Tom. These men were Rocky Mountain Cree guides and wranglers. Dave McDonald worked on the hunting trips in Willmore Wilderness Park. Louis Joachim and Louis Delorme went on the summer trips to the Tonquin Valley where they packed in for the Alpine Club of Canada.

Although there were other men who guided and wrangled for Tom, those mentioned stayed with us the longest. Not only were there good men working for us, but also wonderful lady trail cooks. Alva William, sister of Bill McKinnon cooked on many of the fall hunts. Their mother, Mrs. McKinnon was our cook in the Tonquin summer camps for several years. Lee Hartley cooked several seasons in the Tonquin. Lois *(Anderson)* Berry and Claudette *(Bierney)* Kilgour were trail cooks on fall hunts in Willmore Wilderness Park.

Tom would go up Mt. Robson way on some of the summer trips. I was on one of those trips. That was with Buster Duncan, one of our relations and a B.C. outfitter. Ellie Duncan, Buster's daughter was the cook on that trip. It was Buster, Ellie, Tom and I and guests. *(Buster Duncan was married to Margie Hargreaves, who was one of Roy Hargreaves' daughters.)*

One time Tom told me he wanted me at Rock Lake at eight in the morning, to go out on a trip. That night I had to find someone to look after my children and drove to Rock Lake, so that I could go out on the trail. Tom had hired another cook, so I just helped out wherever needed. I did go on a few summer trips with Tom.

It was a lot of work being an outfitter's wife, because the crew lived with us. I had to prepare meals and lunches. There was so much to do to get ready for the trip. We always had homemade pies and bread and buns. I must say, when the Dixon's bought our summer trail-riding permits, they cooked over the open fire. I really admire people who do that.

My first trip cooking was a trip in the Tonquin Valley. There were twenty of us all together, with sixteen guests. We trailed the horses from the Jasper town site to the Marmot turnoff. We packed up at the turnoff where you go to Marmot Basin. I was dressed in jeans and a jean jacket.

It was raining when we were packing up. Going over Maccarib Pass, it rained and snowed. I was soaked before I ever left. We stopped for lunch somewhere and I ate my sandwich like a buzz saw because my teeth were chattering. I was so frozen that I couldn't feel my hands or my feet. We were close to camp and I begged them to let me lay down. I know now that I was suffering from the effects of hypothermia. I really wanted to go to sleep. The guys told me that we were really close. John Unland was another Jasper outfitter who was our neighbor and

we were able to borrow a camp stove from him, so that there would be two camp stoves. As it turned out, he had a party in and he needed his stove.

Everyone put their wet boots and socks around my camp stove. I cooked supper, which was quite an experience, as I had never cooked on the trail before. Tom taught everyone else how to cook in the bush, but he didn't teach me. Anyway, they ate so much food! Before every meal, they sang grace and the guests sang it in harmony.

The next morning, a guest made the porridge, stirring it with a kindling stick. Boy, these people ate! Everyone had enough to eat, but I wasn't too sure how much to cook for twenty people as it was my first time cooking on the trail. The people in the camp found some plastic bags and stitched them together so that we would have rain gear for our ride out. My introduction to the outfitting business was quite a memorable experience. I got into camp, and I was so soaked and so tired and so cold! After riding all day, my work started by preparing a full meal for everyone.

Sue Did Tom ever tell you about traveling up the Smoky River with Roy Hargreaves when they went to Corral Creek to round up their horses?

Fay   I was expecting Christine, my last child when Tom's uncle, Roy Hargreaves wanted Tom to go in the springtime where the horses were on the winter range. They would take a rubber dinghy up the Smoky River and use it to cross *(at Clark's Crossing).* They would swim their horses across the river. The agreement was, if the baby was a boy, Tom would name him Clay. If it was a girl, I could name the baby: which it was, thus, "Christine".

Tom told me that Uncle Roy was talking away as they were rowing in the rubber dingy and he wasn't looking where he was going. Tom said it was a most harrowing trip that he had with Uncle Roy. When they were crossing the Smoky River in the dinghy, it would sometimes fold over a wave and Uncle Roy would suddenly disappear from sight for a frightening moment. The Smoky was quite a river and needed to be taken seriously. They managed to ford the Smoky in the rubber boat and the horses swam across. It was quite a trip.

Sue   I have seen outfitters, guides and hunters who have crossed the Smoky River in a rubber dinghy and they too found the river crossing distressing, to say the least.

Fay   For many years, Tom took out geological survey trips in the summer months and one particular one was for one hundred and twenty days. The only contact with Tom was a piece

Pictured above:
Tom McCready at
Berg Lake Lodge in 1991.

Photo courtesy of
Fay McCready.

of paper held together with a postage stamp that I received in the mail, after he had been on the trail for some time. Our first baby was just a few months old when he left. The note told me to get Uncle Jack *(Hargreaves)* to drive baby Tess and I out to the McLeod River, where he was going to be camped, which we did for a short couple of days' visit.

Working as an outfitter in the Canadian Rockies was a way of life for Tom. He had such a passion for the mountains and he found solace in the natural elements of the land. Tom loved to ride and take extended trips into the wilderness. It was a way of life for him, as the bush was his home. Tom grew up with outfitting as a boy and was completely comfortable in the hills. Living in a tent in the great outdoors was like being in a five-star hotel. As long as Tom could hear the horses' bells, he could sleep. Tom loved the simple things of life, like the trail, a nice clear stream, or just watching the horses graze in the meadow.

Tom and Larry Nelles both grew up in Jasper. Tom was from an outfitting family and Larry was the son of a Jasper Park warden. Tom and Larry were like brothers. Both of these men had a love of horses, which was a special bond they shared. There is something very special about the spirit of the horse that both Larry and Tom understood. The horse is a lifeline in the mountains and they are your legs. Both Tom and Larry knew how to become one with the horse. I am glad Larry encouraged your coming here.

Pictured above:
Top: Fay & Tom McCready 1994.
Bottom: Todd McCready at 9 yrs.

Pictured on right page (L to R):
Chris, Tom & Todd McCready.

Photos courtesy of
Fay McCready.

Sue There were other Jasper outfitters who had a connection to Willmore Wilderness Park. Some of the early outfitters were Curly Phillips, Bert Wilkins, Otto Brothers, Stan Kitchen, Red Creighton, Johnny Unland, Fred and Jack Brewster—to name a few. I am glad to have this chance to meet with you to show that there were no boundaries between us in the past. There was a historical flow of traffic between the Athabasca Valley, the Smoky River Valley, the Fraser River Valley and the Kakwa River Valley. Today, we have park boundaries and invisible borders created by our governments.

Fay Leonard Jeck was another Jasper outfitter who worked in Willmore Wilderness Park. He was our next-door neighbour and he bought his outfit from Art Allen.

Sue It's hard to write about everybody, but we can show how the travel patterns were in the past, through the eyes of a few outfitters, guides and trail cooks.

Fay It was a good life that Tom lived. The mountains were his life and I am grateful that he could live it to the fullest. He loved to go horseback riding and truly loved horses. He loved the wilderness. Riding a horse on the mountain trails was a truly spiritual connection for Tom. In closing, I would like to leave the last word to Tom. He wrote about ranch life at Mt. Robson from 1925 to 1936 in *Jasper Reflections*.

"Our family spent most of the school holidays *(all seasons)* at the Mt. Robson Ranch with Uncle Roy and Aunt Sophia Hargreaves or with Uncle George Hargreaves at the Sunshine Ranch near Valemount. I particularly remember:

~   Great stacks of Uncle George's sourdough pancakes.
~   Putting up tons of hay in the long barn or haylofts every summer.
~   Taking fifteen horse-loads of grub to a camp at the headwaters of the Muddy Water River with Uncle Dick, Scotty Niven and Brother George. This food was put up on a pole platform cache we built in preparation for the fall hunting trips.
~   Taking care of the cattle on the range and gathering the horses up *(sixty-four head)* for shoeing in readiness for the fall hunting. Uncle George Hargreaves died on one of these hunting trips in 1936 and is buried on Sheep Creek.

"The following summer *(1937)*, Granddad asked us if we could round up all the horses as they were to be sold and to put all the cattle on the 'flats' behind the fences. Our personal horses were taken out and trailed to Jasper—eight horses in all. This was the end of an era for George and me, but the greatest time in our lives." *(Tom McCready 1996)*

CHAPTER THIRTEEN:
Larry Nelles

❧ *Authors Note* ❧

I first hosted a colt-starting and horsemanship clinic in Grande Cache in 1996, bringing Larry Nelles to this mountain community. I had organized the clinic to enable Larry to teach the guides, outfitters and others of this area a new way to start colts. Larry was considered a horseman's horseman, who could gentle any horse he came in contact with. He certainly was the best man to help the trail riders of Willmore start new colts for the trail. To make things better, Larry had an intimate knowledge of the background of the people and peaks of Willmore Wilderness Park.

The clinic turned out to be an enormous success and I opted to continue a yearly tradition of bringing Larry Nelles to this area. I knew that Larry had an in-depth understanding of the local history and in 2003 decided to audio tape Larry, and make a written transcript of our conversation. The interview took place at Kvass Flats, as Larry had come on the trail with my husband, Bazil and me. We were camped at Findlay Springs enjoying some relaxing time in between Larry's busy clinic schedule.

During our interview, Larry encouraged me to audio tape other old-timers, specifically Tom Vinson. He felt it imperative to get the history of this mountain area written down on a first-person basis before it was lost forever.

I decided to follow Larry's advice and have been on a four-year path of preparing this book for publication. Little did I know how much work or technical expertise this project would entail. Since the conception of the People & Peaks of Willmore Wilderness Park, I have been going regularly to the University of Alberta in order to take short-term courses in digital technology—so that I could keep control of the design and feel of this publication. I really wanted the book to exude the true essence of this magnificent park.

During my research, I was able to interview many old-time mountain men and women. I was also able to scan and catalogue a very large database of historical images. This has resulted in a

Pictured above:
Larry Nelles relaxing at
Smoky River Ranch.

Pictured on left page:
Larry Nelles &
his dog Gwen,
at Kvass Flats in June 2003.

Both photos by
Susan Feddema-Leonard.

huge catalogue of information which can be used for future generations. Thank you, Larry Nelles for your encouragement to document the stories about the people and peaks of this spectacular mountain area!

Interview with Larry Nelles

Sue It is June 19, 2003 and I am sitting at Kvass Flats with Larry Nelles and my husband, Bazil Leonard, who is a Willmore outfitter. We are at my trapline cabin, which is situated next to Findlay Springs on the Smoky River—in Willmore Wilderness Park.

I'll just start by asking you, Larry about your life as a youngster and about your grandfather. Could you tell us about your grandfather, the Park Warden in Yellowhead, and your dad, and your life in Jasper National Park?

Larry Well, my *(maternal)* granddad, John Curren came over here from Scotland with Ol' Jimmy Simpson. Jim made quite a name for himself. He shot the famous Simpson ram while hunting. Jimmy outfitteLd on the Bow Summit and had a homestead there. He was one of the original outfitters in the Alberta Rockies. My granddad, Curren ended up as the warden at Yellowhead.

My dad, Alex Nelles was raised in Lacombe in Alberta on a farm. He was the first white child born in that area in 1898. He moved to Jasper and became one of the first *(Park)* wardens in the area. My dad's badge with the Warden Service was badge #17.

My dad married Lottie Swift who already had a daughter from a previous marriage. Her husband was killed. Lottie and my dad were married for four years when Lottie died from tuberculosis. My dad ended up raising Lottie's daughter. Her name was Eunice Carlson. *(Lottie Swift was the daughter of Louis Swift who kept his homestead in Jasper despite the formation of Jasper Park and the coming of the railroad. Lottie Swift was a sister to two well-known guides in the Canadian Rockies: Dean Swift, her brother and Albert Norris, her half-brother.)*

My dad's second wife was Eleanor Curren. She was the daughter of Yellowhead's warden, John Curren. That's where I came along. I grew up as a warden's boy in Snaring.

Sue Could you explain for the people who don't know Snaring, where it is?

Larry Snaring is a warden's post, twelve miles east of Jasper. It was one of the districts my dad was in charge of. He cut a lot of trails in Jasper Park over the years. In those days the wardens were allowed to trap and hunt as well as being a warden. My dad hunted quite a bit in the fall, in the Willmore Wilderness area. He had a string of eighteen head of horses. I have a picture of him hunting on the Smoky River in 1949. The photo was published in the Canadian National Geographic Magazine.

Sue Now at Snaring, there was a family of Suzanne Cardinal and Henry John Moberly.

Larry The Moberlys lived at Snaring—and the Findlays lived across the Athabasca River. Somewhere between 1907 and 1909 the Native people of the Jasper area were moved out to the Grande Cache area—when Jasper became a park. But some of the Rocky Mountain Cree remained in Jasper Park, while some went back to work there. A lot of the wranglers that helped the wardens in those days were the Native Indians that had originated from Jasper. Louis Joachim was one of them that my dad hunted with. There were two Joachim brothers, Louis Joachim and Frank. Miles Moberly was a well-known guide. Outfitters, Curly Phillips and, of course, Tom McCready hired the Native guides.

Sue The old Moberly homestead was close to where you grew up?

Larry Yes, the buildings were still there. Suzanne Cardinal's grave is still there, I believe.

Sue So you have a connection with the people of Grande Cache. Maybe you could share a little bit about your connection to guys like Billy Wanyandie and Gordon Delorme and some of the others, when you came to Grande Cache to do a horsemanship clinic in 1996?

Larry I came up here to Grande Cache eight years ago to teach the people how to start colts. I had an opportunity to meet the Native people of Grande Cache. They are relatives of the people that were friends of my father when he was a young man. I just couldn't believe the connection that we had because our parents had been in these mountains in the early 1920s, '30s and '40s. It was just amazing. And when I started to work horses, it was very enjoyable to be around these people. It gave me the feeling of being a little closer to my dad and being able to experience people that knew him. Every year that I've come back is just like coming home, really.

Sue There was a Jasper outfitter that you were going to bring to the first clinic. His name was Tom McCready. Can you tell us a little bit about how you knew McCready? He died just before he was to come here.

Larry Both Tom and I were raised in Jasper. He was a little older than I. When Tom McCready first started out on the trail, he went with my dad and spent a lot of time with him. My dad took a lot of people out on the trail and started them. Tom ended up becoming an outfitter in Jasper. He was stationed in Jasper but guided and hunted the Willmore Wilderness area for twenty-three years, from the 1950s to the 1970s. I worked for Tom McCready. We took hunting trips out of Rock Lake. We hunted grizzly, black bear, caribou, bighorn sheep, moose and deer.

When someone went with Tom into the backcountry, he would take him in and show him any game he wanted to see. If he wanted to see sheep or caribou, moose or deer, Tom would find the game. He knew exactly where to look. It wasn't a problem to find the animals.

When Tom took people out to hunt, they were given one chance to hunt their game. When they shot an animal, it was theirs. Tom was very conservative and wouldn't let anyone decide that perhaps that ram wasn't good enough to take home and that he'd like to shoot another one. There's no way Tom McCready would allow that. That was the hunter's pick and that's what he would live with. Tom ran a really good camp. He packed out of Rock Lake and went up through Little Grave to Hardscrabble Pass. He hunted all that area.

Tom was a gentleman. He really liked to preserve the natural habitat of the area. He showed me his true nature on different trips into the Willmore Wilderness area. He showed me where there was buffalo buried in the moss and grass. And you could see that there was no way that Tom would touch them. He said that the buffalo had been in this area years ago and there was the proof of it. He showed me different graves where Indian fellows that had died in winters past were buried.

Tom really enjoyed the outback in the years that he hunted. I don't think he shot very many animals for himself, but he always provided well for his hunters. Jack O'Connor was one of the hunters that Tom took out.

Tom was an exceptional guide and his horses were really good trail horses. He didn't have to hobble them. They would stay around a camp. When Tom went into a camp he was like my dad. He said there are just two things that you take when you are in the outback country: you can take pictures and you can leave your tracks, and that's it.

Jim Simpson bought Tom McCready's outfit in the 1970s. George Kelley has since bought Jim Simpson out.

Sue Can you tell me a little about Tom McCready's family? I understand that he is related to the Hargreaves family.

Larry Tom McCready's mother was a Hargreaves. She was a twin sister to Jack Hargreaves. Tom's Uncle George *(Hargreaves)*

Pictured above:
Larry Nelles chopping wood at Kvass Flats - 2003.

Pictured on left page:
Top: Larry taking a break at a clinic - 2000.
Bottom: Larry getting ready to pack up - 2003.

Photos by Susan Feddema-Leonard.

died in 1936 and is buried at the head of Sheep Creek in Willmore Wilderness Park. The Hargreaves brothers were some of the early outfitters in Willmore.

Todd McCready, who lives in Valemount, packed with his dad when he was a young boy. Todd and I are still very, very close friends. Todd came to the Grande Cache clinic in 1996 when his dad was supposed to come. Tom had wanted to visit most of the people in the area because he knew them. He ended up having a stroke. Six months later, Tom passed on. But Todd came up with me to that clinic in his dad's place. Since then, Todd worked for Parks Canada with horses and has worked starting colts. Before that, he spent fifteen years flying for Yellowhead Helicopters. So he knows this country from the air and also from the ground.

Sue   Can you tell us a little bit about the Hargreaves? Can you tell us why they came here to the Smoky Valley from B.C., and how they traveled? Do you know the story about their bringing horses from B.C. and trailing them up and down the Smoky Valley and wintering them here?

Larry   The Hargreaves family had a base camp in Corral Creek. Their horses would range from the Muddy Water River and over to Kvass Flats, as it was the best place in the mountains to winter horses. The Natives knew that. They told us where we could put our horses. They'd say you go in here, there's lots of feed. So you see the Natives had been wintering their horses in this area for a long time.

When the Rocky Mountain Cree left Jasper Park, they came up into this Grande Cache area and they're still here. If you go to Wanyandie Flats or to Victor Lake, you will find the descendants of the Jasper Natives. These people went anywhere they could winter their horses.

After they moved to the Grande Cache area they would have to go to Hinton several times a year to stock up on supplies. When they left the Smoky Valley, it took them two weeks to make a round trip to Hinton to bring food back. There was no road until the 1950s.

Sue   Art Allen, a well-known log-cabin builder in his day, built a cabin on the Jackpine River. Apparently he traveled there with Tom Ross, who later became a Park warden in Jasper. A third man by the name of Red Creighton was there. I understand that Red was an outfitter and that Tom Ross worked for him as a cook in the hunting camps. You knew Red Creighton. Could you tell us what you knew about him?

Larry   Red Creighton and my dad were really good friends. Red was an outfitter and traveled all over the Willmore as there was good game in the Park. Red was one of the early outfitters and so was Stan Kitchen. Red and Stan based their outfits out of Jasper. Some of the first outfitters in the Willmore were Fred Brewster, Jack Brewster, the Hargreaves brothers, Tommy Groat, Stan Clark, Rufe Neighbor and Curly Phillips.

Sue   Can you remember any stories about your dad hunting on the Smoky River?

Larry   In 1926 my dad shot a bear in the Willmore Wilderness area. He told me he thought it was probably one of the last Plains Grizzlies. When they skinned it, they measured the hide and it was eleven foot six from head to tail. They accused my father of stretching the hide. But he said No, it was just a big bear. The locals said grizzlies didn't get that big—that was in 1926.

Sue   What do you mean by Plains Grizzly?

Larry   Plains Grizzlies were bigger than the mountain ones. These bears were the ones that followed the buffalo on the plains. They were a bigger bear; but they were all killed off. But this bear was still alive and it had to be a descendant of them. It was probably one of the last ones. The Plains Grizzly were in the mountain area here because years ago buffalo ran in here for refuge.

Another story I could tell you is about the time my dad was out on a trip and he heard a terrible amount of noise. He tied his horses up, and hiked up over this little bit of a knoll and looked down into this creek bed that was full of buck brush. And there was a bull moose and a grizzly fighting. He watched them for about thirty or forty minutes and said they must have been fighting for a long time for they had about a good half-acre of ground torn up. The bear would charge the moose and jump on its antlers. The moose would put his head down and ram the bear into the ground and then he would toss the bear. He would fling that big grizzly like you'd throw a ball. But in the process, the bear with his claws was gouging the front shoulders

Pictured above:
Larry Nelles at a horsemanship clinic in 2002.

Photo by
Susan Feddema-Leonard

and biting the top of the moose. And then they'd turn around and charge each other again. And at the end of the battle, the bear was gored quite a lot in his stomach. The moose finally died because he bled to death from cuts inflicted by the bear. And the bear crawled about a hundred yards from where the moose died, and he died.

Sue Can you tell us a little bit about your packing experience? You, yourself are an accomplished packer?

Larry I started packing horses and getting paid for packing horses when I was thirteen. I left home when I was eleven and went working with horses. When I was fifteen, I packed for Parks Canada. In the 1950s, I worked as a packer for the miners that were staking claims up Moose Creek, close to Golden, B.C. I worked for George Thagard, an outfitter south of Golden in the Kootenay Valley. I also worked for Rufe *(Rufus)* Neighbor who ran the Athabasca Ranch. Rufe was a friend of my dad's. And of course, I packed when I guided for Tom McCready.

Sue In recent years, you also trained horses for Parks Canada You ended up doing the clinics in Grande Cache in which you eventually helped many outfitters in this area. So you are still touching the outfitters who are packing the horses in the Rockies.

Larry I helped outfitters like Pete McMahon who outfits out of Corral Creek in Willmore and Cody Dixon who outfits out of Jasper. Bob Keen is an outfitter out of Fort Nelson and Phil Dezmase is an outfitter out of Revelstoke. Bazil *(Leonard)* and you *(Susan Feddema-Leonard)* have taken my clinic since 1996. I hosted clinics for the Jasper Park

Warden Service for quite a few years, helping the wardens with horsemanship and starting their horses, and that sort of thing.

Sue Can you talk about some of these horses, how young horses are being packed out into the mountains after you have worked with them?

Larry You can work with young horses in an outfit, if you work with the colts in a non-stressful way. The horse doesn't really learn by being forced to learn. You set it up to let it happen. You don't make it happen. When they go out on the trail, it's more natural when the horse doesn't have to go through a battle to learn how to be saddled or rode or led. A lot of the techniques that were used to train horses have changed since I was young. They would tie a foot up and sack a horse out and then ride them. A lot of these horses were quite wild. If a wild horse that has not been touched by humans is presented with a non-stressful way of being accepted, you can ride them. It is a very simple procedure. These horses will stay close to a camp and even after two or three days, you can go out on to the trail with these horses and kids can start them. You don't have to be a wild, tough bronc rider. You just have to be a person who has a little bit of confidence and some sensitivity and feeling and a little compassion for an animal. This non-stressful approach makes it easy.

Sue Your grandfather was a warden in Yellowhead. Your father was a warden in Jasper. You grew up in Jasper, you packed horses in Jasper, you worked for the Warden Services, you guided in Willmore, and then you ended up coming up to Grande Cache in 1996 to teach the people a better way to work with horses. So you are now training horses to

Pictured above:
Larry Nelles at a clinic at
Smoky River Ranch near Grande Cache.

Photo by Susan Feddema-Leonard

Pictured right:
Alex Nelles' photo of Willow Creek, circa 1940s. At that time the valley floor was an open meadowland, supplying rich grazing for horses and wildlife.

Today, without horses or natural fires, the buck brush has grown in and elimated the habitat.

Photo courtesy of Larry Nelles.

"People used to winter hundreds of horses in here. The Native people that lived here would start fires and burn the bottom part of the valleys out and kill the buck brush each spring, before the snow was gone on the hillsides. It would take all the vegetation and change it so there was a food source for all the wild game and their horses. There was good grazing then for both the wildlife and the horses. The trails were open and easily accessible. The same situation existed at Willow Creek in Jasper. It was exactly the same circumstance as at Kvass Flats. At Willow Creek they had two to three hundred head of horses that wintered in the area for many years."

Quote by Larry Nelles

Pictured left (L to R):
Jasper Park Wardens
on the Smoky River in 1949.
George Camp, Alex Nelles,
Bob Jones and
Mickey McGuire.

Photo courtesy of
Larry Nelles.

go back into the Willmore to re-open all those old trails that your dad and grandfather rode in days gone by. Your life has been in a full circle, so to speak.

Larry Outfitters years ago were right here at Kvass Flats. The Hargreaves wintered horses here. People used to winter hundreds of horses in here. The Native people that lived here would start fires and burn the bottom part of the valleys out and kill the buck brush each spring, before the snow was gone on the hillsides. It would take all the vegetation and change it so there was a food source for all the wild game and their horses. There was good grazing then for both the wildlife and the horses. The trails were open and easily accessible.

The same situation existed at Willow Creek in Jasper. It was exactly the same circumstance as at Kvass Flats. At Willow Creek they had two to three hundred head of horses that wintered in the area for many years. I can remember as a boy after the war that they rounded up all those horses, even in the Jasper Park area. There were hundreds of horses that they caught. These horses had been turned out previously, because most people had gone and fought in the war. Before they left for war, the men turned the studs loose. This resulted in a lot of really good horses. When the men returned home, they had to figure out which horses were which, and brand them. Everybody ran their horses out there at Willow Creek. This whole country was traveled with packhorses. It was just a way of life.

Whether it was Parks Canada or this area here *(Willmore)*, the outfitters and the Warden Service were really closely connected because they both depended on each other to make a living. The Native people that were in this area were an important piece of the puzzle. Without the Natives' guidance, it would be really tough, because they were the ones that could survive easily in the outback.

Pictured above:
Larry Nelles at
Kvass Flats in 2004.

Photo by
Susan Feddema-Leonard.

They showed a lot of the white people that had been in this area how to live in the mountain terrain. The Natives passed on their survival skills, giving the wardens and new outfitters the initiative and the desire to look after this country. The outfitters and the Warden Service hired the Native guides. It was a perfect combination.

Today there is a younger generation that is starting to understand that we should get back to the old ways of managing the wilderness. We need to live on better terms with nature as people used to do.

Sue How do you feel about the Alberta government's no-burn policy over the past fifty years? The government is saying they don't want horses in Willmore Wilderness Park because they are grazing too much of the vegetation off. They biologists feel that the horses are taking away from the elk habitat.

Larry I don't think people understand how the park was maintained on a more natural basis. People don't understand how the environment works because many times a forest fire can heal the land. After a forest fire, the land goes through different growth cycles. First you get your grasses, next you get huckleberries, then fireweed, then alders, and later you get pine. After a fire, the land goes through a transformation. That change enhances the earth. If you leave the land dormant, it gets stagnant. A lot of underbrush creates heavy growth and then the game can't survive. The underbrush just chokes the feed out.

When the country was more open, it made it a little tougher for the wolves and cougars to kill their game. There's less game now in both Jasper and Willmore than there ever has been because of the shortage of vegetation for them to feed on.

With the burns at Kvass Flats, the grasses are coming back to a certain degree. We haven't allowed the natural process of fire to replenish the land. It's a start that they are burning Kvass Flats. Fire makes the whole natural change of the earth better.

Most of the educated people should really come out to the mountains and live and understand the land, before they make decisions. It's really hard to understand what is taking place on the eastern slopes from reading a book or listening to a study. You can't learn how the environment works from documents and reports. You've got to live on the land. Access to a cell phone, a computer and an airplane doesn't fit out here. You need to live it to understand it.

Sue So the old-time outfitters *(Hargreaves)* would trail the horses all the way down here and then in the spring send them back up the river. *Willmore Wilderness Preservation and Historical Foundation* has a mandate to find and restore those old pack trails that your father and his friends used. So we're in the process of finding the rest of the trails back up to Mt. Robson. We want to re-open the trails from the Willmore side right to Jasper Park Boundary, so they connect with the Jasper trails.

Larry In the past, the country was more open and a lot of the trails were made from old game trails. The old mountain men cleared the trails out for horses. The trails were really here because the game used them, but now there's deadfall over the trails. There's not the game that there used to be because there's not the grass. There's not the food source because they've let the undergrowth grow up. They haven't allowed the land to burn. You see, the Natives burnt the land and would let the fire burn out on its own. They would burn the buck brush early in the spring so the fire did not go into the timber. The snow helped keep the fires from under control. They knew that without the game, they couldn't live and without that vegetation, the game couldn't live—so spring fire was a critical part of the of the ecosystem. The Natives used this age old secret in their management of the area.

Sue So, in Jasper, was it the same? Were they burning the valleys?

Larry The same thing occurred in Jasper National Park. The Native people of Grande Cache were originally in Jasper before they were forced to leave when Ottawa legislated it a National Park. You see when they decided to make Jasper a park, they had the indigenous people removed. They took their rifles; took everything, and basically kicked them out of the Park.

When the Park got more involved in trying to create a well-managed Park, they had to bring some of the Native guides back to help them. The Warden Service didn't understand how to do things. That's how the Natives got hired back—to help the wardens learn the ways of the land.

Natives worked with my dad who was a Park warden in Jasper. Miles Moberly was one guide. My father had high regards for both Judd Groat's and Miles Moberly's skills. The Joachims—Louis Joachim and Frank, these men were just naturals and good in the bush. My dad thought a lot of these men.

My dad spoke very highly of Louis Delorme. He said that Louis was probably one of the most intelligent fellows that he has ever traveled in the bush with. Louis could handle horses. He understood how to read the weather. He could track an animal anywhere. He could

Pictured above (L to R):
Dan Leonard,
Bazil Leonard &
Larry Nelles in 2004.
Larry was giving
a six-day clinic
at Smoky River Ranch.

Photo by
Susan Feddema-Leonard.

tell you if a track was three or four days old. If you wanted to know where to get good food or where the game would be, Louis Delorme would walk you right to it. It was not a problem. My father thought of Louis Delorme as an icon. He was a guy who taught a lot of people.

And I'm sure the Natives even helped Jack Hargreaves and other outfitters. They showed them where the game was and where the horse pastures and trails were.

Sue   Louis Delorme is Curtis *(Hallock's) g*randpa and Gordon Delorme's dad, so we're not that far removed from these people. *(Curtis was a guide in camp at the time of this interview.)*

Larry   No, it's not that far away.

Sue   In fact, during the 1980s and early 1990s, every time we traveled from Victor Lake over to Cowlick Creek and Big Grave, Louis Delorme used to stand and watch the pack outfit come and go. He was in his late 80s and 90s back then. I now realize, he was probably wishing he could travel on a packstring back into the mountains.

Larry   He lived to be ninety-six years old. He was top of the line. When you mentioned his name, everyone just seemed to light up. And I never in my life ever heard anyone who had a bad word for him. It didn't matter who you'd talk to. You just mention his name and they just thought—awe! It's the way he was respected!

Others that my dad talked highly about were Judd and Joe Groat who lived in Brule. They were the sons of Tommy Groat, one of the earliest outfitters. I think they've both passed on. My dad packed in the bush a lot with them. They were really good packers like Tom McCready.

Tom was an exceptionally good horseman. One time he had Joe Groat working for him. In the morning when he had forty or fifty head of packhorses, they'd get all the horses caught and they'd start putting packsaddles on to get ready to head out. Tom said Joe would put a packsaddle on quicker than anybody. Joe would probably have packed two horses to his one. And the faster Tom went, the quicker Joe would go. All he told Tom was, "I must be getting old. I'm slowing down!"

I can give you an idea of what he did one time. Tom *(McCready)* told me they ran into a party coming out on the trail and Tom stopped to visit with the fellow. Joe went ahead. Tom said he wasn't twenty minutes behind Joe, but when he got into camp, Joe had the cook tent set up, he had the coffee on, and all the horses were turned out with their hobbles on. The whole camp was set up and he said he wasn't twenty minutes behind him. Joe was sitting underneath a tree having coffee and Tom said, "How did you do that?" And Joe said, "You must have been gone a couple hours, Tom." Tom says, "Joe, I'm not more than twenty minutes behind you." That was the kind of guy Joe was, that's how handy he was.

I could tell you some good stories about him. I could tell another if you'd like. Joe, well he worked for Tom as a packer. Tom had a cook at the time that was--I couldn't tell you the lady's name—anyways, she was a really cranky old gal and she just used to give Joe a hard time. He couldn't do anything right. The wood wasn't cut the right size and the water wasn't there fast enough. And I mean this wasn't done and that wasn't done. She was steady complaining about Joe. But Joe was really handy. Anyway, they packed up one day to change camps and once they were riding down the trail, he's hustling along hurrying to beat heck and Tom said to Joe, "Slow down, you know there's no hurry. We've got all the time to get there." "No, Tom, we've got to get into camp." And this cook's just a-nattering. In the outfit you always had a kitchen horse. It had all the stuff you used just as soon as you get into camp. You'd unpack the kitchen horse first so that the cook could get things set up, get the coffee on, get things going so she could get a meal on the way. Along the way, Joe keeps looking in his pocket at his watch seeing what time it is. When they finally get into camp and they're tying all the horses up, Joe goes over and ties the kitchen horse up and he goes over and takes the lash rope off of it. That cranky ol' cook comes over and says, "You leave this horse alone, Joe. I'll look after everything. You just get over there and mind your own damn business. I'll look after the kitchen horse." He said that old cook walked over and went to take the pan off the top of the thing, when all of a sudden the alarm clock went off in the pack. I mean one of them old Big Ben alarm clocks—made a noise like you wouldn't believe. Well, this horse came apart and it bucked everything off. It was scattering everywhere. There's ole' Joe just a-snickering over there, patching up things. And Tom thought, "Well, now I know why Joe was looking at his watch to get there." That's what he said; it was his own little way of trying to get even with this cook. But those are some of the things that would happen in the backcountry.

Pictured above:
Lita Hallock, Larry Nelles and his dog, Gwen.
Lita is the great-granddaughter of Louis Delorme, who was a well respected outfitter of Willmore Wilderness Park. Louis Delorme worked with Alex Nelles, Larry's father. Lita was a student of Larry's colt starting workshop. She was dancing for an evening pow-wow at the clinic in June 2003.

Photo by Susan Feddema-Leonard.

Sue   What advice do you want to pass on regarding Willmore Wilderness Park?

Larry   If we keep our wilderness intact, I think that's something that our young people will benefit from. Canada is a big country. In the West, we don't have the population. We should do what we can to preserve the backcountry and let people see it. It will do more good than any education that you'll get in university. You'll learn valuable lessons if you walk the same paths that were walked a hundred years ago. It's something you cannot buy and it's an experience you will never forget. However, it doesn't fit everybody.

When you get a taste of the wilderness you're going to find out that it means more to you than anything that you're going to experience in your life. You talk to anybody that's experienced it and they'll tell you the same thing. Backcountry living is something that should be passed on. People need to learn how to live where they don't need all the amenities that you have in a society today.

One Native girl told me when she moved to town that the biggest change she found was this. She said, "When I went to town I found out that the water runned for me and when I lived in the backcountry I knew that I had to run for the water." That was what she said; that's what she noticed. It's the same here. If you want water you have to run over and get it. You don't just have water running for you. And then you conserve water. When you have to carry it, you're less wasteful. It's easy to turn the tap on and leave it running. Those are the little things you'd find out. You'd use less--your clothes, like everything--you conserve; you learn how to get along with less. And you find out that all those things are not that important.

Yeah, and I can't believe that people who are wasteful can do something *(good)* when they don't understand it *(the waste)*. And they don't, you know. Tom McCready took two people from Ottawa into Jasper Park who were environmentalists. He packed them into the backcountry. When he got into the backcountry, he made camp and said, "If you boys have go to go to the toilet, dig yourself a little hole, do your business and cover it. Because," he said, "I want this *(place)* left exactly the way it is. I don't want to see any human trace left here." Pretty soon Tom went out into the back and saw that they had gone to the washroom and there it was, left. So he said, "Oh you better get the shovel and bury that." They informed Tom that they were top high officials from Ottawa and he was just a packer and they would be the ones giving orders, not him. They told Tom this at ten o'clock at night and Tom told them they'd better pack their stuff up, and he packed them up. In the morning they arrived at the head office in Jasper Park and he informed the Chief Warden that these two fellows had to be taken out of the Park. He said, "We're not having trash like this in this National Park."

That just goes to show you the feelings of a man who lived in the bush all his life. He looked after it. You leave tracks and if you want to take anything, you take pictures. That was his motto—my dad's, too.

Sue   Thank-you.

Larry   You're welcome

Pictured right:
Jackpine River in 2004

Photo by Susan Feddema-Leonard.

CHAPTER FOURTEEN:
Leonard Jeck

Pictured above:
Helny & Len Jeck 1977,
Photo courtesy of
Helny Jeck.

Pictured on left page:
Leonard Jeck on
Chief Horse, at the
Alexander River Crossing,
Jasper National Park
circa 1940s.
Photo courtesy of
Jasper Yellowhead
Museum & Archives
89.36.256

❧ Authors Note ❧

I had the pleasure of meeting with Mrs. Helny Jeck on May 13, 2005 at her home in Jasper. She is the wife of the late Leonard Jeck who was a guide and outfitter in both Jasper and Willmore Wilderness Parks. Helny was Leonard's silent partner and worked along side of him. I am very grateful for the help that Helny provided in the preparation of this chapter about her husband
Susan Feddema-Leonard

Leonard Jeck, born in 1917 in New Serepta, Alberta, spent most of his life in the mountains he dearly loved. Leonard worked in the guiding and outfitting industry in the areas of Jasper National Park and Willmore Wilderness Park. He moved to McBride, B.C. when he was eight and re-located to Jasper at sixteen years of age. Shortly after he moved to Jasper, Leonard went to work for Jack Brewster. Jack was a well-respected outfitter who was originally from Banff and had expanded his operation into the Jasper area. In the 1920s, Brewster operated his *Great Glacier Trail* horseback-outfitting excursions. During his employment with Brewster, Leonard took trail riders through the Columbia Icefield area while traveling between the railway outposts of Jasper and Lake Louise. Experienced guides took excursions onto the dangerous glaciers, on foot, snowshoes, or even on horses equipped with spiked horseshoes to better grip the ice.

In 1936, work began on a road linking Jasper and Lake Louise. Jack Brewster recognized the importance of the Columbia Icefield to the tourism industry and built the Icefield Chalet. The Banff-Jasper road was completed in 1939. After the development of the hotel, horses continued to take customers up to the icefield on the Continental Divide, where melted waters feed streams and rivers that pour into the Arctic, Atlantic and Pacific oceans. Leonard took guests on many spectacular trail rides. Horseback was the only mode of travel into the remote area at that time.

After Leonard left this job, Red Creighton, another Jasper outfitter ran the Icefield tours and Chalet. Red Creighton eventually bought Jack Brewster's outfit and Brewster moved back to Banff.

In 1938, Leonard Jeck commenced work at the *Black Cat Ranch*, which is located near Brule, north of Hinton, Alberta. The facility was Fred Brewster's business enterprise that was started in 1935. Fred and Jack Brewster were brothers. Fred had his ties with the *Jasper Park Lodge* and operated day horseback trips out of both the *Lodge* and the *Black Cat Ranch*. He also did some extended summer trail rides into the Rockies. After the season was over, Fred would winter his horses at the *Black Cat Ranch*. (*Fred also established cabins at Maligne Lake, the Skyline Trail and Tonquin Valley, and was instrumental in getting the Jasper ski slopes started.*)

As there were no roads to the *Black Cat Ranch*, all guests arriving and leaving would have to be met and returned by saddle horse to the Canadian National Railway *(CNR)* line, which was a six-mile trip each way. Many times, Leonard would take his packstring and saddle horses to meet the train and new guests. He would greet the dudes, set their stirrups, pack duffle and groceries that were purchased, and return to the ranch.

While Fred operated the ranch, his brother, Jack Brewster offered the more extreme summer trail riding, and a big game hunting business. Jack provided Leonard his training in bighorn sheep hunting during his early years in the outfitting business. Leonard also worked alongside Jack and took summer scenic trail rides to the north boundary of Jasper National Park. On some occasions, the trips originated at the *Black Cat Ranch*, which was a beautiful place to spend a summer vacation. At other times, Leonard picked up guests at the CNR passenger train station in Hinton, and took the trail riders and packtrain over the mountains to Mt. Robson. Upon arriving at the Mt. Robson CNR station, he said goodbye to the guests as they departed by train.

Pictured left:
Top:. Leonard Jeck, at his trapline cabin he built in 1953
Photo courtesy of Jasper Yellowhad Museum & Archives 89 36 256.
Middle: A picture Leonard took of Stan Clark's Cabin
located near the mouth of the Muddy Water River in 1971.
Bottom: Leonard's image of Mt. Sir Alexander from the top of Coffin Top Mountain.
Photos courtesy of Helny Jeck.

Leonard Jeck built the log barn at the *Black Cat Ranch* during the 1940s. It is a different log style than the original buildings at the facility. The first buildings were built in the same style as the *Jasper Park Lodge*. However, the barn that Leonard built was in a Scandinavian style with interlocking corners.

Fred Brewster operated the *Black Cat* until the mid-1950s, when he retired and sold off his holdings to some of his staff. Tom Vinson acquired the backcountry operations in Jasper and the Willmore, and Red Creighton took over the *Black Cat Ranch*. Red operated the ranch much as Brewster had, until the early 1960s when he sold it to Dave Slutker, a member of the Slutker Furs family from Edmonton. Dave was primarily a big game hunting guide, and used the *Black Cat* as a base camp for fall hunting trips. In 1966, the property was sold once again.

Leonard worked for various outfitters until he joined the Royal Canadian Air force *(RCAF)* in 1941. He remained with the RCAF until he was discharged in 1945 when he promptly returned to Jasper. Immediately after the war, Leonard returned to the work he loved, and managed the *Black Cat Ranch*. He also guided for Jack Hargreaves shortly thereafter.

Leonard worked on many occasions for Jack Hargreaves, whom he greatly admired. Hargreaves was also a Jasper outfitter who had an intimate knowledge of the mountains. He was well-known for his exceptional hunting ability of the grizzly bear. In the few seasons that Leonard worked for Jack, seven grizzlies were harvested.

A story that Leonard recounts in the book *Female Grizzly Rights*, which he authored, shows why he admired Jack Hargreaves. The tale is about Jack encountering a big boar grizzly bear one day. While Jack was walking to a fishing hole, a large bear rushed him. Jack kept his cool and smacked the bear on the nose with his fishing rod. This confused the bear, which caused him to retreat for a moment. After a time, the boar made another advance toward Jack who once again swatted the bear's nose. The grizzly retreated again. The bruin circled and made one more advance and Jack gave the bear's nose a swift wallop. With that, the grizzly left. This whole event had unnerved Jack, but he kept calm and the event ended without incident.

In 1953, Leonard married Helny Janson who was from Calgary, Alberta. Leonard was working for Jack Hargreaves at the time of his marriage. For the first year, Helny traveled with Leonard on the pack trips, until she became pregnant and had their daughter, Pamela in 1954. Helny had accompanied her husband as a cook.

Leonard operated the Maligne Lake Pony Barns from 1956 to 1966, while Helny worked as a hostess for Bill Ruddy who owned *Maligne Tours Ltd.* During his time at the pony barns, Leonard built the log washhouse, which is still used today as a gift shop and office. This is another example of Leonard's skill as a craftsman. Leonard worked in the winter season as a carpenter to augment his family's income.

There were many years that Leonard worked with Art Allen, a Willmore Wilderness area outfitter and trapper. In the 1960s, Leonard bought Art Allen's summer trail riding business. He also acquired Art's spring and fall hunting trip operation. The

Pictured above:
Top: Len Jeck with a goat, hunting trophy from Willmore Wilderness Park. 89 36 129.

Bottom: Len Jeck with a record grizzly bear. 999 58 08

Photos courtesy of Jasper Yellowhead Museum & Archives.

purchase included the horses, gear and the area. Art continued to travel with the outfit with Leonard for the first couple of years.

Leonard hired many guides and trail hands over the years. If there were four hunters in a party, they would each need a guide, so Leonard had a fair number of men working for him. Men such as Lee Pittendreigh, John Pittendreigh and Art Allen guided for Leonard. Ted McGuire also guided a number of times. Danny Berry went out on the trail as a trail hand and camp helper, but only off and on due to his young age.

On many occasions, when leaving for a summer trail riding excursion or a hunting trip from Jasper, Leonard would trail his horses to Seldom Inn on the Snake Indian River. Seldom Inn, a cabin that was rarely used, was located upstream from Devona, which was a train stop that some outfitters used to send supplies to. Leonard would trail his horses up the Snake Indian River and over to Willow Creek. He could go from Willow Creek and enter Willmore Wilderness Park at Rock Lake, or go up and over a hump to Rock Creek. Alternately, he could choose to go by way of the North Boundary Trail.

In February, 1967 Leonard survived open-heart surgery. He was well enough in June of 1968 to outfit a summer trip. During that trip, Leonard and two of his companions, Steve Rose from California and Dave Slutker were viciously attacked by a grizzly bear. The three had traveled up the Snake Indian River and made a camp overlooking the snowcapped mountains of the Blue Creek area. On June 5, 1968 the three saddled their horses and took a ride into higher county. They left their horses tied and were travelling on foot when a grizzly bear came running full speed downhill and attacked Leonard. Leonard had warned the others by yelling "GRIZZLY!" Leonard took quite a mauling while Steve climbed a tree and called the bear to try and distract it from Leonard. Upon hearing Steve's yells, the bear left Leonard and climbed the tree, pulling Steve to the ground. He, too, was severely mauled. Dave, who was farther up the mountain, heard Steve's cries of distress, and came running down the mountain to investigate. Before Dave could comprehend what was going on, the bear attacked him, clawing his face, before it turned and ran off. Despite being bitten by the massive jaws, Leonard kept his wits and managed to get the two men back to their base camp. He made sure both men were warm before traveling on to the warden's cabin at Willow Creek, where there was a phone. Through sheer stamina and impeccable bush skills, Leonard managed to push himself beyond thinkable limits and contacted Mickey McGuire, the Chief Warden. After a short time, a helicopter arrived at the warden's cabin and picked up Leonard who showed the pilot where their camp was. When the helicopter circled their camp and landed, both men were in their sleeping bags, still alive and very happy to see their rescuers. It was a seventeen-hour ordeal that miraculously saw all men survive with only a few scars.

Pictured above:
Top: Len helping a small cowpoke.
Middle: Leonard Jeck in 1975.
Bottom: Leonard Jeck in the cook tent.

Photos courtesy of Helny Jeck.

Leonard continued to have respect and a passion for the grizzly bear despite his unfortunate encounter. He felt that the grizzly was normally a non-aggressive animal. He wanted to share his experiences with others and wrote a book about the incident called, *Female Grizzly Rights* which was published in 1982. He also authored *The Bighorn Ram*, which was published in 1979. Leonard gratefully acknowledged his wife Helny for helping him put his thoughts and experiences on paper for the publications.

Leonard continued working and living in the mountains after his encounter with the bear. For the next two years, he went back out into the mountains and ran his outfit. It was in 1970 that Leonard sold his outfit to John Ward. John had worked with Leonard for several years prior to this and knew the area. John's son, Gerald Ward later took over the business from his father and runs the outfit today.

Frankie and Bernie Nelson were the owners of the *Athabasca Ranch* and Leonard guided this family on summer trips for a number of years during the 1970s. He used saddle and packhorses to take the Nelsons into the deep recesses of the Canadian Rocky Mountains. They stayed in tent camps and enjoyed the splendors of Willmore Wilderness Park.

Leonard also made a few trips from the *Entrance Ranch* for Bernie's sister, Ann Bronson in the 1970s. The guests he took from the *Entrance Ranch* would walk into a base camp and go hiking from there. They used packhorses to take gear, food and supplies for hikers into Willmore Wilderness Park. Leonard was the licensed guide and outfitter for the horse-assisted operation.

(The *Entrance Ranch* was bought in 1918 by outfitter Stan Clark who set up a large horse and cattle ranch. Shortly thereafter he acquired the *Athabasca Ranch*. The properties were sold in 1928 to Harry S. Davison who was from New York. Harry and his family spent the summer at the ranch, which was managed full-time by Rufe Neighbor who was also an outfitter. Anne Bronson and her sister, Frankie Nelson inherited the ranches after their father's death in 1961. Frankie and her husband, Bernie still run the *Athabasca Ranch*, and Anne became the owner of the *Entrance Ranch*.)

Leonard traveled widely throughout Willmore Wilderness Park. Mike Moberly, a Grande Cache Rocky Mountain Cree guide recounted a story that clearly shows how extensively Leonard moved through the rugged wilderness terrain. Mike is the great-grandson of Henry John Moberly and grandson of Ewan Moberly. He was guiding for Louis Delorme, a Rocky Mountain Cree outfitter who was based out of Victor Lake, near Grande Cache. Pat Smythe, a Hinton-based blacksmith, wrangler and packer, was the cook on this particular trip. They had four hunters from Edmonton and had bagged two caribou and four bighorn sheep. Their hunting party ran into Leonard Jeck and his Métis guide, Tommy Plante who lived in Marlboro, Alberta. The two outfits encountered each other near Many Faces camp on Boulder Creek.

Mike Moberly recounted how Leonard's outfit had traveled from the Hardscrabble Creek across the Smoky River up to Jackpine Lake and over to Boulder Creek. They were heading to the Muddy Water trail and up to the headwaters of Sheep Creek. Mike Moberly said that Leonard and his outfit were planning their return trip down Sheep Creek to the Smoky River and over to where the town of Grande Cache is now located. They then ventured on to Muskeg River and took the old dirt road back to Hinton.

Leonard realized in the 1950s that the mountain wilderness was in jeopardy of being over-exploited. He became very active in lobbying Norman Willmore, his member of the Alberta Legislature. He wanted to ensure that the eastern slopes of the Canadian Rockies became a protected area. Leonard was one of the men instrumental in getting the Willmore Wilderness Park Act into being. Leonard was an outdoorsman and was involved in anything that had to do with preserving the wilderness. He also had a great concern about the rapid extinction of wildlife in the Rockies and felt that this needed to be addressed.

Leonard Jeck spent over forty-five years riding the Rocky Mountain ranges. He had a tremendous knowledge of the rivers, valleys and mountain ranges, and how to live in the wilds. He cut his teeth learning his trade with men like Jack Brewster and Jack Hargreaves. His skills and knowledge of the mountain way of life were outstanding. His wife, Helny and daughter, Pamela accompanied Leonard many times on the trail. Leonard and his family shared many special experiences and memories in the Rocky Mountain Wilderness.

Leonard also had a passion to share his knowledge of the Rocky Mountain way of life with those he encountered. He taught those who traveled with him how to enjoy the natural beauty of the wilderness without desecrating the natural places he loved so much.

Pictured left:
Leonard Jeck.
Photo courtesy of
Jasper Yellowhead Museum & Archives 999 58 18

Pictured right:
Boulder Creek with one of the Peaks of Mt. deVeber - 2006.
Photo by Susan Feddema-Leonard .

306

CHAPTER FIFTEEN:
Mac Elder

ℰ❧ *Authors Note* ℰ❧

I interviewed Mac Elder at the Canadian Rodeo finals in Edmonton November 12, 2006. Mac worked as a packer and guide for a ten-year period in and around Willmore Wilderness from 1947 to 1956—and left the outfitting industry to become a Jasper Park warden. Mac, like his peers in the Wardens Service, was a competent trail man before he hired on with Parks Canada. He was one of the last of an era of highly skilled 'mountain men' who only needed a 'little polishing' when employed by the Wardens Service. His trail experience put him in good stead to make 'common sense' decisions when he served the Canadian Parks Services for the next thirty-four years. Mac brings into focus some of the other Willmore guides and outfitters who are 'unsung cowboys'—like Stan Kitchen, Red Creighton, Larry McGuire, Gene Merrill, Russell Cooper, Cuff Jameson, Tom Ross, Dorothy and John Williams—along with John and Edith Unland who purchased Stan Kitchen's outfit. These individuals guided and outfitted summer trail rides, hunters and geological survey parties into Willmore Wilderness Park and surrounding areas.

I'm Mac Elder and I live in Cochrane now, but I used to work in the Jasper, Grande Cache and Mt. Robson area.

Before I came to the Jasper country, I was living down between Olds and Sundre, Alberta. I was interested in working in the outfitting business. I had planned on going to work on an outfit for a while—but didn't expect it would last ten years. I was mainly interested in hunting and traveling around with horses. I had talked with Jack Hargreaves and he offered me a job—so I went up there, horse wrangling and packing—and soon I was guiding.

I met Stan Kitchen in 1947 during my first year in Jasper while I was working for Jack Hargreaves. Stan had been working as an outfitter from the late 1930s to the time I met him in '47, and that was the last year he worked as an outfitter. Stan originated from Wainwright, Alberta and came to Jasper.

Pictured above:
Mac Elder at the Canadian National Finals Rodeo in November 2006. Photo by Susan Feddema-Leonard.

Pictured on left page:
Mac Elder Oct 1950. Photo courtesy of Mac Elder.

Bing Crosby had come to Jasper that fall to go on a hunting trip with Kitchen. He had been to Jasper previously to play golf. Bing came another time to make a movie called *Emperor Waltz*. I'm not sure what came first, the golf or the movie but Bing was in Jasper two or three times. He liked Jasper because it was a small town and he liked it because the people didn't pay any attention to him. He was quite a celebrity but he just fit in with everyone. Stan met Bing Crosby in Jasper and got acquainted with him when they sat and visited drinking beer in the Legion. They became friends and Bing decided that he should go on a hunting trip with Stan.

Stan decided to retire from outfitting in '47 and just focus on his trucking business in Jasper. He had trucked on the Alaska Highway during the war when they were building the highway. A lot of people in that era thought that the outfitting business was finished. I thought it was finished in 1954-55-56—but it is still going—nothing like it was, because there aren't those long trips anymore. Stan Kitchen sold out in '47 after he guided the Bing Crosby trip.

During my first year in '47, we spent a lot of time in the spring of the year gathering and breaking horses because Jack had booked a lot of hunting trips that fall. He had three early hunting parties and two late trips. Tom McCready, Jack Hargreaves' nephew also had an early trip and late trip. Tom and I worked out of the same corral that spring getting a bunch of horses ready to work that year.

We did a lot of traveling around in the summer time in '47—in the Tonquin Valley and in different places, taking out tourists and fishermen. We were up around Elysium Pass one time, which was one of the few different summer trips we were on. We left on a hunting trip on August 24 from Jasper. Dick, Jack's half-brother took one of the first hunting parties and had his own crew. Jack's daughter, Evelyn was cooking for that party.

I was wrangling for Jack Hargreaves on the first trip I was on—and we had twenty-two head of horses. There was Jack, his son, Gordon, another fellow who was cooking, two hunters and me. We had trailed horses down to Devona and started our trip from there. Devona was just east of Jasper and it was the staging area—we all pulled out of there. We went north to the Sulphur River. Jack and I and his son hunted all the way over to Winifred (Lakes) from the west fork of the Sulphur. We hunted down the Hardscrabble and into the Winifred and the Kvass Pass area. We got bighorn sheep, goats, mule deer and caribou on that thirty-day trip. We worked our way back to Devona to re-supply for the second trip.

On the second trip, I went with head guide, Gene Merrill. Gene was a fellow who was raised in southern Alberta—but lived up the Smoky River area close to Eaglesham. Gene and his brother had come from that country down to Entrance, and the pair had worked for Stan Clark. They came from that north country down through Grande Cache, working for Stan and several other outfitters before the Second World War, eventually going to work for Jack Hargreaves. Gene was a real woodsman. He'd also trapped down there on the Smoky River with Art Allen in 1942-1943 during the winter months. Gene worked for Jack off and on for many years and he was a crackerjack guy—a really good guy. Gene spent a few years in the Army Pack Troop, which had quite a bunch of horses. They were a mountain commando troop with over one hundred head of horses and were based out of Terrace, B.C. They traveled from Terrace to Jasper, Maligne Lake, the Tonquin Valley, and Yoho. In later years Joe Groat was one of the packers with that group.

Pictured above:

Jack Hargreaves circa 1967. Jack is showing off his retirement project. He made belt buckles and bolo ties and other items out of horn and bone.

Photo courtesy of George Hargreaves who currently resides in Calgary and who is Jack Hargreaves' grandson. He is named after George Hargreaves who is buried in Willmore Wilderness Park near the falls on Sheep Creek.

Gene and I and another guy called Lawrence *(Red)* Ilie, who lives east of Edson, headed out on the second trip that fall. Russell Cooper was on the trip as a guide and wrangler, and Gene's wife, Ellen was the cook. We'd gone over Glacier Pass and down on the Sulphur River. When we were camped at Brewster's wall, one of our three hunters had a heart attack and died about noon. The people were from Pennsylvania *(U.S.A.)* and they wanted to know if we could get him out of there. Gene, Red, one of the other hunters and I had to pack him up out of the basin and down the other side of the mountain. It took us more than half a day to get him packed down to camp. It was interesting because rigor mortis had set into this guy. He was as stiff as a plank and we couldn't bend him. The next morning Gene and I loaded him on a horse and we had to load him on lengthwise—'cause we couldn't bend him. We didn't like to treat him rough, because two of his friends were watching. We packed him on a horse and took him almost to Devona. We were the biggest part of two days getting down to the staging area.

In 1948, I worked for Jack Hargreaves, all spring and summer. Along about August, something happened to the hunting trip that Gene Merrill and I were supposed to take and we ended up going out on a thirty-five day hunting trip with Red Creighton, who was outfitting at that time. Red was in partnership with Larry McGuire who had another party of hunters out. There was Red Creighton, Tom Ross, Gene Merrill and a fellow by the name of Cuff Jameson who were guiding. We had four hunters and I was wrangling.

Cuff Jameson wasn't in the Willmore Wilderness country very long. He worked primarily for Tom Vinson. I think he was from that Caroline *(Alberta)* country.

Marvin *(Red)* Creighton had come from the Maritimes and came out to Jasper as a pretty young guy. I know that he cooked for Jack Brewster on the trail when he first arrived. He worked around on construction like everybody else. Red wound up guiding for Jack Brewster. During the war *(WWII)* he spent some time up on the Alaska Highway working on the Canol Pipeline survey in Dawson Creek, along with Albert Norris, Rex Logan, Judd Groat and Stan Kitchen. After the war, Larry McGuire and Red got together and bought out Jack Brewster's outfit. Creighton and McGuire had a big enough outfit that they could each take a hunting party out. Red Creighton had married Tom Vinson's sister, Nona *(Wynona)* around 1948.

Red had a repeat hunter by the name of Colonel Howard who had hunted in New Zealand and wondered if they could use horses in that country. In the winter of '47 and '48 the Colonel took Red to New Zealand on a hunting trip. He wanted Red to go along to see if they could use horses on the hunt.

Red ended up outfitting on his own because Larry McGuire joined the Warden Service about '50, so Red bought him out. About '51 or '52 Red and Nona went up to Maligne Lake to manage Fred Brewster's camp and they had a little boy by then, called Alfie. Red Creighton was at Brewster's camp at Maligne at the time that I worked with him in '52. We gathered that bunch of Creighton's horses to use on that trip. His horses hadn't been worked for a while and some of them were pretty snuffy.

I was also working with Tom Ross on that '48 hunt. Tom's father was a railroad engineer in Jasper and he grew up going to school in Jasper. He was always interested in the mountains and the trail. Tom Ross and Tom McCready were both crackerjack downhill skiers. They both excelled at skiing—especially with the kind of equipment that they had back in those days. They both did really well. Tom Ross did a little stint in the navy during World War II when he was nineteen years old. He was on a landing barge from which the front was shot off, when they invaded France—with a bunch of people getting killed. I was really good friends with Tom and really liked the guy.

Tom McCready was also in the Navy for a couple of years during the War. I was really good friends with McCready too.

Tom Ross had been down on the trapline with Art Allen one time—on the Smoky, Jackpine and Hardscrabble Creeks. Art and Tom would start from Mt. Robson with a pack on their backs and go down the Smoky drainage, trapping. Art told me that sometimes he started out with two packs. He'd set one down—and take the other one and walk a mile—he'd set that pack down and he'd rest when he walked back to get the other pack. He did everything twice when he was going to his trapline. Can you imagine doing that? Art Allen once told me, "I got my rest when I went back to pick up my other pack."

Anyway, Tom Ross was a very ambitious guy and a very good traveler. In the fall of '49 he and Red went out on a final hunting trip together and I remember seeing them. I think later that fall he went down and joined the Warden Service. He was hired as a fill-in job with Parks Canada. Then he started full-time as a warden in the Tonquin Valley. Tom Ross was an excellent bushman and was one of the men that influenced me into eventually joining the Warden Service.

Pictured above:

Top: Art Allen courtesy of Jacquie Hanington.

Bottom: Tom McCready courtesy of Fay McCready.

Getting back to our hunting trip in '48, we had four hunters out. Red Creighton, Tom Ross, Gene Merrill and Cuff Jameson were guiding. I was wrangling on the trip. We had a long trip—with a lot of people. The bighorn sheep season didn't open that year until September 15. So, they decided that we would go up the Moose River, and make a summer trail ride out of the early part of the trip and hunt later. So we went west from Jasper and up the Moose River—through the head of Blue Creek. We went over the top and out over onto the Sulphur River. We went around to Winifred Lakes—and hunted around there—and back around the back of Mt. Kvass. We eventually worked our way back to Rock Lake.

On the last hunting trip of '48, I was back out with Jack Hargreaves and we were out on the Sulphur River again. Leonard Jeck was out on that trip—and Jack's daughter, Evelyn was cooking—we had a couple of hunters.

During World War II, Jack Hargreaves and Tom McCready had horses running in the Athabasca Valley, wintering there. Some of the horses were in Jasper Park and they ranged all the way down into the green timber where the *Bar F Ranch* is now located near Hinton. Jack was established in Jasper in the mid-1920s and started his own outfit then, after he left the Hargreaves Brothers who were based out of Robson Ranch. He bought out a guy by the name of Ralph James who outfitted in the early days. James was taking people to the Miette Hot Springs on horseback, when there was just a trail up there. So Ralph James decided to sell a bunch of horses that had Morgan breeding in them. There were a lot of sorrels and chestnuts and chocolate-coloured horses—tough horses—my gosh they were tough horses! Ralph James had a place where he ranged his horses at Pocahontas and Jack ended up with the range area. Hargreaves didn't have much help during the war, so he didn't outfit much but had lots of horses at Pocahontas. Five years after I came to that county, we were breaking Jack's old horses. We were working green horses that were six, seven, eight-years-old. They were all broncy range horses. I spent a lot of my time breaking horses and trying to get them ready for the hunting trips—in '48 and '49 and even in '50.

In 1949, I worked for Jack Hargreaves again. I don't remember where we were that summer but we were taking out tourists and fishing trips. Jack had lost one early hunting trip as the hunters had cancelled—and consequently had too many men. I had a chance to go to Mt. Robson and work on a hunt for Roy Hargreaves. I ended up traveling up the watershed from Robson right through to the head of Sheep Creek.

Roy Hargreaves, brother of Jack, was based out of Mt. Robson Ranch. They had two brothers called Frank and George who lived at Jackman Flats near Valemount. Dick was a half-brother who didn't guide that much. Roy wintered twenty-five to thirty head of horses on his brother, George's place, down at Jackman. He kept the big bunch of horses at Corral Creek on the Smoky River for the winter. Each spring, Roy used to take some horses from Jackman and go to the *Range*—gathering a hundred to a hundred and fifty head of horses, and trailing them back to Robson. In the fall, when we were done hunting, they'd trail all those extra horses down the Smoky drainage and put them on the east side of the Muddy Water River. It was a four-day trip down and a four-day trip back again. Roy didn't have enough feed and broke land to grow hay to handle that bunch of horses, so those horses wintered down there. Those horses came out pretty good—if they were able to find them all in the spring. I trailed horses down to the Range in the fall of '49 with ninety or a hundred head. Roy's brother-in-law, Chuck Chesser, Russell Cooper and I trailed the horses that had come off the hunting trips. It was kind of tough as it was getting late in the fall and winter was closing in on us. I never went down in the spring, but Roy Hargreaves usually trailed down to round the horses up as soon as they could get over Berg Lake Summit.

Russell Cooper was a friend of mine that came up from Sundre country. He worked some for Jack Hargreaves, but worked more for Roy Hargreaves and Chuck Chesser out of Mt. Robson Ranch. He did some of the big hunting trips up the Smoky drainage. Russell was a guide in the Willmore area for five or six years.

I was glad to work the first hunting trip for Roy Hargreaves in '49, as I would see some new country. Roy didn't come on this trip but hired me to guide. There were two of us: Carl Mintz was the B.C. guide and I was the Alberta guide. We rode up to Berg Lake, down the Smoky and up Bess Creek to Bess's Shoulder. We dropped onto the Jackpine River, up and over Big Shale Mountain and Little Shale Mountain. We traveled along the Continental Divide through to the head of Sheep Creek. Roy had two parties that flew in and out of Cecelia Lake *(some people called it Surprise Lake)* in a floatplane that year. He had quite a few hunters, but it didn't work because of the weather and of course, in those days, we didn't have radio or telephone communication. The pilots couldn't land the planes because of heavy clouds and poor conditions, and to complicate the situation, they were flying out of Edmonton. Some of

Pictured above:
Mrs. *(Roy)* Sophia Hargreaves,
courtesy of Ishbel Cochtrane.

the hunters made it in, but because it was too weather-dependant, it was not a satisfactory arrangement. Roy decided to abandon the floatplane trips and, from then on, he used horses to transport hunters. We finished our trip and came back to Mt. Robson on pretty much the same trail that we had traveled in on.

When I came in off the first hunting trip, I ended up going into Edmonton with Roy's wife, Sophia Hargreaves to pick up two more hunters for the second trip—who were unable to fly into Cecelia Lake with the floatplane. We drove the hunters back to Entrance to outfitter, Stan Clark's place, where he ran a little store and a restaurant. Mrs. Hargreaves and I were going to drive to Muskeg, as the rough grade road was brand new in '49. It ended at Muskeg at that time. Harold Anderson from Obed came to Clark's store and told us that he was going north with his truck. He was an outfitter who outfitted and trapped the Obed area. He also outfitted in Willmore Wilderness country. Tommy Plante, Felix Plante's brother, worked for him quite a bit. Anyways, he had two hunters, so we hitched a ride with him and with our two hunters. We went to Muskeg where we met Roy Hargreaves' guide, Isaac Plante—who packed the hunters up for the trail. After we dropped off the hunters, we came back to Entrance with Harold Anderson. Boy, was that ever a long day—from Edmonton to Entrance—to Muskeg and back—and on to Jasper!

In '50, I was back with Jack Hargreaves again. In '50, Tom McCready and I traveled in the Mountain Park, Cadomin, Luscar country and south with one of the first geological surveys—working some Devonian limestone. It was Jack Hargreaves' outfit—we used his horses and gear. That fall, Jack and I went out on two hunting trips. Jack's daughter, Evelyn cooked and Leonard Jeck was with us in '50. We had a September trip and an October trip. We were out for sixty-five or seventy days.

In '51, I worked for John Unland. We went out through the Miette and Moose River country and went to Mt. Robson on the north boundary. Then we had a couple of trips to Tonquin. We also had a couple of other hunting trips. Frank Moberly and I were guiding on the hunting trips. We hunted north of Rock Lake and up to Big Grave Flats.

John Unland came from Wetaskiwin and was born and raised around Pigeon Lake. He was a guy who woke up one morning and decided that he wanted to go packing and working in the mountains. Stan Kitchen's outfit was for sale—so John and his brother-in-law, Bill Makenny bought the outfit. Bill was a silent partner until the mid-'50s when John bought him out. The sale was contingent that Stan would take the Bing Crosby trip out. John Unland had a trip out that fall of '47. He hired guides like Dave and Frank Moberly, people who knew the country well. John was a good horseman. His wife, Edith was the trail cook and she became known far and wide for her fine cooking.

John Unland outfitted from 1947 to 1958—when he had a tumor on the brain. His outfit was still operated, however, he hired someone to work it for him as he was in pretty bad shape. This tumor affected him when he walked along, as he couldn't pick up one foot. John had to go into Edmonton and they had a team of doctors look at him. I had gone to see him in the hospital and he was pretty much paralyzed. The doctors told him that he would never walk again—but he did. By 1960, he was riding a horse on the trail again. He wasn't fully recovered but he was able to go out on his trips. He was a gutsy guy and made the best of a bad situation. Everybody that was associated with him admired his congenial ways and determination. He also had a crooked wrist, which was broken when he was a kid, falling off a horse.

I met a doctor from Edmonton, years later, on a boat trip at Maligne Lake. The physician asked me, "Do you know a guy by the name of John Unland?" He wanted to know about how he was doing. He had been part of the panel who had interviewed John about his brain tumor. He said there was a panel of three doctors who asked him, "John did you ever get a bump on the head?' John said, "Oh well, I used to ride horses and do things—and got bucked off a few times." The doctors asked, "Did you ever get hurt?" John replied, "Oh no—nothing like that." The conversation carried on and the medical panel queried, "Are you sure you never got a real hard bang on the head?" John stated, "Come to think of it, I did one time. My brother and I were digging a well. I was down in the hole and a rock fell in and hit me on the head." The interviewer asked how deep the well was and John remarked, "Oh not very deep—maybe eighteen or twenty feet." One doctor asked him how big the rock was. John said modestly, "Oh it wasn't very big—it was only this big *(size of a cantaloupe)*."

John outfitted for quite a few years after that, but he had quite a hard time. Joe Groat worked for him. John Ostashek eventually bought him out but Ostashek went to the Yukon a few years later and became the Premier for one term. John Ostashek was originally from the Coal Branch. Sometime after John sold his outfit, he and Edith left Jasper and bought a farm out by Edson.

My wife, Cathy and I were at Maligne Lake in the Warden Service for a few years—and we had just moved into town *(March 1972)* when I met John Unland on the street one day. He was traveling from Edson to Jasper and it was wintertime. I told him to come on home for a sandwich and a visit—so Cathy made us lunch. Anyway, John had a dry sense of humour. John bemoaned, "It's a bad winter and the wolves are bad. They've killed half of my cattle herd." Unland went on and on about how bad these wolves were. Finally Cathy asked, "How many cows did you have?" John replied dryly, "Two!" John

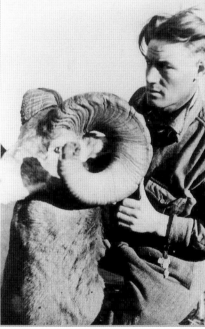

Pictured above:
Top: John Unland , circa 1990s.
Photo courtesy of Fay McCready.
Bottom: Stan Kitchen in 1931,
ram scoring 184 $^{6/8}$th taken with the
Mustard Brother Outfitters
Photo courtesy Jim Babala.

was one of those good-natured guys that it was impossible to fight with. He liked everybody and was a real philosopher. He never got excited about things. He was really a good guy to be around.

In 1952, I guided Jack Hargreaves' outfit and took a geological survey party out. I did a lot of traveling that year. That spring, we had two survey parties out. I had one group out and another fellow by the name of John Williams had the other party. John was raised down around Valemount and ended up a B.C. guide, working for Roy Hargreaves for about ten years. His wife, Dorothy cooked at the same time. She often cooked and worked with Margie *(Duncan),* Roy's younger daughter. They had great fun as she was about Margie's age. Her brother, Bill *(McKinnon)* worked on a lot of those trips too. They were raised there around the Dunster or Croydon area.

That's the summer that Joe Groat was with me and he was a top-notch trail man. He could do anything, cook, wrangle or guide and work bronc horses He knew the country like his backyard. I will tell you a good story about Joe Groat. I was at Pocahontas one day with John Unland. John and I stopped in at a restaurant on the north side of the road. A guy by the name of Len Jones ran that place. John and I stopped in and saw Joe Groat and his wife, Maxine sitting on the stool with these two little kids. Joe Groat's oldest daughter was about four years old and had red hair. Their son, Ken was about two years old at the time. I hadn't seen Joe for a couple of years and I said to him, "Gosh Joe, where did you get this red headed kid?" He said, "Well you know that summer that I was working with you—there was a red-headed guy driving a water truck at Brule and I

think that was his kid." Pointing at Ken, he said, "This one here, I thought that he probably belonged to John Unland—but he don't have a crooked wrist so he probably belongs to Frank Moberly." Joe was a really good man when you got him away from town. He was an excellent trail man. He was fast and he could do anything.

That same year in '52, I was supposed to go on a ninety-day trip and the guy that was going with me didn't show up. I was looking for somebody and I was getting a little desperate about hiring a hand. Joe was with a fellow called Dale Mainprize and they were running around, feeling pretty good. Joe came over and stuck his head over the fence and said, "Hey, I hear you're looking for a man to go out on the trail." I said, "I sure as hell am—are you available?" He said, "Yup." So anyway, we got together and he went with me. We were going out with twenty-two head of horses and three guys. I said, "Joe, do you need a cookbook?" He said, "Cookbook! Hell, I know more about cooking than those guys that make those cookbooks." Joe always had an answer, you know. He should have been a criminal lawyer—he was so sharp—he had all the answers in the world. You know, he was a good man. I always think about the time Joe was stopped by the CNR policeman at Jasper Park Lodge. This was shortly after the big fire at Jasper Park Lodge; the policeman said, "Halt, where are you going?" Joe said, "I'm with the Lloyd's of London. I sell insurance. Have you got any?" And just kept walking right by the guy. I laugh every time I think about it.

We were going down the Rocky River on a game trail. Joe Groat was in the lead and I was in the middle and the geologists were traveling behind. I stopped and counted the horses and saw that I was short one, so I hollered at Joe and told him we had lost a horse. I went back to have a look and this little mare had gone off of

the trail and had gone up in the trees. I was damn lucky to have seen her tracks—but I got her and came back down and got back on the trail. It was probably an hour before I got back to where Joe was waiting. We started out and I said to the geologists, "By God, you shouldn't ride around a horse and leave it behind like that. Next time if you go past a horse and you're going to leave it, let me know about it—so I can go back and get it." Joe never said a word. The next morning, we were getting ready to pack up. Joe was always fast and organized and had everything ready. I had tied this little mare up and was getting ready to pack her. Joe went around and picked up three duffle bags. He put the bags down by the little mare that had wandered off the day before. The party chief said, "That looks like my duffle. Are you going to put my gear on that horse? Isn't that the horse we lost yesterday?" Joe said, "Yeh." The party chief responded, "What are we going to do if we lose her again?" Joe said, "Just see that you don't." That's the kind of guy that he was—he always had an answer. Yeh, we were on that trip in '52. Joe was cooking but he did everything. He was a good trail man.

Joe's brother, Judd Groat was a good trail man too. One time I met Joe Groat and John Unland when I was on the north boundary of Jasper. They had a couple out by the name of McGee. They had come here several years, consecutively. I had gone out with them and knew both McGee and his wife. They were from New York but had retired in Arizona. John Unland and I had taken him over to Mt. Robson previously, that's how I got to know him. I was visiting with McGee and he told me this story. "You know," he said, "That Joe is quite a guy. He always tells us what he sees, saying, 'Did you guys see this or see that?' A couple of days ago I asked John

Unland, 'What animal would be the most unlikely to see on this trail?' John said, 'The most uncommon animal that you would see in these parts would be a caribou.' When they got to camp and were having a cup of tea, McGee said, 'Joe, did you see that cow caribou today?' 'Oh Yeah," he replied without a flinch, "....and there was a calf down there with her.'" Old McGee had made the whole story up. Boy, they had quite a laugh about it.

Anyways, we went way north and around on that geological trip in '52. We came back and went up by Medicine and Maligne Lake, and then we went across and out by Rocky River. We were over in that Rocky country and by Miette, and Fiddle Creek. We went to Luscar and Cadomin, over to Mountain Park, came back around to *Circle M Ranch*. We had been out about ninety days with the geologists. Then I trailed the horses through to Pobokton Creek on the south highway. *Pobokton* is a Stoney word meaning, owl.

Gene Merrill was working at that time on a construction job. That fall, he decided to take some holidays and he joined me on a twenty-one day hunting trip. His wife, Ellen was hired to cook for us. We took two hunters and went to Jobe Creek, which is south of the Brazeau. We were elk hunting down there with our American hunters.

When I got back to Jasper, Red Creighton was gathering horses for a late hunt I was to join him on. Red and I went across the Smoky—pretty near up to Kakwa Lake. This hunter wanted a caribou, so we were going up to Kakwa Lake, but we didn't quite get there. We got a couple of feet of snow; so we started to work our way back down into the lower country. This hunter was a repeat hunter and he didn't really want to hunt. He had built the Banff chairlift and had been out hunting a lot. He really wanted to travel around and look at the country. We ended up heading back on the south side of the Smoky River and up Wolverine Creek to Big Grave Flats. I've crossed over there at Clark's Cache when the Smoky was pretty high. But in '52, when Red Creighton and I crossed the Smoky River—my God, it was deep, deep swimming water that day. That same year, Ed McKenzie and Ken Thompson's son from Rocky Mountain House country were traveling on the Smoky River with another fellow on a geological survey party. They crossed the river at Clark's Cache and got in the river too low down on the 'S' curve there. Young Thompson drowned in there—his dad wasn't on the trip. They found the body the next spring when it washed ashore downstream. Anyways, our party eventually ended up at Rock Lake. I was out over one hundred and fifty days from the time I started until the time I got back.

Pictured above :
Gene Merrill
September 1946
with a small grizzly bear.

Photo courtesy of
Mrs. Ellen Merrill.

In 53' we had two big geological survey parties out. I had one and Russell Cooper and his wife, Mary took out the second party. They were south of the Brazeau River, they were clear down to the Saskatchewan River to the Kootenay Plains *(where Abraham Lake is now)*. I had rounded up all the horses for the two geological survey parties. I think I had twenty-three or twenty-four head of horses and Russell had about the same. I had a guy by the name of Jimmy Joachim with me. He was one of Adam Joachim's sons and was from the Grande Cache area. Lillian Cooper, Russell's sister was our cook. We went clear north to Winifred. Our route took us down through the Sulphur and around down through the Hardscrabble into Winifred Lakes, and down through and back around Big Grave Flats, Rock Lake and the Moose Horn. I was out that fall of '53 hunting with Jack Hargreaves and Leonard Jeck. I wasn't in, in time for the first hunt, but I was back from the geological survey for the late hunt.

In '54 I had a geological survey party out for outfitter, John Unland. That was the year that we worked along the Wildhay and the Berland River. The rivers were swollen and the wooden bridges to Teepee Creek had all washed out. We had to ford the rivers and some of them were pretty deep and high. We worked all along the rock outcrops along the rivers because we were working the **c**retaceous. Cretaceous is the rock that is next to the Coal Age, which is the coal that is mined. We were doing the geological survey right after they discovered the Pembina Oil Field at Drayton Valley. Louis Joachim was with me that year. Louis was good to work with and was a good packer. I think he could track better than anybody I ever worked with. Louis Joachim talked about his Iroquois heritage and was very proud of it. We also had a man cook from down south who had come with the geologist. Louis Joachim lived at what they called Fish Lake, now called Blue Lake. That's where they built the Blue Lake Lodge. They used to have the Air Force survival crews down there and Mike Kelley, father of George Kelley used to train those guys in survival skills. They learned winter survival—went around and snared rabbits and did survival training, this was during the Korean War. *(I know Joachim is referred to as Louis in all of Sue's writings but we always called him Louie.)*

Anyway, Louis had a brother named Frank Joachim. Frank worked with Nickerson some and also worked with Red Creighton. Frank had

been drowned for a few months before I heard about it in '59. He drowned in the Wapiti River when he was moving horses across the river. Frank and Louis had a sister by the name of Rose *(Joachim)* Findlay. She was married to Deome Findlay who guided for Carl Luger a lot. Anyways, we had gone north from Entrance and out by Rock Lake; and north and out around by the Berland River to Teepee Creek; and down the Simonette; then worked our way back. Louis and I were at Teepee Creek on our way to the Simonette when we ran into some of the Grande Cache Natives in July, on their way back from the Pilgrimage at Lac Ste. Anne. They were packing up their horses to go from Teepee Creek to Grande Cache. One of them had a live goose. Where the heck they got this goose from, I don't know. This woman was asking Louis and I if we had ever packed a goose. I think they put this goose in a sack. That poor old goose would have gotten seasick.

Anyway, we went down the Simonette—and that was wilderness country in those days. There weren't any seismic lines or trails that would amount to anything; it was Albert Norris' trapline at that time. We were down there in August and it rained every day, pretty well. The rivers were pretty high and we were in a lot of deep water with lots of beaver dams—which created a lot of trouble. There were a lot of big, old grizzly bears there; these bears hadn't been bothered before. They were still big, old bears with long claws on them and big humps. I saw seven or eight different grizzlies down in there. That's about the only country I've been in where there were any old bears, as the old ones have been killed off in other areas. You can tell these old grizzlies if you look at the pictures of Jack Brewster, George and Roy and Jack Hargreaves on the old hunting trips—they've got those great big, old bears. That's the kind of grizzlies that I saw down on the Simonette that year. You don't see those old bears—even in the *(Jasper)* Park anymore—they're just not around. They were like the old grizzlies from eighty years ago and they weren't tame. They weren't dangerous because they stayed away from humans who hunted them—but now the damn bears are dangerous. They're all half domesticated and used to people.

I came back and went on another hunting trip in '54 with Gene Merrill, and John and Edith Unland, across the Smoky and up to Sheep Creek again. We were guiding the Guinness people from Ireland—you know, Guinness Stout. We started at the Muskeg River and went up to Grande Cache. We traveled past where the Indian houses were—where Louis Delorme lived *(Victor Lake)*. Louis had about nine or ten cows and they were all laying on one of these open side-hills. I was in the lead and Gene Merrill was coming behind with the packhorses. John and Edith and the hunters were coming behind him. I'm sure that we got within a hundred and fifty feet of those cattle—and they were staring at the pack outfit. A couple of the cows stood up, then a few more stood up—then the pack horses had a run-away. They were out of control. It sure was funny to see—the old pack boxes were rattling. We had horses that had never seen a cow before.

I guided a lady who was the daughter of Guinness and she was a real wonderful gal. At that time, Guinness was one of the richest guys in the world, but she was a real dandy lady. She never got frustrated about things and never panicked about anything. I remember coming off a mountain with a goat in that Llama Flats country. It was dark and I was going down through the shintangle and the jungle, looking for two horses that we'd tied in there—and by God, I found them. I wasn't too sure I would, it was so damn dark. Then we rode back to camp. I always admired her because she never panicked about anything—she never worried and said, "Do you think we will get home tonight?" I've had men who would question every move you made when you got into a tight spot like that. That was a pretty nice trip. They were not real big game hunters and were real nice people. They didn't hunt a lot, but they liked to travel. Gene and I were in pretty good shape in those days and we could cover quite a bit of ground. That was in '54.

Both Jack and Roy Hargreaves weren't going out on the hunts by this time, but they hired people to take parties out. Roy was out on the trail until about 1954. I don't think Jack went out after '53 or '54 if he could help it. Both Jack and Roy had a reputation for being very good hunters and for being exceptional grizzly hunters.

In '55, I didn't come north at all. I was in that Rocky Mountain House—Sundre country. I went around and took in a few stampedes. I rode a few horses and went into a few wild horse races about the end of June. Then I took a geological party out for my friend, Russell Cooper. We were in that Rocky Mountain House, Nordegg, and Clearwater, Limestone country until fall.

In '56 I was back up north and I guided a trip for Jack Hargreaves. A young fellow by the name of Joe Timperley was with me that year; he was from Jasper but now he lives in Ardrossan *(Alberta)*. He was a good kid who worked for Unland a lot. My sister, Pat was our cook for the season. I was out on the trail a long time, as we went out in the spring, real early and were out about a hundred days. I remember coming in a couple of times from the Sulphur River by myself with seven or eight pack horses *(for supplies)*. Leonard Jeck and I were on the early hunting trip down around Monoghan Creek. That's about as far as we went. We hunted around Monoghan Flats and around Eagle's Nest.

That same fall, Leonard Jeck had another trip out on his own. Tom McCready and I were out with a late trip with Jack Hargreaves' outfit. Tommy Ross took some holidays and came along and wrangled for us. My sister, Pat was cooking. She cooked on the survey and on two hunting trips and was a really good cook, too. We had three guys out but one man didn't hunt. He was a repeat hunter who was along for the trip. McCready had a hunter and I had a hunter. We spent most of our time around the west fork of the Sulphur River. Tom McCready was out on this trip with his arm in a cast. Tom was a good-natured guy who never complained about anything; he was a well-liked man by everybody who met him.

I was out about a hundred and fifty days that year. I would come into the main valley at the end of the road with a bunch of horses and get a load of groceries. I wasn't shy about going down there, three or four days by myself with seven or eight or nine pack horses, then coming back again. We had a lot of good, old packhorses. If you had two or three broke horses that you could put into the lead, you could follow behind them and lead two or three green horses. We worked some pretty green horses some of that time because they had a lot that weren't too well broke. The horses had been running on an open range and they were old when we broke them. When you had men like Gene Merrill and Tom McCready, you could handle horses like that.

In '56, Chief Warden Mickey McGuire tried to hire me. I told him, "I can't go to work for you this year but talk to me next year." So I went to work for Jack Hargreaves with the idea I would eventually work for the Warden Service. They had been offering me a warden's job for two or three years—and I decided

that maybe I would do that the following year. So in the summer of '57 I ended up packing lumber for the log buildings that Art Allen had been hired to construct. Art and I were both hired to work on a cabin project on Adolphus Lake, at the headwaters of the Smoky River. The second cabin was constructed at Twintree Lake further down on the Smoky watershed. Art was the log man while I worked as a packer. I packed more than seven thousand feet of lumber on packhorses for the two cabins and the two small fire equipment sheds that were built close by. Frank Botham, from Sundre, was the second packer.

In the fall of '57, I started as a District Warden on the Brazeau Lake District. I was there for two years, then moved to the Willow Creek District for five years, then moved to the Maligne Lake District in March 1964 and was there until March 1972, when I moved into Jasper town. The last year that I went guiding was '56. I guided professionally from 1947 to '56. Many of the early day Park Wardens were trail men before they hired on with National Parks. If you go back to the old gang of the Jasper Park Wardens—Mickey McGuire, Bob Jones, Frank Burstrom, Larry McGuire, Tom Ross, George Wells, and some others—you can see a whole era of trail men who were hired by the Warden Service. Frank Burstrom worked with Art Allen on the Jasper Park Boundary surveys. Bob Jones was a packer on one of the trips from Jasper to Hudson's Hope and back again. He was one of the old-timers that had worked on the trail and eventually drowned in the Snake Indian River. Old Bill Peyto started guiding for Tom Wilson but ended up in the Warden Service down in Banff. George Camp was also a trail hand, cooking and working for Curly Phillips. There were quite a number of wardens in the Mountain Parks that were trail men originally. The Warden Service was always looking for men that had been guiding or had trail experience because we were self-sufficient. We could work with horses: track, shoe horses, and pack horses, snow-shoe and winter travel, deal with wildlife problems, and deal with fire. We could climb because we had experience at hunting sheep; we could find someone who was lost, we could cook, and handle ourselves in the mountain wilderness. It was a way of life. The Warden Service didn't need to train us—we just needed a little finishing. That was a whole era—and I was one of 'the last of the Mohicans.' We worked twenty-eight days a month and had two days off. People were used to working like that, and it was a way of life. I was one of the last licensed guides hired as a warden. I made more money working on the trail than I did as a warden. When I started as a warden, I thought that the benefits were worth it. We had medical, compensation and annual leave, and things like that. It's a decision I've never regretted; it was a good career. Eventually we went to a five-day week. Now the wardens only work a thirty-five hour week.

There have been a lot of changes over time. Years ago, Willow Creek was pine and meadow country. Willow Creek is straight west of Rock Lake and has a pretty interesting history. When Jasper House was the fur trade post on the Athabasca in the early-to-mid-1800s, the people that ran the post had hunted out the main valley near Jasper. For many years, the post needed hunters to go north to hunt for meat. Hunters went to places like Willow Creek and Rock Lake and packed meat back down to Jasper House. When I first worked up in the Willow Creek country and went through there with my hunting trips and geological survey parties and so on, there were still teepee poles and meat drying racks, and lots of evidence of that early era. There were about three visible graves in one place over there, and there were six or seven in another place that were easy to see. You can't find them now; because in 2003, I was up there with Rod Wallace. He was doing this human history study for Jasper Park. We were fifty or sixty years late, because I couldn't find a thing, due to the fact that the brush and forest cover had grown up and the evidence was gone. The valley used to be an open meadow and the horses could winter there. In days gone by, when there was a lightning strike, there'd be nobody to put the fire out and it created lots of grasslands. The horses couldn't winter there now because there is way too much brush and small trees.

Pictured above:

"In the summer of '57, I ended up packing lumber for the log buildings that Art Allen had been hired to construct. Art and I were both hired to work on a cabin project on Adolphus Lake, at the headwaters of the Smoky River. The second cabin was constructed at Twintree Lake further down on the Smoky watershed. Art was the log man while I worked as a packer."

Top: Leaving Adolphus - 1957.
Bottom: Packing lumber across the upper Smoky River.

Photos courtesy of Mac Elder.

We're into a cycle and people are realizing that the vegetation in Parks is growing up and that the meadows have grown in. This is not only in our country—but it's all over. Over twenty years ago, they had that big fire in Yellowstone Park. They had the same problem because they had a no-burn policy. They had that big fire and it burnt up a lot of buildings and country. They experienced a heck of a hot fire during a drought. A couple of years later, a lot of the people from the motel and hotel industry in Banff and Jasper town sites started yakking about the same concerns. I'm sure the insurance companies were instigating it. I was Chief Warden of Pacific Rim at the time and I was to a big meeting and there were a lot of superintendents, a few chief wardens and other people. They were trying to think ahead and develop a policy about what will happen, let's say, if Banff caught on fire? What would people do if there was a fire within a mile or two of Jasper—what would be the strategy? The Parks did a little thinning out of trees and a little monkeying around but, it's like everything else: priorities change, pretty soon they didn't have any money to support it and it was another one of those things that died a slow death.

It's much harder to burn areas now than it used to be as there are so many buildings and houses. Policy people don't want you to burn, and the insurance companies don't want burns. Think of burning out around Hinton now that there are houses and acreages everywhere. A couple of hundred years ago it was quite a different story. This morning there was a guy on the radio who was after the government for doing cutting in the Willmore. He said that they were cutting down the old trees because of the Pine Beetle. The guy felt the cutting would chase the caribou out. The caribou like the old growth forests and their decline in population didn't just happen this year or last year. The caribou have been in trouble ever since they built that pulp

mill in Hinton, 'cause all the land that's north of Hinton to Grande Cache—the Berland, Simonette, and Little Smoky—that was an important wintering area for the caribou. In the early days leading up to the 1940s and 50s, a herd of caribou used to migrate from the northwest part of Jasper Park into this wintering area, but now there is only a very small number in the Park herd. In the 1960s, when I lived in the area, the Park herd and the migration had been seriously reduced then. Now it has been logged off and it's full of roads. When you build all these roads and have all this traffic, you make a highway for the hunters and for the wolves. People like the biologist that was on the radio this morning will never blame the wolves for killing the caribou. It's a big thing and it's a very big problem. There's no one solution to fix it. The priorities have changed—and everything hangs on money. I don't have a solution.

The country is red everywhere. If you go up to Williams Lake or go up to Bella Coola and south, the trees are red everywhere—and it has been for a long time. Now the pine beetle infestation is coming into the Willmore country. It's in Banff, Jasper, Grande Cache—everywhere. It will go clear to Saskatchewan. It all started over there in Tweedsmuir Provincial Park and the Cariboo and the Chilcotin area. When I was in Pacific Rim in the 1980s, there was a little patch of pine beetle infestation. B.C. Forest wanted to go in and log it all—and burn it off. The environmentalists wouldn't let them. They launched a media campaign and encouraged public support to leave the trees alone. I have often wondered what would have happened if the Forestry had just cut those trees. Common sense has become illegal.

You know, we had a fire on Rock Creek in Willmore a couple of years ago—in 2003. That's when I was up traveling with Rod Wallace who was doing the human history research. Then they had a big fire on the Rocky River where it flows into the Athabasca—on the east highway there. It went up the Rocky Valley quite a ways. If the conditions are right, there will be a big fire in other areas of the Park.

Grande Cache was open country the first time I was there. The side hills were all open and the trees weren't that big either. When I was last there about 1996, heck, the trees were about thirty feet high. There was a little church down at Susa Creek and that was all wide-open country. When John Unland, Gene Merrill, Edith Unland and I took the Guinness party out in '54, we started there at Teepee Creek. We went from Teepee Creek and crossed Susa *(Sterne)* Creek the next day. The country was wide open and there were hardly any trees. We had gone down to the Native settlement at Susa Creek to ask Adam Joachim where there would be a good ford on the Smoky. Luckily the river wasn't too high that day.

Adam Joachim was a nice man. He was a quiet person. He would travel around the country with his young sons and grandsons and show them the country. One time I ran into him and he had his son, Milton with him and a couple more guys. He went around on some of those forestry trails. The young fellows were supposed to be cutting trails for Alberta Forest Services. Adam went along to see that they got there and got home again. He was doing that in '52, '53 and '54. Adam wasn't any kid then.

The Native guides that came to work in Jasper were Isaac Plante, Louis Delorme, Dave Moberly, Dave McDonald, Louis Joachim, and Jimmy Joachim and there were one or two more. Jimmy Joachim worked in that country a little, but he wasn't a regular. He was the son of Adam Joachim. Isaac Plante, a top-of-the-line guide, lived near Teepee Creek near the Native settlement now called Muskeg Seepee Co-op. He was one of those guys who had been at the

Catholic School in St. Albert. You could tell the people who had been to the residential school because they all wrote so well. They would write in a ledger like a bank teller. I didn't work closely with Isaac but I know he worked a lot for Roy Hargreaves.

Dave and Frank Moberly had worked for outfitter, Stan Kitchen. They also guided for Jack Brewster and Curly Phillips. Younger brother, Ed Moberly worked for Jack Hargreaves and liked him a lot. Another brother called Miles was working around the Hinton mines when I first came into this country in '47. I understand that's where he lost his hearing.

Felix Plante was a Native outfitter who lived on the south side of the Athabasca River, not far from the *Bar F Ranch*—in the sand hills just north of there. Ed Moberly lived close to there too. We used to see him out in the mountains in the early '40s and early '50s. Felix used to go with his pack outfit through the Rockies. He had a good outfit and a good bunch of horses. He was focused on outfitting hunting trips. His boys guided for him, along with his brother, Tommy Plante who was from Marlboro.

Albert Norris was another interesting character that was a guide—and I ran into him from time-to-time. I never worked with Albert, but he worked for Tom Vinson a lot. Albert used to run the *rumly* trip from Jasper Park Lodge over top into Maligne Lake. He was there the years I was the warden. He was back and forth and I saw him whenever he was over there. One time when I first moved into Maligne Lake as a warden, we were getting into construction and had contractors in a couple of camps. We had a pile of grizzly bears in that Maligne country because it was wilderness country then. One day, Albert was looking for his horses in the morning, on his saddle horse. He rode up on a dead moose that a grizzly had just killed. The bear took after Albert and chased him, and he wasn't very far from my house—maybe three hundred yards. He came down just whipping on his horse and yelling, and the bear wasn't too far behind him. It certainly created a bit of excitement. It took him a little while to quit laughing about that. I went up to see where the moose was, because there were a lot of hikers coming into the area. The moose was too close to the trail and I had no way to skid it farther out. So I got a helper and got a chain saw and went up and cut a bunch of standing dry snags that were around. I built a big fire in order to burn this big moose up—as I was afraid that somebody would get mauled. I had a horse and I was riding around checking to see if that damn bear was around there. I had a guy mauled once and I wanted to make sure it didn't happen again. I don't remember what year that bear chased Albert Norris, but in August of '65, a grizzly mauled a Brewster's staff person and he was in pretty bad shape. He got scalped and his eye was torn out, his cheekbone was broke and he just complained about his sore thumb. The grizzly had torn open his upper thigh and his artery was exposed. The reason that the employee didn't bleed to death was because it was snowing and cold. He was in high county and, of course, the man was hypothermic but he didn't pass out. Albert Norris was there when we picked that guy up—and Stan Kitchen, who was managing Maligne Tours at that time for Bill Ruddy, went with me to that incident. We got a stretcher, patched him up and got him out of there. We took him to Jasper to Dr. Betkowski. I have picked up guys that were dead that weren't hurt as bad as this man. He lived, but he needed about five hundred stitches—and ended up in the University Hospital for a long time.

So, back to my story about Albert Norris and the grizzly. I had that fire going good and hot to burn the body of the moose. I knew this would deter the grizzly from coming back for his meal—and hopefully keep him away from the public. While I was horseback riding, checking for signs of the grizzly, one of these modern Naturalists who worked for the Park came along. He said, "What are you doing?" I told him that I had an incident and that a grizzly bear had killed a moose. I advised that I was concerned that somebody was going to get hurt and indicated that I was riding around to make sure that the bear wasn't hanging out in the vicinity. I noted that I had burnt the carcass up. My colleague said, "Oh, I think you made a mistake, grizzlies don't kill moose." I asked him, "What do they kill"? He said, "Oh, they kill ground squirrels." I suggested that I would have to advise the bear that he made a mistake!

Finally I would like to say that Willmore is a great country and a magnificent region. I do believe that I saw it at the best time. Willmore Wilderness Park, like the National Parks, has become an island with development all around it. You can't get up on a hillside in Alberta any more without a sawmill running, an airplane flying over, or a rig moving. There is an analogy I often think of—in that the Park reminds me of a pencil sketch picture. Someone gets a

Pictured left:
Mac Elder in Jasper - 1951.

Photo courtesy of
Mac Elder.

big idea and takes an eraser and rubs a little bit off of each corner—then a few minutes later, rubs a little more off of the drawing. That is what the Park is like. We need to preserve what we have.

Sue, I think you are smart to work with the Willmore Wilderness Foundation to keep mechanization out of the Park. Quads, seismic lines, strip mining and development would wreck it. We need to preserve the traditional activities of hunting, trapping, and horse use. Your best bet to do this is to ensure that the Willmore Wilderness Act is preserved.

CHAPTER SIXTEEN:
Stan Kitchen & the Bing Crosby Story

✌ Authors Note ✌

Stan Kitchen arrived in the Hinton-Jasper area in the late 1920s and gained employment with the Mustard brothers who were based out of Mountain Park, Alberta. He wrangled and guided the latter part of 1920s with Ray and Bill Mustard who had formed a company called the *Mustard Brothers*.

Ray started working in the business as a wrangler for his father and brother, Bill. Bill Mustard was ten years older than his brother. Ray succeeded in getting his guide license in 1924. That year he guided Donald Hopkins and wife. Hopkins was a member of the Boone and Crockett Club. In the fall of 1924 they took a big ram that scored 196 ⅔ Boone and Crockett points. In 1927 Hopkins took another ram with Ray that scored 190 points. In 1937 they bagged a ram that scored 189 ⅞ points.

Stan Kitchen worked his way up in the *Mustard Brothers* business from a horse wrangler to a guide. He worked for the Mustards throughout the Depression years of the 1930s. Stan apprenticed in the outfitting business, working for this highly successful outfit.

Stan and the *Mustard Brothers* primarily hunted in the Brazeau Forest Reserve or the Brazeau River Valley. At the end of the day, Donald Hopkins went on fifteen hunts with Ray Mustard. Stan Kitchen was on most of these hunts.

Jim Babala, a friend of the Mustard brothers, related a story about Stan Kitchen selling a very large ram he had to Bill Foster in 1938. The bighorn measured 196 ⅝ Boone and Crocket Points. The head that Stan sold was listed in the 1971 Boone and Crocket record book. Jim Babala said it was probably a pick-up head.

Stan Kitchen cut his teeth working for the highly reputed *Mustard Brothers* and this apprenticeship put him in good stead to start his own outfit. By the late 1930s Stan decided to form his own outfit. He moved to Jasper in approximately 1937 and established an outfit prior to the war. During this period, Kitchen formed an outfitting partnership with Art Hughes for a short while and operated in what is now Willmore Wilderness Park.

Pictured above:
Stan Kitchen in Jasper.

Pictured on left page:
Stan Kitchen with a bighorn sheep.

Photos courtesy of Gerry Kitchen.

During the war, he worked on the Alaska Highway, and was trucking out of Dawson Creek and Pouce Coupe, B.C. While he was up north, a woman operated his pony barn in Jasper, which he reclaimed when he returned from the Alaska Highway. Later, Stan went into business with Marvin "Red" Creighton. Their outfit was known as *Kitchen and Creighton*, but their partnership eventually dissolved.

Kitchen's most notable trip was in 1947 when he guided the legendary Bing Crosby on a twenty-one-day hunt in what is now Willmore Wilderness Park. Stan retired later that year when he sold the outfit to John Unland and Bill Mackenny. Stan continued his trucking business. In later years, he worked at *Maligne Tours* for Bill Ruddy. Stan died in his sleep at Maligne Lake in 1968.

The following article, *'How I Got My Goat,'* was written by Bing Crosby and published in The Saturday Evening Post, October 16, 1948 edition. Bing kept detailed journals of his hunting trip with Stan. It is reprinted here with permission from The Saturday Evening Post magazine.

༄ *How I Got My Goat* ༄
By Bing Crosby

"He didn't use a stand-in. In a good many cases, articles signed by famous screen personalities are written by someone else. The Old Groaner would like it known that nobody wrote this one but Crosby, who fell down those mountains in person." - Editor of the Saturday Evening Post .

"This is the story of a hunting trip. I went on it in the Canadian Rockies in September 1947. It's a day-by-day account of events that took place, written by myself, with no attempt at fictionalizing or punching it up. We had some laughs and some good shooting. But if you don't think you'll be interested in me following in the footsteps of Carl Akeley or Daniel Boone, you better stop right here.

The idea for the trip took root in 1946. I was in Jasper National Park with Paramount's location company, making shots for The Emperor Waltz.

One of the men Paramount employed to look after the livestock and horses and work as an extra was Stan Kitchen. Kitchen has been a guide for some thirty-five years. Every year he takes parties into the Canadian Rockies in Northern Alberta on hunting trips. *(The area is now known as Willmore Wilderness Park.)* He told us so many stories about the great hunting to be had above the Park that I decided to have a go at it.

I assembled my cast for the hunt in the winter of 1946 and the spring of 1947. I wanted men I thought would be convivial, agreeable and clever in the woods. In the end, the group was made up of a rancher neighbor of mine, Newt Crumley, owner and proprietor of the Commercial Hotel, in Elko County, Nevada; Johnny Oldham, also a rancher from Elko County, Nevada; Dr. Arnold Stevens, a Los Angeles surgeon, and myself. I guess I should amend this by saying that the first two are clever in the woods. The doctor and I left a lot to be desired. But what we lacked in skill we made up for in zeal. I figured the doctor would be a good man to have along in case an ax slipped or if someone got the bends chasing mountain goats around in the stratosphere.

Doctor Stevens is a fine surgeon and a valuable man to have along in wild, rugged country. He is however, absent-minded and he forgot to bring along his medicine kit. But he didn't forget to bring along his movie camera and plenty of film. He shoots a lot of film, either underexposed or overexposed, but never quite right. He is forever posing people for all sorts of shots, usually when they wish they were doing something else. He's the kind of cameraman who would have asked Daniel to step outside with the lions where the light would be better.

We gathered at Jasper Park Lodge and spent the night with Stan Kitchen. Next morning we rode in a truck to our rendezvous with the pack train. There we met the members of our crew. There was

Pictured above:
Bing Crosby had many fans when he was in Jasper.
Top: Yvette Vinson sitting on Bing Crosby's car in 1947, courtesy of Yvette Vinson

Bottom: Bing Crosby, Maxine Groat & friend Belle Kjos. Belle was the daugher of outfitter, Eric Kjos.
Photo courtesy
of Maxine *(Groat)* Thompson.

Don Hoover, about sixty, garrulous but entertaining, a master of invective and contumely. He's a former game warden and forest ranger. During the winter he's a butcher in Banff.

There was Oldham's guide, Frank Joachim, an Indian. He was twenty-four and taciturn, but had ability, resourcefulness, strength of character and woods usefulness. Newt Crumley's guide was a young fellow named Peter McKalip, a husky, sunny, rawboned Canuck. Stan Kitchen was to take care of me and to make sure I didn't blast away at scrub trees or bearded campmates instead of moose.

Our first campsite was on the Hay River *(Wildhay River)*. All of us slept well except Newt Crumley, who had inflated his rubber mattress by mouth, and the moist air in it turned cold at night and made his couch frigid. He tried extra blankets, but the cold air kept right on coming up from the mattress.

Next day we rode to our second campsite, pitched where the waters of the Persimmon *(Range)* dump themselves into the Hay. The following morning, when we came out of Berland Pass, we saw sheep and goats on the cliffs surrounding it. The sheep were ewes, but there were two big billies among the goats, and we matched to see who'd go after them. Doc and John won, and we left them behind with Don Hoover to climb to a spot above the goats. The rest of us reached our permanent camp about one o'clock.

Johnny, Doc and Don got in about six-thirty. Johnny was packing a nice billy. They'd had a tough climb in bitter-cold wind, and when they were completing their climb, Doc had to pull himself up hand over hand and he'd given his gun to Hoover to carry. Oldham and Doc reached the point of the ridge, with Hoover trailing, and found the goats only about seventy-five feet away. The goats took off down the mountainside, and Oldham got a shot from 300 yards. Having no gun, Doc had been forced to sit by helplessly, watching his billy scamper away unharmed. It taught him a lesson: Never let your gun out of your hands when you're close to game, because once you jump a goat or any other animal, he'll hightail it out of there before you can retrieve your weapon.

A big wind blew all that night, but after breakfast Stan, Pete, Newt and I saddled and rode up into the high-cliff area to scout for sheep. The loose shale made it dangerous going for the horses and, after a three-hour ride, we tied up and went on, on foot. During the day we did a lot of climbing over rough country. We saw ewes, but no rams. We kicked up a few nice buck deer, too, but we did no shooting for fear of spooking any rams who might be waiting to be booked for a personal appearance in Hollywood.

After lunch we climbed over a ridge to see what was in the valley on the other side. Newt said he saw a bear down in the valley creek bed, digging grubs. I looked through field glasses, said, "Yep, bear all right!" Newt and Pete took off down the mountainside. After a while they broke into the open below, about four or five hundred yards away from the bear, which was

The handwriting on the tent reads:
COMMERCIAL HOTEL.
NORTHERN BRANCH
Johnny Sick'em
DOG
- MGR.

still digging. When Newt and Pete showed up, the bear disappeared. They walked to where he'd been, so I figured—although I hadn't heard a shot and I couldn't see them any more—that they'd shot him and were walking in on him.

About a half hour later we saw them climbing back up, and when they reached the top they were really cooked. What we had thought was a bear had been just a big old stud porcupine. Newt was bushed after his tough climb, so he rode in with Pete while Stan and I walked.

About a quarter to six we spotted three caribou—a cow, a calf and a young bull. We approached them cautiously. On my stomach I crawled up behind a big rock about a hundred and fifty yards from them. But I dislodged a few stones; the sound spooked the caribou and they ran. I fired, but when I tried to pull the bolt it stuck. It had been lying in the snow and the lubricating oil was frozen. While I tugged, the caribou disappeared over the mountain, moving like pacers at Goshen. That's a fact. Their action is just like a pacer's—smooth and effortless. At the time, however, the beauty of their movements was lost to me.

Our camp was in timber at the base of a mountain. There were big cliffs around us, and a brawling stream ran right through the camp, tumbling over black rocks. Where I'd waited on the top of the ridge for Newt to come back with his tale of the grizzly with porcupine quills, I could see a hundred miles in every direction. What I saw was awesome. There was range after range of snow-capped peaks with deep green valleys between.

Next day thin rain alternated with sleet, but Stan and I decided to visit the Rocky Pass area anyhow. Just before the pass entrance we sighted two billies on a rock saddle. Tying the horses, we started skyward. They climbed up a narrow precipice until they were within scope-sight range of my .30-06, but even if I'd hit one, he'd have been pulp and his horns would have been useless as a trophy by the time he stopped rolling. Maybe I wouldn't have hit them anyhow. I don't claim to be an Annie Lillis Oakley. It was a kick watching them, though, doing a Fred Astaire on places were it seemed hardly possible that a sparrow could come to rest. Even a sparrow couldn't have done an 'Off to Buffalo,' and Buffalo was a long way down.

We rode home in a blizzard and it snowed hard all that night; big, heavy flakes. It was still snowing at six-thirty when we woke up, and the rest of the morning was taken up by a three-handed gin rummy game—Newt, Doctor Stevens and I. Crosby profit, $52.16.

At twelve-thirty the sun came out, and we all took off, hoping that somebody would find where the rams were hiding themselves. Stan and I went up to a pass that led over the mountain. It was blowing a gale, and snow as fine as salt drifted over everything. We saw no tracks, but we did run across several porcupines and treed a big one. In that country, they grow big, fat and sassy. We threw snowballs at him, but it didn't seem to bother him. In fact, nothing seems to bother a porcupine. Late in the afternoon we came upon a couple of big mountain blue grouse watering at a creek. I had my .257 rifle with me, and Stan said, "Go ahead, give 'em a blast."

"I'll just pick his head off, so I won't hurt the meat," I said jokingly. I was bragging, of course, but that's just what I did, from about thirty feet. I don't know how I did it. Ordinarily I'm not one of those right-between-the-eyes boys.

The other bird flew up a tree, and Stan said, "One's not enough for a good mess. Get the other one."

Pictured above (L to R)
Top: Newt Crumley & Stan Kitchen.
Photo courtesy of Gerry Kitchen.

Bottom: Bing Crosby.
Courtesy of the
Jasper Yellowhead
Museum & Archives 999.03.118.

"Oh, no, brother," I said. "That's my shot for the day, maybe for the season. You get it." And that's just what he did too. He took my gun and shot the head right off the other bird.

Morning broke clear and cold, and crawling out of my sleeping bag was an effort. That sleeping bag was getting more and more comfortable. It was on top of an inflated mattress, which rested on the balsam and spruce boughs Johnny Oldham had cut. They were hand-picked boughs with not many limbs, just needles. It was a more comfortable bed than anything at home, and we've got some pretty good ones there.

Breakfast was moose meat and hot cakes, potatoes, canned prunes, hot mush, bacon and coffee. After tucking it away, we started for a point called Big Graves (on the Sulphur River), fifteen miles away on the other side of Rocky Pass. On the way we pushed a grizzly off of the trail, for there were fresh tracks in the snow, and the mud and earth his claws had dug up still oozed. He was a big one; his tracks were catcher's-mitt size. We tried to talk Newt Crumley into leaving the trail with Pete and tracking Mr. Bruin, but Newt said that all prominent grizzly hunters agreed—only somehow he failed to name them—that tracking a grizzly in the timber just isn't done.

A mile farther along we ran into a party guided by Frank Moberly. Frank outfitted out of Entrance, fifteen miles from Jasper Park. He had two doctors with him, a Dr. Malcolm C. Pfunder, from Minneapolis, and a Dr. Frank Knapp, from Duluth. A third member of his party, Charlie Waldo, who ran an opticians' supply store in Minneapolis, was home in camp. They'd spotted seven rams high up in the mountains and, since it had begun to snow hard, they were debating, whether to try for them or wait until the next day. We decided to meet the next morning and do some stalking.

When we reached camp, Doc and Don were already there. They'd had a big day–visually. They'd seen some moose and quite a few caribou, but hadn't been able to get close enough for a shot. I had a hunch that Doc and Don were a little too garrulous for the trail. They talked all the time, and since they generally rode thirty or forty feet apart, hollering back and forth, it wasn't hard to guess why animals spooked out in front of them. The only thing wrong with my theory was that, although we'd been pretty taciturn ourselves, we hadn't done any better.

Next day, Stan and I kept our date with the Moberly party. We found Moberly and Malcolm Pfunder and Charlie Waldo there. The rams they'd

Pictured above:
Frank Moberly

Pictured on left page:
Frank Moberly.

Photos courtesy of
Dusty Groat.

341

spotted the day before were still on deck. But where there had been only seven rams, there were now eleven.

They were on the same mountaintop, alert and watchful. Fortunately, we were in timber, so they couldn't see us. Frank Moberly looked through his glasses and told us that he thought they'd come down to timber to feed when it stopped snowing, and if we started up now we could get into position for a shot. We rode along the trail and then started on foot through the timber. It was steep and we climbed a hundred yards or so, rested for ten minutes, climbed again, then rested again. A third of the way up, we came upon fifteen or twenty blue grouse in the timber. They were perfect for pot fodder, but we couldn't shoot them for fear of disturbing our sheep, so we spent twenty minutes on our hands and knees, trying to catch them or bat them over the head with sticks. When we closed in on them, they jumped ten or fifteen feet away, and the process started all over again. It must have been a comical sight to see a lot of grown men on hands and knees trying to sneak up on a covey of skittish birds.

Finally Frank and Stan went ahead to case the sheep. We broke into a small clearing and, crawling along, came onto a couple of deer feeding. One of them had an enormous chandelier. The other was only slightly smaller and packed quite a hall tree, himself. But with the rams only about three quarters of a mile above us with their ears cocked, it was impossible to shoot them. That last three quarters of a mile was almost straight up and, at some points, we had to pull up hand over hand. I was carrying a gun and camera and wearing a heavy coat. My legs felt like lead, my lungs seemed bursting, and my heart pounded. But each time I felt like stopping I thought of Dr. Pfunder. He admitted to being sixty-one, yet he seemed to be in no greater distress than I. By pulling, hauling, panting and scrambling, we reached a point were we could peer over a ridge at our quarry about four hundred and fifty yards away.

A heavy snowstorm started—big, wet, thick, heavy flakes. We were soaked with perspiration and we clung to the mountain at the twelve-thousand-foot altitude, while our blood congealed, and Frank and Stan debated what to do.

The rams belonged to Frank's party. I was strictly a guest, and as Doc. Pfunder only craved a big head—he had two small ones at home he'd shot on previous trips—we wanted him to have first crack at the biggest specimen. But even with a 'scope site he doubted if he could hit a vital spot, and once his fire had spooked them, they'd light out and that would be the end of our shooting.

Stan decided to circle around over the top of the mountain to see if he could kick them out and head them our way. We watched while he climbed unbelievably difficult places. At last he reached a point where he could get back of them and head them our way. At this moment our rams trotted toward us, outlined against the snow with their heads held high, sniffing suspiciously. The weather cleared suddenly, the clouds parted and the sun shone brilliantly.

Frank and Doc Pfunder got up on the brow of the hill for a shot. The rams were about a hundred and seventy-five yards away when Doc fired. He hit the leader in the hip, but failed to stop him, and the others veered and went up around us. Charlie and I started firing then. I had five cartridges in my magazine, but on the first shot the ejector threw out the used cartridge and one other, and with the second shot the remaining two popped out into the snow. Charlie and Doc were blazing away, the sheep were making for the next ridge, and I was groping in the snow for my lost cartridges. Seeing the sheep getting farther away made me

Pictured above (L to R):
'Taking a Break.'
Johnny Oldham.
Bing Crosby,
Stan Kitchen,
Newt Crumley,
Dr. Arnold Stevens.

Photo courtesy of
Gerry Kitchen.

desperate. Running up to Charlie, I started pulling at his cartridge belt. The confusion was indescribable. I was tugging at Charlie's middle while Charlie's guide was pulling at his shoulder trying to show him where two of the rams had gone. Doc Pfunder was blazing away and, when I wasn't yanking at him, Charlie was blazing away too; and Frank Moberly was yelling instructions.

The sheep were about three hundred yards from us, on another slope, when I got a couple of cartridges out of Charlie's belt. I put one in the chamber and took a pop at a ram. I missed the first time, but the next one must have hit him in the shoulder. He dropped like a stone and slid out of sight down the snow and shale into a deep ravine. Charlie hit another ram in the neck and he fell down a ravine near the one mine had gone down. Doc put a clincher shot into a big fellow and he fell down a third ravine. So now we had three sheep sliding down three slots into the valley below.

But getting to them was quite a job. We had to climb over precipitous and slippery shale covered with snow. If we lost our footing, we'd fall into a gorge or a crevice, but we made it and found our sheep. We got out our cameras and took pictures. Just as we finished, the clouds closed in and the mountains were wrapped in a blizzard. Stan skinned out my head, and we took a couple of quarters and the loins, and started down. The head and cape I was carrying weighed about sixty pounds and I was wobbling, but Stan was in even worse shape. He was carrying the two quarters and the loins. We slid part of the way, fell for additional yardage, stumbled the rest. On this descent, most of it spent on

my extensive derrière, friction burned my hip pocket off, and with it went my brand-new, two-blade, bone-handled knife with leather punch and fishhook disgorger. We reached the trail and the horses about nightfall. The wind was whistling and we got lost a couple of times, and when we sighted our fire, about twelve-thirty, we were cold, wet, tired and hungry. But we had our rams.

The next morning it blew a snowy gale, and we spent the day in camp playing gin rummy. If the storm had kept up, the doctor's instruments would have been mine and I'd have been an innkeeper in Nevada, because though both Stevens and Crumley are reasonably astute men, they would have to have been Gaylord Ravenal, the sharp-shooting gambler in Edna Ferber's Show Boat, to withstand the run of bad cards they were having and the streak of luck I was enjoying. The audit revealed that I was out in front $231.02; Crumley was $58.36 in arrears, and the medic was hooked for $172.66. The snow stopped about four o'clock, and I chopped firewood for a couple of hours. I thought I ought to do something to work off the rich diet we were having—moose meat, grouse, venison, goat, trout, hotcakes and biscuits. Oh my aching girdle!

When we woke at sunup the storm had slackened. After lunch we took off for the next valley, five miles away. Frank and Pete had spotted some pretty good billy goats and had told us where they were. We found them perched up on a ledge, sunning themselves. We tied the horses and started up. During one of our pauses, Stan spotted a well-upholstered billy on the mountain across from us. He was big, maybe a record head. I wanted Newt to have a good trophy, so I persuaded him to go after him with Stan while Johnny and I went up the mountain to stalk the two we'd already seen.

Just as they reached the top, about five hundred yards from their goat, he whiffed them and tore down the mountainside, throwing snow like a rotary plow on a drifted railroad. Our two billies got behind a couple of cliffs, so Johnny and I waited for developments. They weren't long in coming, and were interesting when they came. The goat Newt had spooked off the hill crossed the valley and started up our mountain toward us. He raced up the hill, broke out of the timberline, kept climbing and came out into the open about two hundred yards below us. I aimed at the small of his back about six inches below his shoulder. From that angle, plus the three-inch rise of the 'scope, I figured I'd overshoot about three inches. But I hit him where I was pulling down, perhaps a little lower.

He went down in the snow, slid a few feet, then got up and whipped around the mountain like the girl in the song who was riding all those white horses. This time I caught him in the ribs and knocked him down the hill, about five yards. When he scrambled up, he was going faster, if anything. I was using 180-grain .30-06 cartridges, the distance was only a little more than two hundred yards, and it was amazing the way he could take it. As he reached the crest of the hill, I called to Johnny to put one into him. He had some 220-grain cartridges with him in case we saw a grizzly, and just before he went out of sight, Johnny and I fired at the same time. There was no doubt that he was a gone goat, but the country between us and the spot where he'd disappeared was so steep it seemed almost impossible to reach it.

John found a place where he could climb around the rim of the mountain, but he had calked shoes and mine were rubber, so I didn't dare attempt it. I went down the mountain to the timberline and around the base of the crags, and worked back up. After an hour of scrambling, crawling, panting, climbing and grabbing, I rejoined John and we went after our goat. His trail led down to timber, and a goat goes down only when he's done for. If he can make it at all, he climbs and tries to get up over the mountains into another part of the country. About a hundred yards into the timber we found him still going, but a shot in the shoulder stopped him.

I have never seen an animal of similar size carry the amount of lead that one did. Perhaps it's because they have a very tough hide and don't bleed freely. I don't think I'd care to shoot a beast as game as he was again. I had my camera with me and I got into position and tried to look like a successful big-game hunter trying to seem modest while John took a couple of shots. Then we dressed out the cape and head, and carried them to the bottom of the mountain. I was soaking wet from the workout; it was bitter cold, and we still had an hour's ride home. It looked as if I was a cinch to get at least leaping pneumonia, but I was prepared. In my saddlebag I had a pint of fine old 1929 bourbon I'd bought from Tony Lucey when he ran his restaurant near Paramount Studio. So we had an inner liquid poultice and started home.

I thanked Newt for climbing the opposite mountain and shaking that goat loose and running him over in our direction so I could get a shot at him. My humor might have seemed a little on the wry side, but a hunting trip is no place to pack in tender sensibilities.

Slim had rigged up a pressure cooker out of a couple of pots, and we had a roast cut from one of the quarters of my bighorn sheep. I was in the sleeping bag early, but my sleep was broken at intervals by dreams of falling rocks, snow slides and galloping goats.

The next day Stan and I decided to go with Doc Stevens and Don to see if we could discover what had made their hunting so unproductive. According to Crumley, the sky was cloudless, cobalt blue; according to Stevens, it was copper blue. Being color blind, I made no attempt to classify it, but it sure was blue all right. About fourteen inches of snow was draped over the balsams and spruces, and the Muskeg River, bawling down the valley, frozen over in some places and breaking loose in others, was the only sound we heard other than a clink of a hoof on a stone.

About eleven o'clock Don pulled up, dismounted and unloaded a slew of gear—teapot, cups, meat, salt, lunches, barbecue spits and other culinary articles. The reason for Doc and Don's unproductive forays became apparent. Every day those boys had lugged along what amounted to a portable tearoom and coffee shop, and had been too busy with their cookery to peer through binoculars between eleven and two. It was very restful and, if looked at objectively, probably the smartest routine any of us followed, but it wasn't the type of operation that gets much hunting done.

With considerable prodding, ribbing and kidding, we got them moving about one-thirty and began to comb the big basin. About four o'clock Stan thought he caught a flash of a couple of moose going over a pass a mile and a half ahead of us. We found their tracks, the wind was in our favor, and following them in the soft snow would have been no problem even for a tenderfoot on a Cub Scout patrol. But they kept moving on ahead of us, and we'd just about given up when they suddenly broke out of a thicket about fifty yards from where I was standing.

They were two young bulls. When they split up, one of them almost ran over Don about three hundred yards to our left. He fired his .22 pistol to turn him our way, but the moose bulled right ahead out of the basin. The other broke in front of me and was going up the mountain to our right. He ducked into a patch of timber half a mile away, and as we galloped up to surround it, he started up the mountain again, with Doc blazing away at him. Although he was a long, long way off, I thought I heard a sound as if someone had slapped a bullfrog in the belly with a butter knife. If my ears heard right, Doc had put one into him. When we rode up, the moose was lying on his side. Doc jumped from his horse, and the moose, snorting angrily, started to rise. When those babies snort through the loose gristle of their nose, their face shakes like someone waving an angry mailbag at you. It's frightening to see.

"Hit him!" Stan hollered at Doc.

"Where's the best place?" Doc called back.

"In the shoulder!" Stan said.

He did, and the moose shuddered and tried to rise back again. Doc jumped back, stumbled over a tree trunk and fell into the snow, his rifle falling about ten feet from him. I remember reading that a wounded moose was fairly unpredictable, and I got a cartridge out of my jacket and into my .257. The moose still struggled to get to his feet while Doc ran for his rifle. There was a log between him and the moose, and when he dropped to his knees he aimed so high the shot went over the moose's shoulder. He pulled down lower, and this time he got the moose in the neck. The moose flopped a few times, then lay still.

The Doc was happy. So was I. I didn't want him to go home skunked, and now he had a whole moose to himself. Before skinning him out, Doc had the moose photographed at all angles. We had no sound equipment, otherwise he would probably have made a sound track, complete with a narration of his epic exploit. Looking the moose over, I found myself thinking that although a moose has an ugly puss, his body is beautiful. He has long clean limbs, flat rangy quarters, deep withers, high, powerful shoulders. I couldn't help thinking that if a fellow could fetch a yearling so conformed—a Thoroughbred yearling, that is, no matter how unfashionably bred—to the Saratoga yearling sales, he would bring a fat price.

We stopped at an icy spring en route home and had a Scotch and water in honor of Doc's moose–Doc and Don even carried Scotch and glasses with them—and arrived at camp about eight-thirty. Johnny Oldham had stayed in camp all day doing the laundry—some very nice flatwork.

Next day we started back into Jasper Park and made camp in a pass. About ten o'clock a terrific wind came up. The tent pole fell and hit Doc on the head. Then it hit Newt, me and Johnny. Each time we wrestled it back up, it hit one of us. The gale blew sparks into Don's pillow, set it on fire and burned his hair. It was not a restful night.

The next day we were on the trail at seven-thirty. We wanted to kick up a moose for Newt, and one for me if possible. Newt, Stan, Pete, Johnny Oldham and I rode along, scanning the country with field glasses. After a while we found fresh tracks in the mud and followed them around a hilltop. About a mile away I spotted a big moose with two cows. He ambled up to the edge of the timber, where he paused to watch us. While we engaged his attention, Newt and Pete made a detour and came up on his flank. Through the glasses we saw Newt drill him as clean as a whistle.

He was a big fellow, weighing sixteen hundred pounds, according to Stan, and he had a 50" spread. We left Newt and Pete to skin him while Stan, Johnny and I went off on our own. Our reward was a fresh moose track. We followed it through an old burn and into a moose lick in the muskeg. Dismounting, we got out field glasses and looked around. Sure enough there was Mr. Moose, grazing. Using timber for concealment, we crawled to within about four hundred yards of him. We couldn't go farther without exposing ourselves, and it was up to me to try a shot from that distance. He was on the edge of the timber and if I missed he'd be out of sight in a couple of jumps.

Pictured above:
Stan Kitchen on the trail.

Photo courtesy of
Gerry Kitchen.

I looked through the scope sight and I thought how impossible it was for a marksman as inept as I to make a lethal shot, even with 220-grain bullets, so I started to crawl. After half an hour, we came out above the moose two hundred and twenty yards from him. He saw me and made a break for the timber. He'd gone ten yards when I fired. He shuddered, but didn't go down. I fired again, and hit him in the neck, and he wheeled and ran for a clump of trees in the middle of the clearing. As he reached it, Stan saw his feet go up in the air as he disappeared back of the trees. After a few minutes we walked down towards the trees.

He was a young bull, large in the body, but his head wasn't very impressive. I called to Johnny and asked him to go back to the trail, meet the pack train and pull out a packhorse to carry our moose. The ride into camp was a long one, and Frank set a good pace. I tried every seat known to man on my big, rough-goin' mare, but I couldn't find one that was comfortable. Arriving where the boys were setting up camp, I phoned the administration building in Jasper from the game warden's hut and asked Jim Wood to have a truck meet us the next night and take us into Jasper. We sat round a campfire after dinner and sang a few songs. Somebody got out his camera and took what he claimed were going to be outstanding pictures of the campfire with us seated around it. It was a very colorful group, he thought—a belief in which I couldn't encourage him. Personally, I was hanging on the vine.

When we reached Jasper, the lodge was closed, but one bungalow had been kept open for us, and we got some food at the staff dining room. Next morning we took off for home. But there's one memory that gives me a laugh every time I think about it. When I was trying to catch up with my goat—the one that had absorbed so much lead—I'd slipped and slid a hundred feet into a deep, snow-filled crevice. I thought if my bosses at Paramount could have seen me, it might have ruined a good racket for me. Me, who needs a stand-in so the hot lights won't enervate me, and a double for all my hazardous and semi-hazardous stunts. I hope the studio doesn't get the idea from this that Crosby is the indestructible man and put me to work. Anyhow, it was a wonderful trip. Four weeks without the telephone ringing. And it's a spectacular country—big—and its people are big. Their tastes are simple, but their hospitality is expansive and their motives are honest. I'd like to go back."

THE END

CHAPTER SEVENTEEN:
Jim Babala

I was born in Edmonton on May 21, 1925 and raised in Luscar where I trapped and hunted as a young boy. As far back as I can recall in life, I started fishing and hunting with my father, which was more for sustenance than for sport. This was during the Depression years in the 1930s, which, by many, were referred to as the Dirty Hungry '30s. From that early age, I can truthfully say hunting and fishing occupied much of my time. As a young boy, I always gave thought to becoming a big game outfitter and guide. I eventually got started in this business in 1946 in the Luscar-Cadomin, Alberta area—hunting the mountains of the Brazeau, Clearwater and Athabasca Forest Reserves. A portion of the Athabasca Forest Reserve is now called Willmore Wilderness Park. I outfitted in these areas from 1946 to 1971 with much success—taking many record book bighorn sheep, and building up a reputation as a noted bighorn sheep guide. During these early times, I had no problem booking clients as the Luscar, Cadomin and Brazeau Forest Reserve was noted for producing many record book trophy bighorn. With the war now coming to an end there were many American and European sportsmen and trophy hunters anxious to make pack trips into the remote wilderness areas of Alberta. I could not have chosen a better place and time to get started in the outfitting and guiding business.

During these early times in Alberta, it was not difficult to get an outfitter or guide's license. The only necessities to obtain an outfitter's license, was that one had to have enough equipment and crew in the wilderness to live comfortably for twenty-one days. All equipment had to be inspected once a year by an R.C.M.P. officer before a license would be issued. There were no Fish and Game or Wildlife officers at that time. In order to apply for an outfitter's license, one had to have no past record or any major wildlife violations. There was no problem to obtain a guide's license. All one had to do was write or answer ten common sense questions at the R.C.M.P. or Forestry office. There were no zones or areas assigned to individual outfitters. An outfitter could hunt any part of the Province providing the season was open for the species he wished to hunt. There also was no restriction as to the number of outfitters' licenses within the Province.

During the Depression years of the '30s and early '40s, no major changes were made regarding big game hunting regulations. The winters of '46/'47 and '47/'48 were very severe and hard on big game populations, causing a large die-off of the elk and deer herds. In the area that I had been hunting, the decline of the elk and deer was fifty percent, with moose faring somewhat better. The newspapers' reports of the demise of moose, deer and elk were much higher in other parts of Alberta. The diminishing size of the animal population caused the first major change in big game hunting regulations in years. This resulted in the closing of all special areas for the taking of early antlered animals—with one exception, which was the Athabasca Forest Reserve. This area was kept open to hunt moose, elk, and mule deer—with caribou being closed. Another change included the fact that we were only allowed a choice of taking one antlered animal. During the past years, a hunter was allowed to take one of each species of antlered game. Also during this change in '49, you were allowed your choice of either a goat or sheep—but not both. Grizzly and black bear were opened September 1st with no restrictions on predators: wolf, cougar, etc.

The most serious of all was the die-off of the bighorn sheep population during the winters of '47/'48 due to an outbreak of lungworm. I know I would not be wrong in saying over ninety percent of the bighorn in the area I hunted were affected. The newspapers had many articles regarding the winter kill of moose, elk and deer as reported from Forestry personnel and trappers—but very little was said in the newspapers regarding the die-off of the bighorn sheep. There were no government sources or biological reports other than a newspaper article, which reported an outbreak of lungworm with the bighorn sheep herds in the National Parks. I had never heard of lungworm nor a wildlife biologist or wildlife officer other than the R.C.M.P. or a Forestry officer.

At that time, however, I was aware that the bighorn sheep were having serious problems, as I was trapping the Luscar, Mystery Lake mountain areas with John Haggblad, an old time veteran guide and outfitter. John also trapped Folding Mountain and met up with another guy by the name of John Benson, who also trapped past Folding Mountain. John Benson reported that the bighorn were coughing and having a difficult time getting around in the deep snows. He even made the comment that it seemed that the bighorn had pneumonia. How right he was—and that's exactly what the sheep herd had. But at the time that John Haggblad and Benson reported finding dead sheep on Folding Mountain, we had no knowledge regarding lungworm in wild sheep herds. During that winter, I found one dead ram that had been eaten, so didn't know if it had been killed by a predator or exactly what had happened to it. I did not realize at the time, the serious effects this die-off of bighorn sheep and elk would have on my future and others that were in the outfitting business.

During this winter, there was a loss of many horses throughout the area, as many outfitters and others wintered their horses on the open range. During normal winter conditions, these horses had no problem getting through the winter with the natural grasses they could paw up in the snow. Most of these horses were raised on the open range and knew no other way of life. The '46/'47 winter wreaked havoc, with many saying any animal that survived that year, without help, could survive any weather. However, this winter was more than anyone could have imagined and temperatures were colder than normal. The spring was very late with two extremely heavy, wet snowfalls during the latter part of May. This spring blizzard is what caused the heavy winter kills.

I can truthfully say this winter broke me financially, as I had purchased horses from the prairies of Alberta—and I had to feed them through these two hard winters. I was fortunate, as I only lost six horses during these trying times. Many others lost all of their range stock. People thought that it would take at least ten years for the elk herds to recover—and at least twenty years or longer for the bighorn sheep to increase their population.

These circumstances only left two outfitters operating in the Coal Branch area: Ed Madams of Cadomin and me from Luscar. Three other outfitters working from Mountain Park gave up their businesses after losing ninety percent of their horses. I can honestly say the decimation of the bighorn and elk populations left a big question mark in my mind—if I would continue outfitting. The wildlife south of the Athabasca to the Brazeau River was hit extremely hard, however the impact west of the Athabasca River was not as severe, and more sheep survived.

During the '47/'48 hunting season, I took out a very well-known hunter, Colonel John K. Howard and his companion. Both hunters took out a fine bag of trophies including bighorn, elk, grizzly and black bear. The Colonel had made many Alberta hunts with many well-known guides, trying to take a ram that would better a 40-inch curl—without success. In 1946, Larry McGuire and Red Creighton took the Colonel out hunting and they had a very successful year. The two of them started outfitting in partnership during the '45 season after they bought

Pictured above:
John Haggblad with ram in 1955 at Big Grave on the Sulphur River. B.C. score 180-³/₈.

(B.C. stands for Boone & Crockett Club.) Photo courtesy of Jim Babala.

out Jack Brewster's outfit. Red Creighton was a seasoned outfitter, as he had been in an earlier partnership with outfitter, Stan Kitchen—however, this business venture dissolved in 1943.

After Creighton and McGuire purchased their outfit, they had their work cut out for them. Former owner, Jack Brewster had a number of young, unbroken horses ranging along the Rocky River. These horses had never been handled or halter broke, as Jack hadn't been active for a number of years. He had been fighting a battle with cancer. Larry McGuire had grown up in Jasper and had worked as a guide and wrangler and helped outfitters in many horse roundups. He was also experienced at breaking horses.

Larry and Red took on the job of breaking these horses and they got forty head ready to work that year on the trail. In 1946 they were booked up better than ever. That season, they booked a party of five from Boston—a wealthy businessman by the name of Endicott. Endicott brought along his son, daughter and a friend of his daughter and his attorney, Colonel J.K. Howard.

Colonel Howard had just returned to civilian life from the U.S. Army. He had been a colonel with General Stillwell. Larry McGuire asked his good friend, John Haggblad if he would guide for them during the 1946 season. John was assigned to guide Colonel Howard who was recovering from a bout of malaria. He had made the trip mostly to help regain his strength, so was taking it real easy.

He was leisurely enjoying the trail ride, camp life and fishing. This outing was agreeing with the Colonel and he was feeling better than he had for some time.

John and the Colonel decided to make a try for a goat as they had seen many low down on the mountains and they were everywhere. The Colonel wanted a nice rug for his daughter so they made a spike camp and bagged a goat, as well as a good buck mule deer. While spike camping, the topic of sheep hunting came up. The Colonel was an experienced sheep hunter and had made several trips after bighorns. He had made two trips with the world-famous Jim Simpson from Bow Lake, Alberta, who had taken the legendary Simpson ram in 1924. The best ram that Colonel Howard had taken was in 1929 with Simpson, and it had a 39-½-inch curl with a light base. He told John he wanted a ram with a curl over 40-inch with a very heavy base. John advised he could get one out of the Coal Branch area where he and his brother, Nick used to hunt and outfit. He let the Colonel know that he had promised to guide for Babala Bros. for the 1947 season. The Babala brothers had just started an outfitting business in Haggblad's old hunting area, the Coal Branch and Brazeau River. The operation was a joint venture between my brother, Bill and me.

The Colonel said he would make the hunt the following year, if his health continued to improve, and if John would guide him. He also made arrangements with Red Creighton to hunt elk in the Brazeau River area from September 1-21, 1947, to get an elk that was better than six points to the side. He wanted a seven-point and the heavier the antler, the better. He then would book with Babala Bros. from September 25 to October 15 and would confirm the hunt during February of '47. This all depended on his health.

Colonel Howard phoned me during February to confirm and, better yet, said his daughter would accompany him as a hunter as well. This was Babala Bros.' first hunt for non-residents from outside of Canada. This made John Haggblad the grandfather of *Babala Bros. Outfitting*, and Red Creighton, the godfather. I have much to be grateful for, to both these men. Without their help and the good recommendation regarding the Coal Branch area, I don't believe we would have booked this hunt.

The Endicott party had a very successful hunt with Creighton and McGuire taking a fine bag of mixed trophies. The best rams taken were in the 37-inch to 38-inch class. No 40-inch rams were seen, which encouraged the Colonel to hunt the Coal Branch area.

John Haggblad returned from his trip very pleased with Red Creighton and Larry McGuire. He was very impressed at how well Red was organized and how well he managed his outfit. John suggested it would be good experience for me to work a trip or two with Red and Larry; but due to involvement with my own outfitting business and constant bookings I was unable to.

Pictured above:

Jim Babala with a grizzly taken by Paul Inzanti of New York City at Cardinal River 1960. This was a three-year-old bear.

Photo courtesy of Jim Babala.

In 1947, Colonel Howard and his daughter had an exceptional trip with the *Babala Bros.* The bighorn that the Colonel took was a ten-year-old heavy-broomed ram, that had a curl of 40-¼ inches and 40-½ inches on each horn with a 15-¼-inch base. His daughter took an eight-year-old ram that the Colonel had passed, as the ram only had a 38-½-inch curl with a 16-½-inch base with both horns unbroomed. These rams were fine specimens of bighorns, and I couldn't have taken them at a better time or for anyone better—anyone who would do me more good as an outfitter. The Colonel was one of the last original members of the Boone and Crockett Club and also worked as a scientist with the marine laboratories of Florida. The scientist documented everything regarding the hunt with a complete account of every animal we saw. I can now say he was very impressed with the entire trip and all the wildlife we saw, particularly the number of trophy sheep in the Mystery Lake, Luscar area. His count was eighty-six trophy class bighorns, with three rams measuring over 40-inch curls. These were the best rams that the Colonel had ever seen during all his previous hunts.

Guiding and outfitting hunting parties with my brother, Bill was going well. Red Creighton and Larry McGuire continued to take good rams in the Kvass *(Creek)* area with guide, Ed Moberly taking an exceptionally good head in 1949. Red told me he felt the wrong hunter had taken this fine ram, as he was definitely not a sheep hunter. He said that the goat this hunter bagged meant as much to him as the fine ram. This hunter was not a trophy hunter and it was his first big game hunt—and probably his last. Red said he never heard from the hunter again. Quite often this happens with hunters who make one trip in a lifetime.

In 1951, Larry McGuire joined the Jasper Park Warden Service and Red Creighton bought him out—and continued to run a first-class outfit. He retired in 1964, selling his outfitting business and the *Black Cat Ranch* to Dave Slutker from Edmonton. On his retirement, Red lived in the Brule and Hinton area and worked during the winter months in Hinton and Jasper arenas as icemaker for winter sports. I visited Red one last time in '84—and spent an evening with him. I had just come back from hunting whitetail deer in the Czar-Provost area of Alberta and was feeling pleased as I had taken a fine record-book whitetail scoring 171-⅜ points. I had a great time talking about the good old days with Red. As I had recently returned from New Zealand, we had something in common to talk about. I had bagged a red deer, fallow deer and chamois. Red had made a trip to New Zealand in the late 1940s with Colonel Howard who had hunted there on different occasions. He was very impressed with the number of game animals in that country. The Colonel had made a trip with Red to talk with government officials about starting a hunting and outfitting service for visiting, non-resident hunters. Red decided against starting a business there. As Red put it, "There was too much damn government red tape—bureaucracy and money problems controlled by the New Zealand government."

Pictured left:
Jim Babala
was born in
May 31,1925.
He is age 33,
pictured here
in 1958.

Photo courtesy
of Jim Babala.

When I visited Red, he was eighty-two years old and his mind was very keen and active. His memory could not have been better, even as a young man. His health was failing and he had a severe calcium deficiency and was recovering from a broken arm. His bones were so fragile that when he went to throw out an old portable T.V. set, his arm snapped. As Red told me, "Jim, its hell to get old when your mind wants to do something but your body can't." I looked at Red and said, "Hell, you'll be here next fall and we'll cook up a feed of halibut and salmon. You take care and I'll see you then." Red invited me to spend the night with him but I had promised friends in Edson I would join them on a deer hunt, as I was still hunting for trophy mule deer. I departed, advising Red that I would see him the next October. Red said, "I hope so—but don't bet on it, Jim as there isn't much left in this old hide." I thought of this as I drove to Edson. Red contracted pneumonia and died in the Hinton hospital in early March—another of Alberta's great guides and outfitters, and outdoorsmen, gone.

The Colonel passed the information of the '47 hunt on to other Boone and Crockett club members and the Marine Laboratories of Florida. The trophies were sent to *Jonas Bros. Taxidermy* in New York. As a result of shipping the bighorn sheep, elk and grizzly trophies to be mounted, I had more hunters wanting to hunt with me than I could accommodate—in particular bighorn sheep hunters. There was one big problem now. Since the die-off of the bighorn sheep, there were no trophy rams to be had within the areas that I had hunted in the past. I had scouted and combed the Mystery Lake, Cardinal and Brazeau River areas, finding only a small number of ewes, lambs and two-year-old rams. I found no rams of trophy size that were worthy of mounting. I advised my clients of the lungworm impacts, since I was unable to find suitable live trophies to hunt. I ended up sending back the reservation deposits.

362

During that time, I had found two large ram heads that died over the winter. One ram was 42 inches and unbroomed with a 16-inch base and the other was a broomed ram with a curl just under 41 inches, also with a 16-inch base. Both of these rams, in my estimation would have scored about 190 points or better with today's B.C. measuring system. When I returned the deposits to my clients, I sent close-up photos of the rams. These photos brought much more attention and further correspondence. This made me aware of what a large bighorn ram meant to the outfitting business of Alberta.

Despite this realization, I was somewhat torn. Due to the sheep die-off, I was seriously thinking about getting out of the outfitting business. My brother, Bill decided to quit outfitting and I arranged to buy out his shares that year. I started taking hunters out on my own in '49—and that was the first time I hunted on the Wildhay and Sulphur Rivers.

In 1949, I hired Louis Joachim, an accomplished trail man, as the head guide to lead a hunting party to the Hay and Sulphur Rivers in the Athabasca Forest Reserve. I had tried to hire Frank Moberly, but he was booked up with Johnny Unland. My friend, John Haggblad recommended Louis Joachim, who had been recently hurt in a rodeo accident. Louis was living close to Entrance at that time and he certainly knew the lay of the land. Bill Bodenchuk and I were the guides on this thirty-day trip. George Richmond was the cook and Dave Findlay was the horse wrangler. Louis Joachim was a good guy to have along and seemed to know where everyone was hunting. We trailed our pack outfit up Solomon Creek to Mile 29 where there were a lot of resident hunters. Some hunters I met along the trail advised me that no one was hunting the south fork of the Wildhay River, so we moved and set up a camp there. Bill Bodenchuk and I went up and found three bunches of rams. We spotted nineteen rams in all. Our hunting trip was very successful and we came out with a full bag of trophies, which included bighorn sheep, moose and grizzly. Due to the injury from the rodeo accident, Louis stayed in camp and caped out the trophy heads. That was my first trip into what is now the Willmore area—and that area kept me going for years.

Bighorn sheep hunting in '49 was certainly demanding and virtually no large rams were taken for years in Alberta after the demise of the sheep population. Ed Moberly certainly was the exception to this. He had worked for Red Creighton through the '48 and '49 seasons. It was pretty amazing that Ed guided a hunter to a 41-½-inch ram in '49. I feel quite safe to say this would have been the best ram taken in Alberta. Ed's hunter took this trophy bighorn on Kvass Creek, which was one of Red Creighton's favorite hunting spots.

Ed guided for many years, and the last time I saw him was in '82, when he was walking his dog near his home in Entrance. As I neared him, I stopped and said, "See any sheep, old-timer?" "No," he said, "Can't see good enough any more, Butch." Ed thought he was talking to Butch

Pictured above:

Top: Louis Joachim. Louis guided for Jim Babala 1949 and cooked on one trip in 1960.

Bottom: Bill Bodenchuk guided for Jim in 1949. One of the best sheep hunters ever.

Pictured on left page: "Mustard Brothers' Camp." Stan Kitchen worked for the Mustards in the 1920s. *(See previous chapter.)* Photos courtesy of Jim Babala.

Pictured above (L To R):
Jack Gregg & wife Mary Cardinal. Jack Gregg, founder of Luscar & Mountain Park Mines, lived to 110 years of age.

John & Susanne Moberly, were the parents of Dave, Frank, Ed, Miles & Don Moberly in 1910. Their sons were world famous mountain guides.

Photo courtesy of Jim Babala.

Groat. I laughed and told him who I was. He looked up at me and said, "Nice to see you again, Jim." He went on to ask how things and hunting in the Yukon were. I had moved my hunting operation north in '72 and I was just visiting family and old friends in Hinton. I told Ed that I had retired from outfitting and guiding—and that now I was just doing some writing and fishing in Alaska. Ed invited me to his home saying he would like to talk with me. I accepted his invitation and told him I would appreciate some information regarding the Moberly family history. Ed told me that it was a good time for a talk, while his wife had gone to town.

I had a very good talk with Ed and he shared the Moberly family story. At eighty-one years of age, Ed was quite able—except for his eyesight. He always had a friendly greeting, a laugh and a smile when he met you. He also had a serious, funny sense of humour, more so when he had a few drinks in him. One couldn't stop laughing when he was drinking and telling stories in his own dry way. Ed was a fun guy.

Ed told me that his family was the last direct link to the fur traders—who were the power brokers of their day. This family goes well back to the early 1800 fur-trading days. Ed's forefathers made many hard, strenuous packtrips from Lac Ste. Anne to Jasper House. His grandfather, Henry John Moberly traveled west on a packtrain that had forty head of horses. In his grandfather's journals, he stated the road to Lac Ste. Anne was good, however after they left this post, they followed Indian trails and it was often difficult, rocky terrain. At one point in the journey, their party came to a dead end. The outfit thought they were traveling between two lakes, but it turned out they had traveled down the center of a big horseshoe lake. They had to backtrack many miles but finally made it to Jasper.

Henry John Moberly was the Chief Factor of the Hudson's Bay Co. in charge of Jasper House from 1855 to 1861. He married and became the forefather of the present day Moberlys. Henry moved on to other postings, while his wife Suzanne raised their two sons, Ewan and John—who were born on Moberly Flats, near present-day Jasper. John Moberly was Ed's father.

John Moberly made packtrips in the early 1900s from Lac Ste. Anne to Jasper. It was a great day when John got a moose between Lac Ste. Anne and Jasper, as they were very scarce. The family could always count on getting sheep at Miette, at the East Park Gate near Folding Mountain. During the 1920s, the moose got to be more plentiful, however the Moberlys continued to hunt for sheep and they had no problem getting all they needed. They shot ewes and lambs, as well as rams.

Lewis Swift, an American, settled in the valley near Ewan and John's homestead in 1891, married and started his own homestead. Many a traveler had to pass by his place and often needed to acquire provisions from him—at a time before the railway arrived. Jasper House was the biggest settlement in the valley in the early days.

The boundaries of the newly created Jasper National Park were established in 1907 and the Canadian Federal Government had no tolerance for the people who lived there. The government bought out some of the settlers and pushed others out. All the people that had taken homesteads near the present-day town of Jasper, in the Athabasca valley, were forced to relocate elsewhere. Many arguments and disagreements developed. Some had title to their land and were granted parcels of land outside the Park boundary. Others, who only had a verbal agreement with Ottawa, were evicted and told to settle elsewhere. John Moberly was given a parcel of land east of the East Gate of Jasper Park—at Prairie Creek. John's brother, Ewan Moberly only had a verbal agreement. Adam Joachim, Ewan and others were just evicted with no land settlement. They were told to settle in the forest reserve at Grande Cache on the Big Smoky River, without a written agreement. In years to come, their families had land problems. The old saying is "A verbal agreement isn't worth the paper it's wrote on!" How true!

Along Prairie Creek, where John Moberly settled, was a small shack or tent town. It was a small town consisting of two stores, a hotel, a thirty-bed hospital, a livery stable, and a pack business operated by Fred Brewster. Jack Gregg had a ranch, which was later called the Bar F Ranch, and there were John Moberly's dwellings and land that was allotted to him. The Prairie Creek settlement was short lived.

Pictured above:
Don Moberly, son of John Moberly, was a first class guide.

Photo courtesy of Jim Babala.

The Moberly brothers, Dave, Frank, Ed and Miles, along with their sisters, grew up at the ranch on Prairie Creek. Dave, the oldest child was born at Moberly Flats near Jasper House January 1894 and died on January 7, 1969. Frank was the second oldest brother and was born in 1896 at Moberly Flats and died in 1981. Ed Moberly, the third brother was born on December 29, 1901 at Moberly Flats— and I do not have the exact date he died. Miles was the youngest and was born at Prairie Creek on September 10, 1913 and died May 11, 1983. The Moberly brothers grew up hunting and traveling the mountain wilderness. They knew how to handle horses and were expert trail men. They led many parties hunting, mountain climbing, summer sightseeing, and on packtrips into the Rocky Mountain wilderness.

Ed started guiding for Curly Phillips in 1920 along with his brothers, Dave and Frank, and Adam Joachim. He worked with Curly until the '30s. While employed by Phillips, Ed claimed to have cut a boat in half and moved it by packhorse to Clark's Crossing—and assembled it again. This boat was used for many years by outfitter and survey parties to cross the Big Smoky River. Next, Ed went to work for Jack Brewster for twelve years, then for Jack Hargreaves for eleven years. He also managed a couple of hunts for outfitter, Harold Anderson and one season for Roy and Jerry Anderson after their father died. The Moberly brothers acquired much fame as guides, packers and trappers. It was often said that they were the backbone of the Jasper Park outfitting business. Outfitters in the Athabasca Forest Reserve were also anxious to hire them.

For a short period of time, Ed left the guiding business and went to work for the CNR as a section hand, working out of Brule. I met up with Ed at Entrance during the early 1950s, and on one occasion he said, "This Indian has had enough of working for the railway." He added, "My thoughts are with

the mountains and I have been thinking about how I would like to barbeque a
nice side of sheep ribs over an open fire." Ed asked me if I had work, so I hired
him in '57. The first hunt went very well, as Ed and my hunters both took a ram
each—and the goats were everywhere. Everything was easy and fell into place.
That summer, Ed went to work for Jack Hargreaves taking out summer trail rides.
He met Anne, his wife-to-be, a New York lady of French parentage. Ed and Anne
married in '58 and Ed said that he would work for me for the entire 1958 hunting
season. The '58 season turned out to be a tough one, weather-wise. We had snow
from early September on through October. We had to shovel snow every time we
moved camp, in order to pitch our tents. The first hunt went well and we got our
sheep and goats before the snow. We had no problem getting moose, caribou and
grizzly. During the next hunt, there was more snow than ever, and the hunting
was tough. I don't think that Ed ever guided after that hunt.

Dave Washington Moberly was the oldest brother and I had the good fortune
to have many discussions with him about his family. Dave initially started guiding
with Curly Phillips in 1920 along the Sulphur and Smoky River area. They built
rafts at Clark's Crossing and floated down the Big Smoky leaving food caches
as they floated down the river. They arrived at a place just upstream from the
present-day town of Grande Cache. They unloaded their supplies, their hunters
and backpacks. They used dogs to pack some of their supplies and slowly hunted
back in the direction of Clark's Crossing. It took them a week to ten days to make
the trip back to Clark's Crossing. Dave said the dogs were easy to look after and
feeding them was no problem. The dogs ate just about anything—fish, rabbits,
marmots, porcupine, ground squirrels, or ptarmigans. The dogs worked better
for Curly's style of hunting. They were much more suited than horses to crossing
the mountains, as they could camp any place they wished. With horses, they were
more restricted—camping where there were grasses. It was a tough trip through
these lower mountains—and they got steeper and rougher as one progressed
upstream to Clark's Crossing. Many steep draws and valleys were covered with
lots of brush and timber. All the hunters that made this type of backpack trip
to Clark's Crossing were selected and known by Phillips. Curly was not keen on
horses and he was certainly more of a boatman. He had a lot of experience with
boats in Ontario where he grew up.

Years later, I followed Dave Moberly's directions and took packhorse trips to
the area that Curly and he had hunted with backpacks. I found the area to be
somewhat tough—but eventually found a satisfactory and not-too-difficult route
into the area. The trips into this area proved rewarding, as many fine sheep as well

Pictured above:
Ed Moberly guided
for Jim Babala in
1957, 1958 and 1959.

Photo courtesy of
Jim Babala.

as goats and grizzlies were taken in the mountains—thanks to Dave Moberly and his advice, as his directions were invaluable.

Dave ended up working for Fred Brewster during the 1930s and '40s. After Brewster sold his interest, Dave went to work for Tom Vinson, as well as for Harold Anderson. Harold was an outfitter that hunted the Muddy Water River and Femme Creek across the Big Smoky River. Next, Dave worked for my business, the *Babala Bros. Outfitters* from 1956 to 1962, as a guide and camp hand. Dave and I became very close friends during the time he worked for me. We spent a lot of time talking of past hunting days and old times. Dave told me stories of Ewan Moberly, his Uncle, who discovered Miette Hot Springs, now a very important summer spot in Jasper Park. He also told me of the many subsistence hunting trips that he had made as a boy, to the headwaters of Fiddle Creek Divide. Dave spoke of vast numbers of sheep they saw and the large herds they shot for meat. He said the sheep were much larger than the sheep west of the Athabasca River, namely the Berland, Muskeg, Sulphur and Smoky Rivers—and yet smaller as one proceeded closer to Grande Prairie.

Dave was a talented man. He showed Jack Gregg, the old-time prospector, the first exposed coal seams in the Luscar Mining area. Jack Gregg was the discoverer of *Mt. Park and Luscar Colliery*. He later sold his leases and claims to the Mitchell Bros., from England who developed the mines. Dave Moberly was truly an outstanding mountain man.

Frank Moberly was the second oldest Moberly. Like his brothers, Frank worked for Curly Phillips in the 1920s and the early '30s. Dave, Frank, and Ed Moberly and Adam Joachim were Curly's mainstay in the outfitting business. Curly, himself was a super, well-organized outfitter of the times. Frank later hired on with outfitter Stan Kitchen and worked for him through the '30s until the later part of the 1940s. In 1947, Frank assisted Stan Kitchen when the Bing Crosby party was on a hunting trip in the Willmore region. Frank continued to guide for John Unland who bought out Stan Kitchen shortly after the Bing Crosby hunt.

Frank was also well-known by the coal miners of the Coal Branch for his honesty as a horse dealer. He sold many horses in the area that the miners used for hunting and fishing trips. With my first pay cheque from Luscar Colliery, I bought my first chestnut mare from Frank.

Frank's health began to fail, as he had contracted pneumonia several times while on the hunts, and he, more or less, gave up guiding. I got to talking with Frank in 1960 and he said he wouldn't mind guiding and managing a hunt but would like it to be done early in October, before the cold weather set in. I booked a young doctor and his wife. Frank managed this hunt with Alex Stein as second guide, Harold Woodley as cook, and Ivan Thurner as horse wrangler. Alex Stein was a guide with much experience who always put out a hundred and ten percent. Both Alex and Frank came out with a full bag of trophies, taking record book sheep and grizzly, along with goat and deer.

The next hunter was a lone doctor and Frank guided him to a grizzly, goat and deer, but missed out on the sheep. The doctor was satisfied with the hunt and rebooked for the following season. I received many compliments from clients regarding this outfit, as it was very well managed by Frank. The next year, the doctor took a full bag of trophies except for sheep—and again he rebooked another hunt along with another physician on October 1, 1962. At the last minute, Frank came down with a cold. The result was that I guided this doctor, and John Ostashek guided the other medical doctor. Both hunters took sheep, goat and elk. The doctor I was guiding shot a real heavy ram with over a 16-inch base and a 36-inch curl. He shot this ram from over seven hundred yards and he took the smallest ram out of three. The other two rams, I am sure, would have made the record book, with the biggest scoring over 180 points. These were two of the best rams I ever saw in Moon Creek in the Berland River area. The doctor was quite keyed up to come back again next season to hunt for the rams that got away. I just couldn't take this doctor's ways and told him I was booked full for the coming season and couldn't work him in. Frank had a very good personality as he work with anyone.

Pictured above (L to R): Hunter & Frank Moberly, guide. Taken in the Big Smoky Valley in 1939.

Photo courtesy of Jim Babala.

The doctor wrote to Frank and they remained friends for years. I believe that the doctor was Frank's last non-resident big game hunter. He made a few early September hunts with his son, Allen. I met Frank at the Timberland Hotel just before he passed away. He was, without a doubt, one of Alberta's outstanding guides.

Miles Moberly was the youngest of the Moberly brothers. John Haggblad described Miles to me after working with him on a hunt. "What a man!" John said, "Miles fills the bill any place you put him—as they say in cowboy lingo, 'an all-rounder.'" Miles was an extraordinary guide and a very soft-spoken, quiet man. He was always putting out one hundred and ten percent—or more. He outdid himself in finding bull sheep as he called them. He was known as the best when it came to producing bull sheep—as they say in guide talk, Miles knows all the ram holes. He knew the Hay, Berland, Muskeg, Sulphur and Big Smoky River areas as good as the best knew the area—inside out. Even when finding trophy rams got tough, Miles could always come up with a good trophy bighorn.

Miles started guiding in 1932 for Jack Brewster and later for Fred Brewster. During the war years, Miles went to work for *Sterco Colliery,* which was essential wartime work. He had hearing problems and wore a hearing aid and was not accepted in the army. Miles stayed on with the coal company after the war. He worked there for ten years. In 1952, he again returned to guiding and started with Tom Vinson who had bought out Fred Brewster. Tom had taken over most of Brewster's concessions in Jasper Park. I met and spoke with Miles many times, as we met at different times when he worked for Tom Vinson and for Red Creighton, hunting on the Sulphur River. Miles worked the seasons of

Pictured above:
Miles Moberly
standing in front of a log
house that Freddy Plante
& he were building.

Photo courtesy of
Emil Moberly.

'55 and '56 for me and did a great job. He took good sheep on his second hunt. He guided his hunter to the best goat that my outfit ever produced. It measured out 10-⅝ inches with a heavy base.

During the season of '55, Luscar Colliery asked me if I could put an outfit together, as they had several guests they would like to invite out on a big game hunt. Both my outfits were fully booked. I rented several horses and I pulled an outfit together and hired a fine crew of top men: Miles Moberly, Dave Moberly, Bud Malloy, Norman Woody as guides, John Haggblad wrangler and camp hand, and Tommy Robertson as cook. John Haggblad, a man who had seen everything there was to see in outfitting and guiding, really came to respect Miles on this trip. Tommy Robertson was a fine cook and he turned out gourmet meals. He put out the finest meals—that is if he had lots of time to work with—but had problems at breakfast. He had to get the hunters out before seven in the morning. As John put it, "Miles was the savior, as he pitched in helping with the breakfast." The first couple of days, the hunters were hardly out before ten in the morning. When Miles pitched in, everyone was out hunting before seven. Miles guided and bagged a fine sheep, goat, moose and caribou for his hunter—as well as helping cook meals. He missed out on a good grizzly. They had spotted a grizzly and made a stalk on him—getting to within one hundred yards of the bear. The hunter was shooting from the prone position, and his line of sight through the scope, cleared the rocks in front of him—but the barrel didn't. When the hunter squeezed the trigger, it blew rock and dirt all over the place and scared the hell out of the hunter, Miles and the bear. The bruin took off at full speed and ran through a large basin. The hunter got to his feet, sat down, emptied his rifle at the bear, missing all shots. Miles said it was all downhill and saw the bear run for over a mile. He said, "His feet looked like wagon wheels, as his feet came up past his head when the bear ran downhill!" The same thing happened when they shot their goat but the shot hit the rocks somewhat further out from the shooters. However, they were luckier with the goat. They took this trophy before he made his get-away.

I had many remarkable men work for me over the years. Hunts come and go in the outfitting business, but some hunts leave everlasting memories, especially when outstanding trophies have been taken. The moose hunt I am about to tell you about is not a story of any exceptional trophies taken, but instead is a recount of the exceptional way it was conducted. The hunt was in connection with Felix Plante and John Ostashek.

Felix was an outstanding, determined individual and a self-made man. He wanted to own his own outfitting business more than anything, and dedicated himself to saving many years for this purpose. Felix's determination to become an outfitter became a reality in 1930. When he worked for Brewster's in Jasper, he guided a hunter by the name of Ernest Geese, several times. Ernest said to Felix during a hunt in 1929, "I can't understand why you are not running your own outfit." Felix said that he was planning to start his own outfit in a couple of years, but had not yet saved enough money. Ernest told him to get started in his own business for the 1930

Picture left (R to L):
John Haggblad guide,
Tommy Robertson cook,
Norman Woody guide,
Dave Moberly wrangler,
Front: Bud Maloy &
guide Miles Moberly

Photo courtesy of
Jim Babala.

season. During the next winter, Felix started building his own outfit; carved his saddles and built his pack boxes. The following May, Ernest phoned Felix and asked him how things were going. Felix said he needed three thousand dollars—and Ernest said the money would be right there. He bought more horses, broke out the ones that needed breaking and was ready to go. Felix Plante's outfit was born in 1930.

I took out another hunting party in 1962, with John Ostashek and myself operating in partnership. John and George Ostashek both were born in Mountain Park and were raised in Mercoal, Alberta. In earlier years, I had hired John and his younger brother, George to guide for me. After working for me, George eventually built up his own outfit. George acquired bighorn sheep permits in a zone on the south fork of the Hay River. He ended up with four sheep permits in that area. By 1962, John and I made a business arrangement to split the outfit. I had my regular hunt out and I made a deal with John to take the extra hunters out. I put up half the horses, half of the equipment and John put up the other half, outfitting a second party of hunters. *(John Unland ran an outfitting business and fishing camp in the Tonquin Valley near Jasper— until 1970 when they sold to John and George Ostashek.*[1]*)*

During this trip in 1962, Albert Norris came along as camp cook. Albert was a well-known guide but was getting on in years, so he was cooking for me. He was both a trapper and a guide who resided where Lone Teepee Creek flows into the Muskeg River—near Grande Cache. His mother was Suzette Swift, the wife of Lewis Swift of Jasper. Albert was fluent in Cree, as he learned the language from his mother's people. He

arrived in the area in the 1920s, when there were only a few Native families scattered throughout the region. He became affectionately known as the Mayor of Muskeg.

In 1914, Albert Norris had joined the Canadian Armed Forces and had gone to war. After World War I, he returned home to join the Royal Canadian Mounted Police and was in their service as an interpreter. When he finished his term with the police, he took a job as a fire warden in the mountains northwest of Hinton. After three summers, he left this job to become a guide and remained one for the rest of his life. He spent fifty-five years guiding in the summers and spent the winters on the trapline between the Simonette and Smoky Rivers. He traveled on snowshoes with a pack-dog for company.

So we had Albert as the cook and Fred Plante, Felix's son working as the horse wrangler. Felix had retired from outfitting, but decided to sign onto my outfit as an extra trail hand. John Ostashek was guiding the small German hunter and I was guiding the big German hunter. I had also hired a German interpreter for this hunt.

Fred walked into the cook tent at 9:30 one morning after checking all the horses and said that he had seen a lot of moose sign on the big red willow flat about a mile-and-a-half from camp. Fred saw where a large bull moose had rubbed and polished his horns on a small jackpine tree and had uprooted a few other trees, pawing up the ground. He had also pawed holes in the ground, a sure sign that the rut was on.

The two German hunters had decided to have a day in camp. Everyone was sitting in the kitchen enjoying an extra cup of coffee when Freddy came in. The biggest German, who weighed two hundred and sixty-five pounds, heard Freddy talking moose. He asked the German interpreter to explain to him what Freddy had seen.

That morning both German hunters had previously decided that on their day in camp they would try to catch a mess of trout. Now the bigger German changed his mind and wanted to see the spot where the moose had rubbed his antlers and pawed the ground. Felix said they would get the horses in after lunch and ride to the spot. The German wanted to walk to the spot, as he didn't want to ride a horse. The smaller German, who weighed two hundred and twenty-five pounds, still wanted to go fishing.

After lunch Felix volunteered to take the big German to see the moose sign. The big hunter stashed three bottles of beer, a can of tomato juice, some rye bread, cheese and a German-type sausage in Felix's knapsack. He put on a green hunting outfit, a pair of loose, baggy britches, a heavy sweater, two vests and a heavy coat—also a pair of leggings over his boots. He snapped a three-legged stool with a leather seat onto Felix's belt loop. The stool hung by a light chain from Felix's backside. Felix also carried his rifle and a forked stick that the German used for a

Pictured above:
Alex Person & Jim Babala with a
non-typical score 205 ⅝ B.C. Record Book Whitetail.

Pictured on left page (L to R):
Top: George Ostashek & Jim Babala in 1990.
Middle: George Ostashek and ram in 1990.
Bottom: George Ostashek in the cook tent.

Photos courtesy of Jim Babala.

rifle rest while sitting on his stool. This was a method that the Germans used when hunting red deer in Germany.

John Ostashek took the smaller German and the interpreter fishing. Felix and his German started walking. They had gone hardly seventy-five yards when the German called a halt, took off his great coat and gave it to Felix. They then proceeded on another twenty-five yards and once again stopped. He took off the first vest and handed it to Felix. Another twenty-five yards, and off came the other vest. He had unsnapped the stool from Felix's belt, set it up and sat down, took out a small torpedo-shaped cigar. He even had Felix light it for him and took a few puffs. Then he stretched out his arms and Felix put a vest back on him. In a few minutes more, he stretched out his arms again and Felix put on the second vest, and in a few more minutes, the great coat.

Freddy and I were standing at the cook tent watching this performance and enjoying a good laugh over it. Albert Norris, the cook, had no use for Germans, having fought in WWI. He ranted about the hunters treating us like slaves and bemoaned the fact that we had to cater to them. He said that the S.O.B.s were lucky that he, Albert wasn't guiding them! Then he walked back to his kitchen, ranting and mumbling about Krauts and Germans.

Freddy and I stood there watching these proceedings—taking off and putting on of vests and coats, the

unsnapping of the stool—and setting down and getting up. By then over an hour had passed, and they had not made it to the corner of the flat *(about a mile distance)*. Freddy said they had about three-quarters of a mile more to go around the point onto the next willow flat, where the moose had rubbed and pawed and torn up the ground. When they got to the point they stopped again—and went through the same procedure. This time, Felix opened the German a bottle of beer and lit up another cigar. Freddy and I were roaring with laughter. We would have to get a report later from Felix on the special Canadian moose hunt, hunted in the German red-deer style.

They left the point at three in the afternoon, with Felix planning to stay until dark. He figured they would come back in the evening, however just about 5:30 in the afternoon, Felix and the German appeared back at the point, coming home—using the same procedure. Albert couldn't contain himself watching this spectacle. "Hell, they won't make it back until after nine tonight at the rate they're coming! I'll be damned if I'll give them supper then!" Albert yelled defiantly.

The smaller German, John Ostashek, and the interpreter got back before five with a fine mess of Dolly Varden trout for our supper. I told Freddy to get a couple of horses and go and get the moose hunter. He caught the horses and trotted over to the pair. Felix and Freddy got the German loaded on the poor old horse—and by six o'clock Freddy had the German back to camp. Felix walked back, arrived a few minutes later and he had a grin from ear to ear.

"Felix, you've had many moose hunters in your time, but this German-style hunt—I believe must be the most outstanding," I observed. Felix just laughed and agreed it was. He told us they finally got to the moose tree, as the German called it. The German drank a bottle of beer, ate some sausage and cheese, and took some pictures of the trees the moose had rubbed and uprooted. He also took pictures of the track and pawing. After about an hour, a lone, dry cow crossed the willow flat, from one side to the other. The German snapped a few pictures of her making gestures that she wanted a bull to come out. But no bull came. He then smoked another cigar, drank the third bottle of beer and let Felix know they should start back to camp for supper. Felix tried to get him to stay longer, telling him that the best time for moose hunting was after six in the evening. The German just got up from the stool, snapped it onto Felix's belt and pointed back to camp. Felix figured we would send out a horse once we spotted them.

We all laughed. I asked Felix how many times he had put on and removed the vest and greatcoat. He said he thought probably about ten. He figured we saved him at least six more times, by sending the horse. It was a memorable and outstanding moose hunt that Felix and I chuckled about for years.

Several days later, John Ostashek rode to the east end of Moose Horn Lake where he stopped to glass for moose with his two-hundred-and-sixty-five-pound German hunter. This hunter had difficulty in mounting—and dismounting—the horse and he certainly couldn't ride. John spent most of the morning and afternoon sitting on the north side of the lake watching for moose. Moose tracks were plentiful along the shoreline. The occasional grunt from a bull or a bawl of a cow could be heard from time to time. During the afternoon, everything got very quiet—not a sound from any moose. John knew that later that evening moose would again be active around the lake, so he and the hunter sat. The German had a short sleep and John even dozed off some. They could not talk to each other or discuss anything and they could only use sign language, as the German knew no English. John got a

Pictured above:
Felix Plante with a deer taken in the Moon Creek-Berland River area 1930 by hunter, Ernest Geese.

Photo courtesy of Jim Babala.

message through to the German to stay put at the lake while he went and scouted around some. The German was to watch for moose and not leave that spot. John tied up the German's saddle horse and the packhorse, took his own horse and left to see what was at the second larger lake.

John rode to the far end of the second lake in the direction of Jasper National Park. Moose sign was plentiful, but no better than at the first lake. He rode up to the east end of the second lake, and decided to go up to the Jasper Park boundary. He glassed the Moose Horn valley, where the Park wardens had built a cabin. John, as a student, had hired on a work program and had helped build this cabin. He packed in supplies for the Parks Branch. The Jasper Park boundary sign was only a few hundred yards from the east shore of the lake. John rode past the sign about another hundred yards, to the edge of the timber, where he tied his horse, sat down and glassed the entire valley. It was a warm, sunny afternoon. The only game he saw was a band of goats playing up on the slope and sunning themselves. Nothing much else was moving. It was so nice and warm—John fell asleep.

John was awakened by Bert Rowe, Jasper Park Warden of the Moose Horn district, accompanied by two lady schoolteachers. Rowe asked John what he was doing. John replied, "Sleeping."

"I know that but are you hunting?" the Warden asked.
"No, I am guiding a hunter," replied John.
"There is no hunting here," the Warden stated. "This is Jasper National Park."
"I know that. I'm not hunting here, just scouting around the lake. I rode up here, glassed the Moose Horn Valley, and fell asleep."
"Where is your hunter?" asked Rowe.
"He's at the second lake."
"Are you sure, or is he around here hunting?"
John assured him the hunter was at the second lake.
"We're going that far, so we will see," Rowe warned.

John untied his horse.

"I'll have your rifle," demanded Rowe.
"No, you won't," replied John.

After some discussion, John kept the rifle.

They all rode up to the lake where the German hunter was. He too was sleeping and awakened as the group rode up. Rowe began to ask the German questions, but he just stood there smiling at Rowe. John explained, laughing, "Ask him all the questions you want, but you won't get an answer. You'll have to ride to our base camp, an hour from here and talk through the interpreter. This hunter can't speak a word of English."

Rowe objected that he didn't have time to go to base camp. It would make him late getting the teachers back to Moose Horn cabin. He again asked John for his rifle, but John refused to give it up. Rowe left, advising John he would be hearing more on this episode. *(He knew that John had a concession with Jasper Park. By 1962, John had a trail ride business renting horses by the hour during the summer months at Miette Hot Springs, a summer resort within Jasper National Park.)*

At a later date, John was called on by the Park officials. He was given a strong lecture and read the riot act about hunting in the Park. He was also lectured about not turning over his rifle to Rowe on demand. I'm glad John didn't, as it was my rifle—a pre-war Winchester Model 70 30.06 caliber, which I still have today. I have had this rifle since I was a teenager.

John was teased and kidded most of the winter by all the guides and outfitters—a real good one, falling asleep on the trail and being awakened by a Park Warden. John, to this day, still laughs about it when the topic comes up. Wonder what John was dreaming about when he was so abruptly awakened?

Meanwhile, after an exciting and interesting afternoon, John and the German discovered lady luck was on their side. That same evening, they were rewarded by a cooperative 56", well-

Pictured above:
Jim Babala with a bighorn ram
 from a 1962 hunt.
It scored 181-7/8 B.C. points.

Photo courtesy
of Jim Babala.

palmed moose coming down to the lakeshore. The moose had a few odd-ball, freaky points and all. A good ending and there is nothing more pleasing in camp than a well-satisfied client!

In 1972, I left the Cadomin and Willmore area. The Alberta government had decided to cut down on the number of non-resident sheep hunters to four permits. I didn't feel I could make a go of it—so I decided to move north to the Yukon and start outfitting there. I bought a hunting area at Kusawa Lake, Yukon. My nephew, Randy Babala took over my horses, equipment and trapline in the Coal Branch area. He started his own outfit and guided hunters in my old area. Evenutally, Randy's business expanded and he took summer trail rides into Willmore Wilderness Park.

John Ostashek followed my trail north and arrived in the Yukon one year after me—in '73. He purchased an outfit from Phil Temple. The area he purchased was the same spot that the Jacco Brothers had operated in the Burwash area. John was quite ambitious and got involved in politics and eventually became Premier of the Yukon.

I retired from outfitting in the Yukon in 1980. I have spent my time hunting and writing since that time. Since my departure from actively outfitting, I have authored and published a book entitled, *Arizona Desert King and I.*

CHAPTER EIGHTEEN:
Glen Kilgour

Sue It's May 30, 2004 and I am sitting with Claudette and Glen Kilgour in the town of Grande Cache. Some of Glen's former staff are with us. We have Danny Hallock, cook and Emil Moberly, guide. We also have Bazil Leonard and his son, Dan Leonard who is a professional mountain guide. Glen Kilgour outfitted geological survey parties and big game hunting expeditions in Willmore Wilderness Park during the 1950s and 1960s. (*For clarity we refer to Danny Hallock as "Danny" and Dan Leonard as "Dan L."*)

Glen I was originally from Sundre, Alberta. It was in 1945 that I started with Bill Winter and the horse outfit. Years earlier, Bill Winter and his two brothers had trailed up from California and homesteaded in the Sundre District. On their horseback trip up they wintered on the Snake River —a tributary of the Columbia River. They arrived in Bearberry District in 1910. I got involved with Bill Winter when my dad and I met him on our yearly pack trips into the Rocky Mountains to fish. As the years went by, I bought into Bill Winter's horse outfit. I bought half interest in three hundred head of horses at the price of fifteen dollars a horse. I was not old enough yet to sign any legal papers, as I was not twenty-one years of age. I had to buy the horses on time. I gave Bill the money I had and went into Rocky Mountain House and had a Notary Public make up an agreement on paper. Bill trusted me. Then we went into the hills and started to count the horses. We paid dues on each horse. We counted until we started seeing horses that moved around into groups of horses that already were counted; we stopped and called it three hundred head. Then the cowboying started.

I came north with an oil company, south of the Smoky River. I worked from the Athabasca River north. I went through Little Grave, Big Graves, the Hardscrabble and all that country. I worked with a geological team of four. It was my pack outfit. I hired a cook and horse wrangler and brought them in. We moved our camp all through the mountains.

I hunted in the Willmore for twelve years. On the twelfth year, they built the new town of Grande Cache. Grande Cache was built in 1969. After they built the town site, I never came

Pictured above:
Claudette Kilgour
on Wolf Hill
with her dog Lucky.
Circa 1978.

Pictured on left page:
Glen Kilgour.

Photos courtesy of
Claudette & Glen Kilgour.

back. *(Glen outfitted in Willmore from 1957-1969.)* There were horses also in the Smoky Valley. When I first came to Grande Cache, there were horses on all the hillsides of Grande Mountain and Flood Mountain *(primarily Henry Joachim's horses).* There was a pile of good horses in this country.

There were a few horses that roamed free and wild in the Smoky Valley above the mouth of the Sulphur River. These were horses that had been left when the Hargreaves family wintered and summered horses on the Smoky down-river from the Jackpine River to the Sulphur. *(The Hargreaves family referred to the area between the Muddy Water River and Eaton Creek as the "Range.")* The Forestry Service had given a permit to an older gent *(Ed Benny)* and his girlfriend to capture these horses and remove them. He had a unique method of capturing these horses. He and the girl *(his woman who was a lot younger in age)* built good high corrals, two of them on the flats— one at Kvass Flats and one above Corral Creek. They hung a heavy gate about ten feet wide on a couple of good posts. These gates opened into the corral only. They were tied open and blocks of salt were put into the corrals. The horses roamed back and forth on the flats and would smell the salt. They eventually would go into the corrals and lick salt. After they moved freely in and out, the horse hunters would fasten a rope on a stick that held the gate open. The other end would run across the corral just off the ground, and tied solid to the corral. Of course the horses would go into the corral to lick the salt and, lo and behold, would trip the gate that was built so that it swung shut immediately—and he had a few horses trapped. Then he and the girl would go and catch the trapped horses. He rode a big yellow gelding that was good on the horn, and he would break these horses to lead. He would take them out and picket the horses to the poplar trees. This also helped halter-break them. When he gathered a few horses, he and the girl would tail these horses up and lead them across the river to Muskeg, as that was the end of the truck road at that time. I saw a little outfit of horses that he had captured and let out. At night he just picketed them wherever they were—they were used to this. The horses did not suffer—the ones that I saw were not "barked up" or "rope burned' and were in pretty good flesh. He captured all the horses, as I never saw a wild horse on the range after he was done. I guess there's nothing on those hillsides now.

Bazil   There is a little game. Some elk and deer but it's not like it used to be.

There is a sign on a poplar tree at Kvass Flats that reads "Lola Benny born here 1963." The young woman you saw gave birth to a child while Ed was rounding up Hargreaves' horses. Alice *(Granny)* Joachim *(Henry Joachim's wife)* told Susan and me that story. She was summoned to help clothe the baby after it was born.

Glen   They built the town on some of the hillside—and I was against that. Henry Joachim *(a Rocky Mountain Cree guide and outfitter)* had quite a bunch of horses in the immediate area. Henry had an old stud horse. Alice, his wife would ride that old stud horse across the Smoky, if the river was ever up. She'd ride that old horse across and he'd push water right up to his withers. He wouldn't lose his feet; he'd push that water. She felt safe riding him.

Sue   Rose Findlay *(wife of Deome Findlay, Rocky Mountain Cree guide and outfitter)* told me that when she first came to this country in 1929, Grande Mountain hardly had any trees on it. She lived on the same flats as Alice and Henry Joachim. Rose told me that Henry had horses all over, up and down the valley. He wintered his horses up on Grande Mountain. Now the whole area is treed in, so there's not as much grass.

Glen   The whole country is like that. If you don't set fire, you're going to have nothing but trees and brush.

Sue   Emil, did your people set fire to the flats or valleys? *(Emil Moberly is a Rocky Mountain Cree guide and trapper descended from the Jasper natives.)*

Emil   Yeah, in the spring when there was still snow.

Glen   Up and down the whole mountains they did that. They did it to the whole country—and that is why there were wide-open flats, because they set fire to them and burned them off.

Sue   What was the country like in 1959? In 2002 we rode from Rock Lake to Grande Cache on a seven-day horseback trip. We have also been riding from Grande Cache to the Continental Divide since 1992. The common denominator in Willmore is the fact that

Pictured above:
Top: Glen Kilgour 2006
Bottom: Emil Moberly 2006,
courtesy of
Susan Feddema-Leonard.

Glen & Emil were at the 2006
Willmore Wilderness Rendezvous.
in Grande Prairie, AB. Glen was
honoured as an old-time
Willmore Wilderness outfitter
& Emil was intoduced as being
one of his guides.

Pictured above:
Glen enjoying the
spirit & magic of
Willmore Wildnerss Park.

Photo courtesy of
Claudette & Glen Kilgour.

there are willows everywhere. The only exception to the rule is at Kvass Flats where there have been two controlled burns. Was the country open in the 1950s and 1960s?

Glen   In the early days, Louis Delorme *(a Rocky Mountain Cree guide & outfitter)* traveled around with a pack outfit. The Native people set fire to the valleys. They cleaned it off with a burn every spring when there was still snow on the north side of the mountains. These fires would run their course and all go out. There was lots of grass. Never in this country did I ever have a problem with (lack of) grass. In the Willmore area, we never experienced a shortage.

Sue   In the area of Boulder Creek and Many Faces camp we could see sign of a big burn that would date back to the 1940s. Tom Wanyandie said his father, Daniel Wanyandie went to fight fire in that area when he was nine years old. Tom was born in 1931, so we are pretty sure of the dates. Today that same country is thick with willows. That fire was probably started by a lightening strike.

Glen   The second year I outfitted north of the Smoky River with the same geological party and the same party chief. When we had the oil party, we would move camp every third or fourth day and I had the other days off, so I would play around on the side of the mountains. I usually had colts to ride and I would go for a little ride. That's how I learned the country. The geologists had maps and I could look at the lay of the land. They also had aerial photographs that I could look at. I could tell where I wanted to go, exactly. These photographs were three-dimensional. You took little glasses *(a stereoscope)* and held them over the map. The hills showed up and you could even see the trees—you could see everything. I found trails that were hidden—that no one thought that I would find. Nobody showed me the country; I learned it. I always had enough time to find out where the trails went.

My main party chief of the geological team became president of *California Standard Oil* in Canada and I always got along good with him. They had another doctor of geology and he was a tough guy. He didn't mind if things got pretty rough. We ran out of groceries one time—and that was not a big problem as I had a group of people out with me. We'd just catch some fish or something. We were only supposed to be out for three weeks with the pack outfit, but we stayed six weeks, and were down to eating fish. We came into Muskeg and sent a boy into town *(Hinton)* for groceries. They had a truck ride from Muskeg to Hinton on a pretty rough trail.

We landed in Muskeg and *Imperial Oil* was in here. The other oil company was two days ahead of me. The two oil companies got together and had a big pow-wow there. When I was at the pow-wow I met a grand old man by the name of Adam Joachim and spent several hours with him, where I heard many stories. I was sure pleased to hear from him, as he spoke perfect English. He told me that he had gone to a Catholic Seminary located in Montreal when he was a youth. He spoke four languages: Latin, Cree, English and French. Adam Joachim was the leader of his small band of Mountain Cree. It was when I spoke with him that I found out that there was game north of the Smoky—and no one was hunting it. That's why I came up here. I had come from an area that was taken over by hunters and residents.

I made a summer trip into the country north of the Smoky with the geologists and we found game all over the place. We found moose, elk, sheep and grizzly bears. There weren't many caribou but there was some. We rode right up to Kakwa Lake. That's why I came back and outfitted in the mountains north of the Smoky with hunters.

That's what I told Jim Babala *(an outfitter),* who I saw last night in Brule. We upset the locals in the country, both he and I. He upset more than I did because he was on the south side of the Smoky River. The only one that I upset was Leonard Jeck. Leonard was traveling north and west of the Smoky.

Pictured above:
Adam Joachim in 1935.

"Adam Joachim spoke four languages: Latin, Cree, English and French. Adam Joachim was the leader of his small band of Mountain Cree." G. Kilgour

Adam died April 1 1959.

Photo courtesy of Mary Anne Deagle.

Jim Babala was a coal miner. When he was hunting and outfitting in Willmore, I got to know him a little. I really didn't have to bother with him. He didn't hunt in my area and was not a threat to me at all. One of Jim's areas was Wolverine Creek and the hills up Kvass Creek.

When Jim Babala told people that he was going to take people out and give them a hunt, that's exactly what he did. He turned down game if it wasn't a decent trophy. The hunters had to be in good condition to keep up with Jim because he usually took a fly camp or a little light camp. He'd pull out and he'd travel until night. He stopped at dusk and camped but he'd be up at the crack of dawn and would move on. Jim didn't go five hours back to a base camp. He had camp with him. Some hunters weren't pleased with that way of hunting because they would like a little more luxury and wanted to be pampered in a base camp.

Jim lives in the Yukon in Whitehorse now. He started his outfit in the Willmore area, but eventually moved his outfit to the Yukon. Jim is still in good shape and he looks good.

Sue Who else was in the Willmore at the time you were here, besides Leonard Jeck and Jim Babala?

Glen There was a fellow that came in from Lesser Slave Lake, (*Reinhold*) Eben Ebeneau. Eben was a German fellow who was a good hunter. He wasn't really a threat. He seemed to hunt moose, caribou and different game. I never knew him to take an elk or sheep when I knew him.

Eben had one hunter for seventy days. He had come down to the Willmore with packhorses. He was hunting for about two or three weeks when I ran into him and he didn't have any meat yet. "Holy crow," I said. "We just killed a caribou over the hill and we'll bring in some meat." Later Eben Ebeneau told me that the hunt didn't last. The hunter got a chip in his eye and had to leave. The hunter could have had a good hunt, if he had finished his time out there. With hunting you never know if today's the day you're going to get the big deer, or big moose, or whatever it is—it might be tomorrow. With enough time, you're going to find your game.

Eben wasn't a lazy person. He was a hustler. He was a little bit funny with his crew. He locked his packboxes and things like that, so he always had groceries.

Bazil Eben made the Boone and Crockett Record Book several times with his moose and grizzly trophies. He sure made his mark with the game he took in the Kakwa and Smoky River areas. He only took hunters from Germany, where he was very well known. He was quite a big outfitter in his day.

Eben used to bring his horses from Lesser Slave Lake to Grande Prairie, Alberta by train. He usually filled two boxcars with horses to work for the season. He would unload his horses in Grande Prairie, where he would pack them up with his supplies and gear. There was a ferry that crossed the Wapiti River, which he used. Once across the Wapiti, Eben headed south and spent many months in the Canadian Rockies. I wonder why he locked those boxes—I bet he had some whiskey in there.

Glen   I don't know, but that does remind me of a story about whiskey. Danny Hallock was cooking for me on this trip. I was moving into one of my camps one time. I was moving in with a crew and I got word that a sister-in-law had died. They sent in a helicopter from Muskeg for me. This crew that I was packing for wanted a case of high-priced Scotch whiskey. I had to go to Jasper to get it. I couldn't get the Scotch at any ordinary vendors.

So I went to Jasper, as only the Jasper Liquor Store carried this high-priced Scotch. After I made the big purchase, I came back. I packed this Scotch in two sets of boxes that were identical. I knew the difference between the boxes, but I didn't tell the rest of the crew how to differentiate between them. I had an old sorrel mare that was prone to have wrecks every now and again. Of course they put the whiskey on the wrong horse one morning. They packed up and went down to the creek, which was a good-sized stream. Anyways, the current started washing on the old mare and she was really cinch-bound. She bucked that pack off—and it all landed in the water. It didn't break a bottle. I had it all wrapped and it didn't break. When I got back, I was holdin' my breath when Danny told that story.

Sue   When you went north, what country did you go into?

Glen   I went north of the Smoky River, but never went around the bend (*west Smoky and south of the Jackpine River*). I went up the Muddy Water River, Femme Creek and Sheep Creek.

The first year or two, we would fly hunters into Cecelia Lake, British Columbia. When I first decided to bring hunters into Cecelia Lake, I thought I'd fly them in. We got a camp set up there,

Pictured above:
The Kilgour pack outfit on the trail.

Photo courtesy of Claudette & Glen Kilgour.

and one day, in come the RCMP plane. It was a Beaver airplane. I thought, "Who have I got in camp that they are worried about?" I was wondering if it was one of my crew—or something was the matter. A whole bunch of RCMP jumped out of the plane and came onto shore and beached the plane. It wasn't my boys that they were after—it was me. They asked me where I was at. I told them that I was in B.C. They asked me how I knew. I told them that I had a map that told me where I was. They told me that they had stayed awake all night trying to figure out where I was—and they thought that I might be quite a way inside the B.C. border. I told them that half of the lake was in Alberta and the other half was in B.C. I guess the RCMP thought I was hunting in B.C., but we were packing up and going into Alberta. It was easier to access the good sheep country this way and hunters liked the idea of getting into a wilderness area by this method.

Well, the RCMP told me that I had to pack up and leave the next morning. This was no problem as we were planning on moving anyway. The hunters came in after the RCMP left and I prepared to move camp the next day.

In the morning there was a storm, and the raindrops were coming down and jumping six inches high off the water. The raindrops were so big and hitting that lake so hard that they jumped back up. The crew and I packed up the horses—and after the third horse, we were just soaked. No matter what you had on, you might as well have just taken it off.

Then we had to ride up from Cecelia—up Cote Creek. Holy crow, the wind blew as we went over that pass. It was really, really cold! I was just about beat when we arrived to our camp. We started to set up camp and look after these hunters. We put the tipis up that time.

I got in the tipi and it was still pouring down. I had to stand overtop of the fire to get it going. The rain was coming down through the top of the tipi and putting my fire out. This boy that was with me, named Albert Helmer, came in the tipi and offered me a drink. I asked him if he had a bottle with him and he told me he had some good over-proof rum. I told him that I would have a drink. I remember standing over this fire while he was digging around in his duffle bag—and he came out with that seventy-two over-proof rum. He gave that bottle to me and I pulled that cork off and poured it down. It went down just like water and my eyes never watered. I never coughed or nothing. I was just chilled right to the bone. That fire started right there—and I warmed up at the same time. That was the best drink I ever had.

I used to run up and down Cote Creek, then drop into the Willmore country. That was swampy country, that Cote Creek. There was no one in there except Leonard Jeck. I never bothered Leonard—where he was. Leonard hunted the Muddy Water River and Llama Flats. Leonard hunted that country quite steady. I used to keep track of him because I didn't want to run into him. I stayed away from him. When I hunt, I don't want people around. I want the area to myself. The best way to do that is find out where the other guy is and stay away. Leonard used to have a fit about me—although I don't think I ever held him up much. I would hunt farther away.

Leonard one time came down the Smoky River. We were on the other side hunting. He decided to pack up and move the same day that I did—only, I got down to the river first. There was a boat that we could use to load our

gear and boxes in. That way we could kick the horses across the river empty—without their packs. I had an outfit that I could kick into the river anywhere.

The river was up and Leonard wasn't handy with a boat. I had just moved my last load across the river. I had my horses across and we were packin' up. Leonard, of course, wanted the boat back on his side of the river. So I came over and picked him up—and then we both went back across. Then he was rowing the boat back across, right above the rapids. There was kind of a bend there. Leonard found this rowing quite a lot of work—or job, especially when he was pulling his gear across. So he tied a rope on the front of the boat and went across with it. His crew pulled the boat back and forth across the Smoky.

Leonard told me later that they got the boat out a-ways from the shore and the nose of the boat went up and down into the icy cold water of the Smoky River. He never determined that the rope would get into the water and pull the boat nose up and down. Leonard lost *(trophy)* capes and everything. It was a disaster. They finally had to pull the boat across with oars. Leonard had a lot of trouble that time.

Leonard had a lot of courage and he was a good guy. I had nothing against him and he certainly was not lazy—he was a hustler.

Sue Was there much sign when you first went there? Were there blaze marks? What did you find when you first went in there, regarding trails?

Glen Hargreaves was in there long before I was. The Hargreaves ran all over the country, so yes, there was sign. I am sure there were Native people in the area before that.

Don McMurtry and Eric Kjos told me that the Hargreaves brothers used to come in to hunt on both the B.C. side and the Alberta side for rams. There were four Hargreaves boys in that family: Jack, George, Dick and Roy. The Hargreaves were all hill men who guided and outfitted. Roy had a ranch at Mt. Robson; Jack and Dick outfitted out of Jasper; George outfitted out of Willmore. They had a mountain they called Mt. Bess. Sometimes they came in from Mt. Robson up the Smoky, over Bess Pass to Big Shale Hill, across Shale Pass and along the Continental Divide to Casket Mountain and Sheep Creek.

Roy Hargreaves used to trail his horses up and down the Smoky River as he wintered them at Kvass Flats. Roy had two daughters and both of these girls were good help on the trail. These young ladies would travel on long trips with their father into the Willmore area. One of the girls was Ishbel, who married Murray Cochrane *(B.C. outfitter)*. The other sister was Margie and she married Buster Duncan *(B.C. outfitter)*. The Hargreaves sisters

Pictured above:
Roy Hargreaves' outfit takes
a caribou near Surprise Lake,
on the Continental Divide.

Photo courtesy of
Ishbel *(Hargreaves)* Cochrane.
Photo circa 1940s.

would travel with their father with a pack string of horses from Mt. Robson Park and head downstream on the Smoky River. On rainy days, when they packed up in the morning they would split a bunch of kindling and stuff it in the boxes—this way they could get a quick fire going. The girls knew if it was raining, they'd be ready. The girls did not make it known to their father though—that they were packing wood from one campsite to the next. On some of their trips they would trail horses from where the Smoky River started at Mt. Robson—and trail the horses downstream to their winter range.

Jeff Wilson was a long-time hill man in Jasper Park and Bow Lakes area for old timer, Jimmy Simpson and Jimmy Jr. Jeff told me this story of helping to take the horses up the Smoky River to Mt. Robson Ranch, with Roy and Mrs. *(Sophia)* Hargreaves and Louis Joachim. They had quite a number of horses and Jeff and Louis had chopped off a little bunch of horses to trail. Mrs. Hargreaves came behind chasing the slower end of the string, riding her little flat English saddle. As they started down the Smoky, a Chinook moved in. They had quite a lot of snow in the mountains. This snow started to melt and down the river it went. Well, as they progressed with the horses down the river, it just kept getting wilder and wilder. This story now takes place on the Hardscrabble *(east)* side of the Smoky River. Roy was in the lead and ran out of good bank on that side of the river because the trail had washed away, so he just jumped his horse into the boiling river and crossed. Jeff came with his horses and they all jumped into the current and away they went. Jeff watched this and decided that he could drown in there so he pulled to the side and got his tobacco out and started to roll a smoke.

When Louis Joachim arrived, he was mesmerized by the water and pulled out to the side—and he and Jeff talked about dying in the boiling river. Then along came Mrs. Hargreaves in that little flat saddle and she just rode over to the bank, and over her shoulder she says to the two cowboys, "Come on boys, it's not so bad." In she goes and across the river. Jeff and Louis decided they better follow. That night around the fire they did not talk of being tough guys.

McMurtry and Kjos claimed that one time Roy Hargreaves came down the Smoky River to Corral Creek where they had a corral to round up the horses. That's how the creek got its name. Roy was kind of a funny guy too. He rode bareback sometimes with a rope around the horse—and he stuck his knees in that rope. He'd chase his horses that way. He was a tough guy.

Then one year I got a contract to move the Alpine Club of Canada into Mt. Robson. I set up a camp on the creek trail that leads up to Berg Lake. It was located at the end of the vehicle road in some big heavy spruce. We hauled feed for the horses at the roadside camp—and we could trail the horses from the Alpine Camp down to the head of the Smoky River and graze them on grass at that end of the trail. We only did one trip a day. The Alpine Club Camp was set up just east of the Hargreaves' Chalet.

During the start of this season we met the Cochrane family. Murray and Ishbel Cochrane invited us over to use their shower that they had set up for the family and guests. When we would get a day off, we used their new propane shower, and every time we were over, we were invited into their home for tea or coffee and cookies. We met each of the boys, but the one we got to know the best was Russell, as he was elected to pack the supplies into the Chalet at Mt. Robson that summer. Russell chased a little bunch of horses, packed up the trail to Berg Lake and took guests into the chalet.

At the bottom of the trail next to the Fraser River, was a rain forest. Then you come to the cliffs. Then in about four miles you climb twenty-five hundred feet to Berg Lake. At the base of the cliffs on the trail you come to a little flat—then up you had to go into the cliffs. One day we came behind Russell with his pack outfit loaded, just at the cliffs. Now these horses did not think they wanted to start this steep climb. Russell just stayed behind, picking up rocks and pelted these horses on their rumps. I was sure after watching this performance that Russell easily could have pitched ball for the New York Yankees. He never missed a shot, and it was not long till the horses decided it best to head up the trail. Russell was a good boy. I had my son, Robert with me that summer and the two boys were about the same age. As the summer wore on, I found I had trouble keeping these two boys apart.

On the cliffs going up to Berg Lake, one section of the trail cuts over to the cliffs alongside of the creek that came down into the valley—just below Emperor Falls. When Curly Phillips first started to use this route to go up and over the pass, he built what they called the Flying Trestle. It was actually a bridge that went under the rock bluff.

But when I packed horses into that country, the Forestry had, at Roy Hargreaves' request, blasted the cliff face off—and now the trail goes out to the edge and turns up the mountain farther along. At this very point of the trestle you can look over the cliff and see down into the river, only the river is over halfway under you in an undercut. I was never impressed with looking over the edge of the mountain at that creek—with it being maybe one hundred feet below you.

In moving the Alpine Club of Canada into the top of the valley, we had a favourite person to take into the mountain camp—a Mrs. Phyllis Monday. A botanist in her own right, she also looked after and nursed cripples *(handicapped people)* that climbed and hiked about. A book is written on Phyllis Monday. She was the first woman to have climbed, with her husband, Mt. Waddington *(in B.C. According to Ishbel Cochrane, Phyllis Monday climbed Mt. Robson, in 1924.)* The alpine people had a special tent set up as a First Aid post for their people. Mrs. Monday was in charge of this tent—and the people that needed her help. At Mt. Robson that year, she was a lady of near eighty years of age. Mrs. Sophia Hargreaves, as I recall, was about the same age as Mrs. Monday and was a dear friend.

That summer we had taken Mrs. Monday into the camp, on horseback. The next thing I knew was Mrs. Hargreaves and Ishbel were going to ride up the mountain trail and visit at the Alpine Camp, for a day or two. I did not meet them on the trail with my packhorses. They probably had my schedule about figured out.

Pictured above (L to R)
Claudette & Glen Kilgour
at their farm in Taylor, B.C.
in 2005.

Photo by
Susan Feddema-Leonard.

After they got back home from the top of the pass, we had a day off and went over to the Cochrane Ranch to visit and have a shower. That day I asked Mrs. Hargreaves about the trail up the hill. I asked her if the trail was a lot better than when she first rode up through the pass. She told me that other than the Flying Trestle, the hill was not improved at all. I was certainly pleased to meet and visit with such a fine, upstanding lady as Mrs. Sophia Hargreaves, and her daughter, Ishbel.

While at the Alpine Camp, Bill Harrison told me to go to the draw running out of Mt. Robson's northeast bank, which helped to form the head of the Smoky River. On the east side of this draw near its mouth, was a rocky ledge about ten to twenty feet tall. On this rock wall was a large scratch mark about three or four feet tall—and an inscription was written beside it. This was the front face of the glacier that ran back to the mountain and up its northeast side.

The Alpine people that were in that camp marked this in August of 1911. The markings were very plain and readable when I was there. The glacier, when I looked at this script, had melted back, I am sure, one and a half miles, at that time. We have had global warming on for some time now.

George Hargreaves was Roy Hargreaves brother and he is buried on Sheep Creek. I have been there. The Indians used to ask me, "Where did you go? Were you by George's grave?" You see they used a first name for everything. I'd tell them, "Yes, I was past George's grave." I used to go up into that country for grizzly. You would never run out of them. I really liked to hunt the head of Sheep Creek—as it was good grizzly bear country. The Kakwa River was good too. There were a lot of grizzly bears in there.

Bazil There still is a lot of bears in that country.

Glen I did find a Hargreaves camp, in the avalanche area of Mt. deVeber. There was a broken packsaddle in that camp.

Pictured left:
Claudette Kilgour in
Willmore Wilderness Park.

Photo courtesy of
Claudette & Glen Kilgour.

Sue I believe that we found that camp. There are two camps—at two separate avalanche areas on Mt. deVeber. One is on Boulder Creek and the other is on the Jackpine trail.

Another thing I wanted to mention is that Louis Joachim was Rose Findlay's brother and Deome Findlay's brother-in-law.

Claudette I worked for Tom Vinson in the Tonquin Valley as a cook. Louise Wyant and I both worked there as cooks, as well as cleaning cabins. She had worked there a couple of summers prior to my coming. The tourists either rode in or walked into the Tonquin Valley, depending on what they wanted to do. There were cabins that the guests stayed in which Louise and I maintained.

I also worked with Louis Joachim *(a Rocky Mountain Cree guide and packer)*. Louis was a wonderful gentleman. He was a good worker, very intelligent and was really with it. He was packer for Tom Vinson when I worked in the Tonquin Valley. Wilbert Olsen from the Sundre area was the other packer. Both of these guys were really happy. Both were good with horses. Louis was one heck of a horseman. We worked in there for the whole summer. The guys packed the groceries and supplies into the Chalet.

Sue Did you work for any other outfitter?

Claudette I worked for Tom McCready. Both Tom Vinson *(Sr.)* and Tom McCready were Willmore outfitters. I cooked for both of these outfits.

Tom McCready was a great outfitter who based his operation out of Jasper. I cooked for him in the fall in the hunting camps. We would travel through Eagle's Nest Pass to Rock Creek, Little Grave and Big Graves. We spent time on the Starlight Range. Sometimes we would go past Blue

Grouse up to the headwaters of Hardscrabble Creek. We used to take out small parties on twenty-one day hunts. Tom operated a great kitchen and gave me lots of supplies to work with. One time we were out, and I had just bought a new product called Dream Whip topping mix. One night for supper I whipped it up with my hand egg beater and served it for supper. Boy, the hunters were happy. Tom and the hunters could not figure out where I had gotten the fresh whipped cream from.

Tom McCready kept his horses in real good shape. He had real good hunters the year I was there. Traveling with him was easy. Rod Hardy of Manitoba was guiding for Tom McCready at the time I worked for him. We also had a Jasper teen by the name of Tom Timberly who wrangled the horses.

I really miss the mountains and really loved being in them. It was a great time in my life.

Sue Glen, do you have any stories about the biggest bighorn ram that you ever took?

Glen Deome Findlay *(a Rocky Mountain Cree guide)* worked for me one time. He took the biggest ram that I ever took out of this country. Deome took it right above Kvass Flats. There's a little bump of a mud hill, which is just straight dirt. One day Deome and his hunter were riding along. He looked and there was a big ram. So they made a sneak-up on it and got within fifty yards of it—and they killed it. That was the biggest ram that I ever took in this country.

This sheep had not been on the rocks for a year anyways. Have you seen domestic sheep? Their feet turn up when they have not been clipped—or have not been living on the rocks. That's the way that ram's feet were.

Bazil He must have been old.

Glen He was old and very heavy. He didn't make 40". He made 39 ½". He had a good base. I never did get a picture of him.

I have a story that I tell about Freddy Findlay *(Rocky Mountain Cree guide and son of Deome Findlay).* Freddy worked for me one fall and I had moved a fly camp away from the main camp. We were camped out and had one tent with us, you see. We put the dudes *(hunters)* in the tent. In the day we could cook in this tent; this way we could get inside and keep warm if it stormed. Freddy and I had a few horses with us. I had two hunters. I guided one and Fred guided the other.

Pictured above:
Two outfitters that Claudette worked for.
Top: Tom McCready in 1990 at Berg Lake,
courtesy of Fay McCready.
Bottom: Tom Vinson in 1945,
courtesy of Tom & Yvette Vinson.

Someone said to me, "Why do you like those Indian boys?" I said that it was simple enough. I made the trip with Freddy and one night a blizzard came in. Freddy and I were underneath a fly tarp. Of course you couldn't keep that blizzard from underneath that fly. So here we were in the snow in the morning. Freddy didn't cover his boots under his bed or anything. He took his moccasin rubbers and he just batted them together. He put them on his feet. He never cried. He never said that this is tough or anything about it. He was ready to go and I admired that.

Sue Bazil and I took old Deome Findlay into Big Graves one time when he was over eighty years old. We had our young son, Cody there who was about five years old and daughter, Jaeda who was eleven years old at the time. There was also a German lady who was over seventy years of age and she was as tough as nails. We needed to ride over Hayden Ridge back to Victor Lake, and it was pouring rain at the base of the mountain. The rain was unrelenting as we made our way up the trail to the top. By the time we reached the summit, it was snowing and our clothing was freezing on us. Our jackets became hardened, as did our hats and gear. The change in weather was dramatic and it was bitterly cold. We had ridden up a twenty-five-hundred-foot ridge and we were faced with icy cold sleet that chilled everyone to the bone. You couldn't feel your hands. The weather was totally cruel and wretched. There was nothing to do but keep moving.

It was an hour ride down the east side of Hayden Ridge and over to Cowlick Creek where we stopped briefly before heading to Grande Cache. When we arrived at the base of the ridge, we made a big fire. The heat was welcomed by everyone. As we were standing around the bonfire, Deome turned to me and said, "That boy of yours never cried once when we went over that ridge. Your boy is tougher than any Indian kid that I ever traveled with before."

That's the same bush values that you are talking about. It may be tough, but you don't cry or complain. You cowboy-up and keep on going. So I appreciate your story.

Glen One time I was at Big Grave with the geological party chief and he was going up on the mountain. For some reason he had no one to go with him, so I said that I'd go. We went up there and there was a storm building off to the south of us. We watched this storm and thought that maybe we should pull the pin, but we didn't. We thought it would go by us. At the last minute, the storm turned around and came right at us—and there we were, right on the very top. We had geology hammers—he had a hammer and I had a hammer. This storm hit viciously with lightning and thunder. We looked for shelter and got behind some little shale rock. We got huddled in there while the storm moved on. We put the geology hammers on the rock above our heads. The thunder and lightning was snapping everywhere. It was really, really vicious. I'm not really scared of thunder, but when she gets that way—I kinda wonder if I'll ever live through it. The hammers were going tap-tap-tap-tap-tap on that rock.

Pictured above:
Deome Findlay,
courtesy of Rose Findlay.

They were just plumb full of electricity. In a day or two we packed up the outfit, deciding to move out of there—and went over the shale ridge on the side of the mountain above the Sulphur River. There we ran into another storm and it was another lightning storm. There were thunder and lightning bolts hitting five hundred feet below us—right to the creek bottom. I had five horses abreast on a rock trail that was only wide enough for one. I never dreamt that I would get into that kind of predicament or I would have brought up some help from behind the outfit. You couldn't let the horses get ahead of you or you'd have a wreck. So I had to hold them back. It was quite a panic. That was a vicious, vicious storm that I won't forget! It came right off the Sulphur River.

Sheep Creek was a tough place in the fall. Once you moved into the middle of October, it would storm up there everyday. I don't know if it still does that, but that was the way we found it when I was outfitting. You did not want to be in there. You couldn't hunt because you were in a fog and snowstorm most of the time.

Sue   Have you ever been up into the deVeber basin where they have the beautiful emerald-coloured lakes?

Glen   We hunted that country for sheep. We camped where there were some beaver dams and a big meadow *(Many Faces on Boulder Creek)*. Wherever there were bighorn rams, we found them.

In hot years, the bighorn rams would leave the Corral Creek country, pull out and hit the hilltops over on deVeber. Mt. deVeber is not ewe country. We didn't hunt deVeber the first years that we were in that area. One warm summer, we ran out of rams at Corral Creek. We found out where they had gone, pulled out and into the area on deVeber.

I had one of the most famous hunters in the world venture out with me. We were on Llama Flats. His name was *(Watson)* Yoshimoto and he was one of the first five people in the world to take the twenty-seven rams of the world. At one time they stopped at twenty-seven; I think that they're up to thirty-four now. Watson took his bighorn ram with me and got it at Llama Flats. It was early in the season and it had snowed. That was in September, 1965.

Watson's foreman was with him, and we shot another bighorn ram on the south side of the Smoky. It was around Clark's Crossing—somewhere in that area—and it was an identical ram to Watson's ram. This wasn't a big ram and only made 38", but it was as good as we could find.

We hunted all over and never stayed in one place. A lot of times other hunters would follow my tracks, even on Mt. Stearn. I made a track up off of Kvass. I used to go on the backside of the mountains and come over on the Sheep Creek side. I went into a place called Neighbor Creek

and hunted there quite a little bit. It wasn't long before other hunters were following my tracks over that way—from Kvass Flats. I left the bottom and went through the little poplar trees just so that people wouldn't follow me—but it's easy enough to follow horse tracks if you want.

One time it was a stormy day and I packed up a little light camp and left the Smoky Valley. I went up and over Mt. Stearn—and as you start over, you come to some ledges. You had to get on the right ledge to go over and come out on the flat up top. Anyway, this day it was storming. It was coming down and you couldn't see anything. I got on the wrong ridge. I rode over to the edge of this bank and looked down there—and I think, holy crow, there is no bottom! It looks like it is one thousand feet deep. You can't see anything down there except the snow. I went along with the pack outfit coming behind. Somebody was helping to chase the packhorses. The hunters were looking over that ledge and thinking, oh boy! Then I turned and I saw that I was on the wrong ridge. So I turned around and went back and got on the right ridge. The hunters were convinced that they were up in heaven looking down.

I told Tom Vinson *(Sr.)* about that story. When I got over the other side, going down toward Sheep Creek, there was a draw in there. Tom was talking about the snow and how some years, a long time ago, the snow did not melt. I told Tom that one year I went there in September and went down this draw. It was quite a steep little draw that was located in shale. That September, I came to the draw, and it was snow straight across. I just went across on the snow, as there was no draw at all—it was gone. The snow had never melted that summer. That's the first time I ever saw that. I used to go hunting in there or on another draw that ran up to the head of Corral Creek.

I have another story that I tell about, when I had a hunter with me and we camped at the head of Neighbor Creek. In the morning we went up top and into Corral Creek. So we had quite a lot of mountain to climb. Then we went by a ridge that was a rock bench about forty or fifty feet tall.

We went over and hunted our way down. I hunted and got right down on a ram. There were eleven rams sitting over there that day. I was right on a fairly good ram. During the course of the event, the good ram and his partner ran up the mountain right at us. This was after the hunter shot the first shell. The rest of the rams ran across the valley. So here came the good rams. I had the hunter all ready, and I got out on the bank as the rams were coming. He kind of ran out of sight for a minute and was about twenty-five yards away from us. I had my glasses on him watching for the hair to puff up. Bang—and away went the ram.

Anyway, we were going home again that night. As we went up there, a storm moved in. You couldn't see anything because of the fog. It was a cold, foggy storm and you couldn't see ten feet away. It was really tough. I got up by that rock bench and by God there was a human standing there! He had a tarp wrapped around him. He was hanging onto the tarp because the wind was blowing and it was so cold. He had a long staff in his hand. I'll tell you, we came out of this storm at the base of the rock and there was this man. I didn't know what on earth! I was really goosed up about the phenomena. You know who it was? It was Louis Delorme. He was hanging onto that tarp to keep from freezing to death and he had that long stick with him. He wasn't going to rush home or anything. He didn't know that I was in there and I didn't know that he was in there. I know very well that I scared him—as much as he scared me.

Louis Delorme was the best sheep hunter that was in this country. He was a real top-notch sheep hunter.

Another really good sheep hunter that I knew was Fred Wanyandie. At that time, old Daniel Wanyandie, Fred's father wouldn't let his boys drink or play cards. They were very religious boys and really good boys—but I couldn't keep them with me. They would come on only one trip at a time. Fred Wanyandie guided when he worked for me. He'd work one trip and that was all you were going to get out of him. Fred was over on Sheep Creek with me several times.

Bazil Both Fred and his brother, Tommy were good hunters and guides. Both worked for me.

Glen The boys that worked for me the most were Kenneth Crouch and Larry Trimble. Both of these guys were good guys. I have a story about Kenneth and Fred Wanyandie.

Fred was a good hunter and he knew something that I never figured out. I had a guide one time that was on a caribou, on a lick. This was on the Sheep Creek. They were hiding in the grass and

crawling up on that caribou. The guide told the hunter to shoot the bull on the right. This guy puts the gun up and shot this old cow. Well, I had a rule that anything that we shot, we ate.

Well, Kenneth Crouch brought the hindquarters of this cow caribou into camp. Kenneth and Fred didn't like each other much. Well, Fred picked that hindquarter up and said "cow." How the heck did he know? But I didn't want to be dumb and not know, so I never asked him. I have always wished I had asked him how he knew that that was a cow. I should have said to him to show me how he knew.

Kenneth Crouch used to pull pranks on Fred. He would come into camp and say, "Hey Fred, I saw your wife downtown." Well, holy crow, we lost Fred right there—and Kenneth did that on purpose.

Danny Hallock also worked for me. He was a good bush cook and the son-in-law of old Louis Delorme. Ernie Delorme was the son of Louis Delorme and was a horse jingler. There was never a minute that he didn't know where every horse was. They were both good help and they were friends too. Finally Ernie and Danny quit. I blame myself for that.

A hunter from Switzerland came one year. Being that I was the outfitter, I was in his good books. He was an overbearing person and was down on my help. Everything the crew did was wrong. If Danny made breakfast, he would want something else. This hunter was upsetting everything and everyone.

One morning this guy told me he wanted to walk from the Sheep Creek side over to Corral Creek. He wanted a goat. I told him that we could walk. I'm not much for walking and staying out overnight, if I can help it, but I told him that we could do it. This guy had his wife with him too. We left the camp on foot to climb over the mountain. Danny and the outfit would follow us the next day to Corral Creek. I took this lawyer with me and away we went.

Well, the first day we did fairly good, and we got a goat at night. Then we had to camp out under a tree and the wind blew all night and blew ashes in my eyes. It was one heck of a night. Anyways, the next morning we got up and the hunter had blisters on his feet. We started walking really slowly. He was really crippled up and I struggled along with this for a while. I finally told him, "You can walk as slow as you like—and I'll stay with you until its dark. I'll bed you under a tree and I'm going to camp. I'm not staying out tonight, it's not far to go." After my talk with the lawyer, he spruced up and we made it to camp.

Danny and the crew had trouble getting away on the Sheep Creek side. The pack outfit came in after we arrived at Corral Creek. I had a campsite that I used every time we moved into Corral Creek. Anyway, the hunter and I arrived there first and the pack outfit came in later. We unpacked the horses and threw the riggin' off, just as a storm came along and hit us. We put the cook tent up and I told Danny to go ahead and make supper. I told him that the rest of the crew would put up the other tents. We started a fire and the hunters were in a warm and dry tent. Ernie and I set out to put up the rest of the camp, while Danny started cooking.

That old lawyer hunter jumped on top of Danny and said, "You get the hell outside and help get that camp set up!" Danny told him that he was supposed to cook supper for everyone, as it was eight pm. The hunter didn't listen and told him to go outside

Danny was mad and came over to where I was working. He asked if he could hit that guy on the end of the chin. I was always a diplomatic person, and lots of times I made mistakes. I said, "No Danny, we are not going to have you jump on top of that guy." Danny was so mad; he was just livid. He never worked for me again. I should have said, "Go ahead Danny, hit him as hard as you can; if you can't, I can." That's what I should have done, because I didn't want the guy back with me anyway. He had a really good hunt and he had taken four animals. He even took a black bear after that. I had made up my mind that he was not coming back with me. One trip was enough with him. Danny and Ernie never worked for me after that.

Pictured above:
Glen Kilgour at
Cecelia Lake courtesy of
Glen & Claudette Kilgour.

Pictured on left page:
Top: Fred Wanyandie,
courtesy of
Nanette Hamilton Moseley.

Middle: Dan Hallock
courtesy of
Susan Feddema-Leonard

Bottom: Ernie Delorme
courtesy of
Rachelle McDonald *(AWN).*

Sue How did you two meet?

Danny It was at a rodeo—and Glen hired me as a cook. I worked for him from 1961 to 1964.

Glen Danny was a good cook. He used to make a whole lot of pancakes and good meals. He was good help on the trail too. Danny would eat his lunch after he was on his horse. His theory was that he would eat his lunch only when there was nothing going on, he was not going to get caught eating lunch when a pack needed fixing. He did that the whole time he was with me.

Danny used to chew snoose. The last thing you would hear when you went to bed was tap-tap-tap, with that old snuff can. He put his mouth plum full of snoose and go to sleep. Danny do you still chew snoose?

Danny You bet.

Glen One time we were down on the Muddy Water right where the crossing was. We didn't go up the switchbacks and over to Dry Canyon. We were going in there to the Boat House at Clark's Crossing. All the other rivers and streams were running normal. The Smoky River looked normal for the time of year, but when we came to the Muddy Water, it was really running. It was as deep as up to that mirror *(four feet)*. It was roaring down there with waves. I was in the lead and I crossed—and the rest of the horses came across and followed me.

Danny   I was at the back of the pack horses—pushing the outfit along.

Glen   Anyway, we had an old trail hand that had a hold of a new packhorse that was in the hills for the first year. That horse got in the river and he would not fight the current. He just lay down—and away he went. Finally, as he went away, he gave a shudder and you knew he drowned. Then the pack came off of him as he was bounding along.

We all jumped into the river to try and save our gear. We had a boy working for me who stood and watched Danny's duffle bag come floating by. That bag floated right past him and he didn't grab it. I was really upset with him afterwards. We grabbed everything else. We got the tarps and everything but Danny's duffle bag. We were only a quarter mile above the mouth of the Muddy—and into the Smoky the whole works went. Danny had no duffle bag and it was a tough go for him. I don't suppose that I ever compensated you, did I?

Danny   You brought me in some clothes.

Glen   Did I? But we had those great big clothes that we had to put on Danny. (*Glen is a tall man and Danny is a smaller man.*)

One time I had hunters who wanted to shoot a caribou. So we went up the mountain and picked out two bulls—which were not big bulls. But we thought they were nice bulls, so we shot them. Danny Hallock was in camp with Ted Forshner *(a guide from Faust, Alberta),* and our camp was located close to the mouth of Cote Creek. I had a belief that we'd eat everything we killed—so someone had to go get that meat.

Danny told Ted that he might as well go and get a couple of horses because he would be sent there tomorrow to get that meat. Of course, Ted was hoping that something would happen and he would not have to go. The next morning when I came out for breakfast I told Ted that he might as well go and get a couple of horses because I had quartered that meat and laid it out. I told him to bring the quarters of meat down. It was just like I pulled a rug out from underneath him.

Guys used to say to me, "Why do you bring that Ted along?" I would tell everyone that he would visit with the hunters—and this let me do the work. There was a lot of work around the camp. You didn't have time to entertain hunters. Ted was perfect for entertaining. He was strutting around and tellin' stories. They liked him to entertain—and that's why I kept Ted.

Danny   Do you remember going down the trail one day, and you told Ted that his saddle was crooked? Ted answered, "Which way?"

Glen   That's a true story. Ted was a nice guy, but he sure didn't like me asking him to go and get that caribou.

One other time we killed a caribou east of the Muddy Water and skinned it out. There on the hamstring was a .22 bullet. Some of these guys were trapping in the wintertime and they took a shot at him to break it down. They had a .22 rifle and they thought that they could break it down if they shot it in the hock. That's where that bullet was lodged. I know it was the trappers that did that.

Emil   It was easier to trap with a 22 rifle. If something was alive in a trap, you could kill it right away. Yeah, there used to be a lot of caribou in that country. The caribou would stay in that area all winter.

Glen   All they had was .22 shorts. It was hard to buy shells when these guys were trapping. Every cent was quite valuable. There wasn't much money in the country.

Sue   Did you ever make contact with Carl Luger?

Glen   I got a kick out of Carl. One time I had a horse that fought flies constantly when you rode him. He would fight those nose flies. Years later, I met Carl down at Tom Vinson's place in Brule. Carl had mistaken me for somebody like Rex Logan. When I told him who I was, Carl said, "I remember you. You had the horse that fought flies." By joe, I had forgot about that horse! Yet Carl remembered it. Carl had Joe Groat *(a Willmore outfitter)* working for him that year. I maintain that Joe was one of the great men in the country. He knew where your horses were and where your sheep were.

Rex Logan also outfitted a short time in the Willmore. He has been a neighbour of mine all my life. Rex was a great guy. He floated through the Willmore country. He was partially raised at Moberly Lake, B.C. but his dad and uncle lived in the Sundre district. He has trapped in the Moberly Lake area. He's a wonderful person. Rex is the only one I ever knew that could take an oil party out with every horse green *(unbroken)*. No old horses, just brand new horses that had never been worked. Rex worked out of Jasper and different places. Rex Logan's father worked for years in the Banff and Jasper areas as a top hand for the Brewster family. Tom Vinson and Rex trailed horses all over the mountains.

Danny   I came to the Grande Cache area as a cook on Rex Logan's outfit in 1959. The pack trains left Solomon Creek near Hinton with geologists and headed northward to the Smoky Valley. I came back in 1960 and cooked for Bob Kjos who was also outfitting in Willmore for geological survey parties. After that, I cooked for four years with your outfit, from 1961 to 1964. *(Dan Hallock worked for Jack and Dewy Browning for a fifteen-year period prior to coming to the Willmore area.)*

Glen Bob Kjos worked in the country with geology parties. I don't think he outfitted hunting parties. He was working with geologists the same time that I was. Bob Kjos went into northern B.C., on the Toad River and hunted for years.

Tom Vinson was upset with these outfitters coming in from the south to pack the geologists out. He wasn't scared to tell anybody how he felt. He has sure mellowed a lot since then. He didn't like us boys to pull contracts to get up in this country. If you started to work for an oil company and you handled them right and looked after them, they didn't ask another outfitter to take your place. I worked from the U.S.A. border right to the Peace River. I worked west of Dawson Creek with my pack outfit, with the same oil company. Once the oil companies hired you, they kept you, if you did things properly.

Sue Did you ever have any trouble crossing the Smoky River?

Glen During the twelve years that I outfitted in Willmore there was quite a lot of water in the Smoky River at times. That stopped most of the people in the south from coming across the Smoky. They wouldn't take a chance on the water.

The most water I ever ran into on the Smoky River was at the end of October one year. It had snowed a lot, and all of a sudden a high chinook blew into the valley. It started to bring that water out of the mountains—and holy cow, we had lots of water. It was running pretty good.

Art Allen crossed at Clark's Crossing. Every time they came in with a hunting party, they would ford the river. He told me that many times when they would go home in the fall, they swam the river because it was up and flooding. One year, Art brought hunters in from Rock Lake. He crossed the river at Clark's Crossing three times. He forded the river each trip going to hunt, and swam the river each trip going home.

Art Allen helped me cross Clark's Crossing the first time I went across. He helped me get across. He said, "Don't you cross where the corrals are—you cross up at the bend." That would

Pictured above:
Top: Ferry on the Smoky River in 1965.
Bottom: Glen Kilgour packing up at Henry Joachim's yard at Gustavs Flats.
Photos courtesy of Claudette & Glen Kilgour.

Pictured on left page:
Top: Rex Logan at the 75th Alberta Outfitters Convention in February 2007.
Middle: Carl Luger at Old Entrance Ranch in 2005.
Bottom: Bob Kjos in Brule 2007.
All Photos by Susan Feddema-Leonard.

give a guy time enough to wash out, you see. He said that everyone that got into trouble crossed down below and they would wash into that whirlpool. They'd get sucked in and die. Lucky for me, Art was there that time.

I met Art the first time that I was pulling out of the Park for the season. The geologists I had been working with had pulled out from Kakwa Lake and went home in an airplane. Larry Trimble and I had to move the outfit home. We trailed the outfit into the camp on the Muddy Water River, and we were pushing—making long days. We thought that we would camp at the Muddy; however Leonard Jeck was camped, right in that spot. So we went down below and Art came and helped us pull the riggin' off of our horses. Art was traveling with Leonard Jeck at that time. I think Art had just sold his pack outfit to Leonard Jeck, and he was out helping Leonard get started.

I was packing nine or ten head of horses. We had twenty-seven head of horses all together. The next day we went over Clark's Crossing and up Wolverine Creek. We trailed over the mountain until we reached Big Grave Flats.

Art Allen and Pat Smythe were partners in an outfit. They had their own horses. Art was also quite a cabin maker. All the cabins that are on the upper Smoky River were built by Art. He was the log man. Art Allen was hired by Jasper National Park to build the cabins on the upper Smoky River, which are located inside the Park boundary.

One time at Christmas, Art took off with his snowshoes and he walked into Jasper from the Jackpine Valley. It was a ninety-mile hike that took him twenty-four hours—through the deep snow. A day or two after Christmas, he put his snowshoes on and walked back to his trapline—talk about tough!

Pictured left:
Crossing Smoky River
at the island at
Henry Joachim's.

Pictured on left page:
Ferry on the Smoky.

Photos courtesy of
Claudette & Glen Kilgour.

Sue   I know why he walked out. His daughter, Linda Hokanson of Edson was born just before the Christmas of 1952. She told me that Art walked out to be with his wife for her delivery, but she arrived early before Christmas. He must have been a pretty tough guy to have hiked that far.

Bazil   One of Art's cabins is up on the Jackpine River.

Glen   Well, that is where he was trapping, at that time.

Art Allen was a hill man; there was no doubt about that. Art hunted on the northwestern portion of the Smoky. Pat, Art's partner worked for me for several years and he was in his seventies then. Pat worked with me in the Mt. deVeber area.

Pat was quite a character. He wore a big pair of spurs when he got on his horse. One time we were moving camp when I took the hunter out ahead of the packhorses. I had a boy that was working for me that was jingling horses. He could ride buckin' horses and was a happy trail hand. Before I left, I told him, "You give Pat the stove horse *(the cook's supply horse)* to lead." I always led my stove horse. This boy was to ride the colt.

When it got time to go, Pat took the colt to ride. The colt was gentle enough all right but Pat kinda went to sleep—and the pack got crooked on the stove horse. The stove horse ran up alongside Pat's saddle horse and the pack hit him. The pack got him turned around and made the spur hit the horse's belly. Well this horse made poor old Pat hit the dirt. Pat really

got bucked off and he hurt all over. Pat was a tremendous guy. He worked for Bob Kjos several years after that. That was a good guy. He kept everybody happy.

Glen   Emil Moberly also worked for me. Holy crow, he was a good hunter. Emil was a good man but I couldn't keep him all the time—but Emil could hunt anything. Emil's family was originally from Jasper and his grandfather's house was at Snaring River near Jasper.

(Emil's great-grandfather was Henry J. Moberly who was the chief factor of the Hudson's Bay Company in charge of Jasper House from 1855 to 1861. He had two boys by the name of Ewan and John Moberly. Ewan is Emil's grandfather. Emil's family was forced out of Jasper in 1907 when the Federal government made Jasper National Park.)

Emil   My grandfather's house is on this *(east)* side of the Snaring River.

Glen   That's where Emil's people came from. They moved them out of Jasper and sent them to Grande Cache.

Emil   There's going to be a grand opening of my grandfather's house near Jasper on the twelfth of June *(2005)*. A lot of people will be going. At the grand opening they will be teaching lots of things, like how to make fire in the bush; how to put it out; to cook on an open fire and stuff like that. We'll make bannock and drink tea. My grandfather's mom had a grave there and we called the priest down to bless the grave. They put windows in the old log house two years ago and last fall they made a parking lot. There was nothing there before; you just parked on the road. Maybe we can kill a bighorn sheep on the hillside and eat it (joking).

Glen   Well, that's right close to them sheep hills—where the sheep cross. If one of those sheep fall down out there, Emil, you go out and get me a cape off of one *(joking)*.

When Emil worked for me, he didn't talk much as he didn't speak good English. He spoke in Cree. Some of the other Native guides were quite fluent in English. That wasn't too much of a problem, as Emil did not want the hunters talking on the trail. You could send Emil out for anything and he would bring it back to camp.

Emil was a tough guy. One time he went across the river and killed an elk. It was a really nice elk. Then the German hunter wanted a black bear. Of course, this German couldn't talk much English anyway. They got across the river and, low and behold, there's the bear feeding on the elk carcass—just like that. Emil sneaks the hunter to a good location and he helped his hunter find a good rest for his gun. Emil said, "This is the bear—this is the elk—shoot the bear." You know very well what happened. That German blew that dead elk's guts up in front of that bear. Boy, was Emil ever mad that time. He came into camp and told me about that dumb hunter. Emil said that the bear left so fast that he couldn't believe it.

Emil wasn't only an exceptional hunter, he could make bannock *(Indian bread)*. Every time we had Emil in camp, I had him make up a batch of bannock. He certainly was the bannock king. Emil was good help as he was raised in the hills. That was his trapline over there on the Smoky River. Emil phones me every now and again and he's always surprised to get me on the phone.

Sue   Emil, you said that there weren't many elk in this country before.

Emil   It was 1948 the first time I ever saw an elk in this country. It was at Mile 119, which is one hundred and nineteen miles on the railway line north of Hinton—at the Wanyandies' home place. That year, Louis Delorme was hunting over at Corral Creek. He heard something and he didn't know what it was. The next day he went hunting and he heard something again. He wanted to see what the noise was. At first he thought the wild studs were fighting, because they had a lot of horses. Finally he saw the elk. That's the first time—in 1948 that the elk came up here. Henry had never seen the elk before, either. That was the first time that he saw them too.

And whitetail *(deer)*—it was 1952 the first time they came up in here. I was living at Victor Lake *(near Grande Cache)*. The deer were on the side hills and it was springtime. It was well before the leaves came out, and there was deer there. They were funny looking. My brother Joe lived there as well. I got Joe and we went out to track them. The tracks weren't too far from the house. We saw a long-tailed deer. We couldn't figure out what the heck they were. We looked and looked at them. We figured that they were half mule *(deer)*.

Glen   In 1952, the first whitetail deer and, in 1948, the first elk were seen in this country.

Emil   There used to be a lot of game in this area—but at that time, the wolves were trapped. In the springtime the people would go hunting and get young ones *(pups)*. There was a bounty of fifteen dollars for them. You could find them in the den—sometimes there was as many as twelve. Then we would kill them. Many years ago, fifteen dollars was a lot of money.

Glen   Yes, you got a bounty on the hide. I think it finally got to twenty-five dollars.

Emil   Then it went to fifty dollars.

Pictured above:
Glen Kilgour cutting
Mike McIntyre's hair.
Mike was from
Sundre, Alberta.

Photo courtesy of
Glen Kilgour.

Pictured above:
Claudette Kilgour,
Glen's wife of thirty years,
is an
exceptional horsewoman.

Photo courtesy of
Claudette & Glen Kilgour.

Glen   Emil, when you worked with me, so did Henry Joachim. Henry had a big knife that was quite long.

Emil   I have that knife now.

Glen   There, you have it—there's that knife. Anyway, whenever we camped close to Eben Ebeneau, Henry would lay out his bed. He got into bed and that knife was lying right by his hand—just like that. He could have grabbed that knife in a second.

Emil   Yeah, I got that knife. Alice *(Henry's wife)* gave it to me.

Glen   That's good and I'm glad you have it. I used to watch that big knife when he would lay it out there.

Emil   A long time ago, Eben brought a bunch of horses down to the *(Gustavs)* Flats. These were pretty wild horses for a working outfit going in the mountains. A long time ago, Henry had worked for Eben. Maybe they were good friends at that time. Henry Joachim, Louis Joachim, Frank Joachim and Freddie Findlay were all working for Eben at that time. These guys had to break the horses in order to use them and go hunting. They had to guide their hunter, as well as break the horses.

Glen   Henry had a horse pasture there *(at Gustav Flats)* where the islands are. I used to winter my horses on the Smoky Valley before there was a coal mine. I had made a deal with Henry to winter my horses on the flats. Other times, I made a deal with Louis Delorme of Victor Lake to winter my horses across the Sulphur River, where there is a settlement of Louis's grandchildren. I believe Danny Hallock and his daughter live over in the area where I used to winter my horses.

I used to come to Henry's place a lot as it was a good place to ford the Smoky, so I had the opportunity to know Henry and his family. You see, I used to cross the Smoky River at the islands by Henry Joachim's place. A horse only had to swim a little distance. I crossed there several times.

One time I was rounding up my horses at Henry's home place and had caught them all. I decided to go over to visit Henry. The door was open and I went in and I could see that there were still coals in the fire—so I knew someone must be close by. I sat on the step of his house and waited. It didn't take too long before I saw Henry riding through the poplar trees. Behind him was his wife, Alice and granddaughters, Audrey and Leola Moberly, and niece, Victoria Moberly. This family had been out picking berries and were laughing and having real fun. You couldn't find a family anywhere on this earth that was as close as Henry and his family. It was very ironical because a leading newspaper had just published a story about these poor Indians in Grande Cache. What I observed

Pictured above:
Glen Kilgour.

Photo courtesy of
Claudette & Glen Kilgour.

is that this family was a way ahead of most, as they were loving, caring and obviously very happy. They were close to the earth and were making a living off the land.

Henry's family were real friendly and would visit my camp. One time I had a cook by the name of Eileen McNabb working for me and we had our main camp at Kvass Flats. She was from Bearberry, Alberta. We used to leave her in the base camp alone, when we went out fly camping with the hunters. Victoria, Leola and Audrey used to ride their horses up to Kvass Flats where our camp was. They used to stay with Eileen and keep her company.

Bazil   Lyle Moberly is Henry Joachim's grandson and the son of Victoria Moberly. He grew up on that flat. Lyle and his wife, Denise have operated summer trail rides in Willmore Wilderness Park. They've taken trips from Grande Cache to McBride, B.C. in the past. They go up to Sheep Creek and down the Continental Divide to Pauline Creek. The trail then forks over to the Jackpine and over to the Holmes River road in B.C. So the outfitting tradition is still being carried on today. Lyle still uses his grandfather's brand of J̲H̲.

Sue   Did you ever run into Felix Plante *(a Willmore guide and outfitter)*? He got started in the outfitting industry when he worked fifteen years for Fred Brewster. He worked for Brewster out of the *Jasper Park Lodge* and catered to tourists who wanted to go out on twenty-one to thirty-day hunting trips.

Dan L I once saw a picture of Felix Plante crossing the Athabasca at Entrance with a whole packstring of horses. He had quite a reputation as being a first-class outfitter. Felix first came to the Hinton and Jasper country in 1914 from Lac St. Anne. At one point in his life, he lived in Jasper and spent fifteen years guiding for Fred Brewster. Jack outfitted guests who wanted to go on twenty-one-day to thirty-day trips in the Rocky Mountains.

Bazil Felix hand-carved the packsaddles and they were a fine piece of art. He was known all over the country for his exceptional packsaddles. Felix was one of the best outfitters in his time. Johnny Groat and Felix Plante must have had green, young horses on that trip.

Glen You know, I bought a couple of packsaddles off of Felix for my packhorses a long time ago.

Dan L In 1927, Felix had saved eleven hundred dollars to buy his own outfit, which consisted of fifty horses. He went on to start his own outfit and took geologists, hunters and tourists into the hills. He based his operation out of Entrance.

Sue   In fact, in 1950, Felix Plante outfitted a forty-four-day hunting trip north of the Smoky River where outfitter, Carl Luger and his new bride packed and cooked—for their honeymoon. Carl was an outfitter in his own right at that time, but he worked for Felix on that trip.

Dan L   He was one of the most reputable outfitters of his day. Felix ran his own outfit for twenty-five years.

Glen   Tommy Groat was also a well-known outfitter who married a Moberly girl. Emil, how would she be related to you?

Emil   That was my dad's sister and her name was Clarisse.

Glen   You see the Groats were really old timers out of Edmonton *(Alberta).* That's why there is a Groat Road in the city and a Groat Bridge on the Saskatchewan River. It's named after that Groat Family. Groat Road is named after Malcolm Groat, Tommy's father. There were seven children in the Groat family at that time and they lived on an estate on the Saskatchewan River.

Tommy Groat rode away one spring with a pack outfit. He went west with the Grand Trunk survey team. He told his folks where he was going—but he didn't come back that fall. So the next spring the Groat family sent the other two boys down to see what happened to Tommy. These two brothers packed up their outfit and left Edmonton. Tommy Groat had married Clarisse Moberly at Prairie Creek and they were living in the Hinton-Brule area. Anyways, Tommy's two brothers had to turn around and go back to Edmonton. When the two brothers got home they were asked where Tommy was, and were told that he was not coming back. Tommy Groat worked as a guide and outfitter in the Jasper and Willmore mountains. Some say that he was the best outfitter in the country. Tom and Clarisse had nine children. Two of his sons were Joe and Judd Groat. Both Judd and Joe worked in the guiding and outfitting industry.

Joe Groat was a bushman. He was one of those guys where it didn't matter what kind of job he had. He knew where all the horses were; he knew where the rams were; he knew how to cook. He could cook everything; there was nothing that he couldn't cook. One time I went into his camp when he was with Carl Luger. He was cooking for Carl this summer—and I rode by for a visit. Here Joe had built a great big cake and it was sitting on the counter. He had baked some pies and they were sitting on the counter. They had a geology party out, you see. There he was poking sticks in the fire. He was cooking fresh bread—all in the morning. He was feeding that wood stove with kindling wood to get just the right temperature. Joe was a professional hill man.

Joe and Judd Groat both were born hill men. They learned from their father who was an outfitter and their mother who was born and raised in the mountains.

Sue   Emil, that picture that you gave to me, who were the people in it?

Emil My dad *(Adolphus Moberly, on the left)*; Tommy Groat is the next one; then Phillip Delorme; Adolphus Joachim; and William Moberly. William was the father of Ed, Roddy, Malcolm, and Paul. His daughters were Helen, Rose, Evelyn and Victoria. Victoria is still alive and her son, Lyle Moberly is a Willmore Wilderness Park outfitter.

(Adolphus Lake, which forms the source of the Big Smoky River flowing from Robson Pass was named by mountaineer, Arthur Coleman. He named the lake after his Métis guide Adolphus Moberly. Adolphus was Emil's father.)

Sue This is such an awesome picture, Emil. Your father Adolphus and his brother-in-law, Tom Groat were sure handsome men.

Emil Yeh, that's sure an old picture.

Sue Glen, Jerry Stojan was an outfitter in this area. Did you ever run into him?

Glen Jerry Stojan from Sexsmith, Alberta—he was here. I have a story that I tell about him. He got this bunch of horses that he got started, and they were going good. He moved down from the north and came out on the flats close to Henry Joachim's home place. The horses had trailed a long way and had hit the flat on the Smoky River. They had been confined to the trail in the trees before that. When the horses hit the meadows, nobody was ahead of them. The packs on the horses were loose because they had travelled all day. The horses had gotten ahead of Jerry, who was the lead man. When these pack horses reached the open field they were rompy and playful. Anyway, there the horses went, kicking and romping—with nobody ahead of them and they started running. Pretty soon the packs started coming loose. Well, they scattered packs all over that flat. You never had seen such a mess as that one. It took the rest of the night to gather that gear up and set up camp. That was the greatest scatter that I ever saw in my whole life. I knew Jerry Stojan all right. I just happened to come along there with my saddle horse just when that wreck happened.

One other outfitter that came from up in that northern country was Abe Reimer. He was an early outfitter who started out at Wembley, and ended up in Hinton, Alberta. Abe died and his wife passed on a short time later. She donated their land for what is now the present day rodeo ground in Hinton. Abe had interesting names for dudes or greenhorns. He used to call them "pilgrims." If he didn't like someone, he would call them a pilgrim.

Bazil We used to call dudes "prune pickers."

Claudette That's what we could call any greenhorns— "prune pickers."

Glen My old horse partner used to call our dudes "prune pickers." It's funny how we would use these old terms on the trail.

It's great to think of the old times. I would love to go into Cote Creek and shoot a ram. There are some bighorn rams on the B.C. side—on the one side of that mountain. Sometimes they change their territory. We hunted the Alberta side and I didn't make a habit of going into B.C. The only other place I used to get into B.C. sometimes was by Compton Mountain, because there was nobody on the other side. We were hunting grizzly. There was goat up there too. Then there were lots of goats all over. One time below where the town is, there were forty or fifty goats on a ridge right above Henry Joachim's.

Bazil There was over sixty head of goats there.

Glen I had good years outfitting in the Willmore. I maintained that we should have left this area a wilderness. We didn't need this town. We had a resource here. There was money to be made off of the hunting industry in this area. The money from hunting was being spent in Alberta and we had a natural resource right here. I thought that this was a beautiful country.

Pictured above:
Jerry Stojan circa 1960s.

Photo courtesy of
Chuck Stojan.

A lot of decisions are being made regarding the wilderness area by people who are sent away to schools and who spend very little time in the mountains. Last night and this morning we were talking about the grizzly bear. Somebody made mention that twenty years ago there was a grizzly study and that the Alberta government is doing another grizzly study now—but we have these new biologists that have to learn it all again.

Shutting the hunting season off on these bears is unwise, because all we are going to do is increase the bear population until they become a headache. Our biologists are getting information that lacks the old-time knowledge. These guys go to university and have professors who have little experience in the wilderness. That's who these biologists are learning from. You can't really blame the kids. I blame the education system. Living in the wilderness gives a person a whole different perspective. Common sense seems to be a thing of the past.

A bunch of years ago, the Alpine Club was moving into this mountain area—thirty or forty miles south of Jasper. I was crossing the Athabasca River on my horse. Somehow I told somebody that a pack of wolves had moved in and was living right with our horses. I was quite worried about the horses being there.

It wasn't long after this that a man showed up in the area in a vehicle. In the back of his panel truck he had everything to camp with—everything you can imagine. He had the most modern equipment that you could buy. He was doing a wolf study.

I had been up the mountain that day and was riding back to camp, but the wolves had pulled the pin and had gone. Naturally they do this—it's the way of the land. They pull into a country for a day or two and then pull out. Wolves are travelers and they travel all the time. Anyway, that day down the mountain, not a wolf track, right to camp. I was right on the banks of the Athabasca. No wolf tracks anywhere.

I met this boy almost at camp and I asked him what he was doing. He told me that he was on a wolf study. He heard that there was a pack of wolves in there and he had come to study them. I asked him what he saw. He told me that he saw wolves that day. I didn't correct him or anything—but the wolves were gone. He never saw a wolf. That night instead of camping there with all these wolves he said he had seen, he went into Jasper and got a motel room. The government was paying for it. He was living a life of luxury—and lying to me about those wolves. He never saw wolves that day. I know he didn't. Wolves leave tracks, you know—and I watch for tracks.

Now the B.C. government is doing another big wolf study. This study is supposed to be a new thing. I believe that we are in trouble with the way we study these animals.

One time the authorities wrote me and asked if I had ever seen any caribou in the Sheep Creek area. I wrote back and told them that I had seen quite a bunch of caribou up there—up to one hundred and twenty on one ridge. The caribou would come out of British Columbia and climb a ridge there at the headwaters of the Sheep. The authorities did not believe me.

We had a caribou man in British Columbia that had really studied caribou. The authorities made fun of him to me. I knew that this guy knew more about caribou than anybody in this country. At that time, there were many caribou in Willmore. Then the authorities claimed that there was none. There's no use to talk to them. They're not going to pay any attention to what you see or what your knowledge of the species is.

Sue   There sure needs to be a voice from the mountain people who spend a good portion of their lives in the wilderness. The people of the earth have a right to be heard. Their knowledge should be respected and not rejected.

Glen   It was a great country before they built this town. I had lots of good people work for me over the years. Now I live in Taylor B.C.—and I'm a long way from the mountains. It bothers me to come down here to Grande Cache. Tom Vinson (Jr. outfitter) has a short summer trip that is going on Tuesday—and I would love to go with him.

ᑫ   ᑫ   ᑫ

THE INDIGENOUS PEOPLE, OUTFITTERS & TRAPPERS SEE THEMSELVES AS THE

"WORLD'S BEST ENVIRONMENTALISTS."

Pictured above:
Canadian Rockies 2006
"Looking Towards Willmore Wilderness Park."

Pictured on page 422
"Woodpeckers on the Smoky River."
Both photos by Susan Feddema-Leonard.

EPILOGUE:

The indigenous people, outfitters and trappers see themselves as the *'World's Best Environmentalists.'* Who else notices if the mouse population is up or down—and understands the profound impact that a small change can have on the entire ecosystem? These people have a finger on the pulse of the land and understand *'mother earth'* in a very intimate way. They know that the planet is a *'living organism'* and not a static object. They understand the earth spirit—*'the Gaia spirit'*—and how to listen to her subtle signs.

With so few wilderness areas left in North America, the *Willmore Wilderness Act* is a critical piece of legislation, which ensures the age-old traditional activities of hunting, fishing, trapping and horse use in this region. Willmore Wilderness Park is a haven for both the *'earth people'* and those who yearn for a closer connection to the vast mountain wilderness. This magnificent area offers an incredible place to experience the *'great planet earth'*— without the interruptions of the industrialized world. It is a timeless oasis of mountain streams, alpine meadows and wildlife. It is truly one of the great wonders of the world.

Happy Trails, Susan Feddema-Leonard

INDEX:
People & Peaks of Willmore Wilderness Park

∾ *Special Thanks* ∾

When all is said and done, I would like to especially thank Estella Cheverie for her incredible work, her meticulous attention to detail, her perseverance and her ability to work through an exceptionally heavy work load.

Thank you, Estella Cheverie. This book would not be possible without your dedication and endless support You are truly a very special friend.

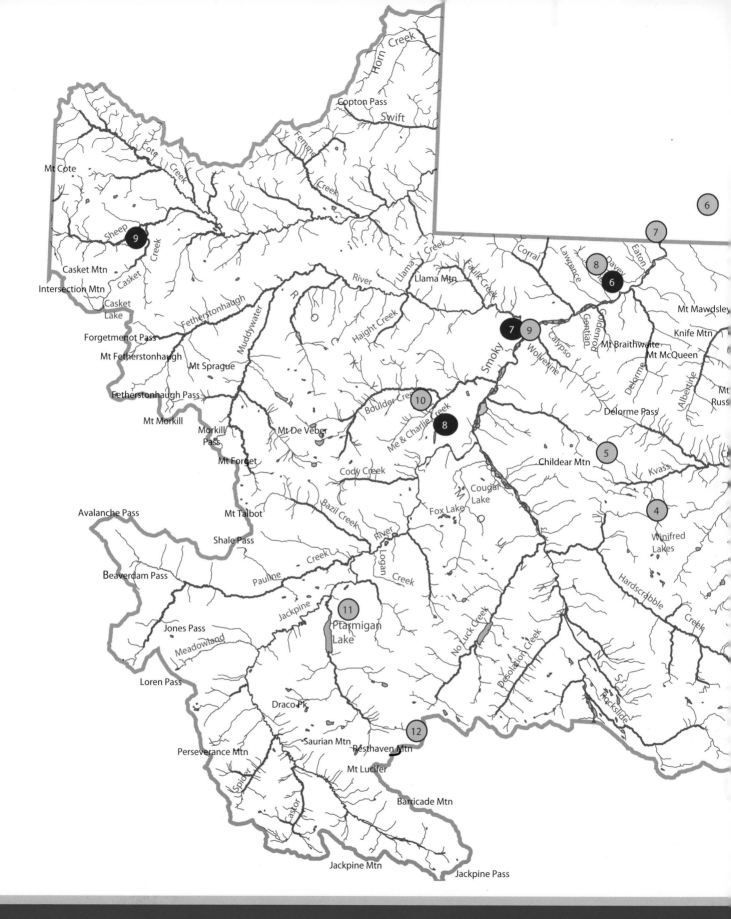

Willmore Wilderness

Willmore Wilderness Park is bordered on the west by British Columbia and on the south by Jasper National Park. It is 4,597 sq. km. The Park was created under the Wilderness Provincial Act of 1959, which was later renamed the Willmore Wilderness Act after Norman Willmore.

Points of Interest

1. Rock Lake
2. Mines at Thoreau Creek - circa 1928
3. Adam's Creek Lookout
4. Winifred Lakes
5. Kvass Lookout - closed in 1972
6. Town of Grande Cache
7. Sulphur Gates Staging area
8. Kvass Flats - named after trapper Fred Kvass
9. Clark's Cache and (boat) crossing
10. Many Face Carvings - Coyote Cliff's camp
11. Ptarmigan Lake - largest lake in Willmore Wilderness Park
12. Resthaven Mountain - highest point in Willmore at 3,125 meters

Grave Sites

1. Mother of Adam Joachim died 1904
2. Daughter of Washy Joe Agnes died 1901
3. Baby Delorme died in 1908 now called 'Little Grave'
4. Thappe, a Beaver Indian who was Joe McDonald's father
5. Louis Delorme, grandfather of Louis Joachim at 'Big Grave Flat'
6. Pierre Delorme's sister buried at Findlay Springs on Kvass Flats
7. Unknown baby on the Muddy Water River
8. Unknown grave near Boulder Creek
9. George Hargreaves died Sept 17, 1936 and is burried near Sheep Creek Falls

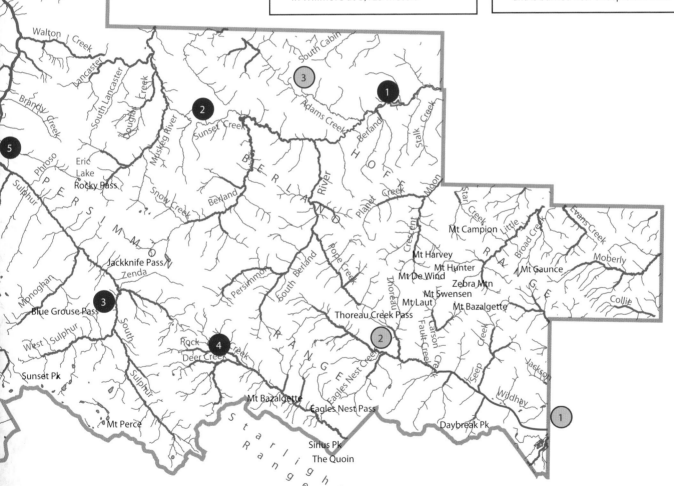

WILLMORE WILDERNESS MAP:

Thanks to Gwen Edge, Graphic Designer for Alberta Sustainable Resources for the basic map file.

∽ LET IT BE ∽

a poem about the Willmore Wilderness
written by Harry Edgecombe November 1982

I am patrolling the Willmore
For the Alberta Forestry,
Following the track of the horse and pack
The way it used to be.

The years have slipped by,
All too quickly it seems.
Many changes have been made in the forestry trade.
For the past it is memories and dreams.

Today I am back where I started
Patrolling the mountains once more;
With horses three, and only me.
It is the same as it was before.

Time has no real meaning,
Today is all that is real.
You find your way through the mountains gray.
Happy is the way I feel.

There is a message carried in on the breeze
A meaning that is easy to see;
A message told by the mountains old,
LET IT BE.   LET IT BE.

This is not the land for loggers
Who fells and cuts up the tree,
Not for oil or ore -- they have been here before.
LET IT BE.   LET IT BE.

The message rings loud and clear:
This is not the land of industry!
No motel or store on the valley floor.
Just LET IT BE.   LET IT BE.

All around me the world is gleaming,
The streams are rushing along.
Spring has aroused the bear from its mountain lair,
The valley is singing a song.

Background photo by Susan Feddema-Leonard
Small photo is Harry Edgecombe courtesy of Mavis Holroyd.